THE *PUEBLO* INCIDENT

Modern War Studies

The
PUEBLO
Incident

**A Spy Ship
and the Failure of
American Foreign
Policy**

Mitchell B. Lerner

University Press of Kansas

The chapter epigraphs are from "Bucher's Bastards," a poem composed by the crew, especially by Communications Technician Earl Kisler, while in captivity. The whole poem is reprinted on the *Pueblo* Web site at www.Pueblo.nethelpnow.com.

Published by the University Press of Kansas (Lawrence, Kansas 66049), which was organized by the Kansas Board of Regents and is operated and funded by Emporia State University, Fort Hays State University, Kansas State University, Pittsburg State University, the University of Kansas, and Wichita State University

© 2002

by the University Press of Kansas

All rights reserved

Library of Congress Cataloging-in-Publication Data
Lerner, Mitchell B., 1968–
    The *Pueblo* incident : a spy ship and the failure of American foreign policy / Mitchell B. Lerner.
        p. cm. — (Modern war studies)
    Includes bibliographical references and index.
    ISBN 0–7006–1171–1 (cloth: alk. paper)
    ISBN 0–7006–1296–3 (pbk: alk. paper)
    1. Pueblo Incident, 1968. I. Title. II. Series.
    VB230 .L47 2002
    359.3'432'0973--dc21   2001006733

British Library Cataloguing in Publication Data is available.

Printed in the United States of America

10 9 8 7 6 5 4

The paper used in this publication meets the minimum requirements of the American National Standard for Permanence of Paper for Printed Library Materials z39.48–1984.

Contents

A photo gallery follows page 122.

Preface

This is a book about the USS *Pueblo,* an American intelligence ship captured by North Korea in January 1968. Despite the fact that the *Pueblo* was the first American ship to surrender in peacetime in over a century and a half; despite the fact that the incident threatened to spark another Korean War; despite the beatings, torture, and humiliation the North Koreans meted out to the eighty-two American survivors, the *Pueblo* and her crew slipped from public attention with an almost shocking alacrity. The literature on the subject has reflected this dearth of interest. After an initial rush of memoirs and a few journalistic accounts, the *Pueblo* Incident faded into oblivion, where for almost thirty years it has remained a virtually unexamined topic. No scholarly study of this dramatic event has ever been published, nor has the ship garnered even a mention in most surveys of American Cold War foreign policy. It is my intent to breathe some life into this important story—and in doing so to answer some of the questions that for too long have gone not only unanswered but also unasked.

However, this is also a book about American foreign policy during the Cold War. The *Pueblo* Incident, I believe, can serve as a window through which we can examine the underlying source of many of America's policy failures during the Cold War—the inability to recognize the importance of national values and indigenous belief systems in international relations. In designing the *Pueblo*'s mission, preparing the ship for launch, and attempting to resolve the crisis, American policy makers consistently failed to treat the North Koreans as North Koreans, instead viewing them only as one cog in a greater communist conspiracy that consisted of virtually interchangeable parts. Had American officials accepted the possibility that a communist nation could act for reasons distinct from the struggle between the global superpowers, the *Pueblo*'s career would likely have followed a very different path. Instead, they clung to this comfortable worldview that reduced complex events to simplistic shades of black and white and saw everything as part of a zero-sum contest for world domination. Earlier, this same myopia had driven the United States to intervene in Vietnam, in Cuba, in Guatemala, and elsewhere; in 1968, it condemned the eighty-three *Pueblo* crewmen to a tragic and unnecessary fate.

* * *

It is ironic that after writing 130,000 words on the *Pueblo* Incident, I should find myself unable to find just a few more that would adequately thank the many people who helped make this project possible. I hope they will settle for a simple acknowledgment until someone more eloquent than I gives me the words to express my gratitude.

Many friends, advisers, and colleagues read parts or all of this manuscript. Others listened to my ideas, offered advice and criticism, and helped me to develop my thoughts. Although I am sure I am inadvertently omitting a few, I would like to thank Matthew Aid, Trevor Armbrister, James Bamford, Gordon Bennett, H. W. Brands, Dae Sook-suh, Roger Dingman, Ed Drea, Steve Galpern, R. Scott Harris, Byron Hulsey, Sean Kelley, Clarence Lasby, Mark Lawrence, Allan Millett, Mike Parrish, John Prados, Nicholas Sarantakes, William Stueck, and Randall Woods for their valuable suggestions. Undoubtedly, the work would have been better if I had followed them more closely. Two scholars and friends deserve special mention: Robert Divine and Michael Stoff, who together showed me how to be a historian. Both were influential in every step of my graduate school career in ways that far exceeded the assistance they provided on this project.

Any historian who undertakes a lengthy project quickly realizes the importance of good archivists. I was lucky to have been aided by the wonderful staff at the LBJ Library in Austin, Texas; among others, Allen Fisher, Regina Greenwell, Mike Parrish, and Linda Selke provided the kind of support that has made the Johnson Library one of the finest research facilities in the nation. Regina Akers at the Naval Historical Center in Washington went far beyond the call of duty in providing materials, answering questions, and offering suggestions. Others whose help proved invaluable include Paul Stillwell at the U.S. Naval Institute, Karen Gatz of the State Department Historical Office, and Milton Gustafson at the National Archives in College Park, Maryland. Rich Mobely generously shared his research on the *Pueblo* from the Public Records Office in London, and Stu Russell of the *Pueblo* shared a wealth of information on topics too numerous to list. Without their help, I would likely still be digging through old files looking for documents. The people at the University Press of Kansas proved knowledgeable, supportive, and (most of all) patient. Senior editor Mike Briggs was everything an author could ask for in an editor and a friend. Among others, Melinda Wirkus, Susan Schott, and Linda Lotz provided the type of assistance that justifies the exceptional reputation of this press. Valuable financial assistance was provided in the form of grants and fellowships by the Lyndon Johnson Library Foundation, the John F. Kennedy Library Foundation, the University of Texas, and the Ohio State University.

The final debt, to my family, is by far the largest. The support of my mother and sister has been crucial to my success in many ways. My father, who died shortly before I began this project, nevertheless helped in ways that are too valuable to be forgotten but too painful to be expressed. My two daughters, Camille and Julia, usually understood when I turned off their computer games in order to do my own work, and my infant son, Maxwell, rarely spit up on either the manuscript or the computer. They also provided a constant reminder of what is truly important. Most important, my wife, Michelle, lived these past years as my partner, taking as much joy in my successes and as much unhappiness in my failures as I did myself. Throughout it all, she cheerfully served as wife, mother, proofreader, audience, and friend; it is for her sake above all else that I wish I was capable of producing something better.

Abbreviations

AGER	Auxiliary General Environmental Research
AGI	Naval Auxiliary Intelligence Collectors
AGTR	Auxiliary General Technical Research
AKL	Auxiliary Cargo, Light
CIA	Central Intelligence Agency
CINCPAC	Commander in Chief, Pacific
CINCPACFLT	Commander in Chief, Pacific Fleet
CNO	Chief of Naval Operations
COMINT	communications intelligence
COMNAVFORJAPAN	Commander of U.S. Naval Forces, Japan
COMSERVPAC	Commander of Service Forces, Pacific
COMSEVENTHFLT	Commander, Seventh Fleet
CT	communications technician
DIA	Defense Intelligence Agency
DMZ	demilitarized zone
DPRK	Democratic People's Republic of Korea (North Korea)
ELINT	electronic intelligence
ICBM	intercontinental ballistic missile
IFF	Identification Friend or Foe
INSURV	Inspection and Survey
IRC	International Red Cross
JCS	Joint Chiefs of Staff
jg	junior grade
JRC	Joint Reconnaissance Center
JRS	Joint Reconnaissance Schedule
KTF	Korean Task Force
KWP	Korean Workers Party
MAC	Military Armistice Commission
MAP	Military Assistance Program
MSTS	Military Sea Transportation Service
NAVSECGRP	Naval Security Group

NSA	National Security Agency
NSC	National Security Council
ORI	operational readiness inspection
POW	prisoner of war
PRC	People's Republic of China
ROK	Republic of Korea (South Korea)
SIGINT	signals intelligence
SICR	Specific Information Collection Requirements
SITREP	situation report
SOD	Special Operations Department
TRAPAC	Training Command, Pacific
TRSSCOMM	Technical Research Ship Special Communications System
UN	United Nations
XO	executive officer

THE *PUEBLO* INCIDENT

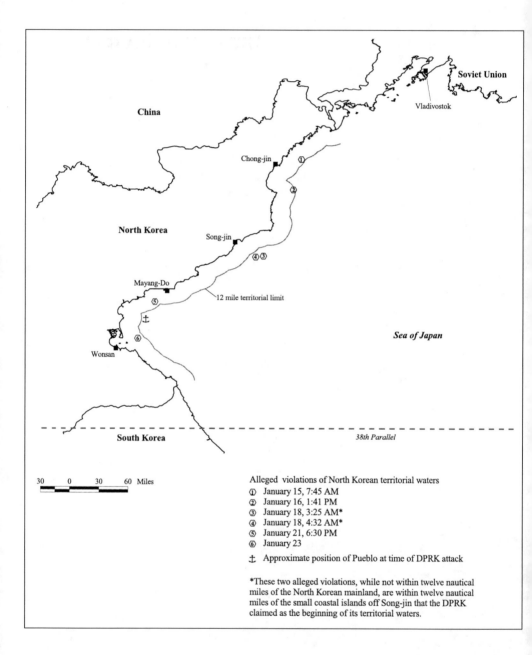

China

Soviet Union

Vladivostok

Chong-jin ①

②

North Korea

Song-jin

④③

Mayang-Do

⑤

12 mile territorial limit

⚓

Sea of Japan

Wonsan ⑥

South Korea

38th Parallel

30   0   30   60 Miles

Alleged violations of North Korean territorial waters
① January 15, 7:45 AM
② January 16, 1:41 PM
③ January 18, 3:25 AM*
④ January 18, 4:32 AM*
⑤ January 21, 6:30 PM
⑥ January 23

⚓ Approximate position of Pueblo at time of DPRK attack

*These two alleged violations, while not within twelve nautical
miles of the North Korean mainland, are within twelve nautical
miles of the small coastal islands off Song-jin that the DPRK
claimed as the beginning of its territorial waters.

Introduction

Two days before departing the port of Sasebo, Japan, Commander Lloyd "Pete" Bucher of the USS *Pueblo* received a final piece of advice: "Remember," cautioned Rear Admiral Frank Johnson, "you are not going out there to start a war."[1] It appeared to be an unnecessary warning. The *Pueblo,* a small and dilapidated ex–cargo vessel that the navy had only recently rescued from mothballs and christened for oceanographic research, seemed uncertain to make it out of port, let alone spark an international incident. Yet, those aware of the ship's real purpose knew that Johnson's admonition was not unwarranted. In fact, the *Pueblo* was a research ship, but not the type the navy claimed; instead, she was an electronic intelligence ship operating under the joint direction of the National Security Agency (NSA) and Naval Intelligence, about to depart on her first mission. It was a trip from which she would never return.

The *Pueblo* left Sasebo on January 11, 1968, destined for the Sea of Japan. The crew had two main objectives: to monitor and collect North Korean and Soviet electronic communications such as radar, sonar, and radio signals; and to study naval activity along the Korean ports of Chongjin, Songjin, Mayang-do, and Wonsan. If possible, they were also to shadow Soviet ships in the Tsushima Strait to collect further communications information. Should everything go smoothly, the ship would return to Japan on February 4, full of valuable communications intercepts, photos of new Soviet ships, and eighty-three sailors desperate for some shore leave. Unfortunately, things never seemed to go smoothly for the *Pueblo.*

The ship had a history of serious equipment problems, especially in the critical areas of navigation and communication, that had never been fully repaired. The sole means of defense, other than a limited number of individual firearms, were two small .50 caliber machine guns mounted on the deck. Besides being antiquated and temperamental, these guns took anywhere from fifteen minutes to an hour to ready for combat, offered no protection for the shooter, and were not accurate beyond fifty yards. The crew was young and inexperienced, the chain of command muddled and confused, and support preparations sorely inadequate. Despite the estimate from Naval Intelligence that the mission was "routine" and the risk "minimal," the crew was understandably worried. "What happens," asked Seaman Stu Russell as the *Pueblo* cruised North Korean waters, "if someone decides to come out and pick us up?" "You're crazy," replied Communications Technician Anthony LaMantia. "The chances are one in a million."[2]

Tragically for the crew, Russell's unease proved prescient. On the afternoon of January 23, North Korean ships and jets approached the 176-foot intelligence ship while she lay dead in the water off the eastern coast of North Korea. Anticipating the routine harassment common in the intelligence-gathering field, Commander Bucher maintained his position until the lead ship suddenly demanded, "Heave to or I will open fire." Gunfire met the *Pueblo*'s attempts to escape, and Bucher soon surrendered with one dead and four wounded. In a struggle that had taken less than two hours, an American captain had surrendered his ship in peacetime for the first time since Commodore James Barron surrendered the USS *Chesapeake* to the British in 1807. It would require almost a year of difficult negotiations before the two rivals found a diplomatic solution, which returned the men, but not the ship, to the United States just in time for Christmas. The ship remained in North Korea, where it eventually became a tourist attraction.

On the surface, the story of the *Pueblo* seems simple and straightforward: spy mission, sudden capture on the high seas, torture, negotiations, release, American heroes, communist villains. It had all the elements of a made-for-TV movie, which it was in 1973.[3] Yet there are certain lessons that can be drawn from the crisis, lessons that become clear only by moving beyond the simplistic dichotomy of good and blameless Americans abducted by bad and scheming North Korean communists and addressing the more complex reality of the seizure. Only through such an examination can one recognize that responsibility for the *Pueblo* Incident went beyond a communist dictator on the Korean peninsula. Instead, a succession of American military and political errors combined to create the greatest tragedy of the *Pueblo:* the fact that it should not have happened. That it did reflects above all the inability of those who planned the mission, as well as those who reacted to it, to overcome their basic assumptions regarding the Cold War. American policy makers clung to the belief that all communist nations were the same—servile duplicates of the Soviet Union unified in a plot to dominate the world. This simplistic Cold War mentality divided the world neatly into two armed camps—the "free" world and the "communist" world—and those in charge of the *Pueblo* saw no need to draw distinctions within the communist side. Accordingly, they ignored the specific North Korean circumstances that should have indicated an increased risk to the *Pueblo* and confidently launched a ship and crew that were far from ready for their mission. Twenty-five years after the release of the men, one of the engineers in charge of the ship's preparation wrote, "Many sordid stories have been written on the *Pueblo*. None have told the true story. Pete and the crew were tasked with 'Mission Impossible.'"[4] Under these circumstances, a "Mission Impossible" it truly was. The real tragedy for the men of the USS *Pueblo* lay in the failure of American policy makers to recognize this fact until it was too late.

CHAPTER ONE

A Classified Operation

Out of Japan,
On the Fifth of Jan.,
The Pueblo came a-steaming.
Round Kyushu's toe,
Past Sasebo,
You could hear the captain screaming.

The message arrived at Submarine Flotilla Seven headquarters one cold December morning, addressed to Assistant Operations Officer Lloyd "Pete" Bucher. It contained a naval officer's most sought-after prize, ordering Bucher to leave his position in Sasebo, Japan, and "report to Commander Service Force, U.S. Pacific Fleet, for temporary duty as prospective commanding officer in connection with reactivation [of] USS *Pueblo* . . . and duty aboard that vessel when placed on commission as Commanding Officer."[1] He immediately phoned his wife. "Hey Rose," he announced. "I've got my own ship at last."

She let out a cry of delight: "Wonderful. Which one?"

"She's the USS *Pueblo*."

"The *Pueblo*. . . . What's that?"

"An AKL . . . that means Auxiliary Cargo, Light."

"Oh." Rose Bucher had a hard time hiding her disappointment. Pete had dreamed of commanding a submarine, or at least a diesel snorkel boat, and instead had been assigned a small transport vessel.

Her husband of sixteen years caught the note in her voice. "You can disregard the 'cargo' part of her designation," he reassured her. "I'm not going to become the skipper of a freighter. It's part of a classified operation."[2]

His words comforted her. Yet, had she known the history of the program that now beckoned them back to the United States, Rose's unhappiness would surely have returned. Lieutenant Commander Bucher was right; the *Pueblo* was no ordinary cargo ship. Instead, she was part of the top-secret Operation Clickbeetle, an intelligence-gathering program run under the auspices of Naval Intelligence and the National Security Agency (NSA). Clickbeetle and its predecessor, a similar program run primarily by the NSA, transformed antiquated transport ships into signals intelligence (SIGINT) collectors and then dispatched them to various coastlines as mobile eavesdroppers.[3] These operations had seen some triumphs; in 1962, one such ship provided the first evidence of Soviet medium-range ballistic missiles in Cuba.[4] Yet they also possessed some serious shortcomings, most notably the tendency of those in charge to presume a lesser degree of risk than actually existed. As a result, Rose Bucher would soon wish that her husband had in fact received command of a cargo vessel.

This specific form of seaborne intelligence collection originated with the NSA. The NSA, in turn, was the product of earlier American intelligence failures, especially the 1941 Japanese attack on Pearl Harbor and the North Korean attack on South Korea in 1950. In both instances, American SIGINT programs, run independently by the separate military branches, had obtained evidence pointing to the attacks but had failed to interpret or disseminate the information properly.[5] To prevent such a recurrence, President Harry Truman established a committee to evaluate and recommend means of improving the performance of American SIGINT programs. Headed by George Brownell, a former special assistant to the secretary of the air force, the committee's 239-page report proposed the creation of a sole authority to collect, evaluate, and disseminate SIGINT. This agency would be directed by an individual appointed for a term of four to six years, who would have almost total operational control of the nation's SIGINT programs. The director would report to the secretary of defense, who in turn would report to a special committee of the National Security Council (NSC) consisting of the secretary of defense himself, the secretary of state, and, when necessary, the president. On October 24, 1952, Truman signed a memorandum that became National Security Council Intelligence Directive No. 6, essentially putting these recommendations into effect. Thus, the NSA was born, ordered to "provide for the SIGINT mission of the United States, to establish an effective unified organization and control of all SIGINT collection and processing activities of the United States, and to produce SIGINT in accordance with the objectives, requirements and priorities established by the Director of Central Intelligence Board."[6]

From the beginning, the NSA was shrouded in secrecy. Not until 1957 was it even mentioned in the *U.S. Government Organization Manual,* and the agency's funding never appeared in the federal budget. When NSA officials attended White House meetings, the published lists of participants omitted their names; "NSA," ran one inside joke, stood for "Never Say Anything" or "No Such Agency." Congress not only accepted this secrecy but encouraged it, passing Public Law 86–36 in 1959, which permitted the organization to refuse to disclose any information that might impair its objectives, including, "any information with respect to the activities thereof, or the names, titles, salaries, or number of the persons employed."[7] With little to answer for, and few to answer to, the agency was left to run its operations almost devoid of scrutiny; in the 1980s, for example, the NSA assisted the CIA's illegal Iran-contra operation and then refused to respond to an inquiry from the secretary of defense on the grounds that its actions did not fall within his "need to know" purview.[8]

In order to perform its primary task, the interception of foreign communications, the NSA developed a vast network of over 2,000 listening posts designed to capture signal waves broadcast over foreign transmitters. Communications between distant nations and their American embassies, for example, could be easily intercepted by listening posts in suburban Maryland and Virginia. However, most posts existed abroad, with the Soviet Union receiving the bulk of the attention. These stations supplied invaluable information; in the early 1970s, they intercepted radio and telephone communications of Soviet leaders speaking from limousines and later managed to obtain advance knowledge of the Soviet bargaining position for SALT I. Yet they also had severe limitations, most notably in their geographical restrictions, since stations were obviously immovable and therefore hindered by location and natural barriers. They were also unable to provide emergency coverage of smaller nations; the communications base in the Himalayas, for example, could hardly be rushed to the coast of Malta if needed, yet it made little sense to have a costly and attention-drawing base dedicated solely to Malta. As a result, these stations provided a myopic view of the world. By the early 1960s, NSA facilities virtually encircled the USSR, yet only two existed in all of Africa and none in South America. The obvious solution was to create mobile listening posts, and in 1960 the agency began a program of converting noncombatant ships for just such a purpose.[9]

The idea of using ships as information collectors was hardly new to American intelligence, but earlier missions had been undertaken largely by combat ships. This policy left both the NSA and the navy dissatisfied. Such missions required the sudden withdrawal of combat vessels from their normal duties, which not only disrupted the navy's routine but also ruined the element of surprise, since it was difficult to conceal the abrupt departure of a destroyer from her standard operating area. Because of their military capabilities, combat ships were also more likely to be judged threatening by other nations, and thus risked a response should they stray too close to sensitive areas. Furthermore, warships were bound by various maritime treaties and conventions from which noncombat ships were exempt. Hence, converting old cargo vessels seemed a much better option; they were cheaper to operate, more mobile, less threatening, and, unlike airborne surveillance, could be on station twenty-four hours per day. They did not affect other naval operations and, it was assumed, were assured safety as long as they stayed within international waters.[10] These ships, concluded Secretary of Defense Robert McNamara, were "less provocative ... [with] more of a chance of obtaining the information [and] ... less of a risk of hostile action and escalatory response."[11]

In using these small noncombat vessels, the NSA was actually emulating the Soviet Union, which had been sending such ships off the American coast for years. Other nations would later use such vehicles; East Germany, for example, had one near the Baltics by the mid-1960s, and Algeria had one in the Mediterranean. However, Soviet ships, called Naval Auxiliary Intelligence Collectors (AGIs), were the first to be employed for SIGINT missions. AGIs frequently operated near American military bases during the 1960s; in April 1960, the Soviet trawler *Vega* appeared off the New Jersey coast during the testing of the *George Washington,* the first nuclear submarine equipped with the 1,200-mile-range Polaris missile. The *Vega* later materialized off Cape Henry, Virginia, within easy intercept range of the American naval base at Norfolk.[12]

The Soviets increased their use of AGIs following the 1962 Cuban Missile Crisis, even at the risk of violating American territorial waters.[13] In 1965, the trawler *Barometr* intruded within three miles of U.S. waters near Puerto Rico and then blamed the U.S. Coast Guard, whose sailing guide it claimed to be following.[14] Later that year, the *Arban* violated American waters off San Pedro, California, and soon after, the *Teodolit* did the same near Puerto Rico.[15] In another incident, a Soviet ship crossed into American territory with an unusual problem for an intelligence vessel, one solved when a U.S. helicopter arrived with personnel to assist in the delivery of a baby.[16] AGIs also operated near American bases in South Carolina, Hawaii, and even Rota, Spain, and Holy Loch, Scotland.[17] In fact, for most of the Vietnam War, the Soviets kept such boats off the coast of Guam, tracking the departure of American B-52s heading for Vietnam.[18] With this example, the NSA set out to create its own espionage fleet.

The first generation of NSA ships was born in 1960, beginning with the USNS *Private Jose F. Valdez,* a former coastal transport with the Military Sea Transportation Service (MSTS). The *Valdez* was quickly followed by the USNS *Joseph E. Muller,* an ex–supply ship retired in 1956 after a career of ferrying cargo in the Far East. Small, old, and innocuous, these ships seemed unlikely to alarm anyone, fitting NSA requirements perfectly. "What we wanted," recalled a leading official, "was a slow tub ... that could mosey along a coast relatively slowly, take its time, and spend time at sea."[19] They were also both run by the MSTS and thus manned by civilians, exempting them from required liberty calls and allowing their home ports to be far from an American naval base.

Eventually the NSA stationed the *Valdez* at Capetown, where she spent her time cruising the coasts of South Africa. The *Muller* remained closer to home in Port Everglades, Florida, keeping an eye on Fidel Castro.[20]

This first group of ships was the only one under the National Security Agency's sole direction. Following the program's early success, the navy demanded an active role. After some bickering, the two branches reached a compromise: future generations of SIGINT ships would be manned and operated by the navy, under the direction of the Naval Security Group. The NSA would still select most of the targets and the objectives, but the navy would be allowed to choose a small number for itself.[21] Under this new arrangement, the next generation of ships began to emerge in 1961 with the conversion of Victory and Liberty class cargo ships designed in World War II. Each weighed over 7,000 tons, measured approximately 450 feet long by 60 feet wide, and carried a crew of less than 300 men.

The fleet's first member was the USS *Oxford,* assigned to the eastern coast of South America and later to Southeast Asia. Bigger and faster than her predecessors, the *Oxford* warranted designation as the first ship of a new model, and on July 8, 1961, she was christened the first Auxiliary General Technical Research ship (AGTR-1). The navy commissioned two more AGTRs in 1963, the USS *Georgetown* (AGTR-2) and the USS *Jamestown* (AGTR-3), both of which spent most of their early years off South American coasts. The final two, the USS *Belmont* (AGTR-4) and the USS *Liberty* (AGTR-5), joined the group in late 1964. These last two received the most consequential assignments. The *Belmont,* on her way to Africa in 1965, was suddenly diverted to the Dominican Republic, where she helped evacuate American citizens during an attempted revolt against the regime of Donald Reid Cabral. The *Liberty* was less successful; assigned to the Mediterranean Sea, she was attacked and badly damaged by Israeli forces during the 1967 Six-Day War.[22]

Overall, the program pleased the National Security Agency but not the navy. Although seven SIGINT ships existed, all worked almost exclusively for the NSA. The agency permitted the navy to use them only if doing so did not interfere with the ships' primary function, the collection of intelligence for the NSA. The NSA had the authority to decide when the ships could spare such time, and perhaps unsurprisingly, the agency rarely accommodated navy requests. As a result, the navy once again found itself dependent on combat ships for intelligence operations. In 1965, Assistant Secretary of Defense Eugene Fulbrini took up the navy's plight and led the charge for an intelligence fleet for naval use only. On April 20, 1965, Fulbrini and Chief of Naval Operations David McDonald met with Director of Naval Intelligence Rufus Taylor and Rear Admiral Frederic Harlfinger, the assistant director of the Defense Intelligence

Agency. Explaining the need for their own source of signals intelligence collection, the two men proposed the establishment of a naval fleet of thirty reconverted tuna boats at a cost of about $1 million each; later, they planned to add forty more built from scratch.[23]

The navy responded to Fulbrini's plan with enthusiasm for the idea but worries about the expense. Recognizing Secretary of Defense McNamara's tight budget restrictions, naval leaders decided instead to request only enough funds for a trial run of three ships, to be followed by approximately a dozen more if these proved worthy. Officials at the Naval Ships Systems Command further rejected the idea of converting tuna boats for the fleet, citing both the expense and their structural inability to bear the heavy SIGINT equipment. Still, the navy liked the idea and launched a more specific feasibility study that eventually proposed implementing Fulbrini's flotilla in three phases. First, one ship would be built and operated in the western Pacific. If it proved successful, two more would be added the following year; if no problems emerged, the fleet would be expanded by about a dozen. Quickly, this plan was approved by Harold Brown, the director of Defense Research and Engineering, and Cyrus Vance, deputy secretary of defense.[24]

With approval in hand, naval authorities rushed ahead. In September 1965, the Office of the Commander in Chief, Pacific Fleet (CINCPACFLT) laid out the program's general concepts, and in March 1966, it provided the specifics. CINCPACFLT directives called for the creation of a program of "seaborne surveillance by a small ship acting singly." Ships were to remain at all times at least one mile beyond the territorial waters claimed by the target country, usually twelve miles. Although the program would be under the control of the Office of the Commander, Seventh Fleet (COMSEVENTHFLT), missions themselves would be under the control of the Commander of U.S. Naval Forces, Japan (COMNAVFORJAPAN), headquartered in Yokosuka, Japan. Specific mission proposals would originate with COMNAVFORJAPAN, which would relay them for further evaluation to the Joint Chiefs of Staff (JCS), the Commander in Chief, Pacific (CINCPAC), and CINCPACFLT, as well as the government's senior review board that approved all such covert operations. If all endorsed the mission, the JCS would issue specific sailing orders and authorize COMNAVFORJAPAN to oversee the details.[25]

The first phase of the program, designated Operation Clickbeetle, required the creation of a single ship to serve as the program's prototype. Like the AGTRs, this ship and its offspring received their own designation, Auxiliary General Environmental Research (AGER) vessels. Although similar to AGTRs, AGERs were smaller and cheaper; hence their intelligence-gathering abilities were more restricted. Only three were built: the USS *Banner* (AGER-1), the USS

Pueblo (AGER-2), and the USS *Palm Beach* (AGER-3).[26] All were former light cargo ships, approximately 180 feet long, with maximum speeds approaching thirteen knots. All were specifically reconfigured to collect SIGINT and general hydrographic information, and all were assigned the task of "naval surveillance and intelligence collection in support of high priority national intelligence objectives." Further, they were to "test the effectiveness of a small ship acting singly, and primarily, as a naval surveillance and collection unit [by] . . . collect[ing] photographic, acoustic, hydrographic, and other intelligence materials . . . and report[ing] any intercepted information of CRITIC or spot report nature." Eventually, the navy hoped that they would "provide continuous coverage of areas in which collection deficiencies exist."[27]

These goals soon proved unreachable, due in no small part to the navy's handling of the program. Having stolen the idea for these ships from the Soviets, and having built them primarily for use against the Soviets, American officials now failed to evaluate the operations apart from the U.S.-USSR rivalry. When Soviet intelligence ships were caught within the territorial waters of the United States, American officials simply asked them to leave—no military showdown, no political crisis, no public ultimatum. The U.S. government recognized the right to operate spy ships on the high seas and demanded only that they avoid American territorial waters, as elucidated by the 1958 Geneva Convention on the Territorial Seas.[28] Anticipating similar courtesy from its rival, the navy limited early operations to the Soviet coast, where safety seemed assured.[29] Flush with success, however, intelligence planners quickly extended Clickbeetle's range, blithely assuming that this safety net extended to all communist countries. In doing so, they failed to consider the likely response of each individual nation based on the indigenous values and circumstances of that nation. Instead, they presumed that these ships would be as safe near Pyongyang as they were near Vladivostok, an assumption that would eventually haunt the crew of the USS *Pueblo*.

Convinced that the mission carried negligible risks, the navy saw little need for expensive ship conversions. The AGERs, it seemed, needed only to be seaworthy, as navy officials ignored problems in important areas such as defense, navigation, and communications. The ships' overall abilities were almost completely disregarded; even Chief of Naval Operations McDonald admitted, "This was sort of a minor ship, you know—the nearest thing you could get to a fishing boat. . . . With all the other things we had to worry about in 1964 and 1965, this was pretty low on the totem pole."[30] Naval authorities had rushed full speed ahead to create their fleet, but by failing to focus on the quality of the ships themselves, they would produce an impressive program of international espionage without producing the vehicles necessary for its success.

This problem was apparent even before work on the ships began. Having dismissed tuna boats as unsuitable for conversion, the navy needed a replacement model. The task of choosing a new ship fell to Vice Admiral John Colwell in Naval Operations, who assigned it to a staff member, Captain John Oseth. Oseth received no help in making his decision, yet because the project was so highly classified, he could not be informed of the purpose of the vessels whose future he was deciding. Further, the navy told him only that they would carry some "special equipment," but not what it was or even how much it weighed. In the summer of 1965, he reluctantly settled on AKLs, calling them "the least unsuitable hulls that could be made immediately available."[31]

The AKL chosen as the guinea pig was the USS *Banner*. Smaller than most tugboats at 176 feet and 960 tons, the *Banner* had recently been ferrying cargo in the Mariana Islands and had just departed for retirement in the United States. Oseth's decision spared her. Instead, the navy sent a team of cost estimators to meet the ship at Midway Island, to ensure that conversion could be accomplished within the allotted fiscal constraints. Reflecting their assumption of the ship's safety and their concern with cost above all else, naval authorities sent no such team to evaluate her overall worthiness for the operation. With the approval of the number-crunchers, retirement plans were scrapped, and the *Banner* was redirected to Puget Sound Naval Yard in Washington for conversion into a SIGINT vessel.[32]

In spite of the inherent dangers of covert intelligence operations, the navy rushed the *Banner*'s transformation. Clickbeetle restricted missions to the Sea of Japan, where winter weather greatly hindered surveillance operations. Naval authorities thus had two choices: delay the mission until the following spring, or speed the conversion in time for a September departure. Eager to develop their own intelligence armada and dismissing the chances of a military encounter, they chose not to wait, transforming the *Banner* from an old cargo carrier into a top-secret SIGINT vessel in less than seven weeks. On October 1, 1965, she sailed out of Washington, carrying on her small decks the navy's hope that many more would follow. However, the navy's rush to get the prototype to sea had some serious ramifications, ones that should have been apparent. Instead, the navy turned a blind eye and launched a ship that, as Captain Oseth himself recalled, "was literally put together like a plate of hash."[33]

The ship's deficiencies were many. There was no ventilation or air-conditioning, and the well deck, once open to the crew, had been replaced by a classified box-shaped room called the SOD-Hut (Special Operations Department), where communications technicians (CTs) performed their intelligence operations. The quarters had to accommodate three times their normal allotment of men, forcing some drastic modifications; the small forward berthing compartment, for example, was formerly a refrigeration area. The bridge was so crowded that it was impossible to move directly between the port and starboard wings without taking long detours around various types of equipment. No guns were provided—an especially significant problem, since the emergency destruct facilities were also inadequate. Scuttling the ship required the slow process of flooding the engine room by opening the cooling water intake valves; even the chief engineer lamented that after opening the valves, "Nobody will be able to stop it from going down, but it might stay afloat for another two hours."[34] Nor had the navy considered it necessary to hold the normal shakedown training and inspections designed to ensure the quality of the ship and crew. In fact, Vice Admiral Edwin Hooper, commander of Service Force, U.S. Pacific Fleet, recalled that although his staff reported that the conversion had gone well, they had not been allowed into a number of areas because of security classifications.[35] For the *Banner,* it seemed, everything from training to testing to equipment to comfort had been sacrificed to the gods of thrift and expediency.[36]

The ship's first mission called for a series of patrols in the Sea of Japan to "conduct tactical surveillance and intelligence collection against Soviet Naval Units and other targets of opportunity."[37] Specifically, her first task was to operate off Cape Povorotny Bay near Siberia, to test the Soviet response to her presence. Problems emerged from the start. The ship collected ice on her superstructure as she steamed north, and, lacking steam hoses, the crew had no way to remove it. With the ship close to capsizing because of the weight imbalance, Lieutenant Robert Bishop radioed COMNAVFORJAPAN that he planned to withdraw; the navy responded in no uncertain terms that he was to continue. Soviet destroyers and patrol boats surrounded the *Banner* before she reached her target, some closing to within twenty-five yards, and only Bishop's skillful helmsmanship prevented a collision. The weather worsened, and the ship steamed directly into a storm for the next twenty hours; the *Banner* not only failed to make progress but actually lost two miles. Eventually, the ship returned to the United States without reaching her target, but naval authorities, jubilant that the Soviets had not responded with force, took enough satisfaction in confirming Soviet acquiescence that they paid little attention to the mission's ominous harbingers.

The *Banner* completed sixteen such missions over the next three years. The results were deemed so successful, recalled Admiral Hooper, "that Washington then wanted to convert two more."[38] However, there was also an unwanted consequence. After the *Banner*'s first few missions off the Soviet coast, the NSA received copies of the intelligence collection and suddenly demanded a role in the AGER program. Rather than debate such changes with the entire military chain of command, NSA authorities directly contacted CINCPACFLT head-quarters in Hawaii to suggest that the *Banner*'s missions be expanded to include some NSA targets. CINCPACFLT erroneously assumed that Washington had already approved this request and thus forwarded approval to COMNAV-FORJAPAN. In the ensuing confusion, a compromise was struck; the AGERs would remain under the navy's operational control and would be run solely by navy personnel, but the NSA would be allowed to choose a number of missions for its own use, even if this meant sending the *Banner* into regions not previously envisioned.[39]

Of the *Banner*'s operations, the first eight were conducted in the Sea of Japan, primarily monitoring the Soviet naval base at Vladivostok; the last eight included return trips to the Sea of Japan, as well as others off the Chinese coast in the East China Sea. The ship encountered harassment on ten of her missions, most seriously near Shanghai, when eleven Chinese trawlers surrounded her, coming close enough for the crew to almost touch them. In advance of the three trips to the East China Sea, COMNAVFORJAPAN requested that air and surface support be ready if necessary; as a result, the commanding general of the Fifth Air Force, headquartered in Fuchu, Japan, provided several aircraft on alert, and COMSEVENTHFLT assigned a destroyer for emergency protection. On the missions where no such advance arrangements had been made, the *Banner* depended on the same forces for assistance, although they would likely take longer to arrive.[40]

Although the missions had been without major incident, signs of trouble should have been apparent. Physically, the *Banner* was a mess. On one mission she lost both engines and drifted nervously off the coast of her target until a tug arrived to drag her home. On another occasion, both engines broke down while the ship was surrounded by Chinese vessels, leaving her floundering helplessly until the engineers restored them. Steering controls failed four or five times per trip, making them only slightly more reliable than the engines, which failed regularly because of problems in the air compressor unit. Both of their main navigation systems, radar and loran (long-range aid to navigation), were so untrustworthy that Captain Charles Clark ordered his officers to keep the ship beyond eighteen miles of land unless he was on the bridge, even though their orders authorized them to approach to thirteen. The communication system, a KW-7 code radio, transmitted messages only when set at precisely the same frequency as the receiving base. Although this made interception difficult, it also required the *Banner* to calibrate its frequency so specifically that communications were unreliable, especially during harassment or rough seas. It often took over twelve hours for the ship to get messages to COMNAVFORJAPAN, and on some occasions, it had taken over twenty-four.[41]

The missions continued in spite of these problems, even as their risks became more apparent. Harassment by other ships was common, and in 1966, the *Banner* even collided with the Soviet ship *Anemometr*.[42] Other incidents followed; the *Banner* was once signaled, "Heave to or I will open fire," once shouldered off course, twice surrounded by enemy trawlers, twice buzzed by Soviet aircraft, and three times approached by enemy ships with guns manned and trained on her.[43] Under these circumstances, it seems reasonable to expect that every effort would have been made to get the ship in better working order, especially in late 1967, when the engineering officer refused to approve further trips without some repairs, but the demand went ignored.[44] The *Banner* was not scheduled for major repairs until the summer of 1968; in late 1967, the navy considered granting an earlier date, even admitting that such a change was "preferable." Yet, it concluded, "funding and work schedule makes earlier time frame prohibitive."[45] "I cannot understand why the NSA didn't do anything [to protect the ships]," recalled one watch officer stationed at Kamiseya who was involved in the Clickbeetle missions. "They read all the reports. Everyone knew it [an attack] was just a matter of time."[46]

The *Banner* succeeded despite these obstacles, a tribute to the skill of the captain and crew, as much as to the vagaries of luck. Intelligence authorities at the NSA and COMNAVFORJAPAN considered this confirmation that the forays were safe, regardless of where they were assigned, despite the obvious dangers that accompanied almost every mission. This complacency obscured some clear problems in the mission assessment process, especially with regard to the provision of support forces. The *Banner*'s missions were all classified as "minimal risk" by COMNAVFORJAPAN, which had sole discretion regarding the placement of backup forces on alert. In making this decision, no formula for weighing risks was used, no detailed studies of the target nations were compiled, no experts were consulted. COMNAVFORJAPAN assigned backup in accordance with the feelings of Commander Frank Johnson and his aides, who were charged with overseeing many other projects as well. Subjectivity thus marred the assessment process. Johnson requested forces for one mission, he recalled, because "I personally was unhappy about the geographical location. . . . I didn't trust the area, I didn't trust the foreign countries involved."[47] Although Johnson was an experienced naval officer, these operations involved the lives of hundreds of crewmen; his personal feelings were hardly an adequate method of determining risk. Furthermore, he appraised the hazards without seriously considering the possibility of attack, admitting in 1969 that the risk evaluations considered "various emergency situations, but did not contemplate, in my planning, the unlawful seizure of a ship." Foreseen situations, he added, were those that "would result from an intentional or inadvertent collision or where mechanical casualty might result in drifting into territorial waters."[48]

At times, COMNAVFORJAPAN even ignored the opinions of those whose greater expertise should have been clear. The *Banner*'s tenth mission, for example, sent her off the North Korean coast for a short time. Despite the fact that this was the first mission in this dangerous area, COMNAVFORJAPAN saw no need for concern and chose not to request strip alerts. When he discovered the mission's destination, Lieutenant General Seth McKee, commander of the Fifth Air Force, became concerned, noting the frequent hostility with which the North Koreans treated approaching aircraft. McKee specifically warned the *Banner*'s commander of the danger and then sent a message to the 314th Air Division at Osan, South Korea, requesting that planes be placed on alert while the ship was in the area. When, less than a year later, the *Pueblo* would return to the same waters, COMNAVFORJAPAN again classified the mission risk as "minimal" and requested no alerts. The fact that a general who dealt almost exclusively with this region had recently dissented from this conclusion had been swiftly forgotten.[49]

Even when Johnson did want protection, the navy proved deficient. COMNAVFORJAPAN had no support forces of its own; instead, assistance had to be sought from the Fifth Air Force and the Seventh Fleet. This created problems in ensuring timely support. On one mission, COMNAVFORJAPAN requested that a destroyer be stationed within thirty miles of the target area near Shanghai; instead, the commander of the Seventh Fleet could not provide one any closer than 450 miles. Twice the *Banner* called for help during occasions of severe harassment in the East China Sea, but neither time did help arrive before the crisis ended. Still, the navy made no effort to adapt its procedures to ensure that support could arrive rapidly enough to make a difference.

Although never the target of a serious attack, the *Banner* encountered enough resistance to suggest that Clickbeetle operations might be more dangerous than originally believed. The navy, however, refused to recognize this possibility. In fact, not only were the danger signs from the *Banner* overlooked, but so were the more ominous harbingers from two more infamous SIGINT missions, one occurring in the Mediterranean Sea and the other in the Gulf of Tonkin. In 1964, the destroyer USS *Maddox* was operating in the Tonkin Gulf, along the eastern coast of North Vietnam. The operation was part of the DeSoto program, designed to collect electronic intelligence by monitoring local radio communications and by locating and tracking the frequency of coastal radar stations. Among other aims, American intelligence designed these patrols to gather information in support of OPLAN 34A, a series of covert operations secretly organized and supported by the United States and performed by the South Vietnamese against North Vietnam.

On July 30, South Vietnamese commandos operating under OPLAN 34A attacked North Vietnamese radar and military sites at Hon Me and Hon Ngu, two offshore islands in the Tonkin Gulf. The *Maddox* entered the gulf the next morning and headed north, approaching dangerously close to the areas just shelled by the commandos. As the destroyer approached Hon Me on the evening of August 1, she intercepted a series of messages indicating the imminent launch of an attack on the *Maddox*. Citing the "unacceptable risk" now presented by North Vietnamese plans, Captain John Herrick advised his superiors that the mission should be terminated and steered his ship toward open sea. The naval hierarchy, much as it would do during the *Banner*'s first mission, ignored the concerns and ordered the *Maddox* to resume its patrol. The next morning, the *Maddox* was approximately fifteen miles off Hon Me when Herrick spotted three North Vietnamese patrol boats approaching from the southeast. When the boats closed within 10,000 yards, the American vessel opened fire, launching almost 300 explosive shells of various types. In the end, one Vietnamese ship was badly damaged, and the other two broke off their attack. The fighting ended quickly, and the Johnson administration ordered no further retaliation. "The other side got a sting out of this," concluded Secretary of State Dean Rusk. "If they do it again they'll get another sting."[50]

Two nights later, the *Maddox*, now accompanied by the destroyer *Turner Joy*, was still in the Tonkin Gulf. Operating in bad weather, the two ships reported (erroneously, as was later demonstrated) that they were under attack. After this news reached Washington, President Johnson launched Operation Pierce Arrow, a retaliatory strike against North Vietnamese torpedo boat bases and oil storage facilities. Johnson also used this opportunity to push the Gulf of Tonkin Resolution through Congress, authorizing him to "take all necessary measures to repel any armed attack against the forces of the United States and to prevent further aggression."[51]

The issues surrounding the Gulf of Tonkin Incident and its impact on the Vietnam War have been well studied by historians and need no further elucidation here.[52] What is worthy of scrutiny is the navy's failure to comprehend and apply the lessons offered by this example. Although the *Maddox* was in different waters at a different time, on a slightly different mission from the *Pueblo*, striking similarities still exist. Both ships were conducting SIGINT operations along the coast of an Asian rival when they were unexpectedly attacked. Both missions' risks had been underestimated, and the officers and crew were thus somewhat unprepared. Both ships also suffered from problems in crucial areas such as communications and defense. Although the end results were different, the *Maddox* attack should have alerted naval authorities to the inherent risks of seaborne SIGINT missions and the need to prepare for the unexpected.

Perhaps most clearly, the Gulf of Tonkin Incident should have demonstrated the importance of keeping the ships in good physical condition. The *Maddox* was poorly built for her mission, turned from simple destroyer into spy ship by the addition of a special intelligence-collection room, similar to the SOD-Huts later installed on AGERs. Yet, even though intelligence gathering was the ship's primary function, the intelligence addition was treated as an unimportant item. "It had been built," recalled the officer in charge of the communications facility, "on a shoestring budget—primarily using equipment discarded by other operating facilities."[53] Crucial equipment malfunctioned at critical times. The sonar, for example, functioned poorly on the morning of August 4, prompting the captain to complain to the navy of "material deficiencies."[54] The Identification Friend or Foe (IFF) system that distinguished the status of approaching vessels had failed the same day. The ship also lacked automatic encryption machines for translating messages into code. Instead, whenever Captain Herrick needed to communicate with his superiors, he had to assign one of his officers to work the code through slowly by hand. The navy's decision to send a ship on a covert intelligence mission with unreliable navigation and identification equipment, as well as inadequate communication abilities, clearly demonstrates the extent to which it believed these missions were safe; yet, as the North Vietnamese response should have shown, seaborne intelligence operations near unpredictable enemies always involved risks.[55]

The crew was as underprepared as the ship. Suffering from a manpower shortage, the navy routinely dispatched vessels with smaller crews than were recommended for combat. As a result, the *Maddox* carried only 212 men, rather than the suggested wartime complement of 296. This badly hindered her defensive abilities; during the August 2 attack, her guns performed far below peak efficiency, largely because there were not enough men to maintain a steady supply of ammunition. The crew was also mentally unprepared for combat, having been briefed on July 27 that the mission involved little risk; it was going to be, as one officer thought, "a leisure cruise."[56] Yet, between July 30 and August 2, the United States had authorized a number of naval attacks off North Vietnamese coastal installations and was now sending the *Maddox* into the same region. The close timing of these missions was no coincidence. The North Vietnamese often turned off their radar when a DeSoto patrol appeared, so as not to reveal specific defense information. CINCPAC and CINCPACFLT thus decided to send OPLAN 34A raids near the DeSoto patrols, enabling the smaller attack vessels to utilize the advantage of surprise. Clearly, this made the DeSoto patrols more provocative, especially since the July 30 OPLAN 34A raid was the first to shell a North Vietnamese target directly. In fact, the North Vietnamese did link the two operations and assumed that the

Maddox had now returned to finish the job. Still, the navy minimized the risks to the *Maddox*, leaving the crew confident and relaxed as they cruised these dangerous waters.

Another lesson that went overlooked was the need to maintain support for these operations. Although the navy did not anticipate trouble, it stationed the aircraft carrier *Ticonderoga* near the *Maddox* during her mission and sent the *Turner Joy* to accompany her following the August 2 attack. It was unlikely that the three North Vietnamese patrol boats would have inflicted severe damage on the *Maddox* in any event, but had they scored a lucky hit, the *Ticonderoga*'s Crusaders would likely have arrived in time to ward them off before they could destroy the ship. Here was one aspect of the mission that the navy had conducted correctly, but even this example was evidently forgotten. Four years later, it would send a much weaker ship into dangerous territory without such protection, sparking much more damaging results.

In 1967, the USS *Liberty* offered similar lessons. Operating as part of the National Security Agency's AGTR program, the *Liberty* was more closely related to the *Pueblo* than the *Maddox* had been. Originally a World War II freighter known as the SS *Simmons Victory,* the ship had retired to the national reserve fleet in Olympia, Washington, in 1958, only to be reactivated by the navy five years later. With a new name, new equipment, and a new mission, the *Simmons Victory* was reborn in 1964 as the USS *Liberty,* the fifth ship in the NSA's SIGINT program. In May 1967, she was dispatched to the eastern shore of the Mediterranean Sea to monitor growing hostilities between Israel and its Arab enemies. By the time the *Liberty* arrived on the scene, the Six-Day War was winding down. On the afternoon of June 8, while the *Liberty* floated fourteen miles off the Sinai coast, Israeli planes suddenly swept from the skies, bombarding the ship with shells, rockets, and napalm. Minutes later, three torpedo boats appeared, firing torpedoes and armor-piercing bullets. One torpedo with a thousand-pound warhead struck the ship forward of her starboard side, opening a forty-foot hole in what used to be the SIGINT compartment. As the crew scrambled to put out the flames, Israeli soldiers gunned them down, just as they did the *Liberty*'s three rubber life rafts when the crew tried to evacuate the ship. The Israelis departed after destroying the vital communications equipment, leaving 34 dead and 171 wounded. The survivors patched the ship together as best they could and miraculously guided her through the night, using the North Star as their compass, to an eventual rendezvous with two American destroyers.

Like the story of the *Maddox,* the *Liberty*'s tragic tale has been told in much detail elsewhere.[57] What is important here, however, are the striking similarities between the *Liberty* and the *Pueblo*. Like the *Maddox,* and later the *Pueblo,* the *Liberty* suffered from major mechanical problems. Communications difficulties were perhaps most troubling, especially since the ship would be operating in a war zone. The ship's transmissions were operated through a Technical Research Ship Special Communications System (TRSSCOMM), a complex network of computers, sensors, and antennae that dispatched a 10,000-watt microwave signal to the moon and then back down to receiving stations in the United States. The *Liberty*'s system had been in place for almost a year and had never worked properly. To be effective, TRSSCOMM required the antennae to be fixed directly at the moon—always a difficult task on a rolling ship. Even had this been possible, the hydraulic system that maneuvered it had been improperly installed. Not only did it fail consistently, but it often covered the deck with purple hydraulic fluid, leaving the ship more colorful but less effective. During the most recent repair session, the shipyard had mistakenly installed the wrong piping into the system, which, in spite of a temporary repair at sea, quickly failed again. As a result, the *Liberty* had sent position reports to the navy each of the four days since she left Spain but was informed on June 6 that none had been received.[58] TRSSCOMM might have been a reasonable idea, but it was still experimental and thus hardly appropriate for ships so dependent on reliable communications. Yet the navy was so certain about the safety of these vessels that it used them as guinea pigs for an unproven communication system; in fact, the first ship to receive one had been the original AGTR, the *Oxford*.[59]

Another significant problem lay in the ship's emergency destruct system. During the attack, the crew's attempts to destroy classified documents were slow and ineffective, largely because the navy had provided inadequate equipment. Weighted bags to be filled with papers and discarded over the side were too heavy to carry, and the person throwing them was exposed to hazardous fire. Even had the bags been jettisoned, the water was simply too shallow to prevent their recovery. The ship's incinerator was not only too small to be of much help but had also been placed on an exposed deck. In the end, the crew was forced to try to destroy their classified materials by hand while they were under attack and sinking.

Other problems plagued the ship, most notably in the realm of communications. When the NSA discovered how close to shore the navy had sent the ship, it demanded that it be moved away. The navy reluctantly concurred, and the JCS message center in the Pentagon composed a message requiring the *Liberty* to move at least twenty miles from shore. However, this order waited in the communications center for over fourteen hours before being transmitted. When finally sent, it went not to the *Liberty* but was instead misdirected to the naval communications station in the Philippines, where it remained until after the attack. Still, the JCS were worried, and a few hours later they sent another message, this time directing the ship to stay 100 nautical miles from the coast. This one was also misdirected to the Philippines station and then rerouted back to the Pentagon, which sent it to NSA headquarters in Fort George Meade, Maryland. This message also requested that the receivers acknowledge its receipt, but no one noticed that the *Liberty* never responded. Finally, the JCS sent one more communication. This one was designated "top secret" and of "immediate precedence" and was to go directly to the *Liberty*. The Pentagon message center selected a "top-secret" message delivery system for conveyance, inadvertently choosing one to which the ship did not subscribe, and once again the message missed its intended target.

Problems existed in the area of support as well. Armed only with four ineffective .50 caliber Browning machine guns, the *Liberty* relied on promised backup in case of trouble. During the Israeli attack, *Liberty* radiomen sent a distress call to the Sixth Fleet, which sent four F-4 Phantom jets from the USS *America*, operating near Crete. Yet the planes carried only nuclear weapons and consequently were recalled by Secretary of Defense McNamara. Upon returning to their ship, they had to undergo the lengthy process of switching to conventional weapons and were therefore unable to arrive in time. It was not unreasonable for the navy to maintain a small number of planes so configured, but there were two aircraft carriers, the *America* and the *Saratoga*, within range of the *Liberty*, carrying a total of over 150 aircraft. Somehow, every plane was either configured for nuclear strikes, being repaired, or had been reserved for a specific mission. Despite the fact that a poorly armed intelligence ship was operating in a hazardous situation nearby, no one had readied any of these planes for its defense, even though the *Liberty*'s captain requested on June 5 that a destroyer be sent as an escort while his ship operated in this region. In fact, the navy rejected his request the following day, explaining that "*Liberty* is a clearly marked United States ship in international waters, not a participant in the conflict and not a responsible subject for attack by any nation."[60]

Following the difficulties experienced by the *Banner*, the *Maddox*, and the *Liberty*, it seems logical to assume that the Clickbeetle program would be altered, or at least reexamined, with an eye toward reducing the degree of risk. Yet the navy not only failed to do so but later even justified this inaction. In testimony before a congressional inquiry into the *Pueblo* Incident, Frank Slatinshek, assistant chief counsel for the Special House Subcommittee, criticized Admiral Frank Johnson's judgment: "A commanding officer is required not to hazard his ship. He is supposed to exercise his judgment as to anticipating hazards, and what was involved here is your assessment of risk concerning the *Pueblo*, and as shown here, you obviously made a bad guess." Johnson interjected to defend his decisions, "Based on 150 years of never having happened." Chairman Otis Pike (D-N.Y.) cut him off by asking, "You don't think what happened to the *Liberty* disturbed that precedent in any manner?" Johnson responded weakly: "That is a different situation, but that is correct."[61] A similar exchange occurred between Pike and Chief of Naval Operations Thomas Moorer during the same hearings, when Pike asked if any changes had been made as a direct result of the *Liberty*. Moorer answered that the navy had learned that these missions could be more dangerous than originally believed, but when pressed to cite specific examples of how this realization had been applied, he could only point to the addition of guns to the ships, a change that was of no help to the *Pueblo*.[62] Moorer could say nothing about making changes in support, upgrading the equipment, ensuring adequate communications, or reassessing the missions' risks, because no such steps had been taken.

Nothing demonstrates the navy's failure more clearly than a series of comments made by Admiral Moorer, who was COMSEVENTHFLT at the time of the Gulf of Tonkin Incident and chief of naval operations at the time of the *Pueblo* attack. Speaking over ten years apart, he defended the navy's apparent lack of concern in both cases. Regarding the *Maddox*, he attributed this complacency to the fact that the ship would be in international waters and pointed to the presence of Soviet ships off the American coast, concluding that the mission was therefore "routine," since, he explained, "at the same time, the Soviets . . . were doing identical things with their trawlers." These reasons proved fallacious, especially since North Vietnam, not the Soviet Union, was the target. Regarding the *Pueblo*, Moorer again defended the navy's complacency, and again with the same themes. The navy was justified in not foreseeing trouble, he concluded, because "the ship was going to operate totally in international waters" and because "the Soviets . . . employ about 40 unarmed intelligence collection ships. . . . Some of these AGIs occasionally have violated our territorial waters but none has been attacked or fired on by our forces."[63] Even if one accepts Moorer's explanation for one incident, it is difficult to accept it to justify both. In 1979, Moorer jumped into the fray again, writing the foreword for a book on the *Liberty*. He began with the advice that the book "should be read by all Americans."[64] Perhaps the men of the *Pueblo* would have been better served if Moorer, and the navy itself, had taken this advice and followed these events a little more closely.

President Franklin Roosevelt once remarked of the navy, "To change anything in the navy is like punching a feather bed. You punch it with your right and you punch it with your left until you are finally exhausted, and you find the damn bed just as it was before you started punching."[65] FDR's complaint was as valid in 1968 as it had been thirty years earlier. Recent events had clearly demonstrated that these missions were not what had been anticipated. The fundamental assumptions that underlay the program had been proved either false or irrelevant: the operations were riskier than had been assumed, the ships were not always safe in international waters, and the quid pro quo with the Soviets did not always matter. The *Banner* had been harassed to the point of near disaster; the *Maddox* had been attacked in international waters, and the *Liberty* had almost been destroyed by an ally. Clearly, the program needed to be reexamined to provide for better-equipped ships, better-trained crews, better risk assessments, and better protection. The facts were punching with both hands, but like Roosevelt's feather bed, the navy remained unaffected.

CHAPTER TWO

The Ugly Duckling

From morning to dark,
A gray Noah's Ark,
We bounced and quivered along.
But instead of a pair
Of animals rare,
We carried agents, about 83 strong.

It was a rainy January day when Pete Bucher's plane landed in Seattle, but even the poor weather could not dampen the new skipper's high spirits. Quickly he dashed to the Puget Sound Naval Shipyard in Bremerton, eagerly anticipating a glimpse of his new command. His mood plummeted as he approached the shipyard's basin:

> I spotted . . . the unmistakably ugly shape of a pair of AKLs, made even uglier by their molding green blotches of anticorrosion paint with running sores of bleeding rust. One of them had to be the USS *Pueblo.* Which one did not matter as they both looked like abandoned derelicts when compared with the great warships being serviced in the yard, or even with the *Banner.* . . . She still had the musty smell and disarrayed appearance of one recently resurrected from a mothball fleet. Her decks were cluttered with tools and scaffoldings of half-finished projects. Her interior spaces were unworkable and unlivable; her main and auxiliary engines torn down for repairs; the complicated electronic installation of her all-important SOD-Hut barely begun, and most discouraging, much of the modification work that should have been included was not, while such that had, had been done inadequately.[1]

The introduction provided an important lesson about the ship's position on the navy's list of priorities. The *Pueblo,* then sporting the less colorful appellation *FP-344,* had not been a functioning vessel since 1954 and needed extensive work to even be considered seaworthy. For the last six months, she had been docked in Bremerton for just such a purpose, supposedly being converted from dilapidated ex–cargo carrier into sophisticated intelligence interceptor. Instead, as Bucher so unhappily discovered, she had been virtually ignored, receiving significant attention only when moving from slip to slip to accommodate repairs on the many vessels deemed more important.

Still, Pete Bucher had faced long odds before, and his energy and enthusiasm had always triumphed. Born in 1927 to parents he never knew, he was soon adopted by an Idaho couple, Austin and Mary Bucher. Fate was unkind to the Buchers. Mary died of cancer in 1929, about the same time that Austin's restaurant failed, crushed by the joint pressures of the Great Depression and his own gambling habit. At the age of three, Pete moved to his grandparents' farm, which went the way of his father's restaurant in 1933. Austin Bucher, who had never recovered from the loss of his wife and his business, remained in Idaho while Pete and his grandparents traced the path of thousands of other farmers moving west to California.

Pete's grandfather died in 1934, leaving his grandmother unable to care for him by herself. He returned to his father, who lived with a group of itinerant men in a shack on the banks of Idaho's Snake River. The young Bucher soon was skipping school and stealing, and he joined a gang. After local police arrested him for shoplifting, state welfare officials placed him in an orphanage in Boise, which transferred him to St. Joseph's Orphanage in Culdesac, Idaho, in 1938. Three years later, Pete moved on to the Boys Town orphanage in Nebraska, where he began to blossom, becoming a starter on the football team, a solid student, and twice the president of his class. He left Boys Town on October 2, 1945—eight months before graduation—and enlisted in the navy. After two years of service on a supply ship, he returned to Boys Town to collect his diploma, and in 1949 enrolled at the University of Nebraska. Four years later he returned to the navy, this time with a bachelor's degree in secondary education, an associate's degree in geology, experience in the Naval Reserve Officers' Training Corps, and a wife, the former Rose Rohling, who had become Rose Bucher on June 10, 1950.

After a number of different assignments, Pete reported for duty aboard his first submarine, becoming the supply, communications, and weapons officer for the USS *Besugo* in December 1955. He remained there until 1958, and then after various shore positions he joined the USS *Ronquil,* a diesel-powered submarine, in 1961. His skills and leadership abilities impressed the wardroom, and he eventually ascended to the position of executive officer. In 1964, Bucher left the *Ronquil* to become the assistant operations officer for Submarine Flotilla Seven in Yokosuka. His career had progressed steadily, and in 1966 he was not surprised to discover that he was under consideration for command of his own submarine. The surprise came later, when he learned that he had been rejected. Thirty-five men had been examined for only seventeen spots, and Bucher had been found wanting. Years of loyal service paid off, however, as his former superiors pressured the navy to reconsider. The authorities agreed, but since it was too late to assign him a submarine, they decided to grant Bucher the next available command position for which he was qualified. In late 1966, they ordered him to assume command of the USS *Pueblo*. Pete Bucher had made the long journey from orphan to officer, and although the *Pueblo* was not a submarine, it was still a symbol of how far he had come. He was determined not to let some wear and tear spoil the opportunity.

Still, he could not help but be aghast at the lack of progress. "They had finished the structural work," he recalled, "but none of the guts were in there. And they weren't working on it. There was just these two or three guys who went down to the ship every day and farted around." Equally distressing was the fact that he seemed alone in his concern about the vessel's obvious inadequacies. Shortly after arriving, Bucher complained about the lethargic conversion to the shipyard commander, Rear Admiral Floyd Schultz, who responded with a clear message about the navy's priorities. "The admiral told me that he didn't know much about the program, and said he didn't want to know," recalled Bucher. "He gave me every indication that he wasn't very damn interested."[2] In the end, the captain's repeated pleas only alienated the shipyard staff. "At times," noted Bucher's 1967 fitness report, "he became overzealous in requests for certain work he wants accomplished on *Pueblo* and overtaxed the patience of shipyard workers."[3]

Bucher's concerns about his ship's condition went ignored largely because the navy foresaw little danger in the Clickbeetle operations. "[The] risk," explained COMNAVFORJAPAN, "is estimated to be minimal since operations will be conducted in international waters."[4] This opinion was held not just at this immediate command level, noted Admiral Johnson, but was "concurred in by all commands in the chain of command, including JCS."[5] Accordingly, the navy had no interest in spending time, money, and effort on improvements. Despite the obvious harbingers offered by other SIGINT missions, and the *Pueblo*'s even more obvious problems, the navy turned a deaf ear to Bucher's complaints, a blind eye to signs of danger, and a closed mind to any suggestion that the ship be upgraded.

The navy's attitude was clear from the start of the conversion process. Inspired by the *Banner*'s results, authorities decided to launch phase II of Operation Clickbeetle in 1966 by adding two more SIGINT vessels to the program. Two retired army coastal freighters were chosen: *FS-389*, moored at Charleston, South Carolina, would soon become the USS *Palm Beach*; *FP-344*, moored at Rio Vista, California, was to be the more well-known USS *Pueblo*. The two ships were towed to Bremerton without any careful scrutiny; in fact, the navy assumed that they were twins and prepared only one conversion plan for both, despite the fact that their different physical structures were obvious at even a cursory glance.[6]

Originally built in 1944 as a general-purpose supply vessel for the Army Transportation Corps, *FP-344* had performed well in this capacity until her 1954 retirement.[7] After collecting rust at Clatskanie, Oregon, and Rio Vista, California, for over a decade, she was transferred to navy control in the spring of 1966. At 177 feet long and just under 33 feet wide, the ship was tiny by navy standards, as was her recommended complement of forty crewmen. Her propulsion system consisted of two eight-cylinder diesel engines with twin screws, which could reach a top speed of thirteen knots, about one-third that of a conventional American destroyer. Years of inactivity had taken their toll. When the USS *Tatnuck,* the tugboat charged with transporting her to Washington, arrived to take possession, her skipper wondered if his orders had somehow been mistaken. *FP-344* looked so dilapidated that he doubted she would survive the short trip.[8] Still, he had his assignment, and on April 22, 1966, *FP-344* arrived at Bremerton at the rear end of a tugboat. It was a position she would assume regularly over the next twenty months.

The *Tatnuck*'s captain had not underestimated the ship's condition. Rust had corroded her hull so badly that sunlight poured through the deck in the aft spaces. Sounding the foghorn drew compressed air from the air clutch in the main propulsion drive system, sometimes leaving the ship without sufficient air to change direction. Most ships requiring adroit maneuvering were controlled directly from the bridge, but *FP-344* required the bridge to relay orders to the engine room through a system of bells. Even when commands were successfully transmitted, the steering engine failed so frequently that there remained a good chance they could not be carried out. No space was available for the test equipment that usually accompanies complex electronic gear, nor were the research areas adequately ventilated. Ship-to-shore communication was horrid, making it only slightly worse than internal ship communication, which was merely inadequate. *FP-344* might be made seaworthy with some time, money, and effort, but readying her for sensitive intelligence operations would clearly require a more herculean performance.[9]

Bucher doggedly tried to transform his ugly duckling into a swan, or at least a less ugly duckling, but he had little success. A few months after arriving, he recalled, "actual progress on the *Pueblo* was hardly visible."[10] Funding was one obstacle, as the allocation provided fell far short of what was deemed necessary by even the navy's own estimates. The Navy Plans and Programs section originally requested $15 million for the conversion of the two ships. Instead, navy comptrollers allocated only $11.5 million, later reduced to $8.6 million by the

Defense Department. Of this amount, the *Pueblo* received $4.5 million.[11] Faced with these budget constraints, the navy repeatedly rejected requests for improvements. Among other things, the ship's officers sought an intercom to link the engine room with the pilothouse, improved living quarters, a set of damage control plates and a damage control book, a collision alarm, and watertight hatches for the office spaces and the forward berthing compartments. All the requests were denied.[12] After the *Banner* experienced serious engine and power failures off the Shanghai coast, Bucher unsuccessfully sought an engine overhaul.[13] Citing the real threat of capsizing, he asked to be allowed to remove the twenty-six-foot motor whaleboat, which raised the ship's center of gravity without serving any real purpose, since adequate life rafts were already stored, but again he was overruled.[14] After the steering system failures became hourly, he sought a complete overhaul of the steering engines, and again the navy found his arguments unpersuasive.[15]

Money was not the only obstacle, however. The navy deemed the ship and her mission to be so highly classified that it briefed only those few authorities who had a clear "need to know." Accordingly, many of those charged with preparing the ship never knew what they were preparing her for. Shortly after the navy cut $1 million from the conversion budget, Bucher watched the shipyard spend $5,000 to bead in the "AKL" designation on his ship's bow, even though he knew it would have to be replaced by "AGER" before leaving port. But since no one in Bremerton was cleared to know of the existence of the AGER program, he could do nothing to avoid the unnecessary expenditure.[16] This problem hindered operations throughout the conversion. As late as two days before departure, Bucher met with Rear Admiral Norvell Ward of Service Group Three, which had administrative control of the *Pueblo*. When Ward asked about any last-minute problems, Bucher declined to name any, leaving the admiral convinced that the ship was fully functional. In fact, Bucher might have said plenty, but Ward, despite being commander of Service Group Three, was not cleared to receive information about the vessel's actual operations.[17]

Bucher had similar difficulties in dealing with the Bremerton leadership, since both Admiral Schultz and the ship's superintendent, Lieutenant Commander Leo Sweeney, lacked the necessary security clearances to be told about the ship's mission. Finally, Bucher went to Al Johnston, a civilian in Naval Ships Systems Command charged with designing the *Pueblo*'s specifications, and discovered that Johnston was converting the ship into a standard AKL, simply because no one had ever informed him that it should be otherwise. Accordingly, the naval yard had accepted Johnston's orders without question and thus rejected items Bucher considered vital, such as a self-powered incinerator and a storage area for classified publications, since they did not fit AKL design specifications.[18] "We had," complained Edward Murphy, the *Pueblo*'s executive officer, "a staff above us who had little or no appreciation for the kind of ship they were supporting. . . . This was apparently due, at least in part, to the need for security, but that security was carried to such a degree that no one seemed to know what was going on."[19] Ironically, while the navy demanded such tight security, shipyard workers routinely tossed top-secret design blueprints and other materials into a nearby dumpster, where the ship's communications technicians tried to fish them out before they fell into the wrong hands.[20]

These security problems hindered the conversion in other ways. For much of the effort, the navy had not approved Murphy to know the details of the *Pueblo*'s mission, forcing him to fulfill the difficult assignment of outfitting the ship without knowing its objective.[21] Subsequently, Operations Officer Frederick Schumacher was charged with requisitioning supplies, and although eventually cleared for the ship's mission, he lacked the Special Intelligence clearance required for entry into the research spaces, making it hard to determine what supplies the CTs needed and when.[22] Security restrictions kept most of the crew in the dark as well. In early 1967, seventeen men other than Bucher had reported for duty, none of whom could be told anything except that they would be undertaking "special research missions."[23] All they knew, one remembered, was that they "were on a ship that would at some time, go somewhere, to do something, for someone."[24]

In some cases, conversion problems stemmed from simple bureaucratic error, an occurrence especially prevalent with the *Pueblo*. Since so few people were aware of her existence, the ship had few advocates in the lower echelons of naval paperwork and was thus often overlooked. Early in the conversion process, Murphy requested more crewmen to complete the ship's complement, and more bunks to accommodate them. However, Ships Systems Command refused to send the bunks until the men arrived, and the Bureau of Naval Personnel would not assign the men until their bunks were ready. Since such a minor issue was insufficient to warrant the attention of the high-ranking admirals in nominal charge of the ship, and since few people at lower levels had even heard of the *Pueblo*, Murphy could only wait until one side relented. Finally Naval Personnel sent the men in October, but the bunks still did not appear, until Murphy "appropriated" some from a nearby reserve ship about to be scrapped.[25] Even when the navy bureaucracy tried to provide support, secrecy and inattention still hindered the results. Shortly before departing, Bucher requisitioned rock salt to melt any ice that accumulated on the ship while in the Sea of Japan. Rather than sending him the requested granulated salt, navy officials delivered 600 pounds of large blocks, which, as salt licks, would have provided an effective diversion if cattle ever attacked but were of little use in a blizzard.[26] Although such minor incidents had no bearing on future events, they reflected the navy's general attitude toward *FP-344*. Having dragged the ship from retirement and ordered her prepared for a secret mission, navy leaders turned their focus elsewhere. At the same time, they classified the project too highly for most of the relevant parties to be informed of its details. The end result was one of the omnipresent realities of the *Pueblo*'s conversion: those who paid attention to the ship could not know anything about it, while those cleared to know about it did not pay it any attention.

Perhaps no improvement was more warranted than an upgrade of the ship's facilities for the destruction of classified information. In case of emergency, the *Pueblo*'s primary method of material destruction consisted of twenty-two weighted sacks that could be filled with papers and thrown overboard. These sacks may have been adequate under peaceful conditions, but they were less useful under fire, since they required manual jettison from the unprotected main deck, thus exposing the bearer to hostile fire. They were also slow to fill, hard to carry during unsteady conditions, and practical only in water deep enough to prevent easy recovery. Since the *Pueblo*'s sole purpose required her presence close to enemy coasts, the chances of her being in such depths were minimal. Even if she was not attacked but was merely harassed or broke down near enemy territory, the bags were an unlikely solution. Emergency destruction would be ordered only if a threat to the ship emerged; yet the presence of such a threat, most likely hostile ships that could easily retrieve the materials, defeated the purpose of such a procedure. As a result, the only time that the destruct facilities would be useful would be during those occasions when there was no need for them.

The *Pueblo*'s destruct system had other components, but they were similarly inadequate. The ship carried two slow paper-shredding machines in the forward electronics room, each with the capacity to shred only three or four sheets of paper at a time. The navy did not install an incinerator, and after Bucher's repeated requests for one were ignored, he purchased a hand-fed commercial model with $1,300 of the $4,000 the navy allotted for crew comfort.[27] Still, the incinerator could handle only four pounds of paper at a time and required that the pages first be shredded. Since it was not fuel fed, it needed to be watched carefully; too much paper at one time would smother the fire, and too little would extinguish it. It could also destroy only individual sheets, obligating the crew to tear apart hundreds of bound reports by hand. Shortly before departure, a Naval Security Station representative proposed upgrading the incinerator, but the shipyard, citing the standard concerns of time and money, rejected the idea.[28] Considering that the *Pueblo* left port with almost 450 pounds of paper materials and was expected to add another 150 pounds of its own research, destruction by these methods would clearly take longer than could reasonably be expected during a crisis. One officer estimated that complete destruction under the specific conditions of the seizure would have taken between nine and twelve hours, an estimate that actually appears overly optimistic.[29]

The navy ducked charges that the ship had been inadequately prepared. The Office of the Chief of Naval Operations (CNO), for example, somehow claimed that all materials could have been destroyed in one hour.[30] Instead, the navy blamed the inadequate destruction on the officers' "lack of initiative and leadership."[31] Bucher was singled out for reproach. Admiral Sharp lambasted his poor performance, stating, "especially with all the highly classified documents he had on board, . . . he took no really positive steps to get rid of them"; Admiral Johnson even blamed him for not unloading more before departure.[32] Such criticism was unmerited, especially since the shortcomings of the SIGINT destruct systems should have been evident well before the *Pueblo* seizure. Commander Clark of the *Banner* had frequently voiced concerns about the inadequacy of his ship's destruct capabilities, and the *Liberty*'s experience with virtually the same equipment had proved its shortcomings under attack.[33] Perhaps destruction could have been performed efficiently under ideal circumstances, but doing so during an attack at sea on a poorly balanced and barely steerable ship was a more daunting task. Reflecting the navy's attempt to transfer blame, one CNO expert maintained that the officers should have started a fire to aid them in burning papers, a "small controlled one that doesn't endanger the ship."[34] Such a tactic might have been reasonable at CNO headquarters, but common sense suggests that a fire on board a small and poorly ventilated ship while under attack might not have been so easily controlled. In fact, the CTs did set some fires during the seizure, but since the navy, for security reasons, had refused to allow portholes in the SOD-Hut, there was no way to clear the smoke from the room and enable the crew to see (and breathe) while they burned documents. The navy's claims fell apart under close scrutiny, as demonstrated when Admiral Johnson testified before House hearings on the seizure.

MR. LENNON: Your command was charged with the responsibility—and I am reading from your statement—to verify that suitable facilities and procedures exist for the rapid destruction of classified material. . . . Now answer the question "Yes" or "No." Did we have the facilities and procedures for the rapid destruction of classified material on the *Pueblo?*
JOHNSON: Mr. Lennon—
LENNON: Just "Yes" or "No," and then explain it.

JOHNSON: The answer is "Yes" under certain situations which I had envisioned would be the situation that would develop, and "No" under others, such as unlawful seizure. . . . There would be reasonable time in the case of drifting or in other situations.

MR. NEDZI: Under no conceivable circumstances to me, you would have sufficient time to adequately destroy the classified material. . . .

JOHNSON: Yes, sir; I think you could do it in about three hours.

NEDZI: Well, how could you anticipate getting three hours time? . . . When in immediate danger, they have only a few minutes.

JOHNSON: I get your point. That is right.[35]

The lack of an efficient destruct system was especially significant because the *Pueblo* carried a staggering accumulation of classified publications on her maiden voyage, most of which were irrelevant to her mission. Originally, naval authorities mistakenly sent her a full set of publications for an AGMR, a converted escort carrier. Without any being removed, the *Pueblo* received a set for an AKL, despite the ship's recently changed status to an AGER. Subsequently, naval bureaucrats inundated the ship with other materials, including paperwork from COMSEVENTHFLT, CINCPACFLT, COMNAVFORJAPAN, and the Pacific ELINT (electronic intelligence) Center at Fuchu Nobi, Japan. Many were inapplicable; others were merely superfluous, like the ten copies of Naval Warfare Publication #33 the ship received instead of the allotted one. Further adding to the burden was the number of different intelligence specialists the ship carried, all of whom required the relevant publications for their individual fields and machines, including manuals for the top-secret KW-7, KWR-37, and KL-7 coding and decoding machines. Just before departing on the mission, Murphy wondered if all the materials were really necessary and answered his own question: "To that there is a simple, emphatic answer: no. But with an important qualification; since no one either aboard or ashore appeared to know for sure which ones were necessary and which ones weren't, we had to sail with them all."[36]

Bucher and his officers complained incessantly about the allotment, but the Office of the Commander of Service Forces, Pacific (COMSERVPAC) refused to permit their off-loading. Nor would the Pentagon approve the addition of improved destruct facilities. When Dan Hearn, the civilian engineer overseeing the conversion, informed the Defense Department that his staff had decided to install automatic systems, navy authorities overruled him. "When was the last time a U.S. Navy ship was captured?" asked a senior officer.[37] The hierarchy finally relented a mere three days before departure, allowing the *Pueblo* to remove some excess publications. The victory was brief, however; at 5:00 the next morning, five more boxes of communications publications arrived, all with the highest security classification. The new shipment, in fact, exceeded the number that the crew had just removed. By the time the ship left, there were classified documents literally stacked in the aisles.[38]

The *Pueblo* itself also merited a destruct system, since her SIGINT equipment and intelligence specialists made her a considerable prize. On most intelligence ships, explained one navy official, "You push two buttons and all they get is a mass of melted metal."[39] Yet when Bucher arrived in Bremerton, the ship carried only a set of sledgehammers and fire axes for the destruction of intelligence equipment—a somewhat useless provision, since most of it was encased in heavy metal jackets.[40] There were no seacocks, valves affixed to a ship's hull that, when opened, create quick internal flooding; instead, scuttling could best be achieved by removing the saltwater cooling intakes in the main engine room, thereby flooding it until the bulkheads burst. Under ideal conditions with an experienced crew, the procedure would take over an hour; done by the *Pueblo* crew while under attack, it would likely have exceeded twice that.[41]

Bucher's requests for an improved means of self-destruction went ignored until he sent a strongly worded letter to Naval Operations in June 1967, firmly declaring, "The scope of the security-sensitive equipment installed aboard, together with other classified material, renders their quick destruction impossible using conventional destruction means, i.e. fire ax, sledgehammer, destruction bags. An explosive destruction means should be provided to the ship which will enable the commanding officer to thoroughly destroy all sensitive classified material."[42] In response, the chief of naval operations asked Naval Ships Systems Command to review the situation. On July 17, authorities replied that an upgraded destruct system was considered "highly desirable." Yet they doubted that one could be added, since standard procedure was to build the ship around the explosive, not the other way around. However, they concluded, the army had recently developed a method that might be applicable to ships like the *Pueblo*. Accordingly, they recommended that no action be taken until the army system could be further studied. The chief of naval operations agreed.[43] Such an improvement might be merited, but there seemed no immediate reason for concern. Meanwhile, the *Pueblo* would just have to wait.

Finally, Bucher took the matter to Admiral Johnson, who sent an explosives expert to the ship. The specialist, Lieutenant (jg) Lynn Pickard, recommended the placement of about a dozen thermite bombs in strategic locations throughout the ship, which could quickly blow a hole in the hull if necessary. Bucher rejected the idea. Not only were thermite bombs extremely hazardous at sea because of the ease with which they could be accidentally triggered, but navy security publication KAG-1D forbade their presence on these ships.[44] Instead, he tried to obtain TNT, which was more stable and easier to handle, but which the ammunition depot proved unable to obtain (thermite, of course, could have been acquired easily). Finally, he gave up. "All I could accomplish by pressing it further was to upset Admiral Johnson and his staff by giving them the impression they had a skipper on their hands who seemed obsessed with the capability to blow up his own ship. I didn't want to cross the boundary between chronic worry-wart and outright nut!"[45]

The navy subsequently claimed that it had done all it could on this issue, having provided "everything that was suitable that was available at the time."[46] Such a claim was hardly accurate. Despite much evidence of needed improvements, the navy refused to consider an upgrade. In fact, subsequent actions suggested that such changes might not have been as difficult as the navy leadership contended; in a clear case of closing the barn door after the horse had escaped, they began a program to upgrade the destruct capabilities of SIGINT ships shortly after the *Pueblo* capture and had refitted them all by early 1969.[47] Similarly, it was no coincidence that the provision against thermite was reversed soon after the *Pueblo*'s capture, nor that many secret documents began to be printed on water-soluble paper.[48]

Problems existed in other areas. Despite Admiral Moorer's subsequent claim that "We had real fine communications," the *Pueblo*'s antiquated system was sorely inadequate for an intelligence ship.[49] A public-address (PA) system, built prior to World War II and operating through the same speakers as the general alarm, handled internal ship communication. As a result, there could be no on-board communication over the system while the general alarm was ringing; like the emergency destruct system, this aspect of the ship worked best when it was needed the least and was virtually useless when it was most vital. Even without the alarm, the PA system could be heard only in areas where speakers already existed. Although the navy had added numerous rooms during the conversion, it had neglected to equip them with speakers, leaving some locations, including the research spaces, without a link to the ship's major form of internal communication. Accordingly, the only communication between the SOD-Hut and the rest of the ship was a 1-JV sound-powered telephone system mounted in the hall outside the door, which the navy required be kept closed and triple-locked at all times. Installed during World War II, this phone system connected over thirty areas of the ship, and during a crisis, it would likely be overwhelmed with conversation.

Again, Bucher's repeated requests for improvements went ignored. Among other things, he petitioned for a general announcing and alarm system, an intercom between the pilothouse and the signal bridge, a collision alarm, and a set of remote unit radio telephones, but he was routinely denied, usually for budgetary reasons.[50] Finally, after almost coming to blows with the ship's planning officer, Bucher received an extension phone on the signal bridge and some basic wiring and telephone instruments with which to create a homemade internal communication system.[51] In the end, the ship left on a top-secret espionage mission in dangerous waters; yet had she come under attack, the only way for the bridge to send orders to the research spaces was to send a messenger, who would have to be admitted from the inside, since it was unlikely that he would know the combinations to the SOD-Hut locks. In a crisis situation, such inefficiency could (and would) prove costly.

External communications were also problematic. The *Pueblo* carried a modern communication system, primarily run through a KW-7 code radio, a state-of-the-art machine that could code and decode messages transmitted over secure HF teletype circuits. The ship could also send and receive messages on a voice circuit, on a teletype circuit, through Morse code, or even on uncovered telephone lines.[52] In theory, when the ship needed to report, crewmen would call the Naval Communications Station in Kamiseya, Japan, on an open Morse code line and request the opening of circuit 21P, a special teletype line reserved just for them.[53] However, the *Pueblo*'s transmitting power was limited, and Kamiseya had trouble hearing her. Even when the ship was within range, newer vessels with more powerful transmitters often obscured her messages.[54] Propagation anomalies in the Sea of Japan also made it difficult to find frequencies consistently, especially since the system required almost perfect calibration between the ship and the receiver to begin transmitting.[55] Communication was especially difficult in the early morning, when the rising sun created atmospheric problems, and late at night because of ionospheric disturbances. "It seemed," recalled one CT, "as if there was an invisible shield that would surround the ship after dusk."[56] Even when links were established, they created other problems, because the transmissions often affected the sensitive SIGINT collection equipment.[57] Yet, when the crew brought these problems to the attention of the navy, they were ignored. "They had an attitude," recalled CT Don McClarren, "of 'Oh well, we'll fix it later,' but later never came."[58]

Problems also existed with the steering engine, which had the not insignificant task of turning the ship's rudder. Unlike the hydraulic steering systems common in most ships, the *Pueblo*'s was electromechanical, the creation of a Wisconsin elevator company that went out of business shortly after World War II, taking most of the spare parts with it. The engine failed frequently, leaving the ship dependent on manual control. An extensive study at Bremerton concluded that the flaw was inherent in the design, and since replacement parts were difficult to obtain, nothing short of a total renovation would alleviate the problem. However, since such work would cost hundreds of thousands of dollars and delay the mission by at least a few weeks, naval authorities rejected the idea. If they thought the system would suffice, however, clear evidence should have indicated otherwise. Not only did the *Pueblo's* system consistently fail during her trials, but the *Palm Beach,* on the way to her first assignment, had a complete steering failure in the Atlantic and had to be towed back to dock for a total overhaul.[59]

Difficulties also existed with the SIGINT equipment. Installation began in February 1967 and was almost completed in the spring. As always, unexpected complications emerged. In April, Lieutenant Stephen Harris, who was in charge of the ship's intelligence detachment, realized that the equipment had been installed in the wrong positions. Those devices monitored most frequently had been placed along the baseboards or high above the deck, while the more useless equipment stood at eye level. In this arrangement, the CTs would spend most of their time lying flat on the floor or standing on ladders. A furious Bucher found himself unable to blame the shipyard staff; they had actually installed the equipment as ordered by Naval Ships Systems Command, which had designed the installation without considering the practical applications. Fixing the blunder took over $250,000 and almost two months of extra work, yet problems continued. Some of the machines still needed to be operated on hands and knees, and no space was provided for test equipment or for the accumulated results. On those rare occasions when the CTs could perform their jobs while seated, they found the chairs less than cooperative, since Naval Ships Systems Command had forgotten to have them secured. The seats "wouldn't stay in one spot longer than three seconds when we were under way," recalled Bucher. Since the SOD-Huts also lacked grab bars, some CTs tied themselves into their chairs during rough seas and then tied the chairs to the heavy racks that contained the machine they were using.[60]

In time, the navy would correct some of the problems. During the summer of 1967, the commander of the Puget Sound Naval Supply Center labeled the mess decks a health hazard. At Bucher's urging, he described the conditions in a letter to COMSERVPAC, which responded with $65,000 for repairs.[61] Still, many problems remained in more critical areas. The loran navigation system was inaccurate, sometimes off by up to five miles, and the compass's directional errors could exceed 20 percent. The ever-worsening balance problem also went unresolved. The situation became so severe after the lengthening of the forward mast and the addition of the research spaces that the accumulation of a mere four inches of ice on the ship's decks would cause her to capsize. The laundry machines took five hours to do one load, there were only four shower stalls and six washbasins for eighty-three men, and the toilet in the forward berthing compartment (nicknamed "the shooter") backed up frequently, sending feces and urine over the deck. The *Pueblo* was still in such poor condition at its commissioning ceremony on May 13, 1967, that Bucher approached Monsignor Nicholas Wegner, an old friend who had delivered the benediction, with an invitation to tour the ship and a comment made only half in jest: "You might as well get a good look at what you just blessed and know how badly it needed it."[62]

To some extent, the navy's antipathy was understandable, since the *Pueblo* had the misfortune of being transformed during the escalation of the Vietnam War.[63] In March 1966, approximately 4,500 naval personnel were active in Vietnam; by the end of 1967, the number had grown to 31,000. Minesweepers arrived in Vietnam in March 1966, and in June, navy pilots took to the air to provide helicopter support for joint army-navy operations along the Plain of Reeds. Operation Market Time, an attempt to interdict seaborne infiltration along the South Vietnamese coast, employed navy personnel at the ports of Danang, Cam Ranh Bay, Qui Nhon, Nha Trang, Vung Tau, and Saigon by the end of 1966. In 1967, their field of operations was expanded to include surveillance in the Gulf of Thailand to monitor traffic to and from Cambodia. In 1966, Market Time personnel inspected 223,483 ships, boarding 181,482 of them, and engaged in almost 500 firefights; in 1967, their activities increased to over 500,000 boardings. The Riverine Assault Force (TF-117) began in December 1966 to support the army's "search and destroy" operations in the Mekong Delta, and by the summer of 1967, it was engaging in major assaults alongside both American and South Vietnamese troops. In September 1967 alone, TF-117 killed over 400 enemy soldiers and destroyed tons of supplies. By comparison, the conversion of a ship safely docked in Bremerton Harbor was not a major concern. "*Pueblo*," explained the Bremerton shipyard commander, "was just another job, and a minor one at that."[64]

The conversion was largely complete by the summer of 1967, and the ship was deemed ready for test runs. Her first sea trial had actually been scheduled for early 1967, but physical problems delayed it until the summer. Finally, the fateful day came in late June.[65] With a collection of skeptical onlookers—and an expectant tugboat—watching, Bucher ordered "Right full rudder—Port ahead one-third," and the ship, belching diesel smoke, pulled away from the dock. Confidently, Bucher ordered the first test, the dropping of the anchor, and the crew obeyed, until the anchor chain dislodged from the windlass and flopped about uselessly. A more appropriate harbinger could hardly have been imagined. After a few hours of uneventful cruising in Puget Sound, the skipper began testing the engine. Responding well at first, the ship reached a top speed of 12.7 knots, until Bucher ordered, "Left full rudder." Suddenly, disaster struck:

"She does not answer the helm, sir," bellowed the helmsman. "Rudder frozen." The cable connecting the rudder to the steering engine had shattered. Without the steering controls, the ship careened crazily until finally stopping dead in the water. Repair attempts failed, and Bucher reluctantly summoned the tugboat. Three days and one new steering cable later, the *Pueblo* made a second attempt, which was once again cut short when the ship tried to change directions abruptly. This time the cable was intact, but the steering engine had failed nonetheless. Although the crew eventually restored it, thereby avoiding the indignity of another tow, the exercises hardly helped the confidence of the captain or the crew.

The tests continued, as did the ship's poor performance. On August 23, the *Pueblo* underwent her first major inspection, the Board of Inspection and Survey (INSURV) tests. Three days of continuous testing by a team of nine officers produced an eighty-five-page report documenting her condition. The results were dismal:

> The adequacy of stability of *Pueblo* appears deficient . . . steering gear unreliable and failed repeatedly during trials . . . the emergency steering arrangement is ineffective . . . full power ahead and astern steering trials not satisfactorily demonstrated . . . phone system is a potential danger during sea details because of the many stations on the line . . . there is no reliable means of communication between the navigator's chart desk and captain's open bridge conning station . . . the 1MC system power amplifiers are not suitable for shipboard use . . . quarters are cramped and congested . . . no Sick Bay/Pharmacy aboard . . . water leaks from flying bridge deck . . . boat compass had deviation errors in excess of twenty percent.

Overall, the INSURV team found 462 separate deficiencies, 77 of which were so severe that inspectors ordered that they "must be corrected" before the ship began a mission. "Material deficiencies," they concluded, "exist in the ship that substantially reduce her fitness for naval service."[66] However, the INSURV board did not recommend a complete engine reconversion—a surprising omission, considering that the steering engine had failed 180 times during the three days of testing. "I think INSURV passed us," recalled one CT, "just to get us the hell out of there."[67]

On September 11, the ship departed Bremerton for San Diego, where she was to receive shakedown training, a regimen of drills and tests specifically geared toward her mission. Although the Bremerton yard worked hard to correct most of the deficiencies uncovered by INSURV, the ship was, as Murphy lamented, "far from RFS—Ready for Sea."[68] On the trip, he recalled, "the steering continued to break down, no matter how many hours were spent on its repair.

Except for the installation of an extension phone on the signal bridge . . . we had made almost no headway in improving our internal communications. As for securing the seats in the research spaces, we had no luck whatsoever. Steve [Harris] was having unforeseen difficulties with his secret gear, which wasn't working as it should."[69] So bad was the steering system, in fact, that by the time the ship reached San Diego on September 21, it was failing every hour.[70]

Five weeks of shakedown training commenced in San Diego. Inspectors from the Training Command Department of the navy's Anti-Submarine School oversaw the tests, sailing with the ship while simulating situations that might be encountered on the mission. Again the *Pueblo*'s top-secret status created problems, since the inspectors could not be informed of her specific purpose. "The trouble was that there was nothing in the huge library of manuals which even vaguely covered her class of ship," Bucher complained. "We were the first AGER-2 in their experience. Security had done its job so well that nobody in the Office of Training Command, Pacific (TRAPAC), had any notion of our true purpose."[71] Without any specific instructions, inspectors followed the standard format for an AKL. Some drills were useful for any naval vessel, including man overboard, damage control, and general quarters. Others, however, were completely irrelevant. The ship practiced towing and steaming in formation, despite the basic premise of solitary operation that underlay her mission. She was also expected to demonstrate proficiency in under-way refueling, but since the *Pueblo* lacked the equipment for such a maneuver, the inspectors arranged for a fuel ship to pull alongside and then watched as the men pretended to refuel. "Everyone," recalled one crewman, "was pleased with our acting abilities."[72] In the end, the training tested the crew's reaction to a nuclear blast but not their response to harassment off an enemy coast or their ability to evaluate intercepted intelligence.

Still, Bucher pushed his crew hard throughout the tests, and the overall performance exceeded reasonable expectations. Inspectors were impressed; "USS *Pueblo* (AGER-2)," they concluded, "is considered ready for unrestricted operations."[73] Although comforting, the evaluation did not reflect the ship's true condition. The steering problems continued throughout the training, yet the *Pueblo* somehow received a ranking of "good" in the category "Ship Control." Internal communications were still confused, and the research spaces had not been linked to the PA system, yet "Communications" were marked as "satisfactory." At top speed, the ship's vibrations were visible to the naked eye, yet TRAPAC declared her "excellent" in "Main Propulsion and Electrical." Other areas went uninspected, as security restrictions rendered off-limits the research areas and the competence of the CTs themselves. Still, TRAPAC was largely unconcerned, since it believed that the ship's safety was guaranteed as long as she remained in international waters. The possibility of attack seemed so far removed, recalled a TRAPAC lieutenant, "that nobody was even worried about it."[74]

Following the shakedown training, the navy ordered the *Pueblo* to Hawaii. The journey, marked by repeated failures of the steering engine and the SIGINT equipment, provides a more accurate picture of her condition. An entry in the ship's deck logs dated November 12, less than two months before departure, disputes TRAPAC's conclusions:

> 0800–1200 Underway as before . . . 0825 lost electrical steering, all engines stop. 0826 regained electrical steering, all ahead full. 0829 lost electrical steering, 0830 all stop. 0833 shifted to manual steering. 0834 all ahead standard, shifted to electrical steering, 0839 all ahead full. 0909 lost electrical steering, all stop. 0910 shifted to manual steering. 0910 regained electrical steering. 0911 all ahead standard. 0913 all ahead full. 0914 lost electrical steering, all stop. 0915 all ahead standard, 0916 port ahead full, starboard ahead standard. 0917 all ahead full regained electrical steering. 1005 starboard engine overheating, port ahead standard, starboard ahead 2/3. 1007 port ahead one-third, starboard stopped.[75]

Two weeks later, the deck logs noted that the ship was "experiencing considerable and repeated casualties to electro-mechanical steering, causing ship to veer up to 110 degrees off course."[76]

The problems that had marked the ship's conversion also characterized her last few months in port. On test runs from Pearl Harbor, Kamiseya reported difficulty receiving her transmissions, and the navy continued to reject Bucher's pleas to off-load classified documents and refurbish the men's quarters.[77] Meanwhile, the crew waited for the arrival of an auxiliary air supply system intended to improve steering, but navy bureaucrats misdirected it to Japan—a not unprecedented occurrence, since it had earlier failed to show up as promised in San Diego.[78] During a two-week trip from Pearl Harbor to the naval base at Yokosuka, Japan, the steering engine continued to fail, the loran was inaccurate, the generator caught fire, clogs in the oil coolers drove the engine temperature up to 200 degrees (twenty-five degrees higher than normal), and faulty regulators in the engines made it difficult to maintain fuel pressure.[79] Communication with Kamiseya remained a problem. One CT tried to send a message to Japan from fairly close range, but found it impossible to make contact and instead had to route the message through Keflavik, Iceland.[80] The ship rolled so badly that the cooks abandoned their attempts to prepare hot meals, which was not a major problem, since many of the inexperienced crewmen were too seasick to eat. Upon entering the Yokosuka Channel on December 1, both the electrical and the manual steering systems failed, leaving the ship floundering until pusher boats arrived to guide her into the harbor. The trip was so unpleasant that along the way Bucher considered aborting the voyage, and upon arrival, he reflected that his ship was "far from ready to go on her first operational mission."[81] Unfortunately for Bucher and the crew, the navy did not share his opinion, not even three weeks later (and less than three weeks before departure for their mission), when tugboats were required to drag the *Pueblo* back in after the steering system failed thirty minutes into a test run.[82]

While in Yokosuka, Bucher continued to demand improvements and continued to be refused. Yet the navy found time and money for one change that he had neither requested nor wanted. Originally, the AGERs carried no overt weapons, on the assumption that armed ships might spur an overreaction from a target nation. Even if the vessels were armed, the navy decided, their small size, their need to operate alone, and their position close to enemy territory made it unlikely that they could defeat a determined attack, regardless of their armaments.[83] This policy, however, was abandoned following the 1967 attack on the USS *Liberty*. Outraged by the assault, Vice Chief of Naval Operations Admiral Horacio Rivero ordered "the installation of defensive armament (not less than .20 millimeter guns) on commissioned navy ships not now so equipped."[84] In doing so, Rivero eliminated the *Pueblo*'s clear status as a noncombatant and thus fundamentally changed the risk of her mission.

On January 3, a mere eight days before departure, two gun mounts were attached to the ship's forward forecastle, and a third aft on the boat deck. Two .50 caliber machine guns were provided, along with over 600,000 rounds of ammunition stowed in locked boxes below deck. This was in addition to the ten Thompson submachine guns, seven .45 caliber pistols, and one .30 caliber rifle already carried. When informed of the decision, Bucher recalled, "I almost threw a fit." The orders, he concluded:

> introduced some subtle considerations which evidently CNO did not think about. First and foremost, we were to operate on the high seas where tradition and International Law hold that we had a right to conduct peaceful operations without interference. Secondly, our ships would in fact be engaged in the collection of hydrographic and oceanographic information, which, regardless of the fact that it would be a cover, had peaceful applications and connotations. With this in mind, it followed that ships like *Pueblo* should be entirely non-provocative and never appear hostile, or act aggressively. The justification for not arming the AGERs was, of course, that the Soviet Union had been sending unarmed trawlers near (and sometimes inside) our territorial waters for almost twenty years. . . . Thus any order to arm the AGERs

would represent a major change of policy, and a departure from one of Operation Clickbeetle's fundamental concepts.[85]

Accordingly, Bucher and his officers opposed the addition, as did Admiral Johnson, but Naval Operations ignored their pleas.[86] Somehow, the navy had decided that the ship, which would be operating in hostile territory without close support, would be better served by a few guns than by a working steering system.

The new armaments increased the risks without increasing the security. Originally designed to be carried by infantrymen, .50 caliber machine guns are light weapons and are thus of limited use on a rolling ship, especially one like the *Pueblo,* whose gun mounts had been poorly installed. They jam frequently, especially in conditions of salt water and icing, and the firing pins need frequent adjustments, often taking up to ten minutes to prepare for discharge. The ship's small surface area created other problems. Three hundred sixty–degree coverage could not be achieved even if all three mounts were used—an impossibility, since the navy had provided only two guns. Even worse was the fact that the gun operators' exposed position on the forecastle made them easy targets for an enemy ship; even getting to the forecastle mounts was dangerous, since it required the gunners to rush across an exposed deck.[87] Providing armor topside was impossible because of the ship's poor stability, and, citing time constraints, the ship repair facility denied Bucher's request for gun tubes.[88] Recognizing the increased risks, Admiral Johnson ordered that the guns be kept stowed or hidden under tarps, so as "not to elicit unusual interest, and to employ weapons only when threat to survival was obvious."[89] Although this order at least reflected an awareness of the problem, it actually worsened the situation, since covering the guns was unlikely to fool anyone but would hinder the crew's ability to move them quickly in case of emergency.[90]

Nor were the men adequately trained in the weapon's operation. Senior Gunner's Mate Kenneth Wadley had never handled a .50 caliber machine gun, and only one member of the gun crews, Seaman Roy Maggard, had received even basic training in its usage. Rather than delay the mission to provide thorough preparation, the navy sent marine instructors to give basic familiarization lectures and then sent approximately half the men to a firing range to shoot three or four rounds. The crew conducted no general quarters exercises after the guns were added, leaving certain crucial roles unpracticed. Storekeeper Second Class Earl Phares, for example, was expected to load the forward machine gun but had "no idea" how to get the ammunition, since no one had thought to arrange a way for him to open the locked storage bins.[91] On the first few days of the mission, Bucher tried to compensate for this inexperience by running drills involving the use of the weapons, but the results were dismal. The guns were never fired in less than ten minutes, and it sometimes took up to an hour. Nor, despite the navy's claim that the effective range was 2,200 yards, could the gunners hit targets from beyond 50 yards.[92]

After the seizure, the navy defended the decision. The .50 caliber machine gun, argued Admiral John Hyland of CINCPACFLT, was "a mighty tough weapon to face if operated properly. It shoots a lot of pretty good bullets, and it will kill people right and left if you use it."[93] The official navy inquiry into the seizure agreed, lambasting Bucher because "there was no intention or attempt to use the small arms or the fifty caliber machine guns. . . . The commanding officer never knew what success he could have achieved through using any or all weapons available to him because he simple [sic] never tried to use them. He capitulated without firing a shot."[94] These claims were self-serving. Because of the positioning of the guns and their lack of protection, any attempt to reach them was doomed to fail. Even if they had somehow been loaded, they would not have been a serious deterrent, nor was it likely that someone could have fired them for longer than a few seconds without being shot himself. In one hasty action, the navy had altered the mission's underlying premise and invalidated the basis for its risk evaluation, without ever considering the ramifications for the Pueblo. "In short," Bucher concluded, "our noncombatant status had been compromised without providing us adequate means of repelling any serious attack."[95]

On January 5, the Pueblo departed Yokosuka for Sasebo, Japan, a brief stop before beginning her mission. A prelaunch inspection convinced Johnson that the ship was "in a satisfactory state of readiness and could carry out her assigned mission."[96] Yet even the short trip to Sasebo suggested otherwise, as the steering engine and the loran continued to perform poorly, and a storm cracked the ship's weak hull, leaving part of a direction-finding antenna lying in the Pacific. One of the two sixty-kilowatt electric generators that powered the SIGINT equipment in the research areas failed completely, and the other was kept operational only by replacing its malfunctioning pieces with their counterparts from the broken one. The ship was still overloaded with publications and lacked an effective means to destroy them or itself. Other problems remained. "Our internal communications still left much to be desired," recalled Murphy. "Also, we were still top heavy. And we had failed to find a way to secure the chairs in the Sod-Hut. So it went down the list of unsolved problems."[97]

In the wake of the Pueblo seizure, the navy denied that the ship's condition played a role in the tragic results. "The U.S.S. Pueblo," pronounced Admiral Johnson, "was in a satisfactory state of readiness and could carry out her assigned mission."[98] Although admitting to some physical shortcomings, the navy's final report on the incident concluded that they were minor problems, "common to most naval projects," and Vice Admiral Edwin Hooper of COM-SERVPAC claimed that "almost everything that Bucher asked for was approved."[99] Instead, a convenient scapegoat was found. The capture, explained Admiral John Hyland of CINCPACFLT, was "all the responsibility and the fault of one guy, and that was Bucher." "Bucher," agreed Admiral Moorer, "did not conduct himself in a way that a captain of a ship is expected to conduct himself."[100]

Again these claims were disingenuous. Although Bucher's decisions were not beyond reproach, his options were drastically curtailed by navy decisions made well before departure. "I know," Bucher lamented two decades after the seizure, "that the incident would never have come to pass as it did had the U.S. Navy done its job before, during, and after it occurred."[101] A look at the twenty-month conversion process demonstrates the accuracy of this assessment. Although it is unrealistic to expect the navy to anticipate every possibility for every ship on every journey, it is not unreasonable to demand adequate preparations based on similar missions, the specific nature of the target, and the limitations of the ship and crew involved. In failing to make such an evaluation, the navy left the *Pueblo* officers in an impossible situation and then criticized them for not producing impossible results.

The vessel, however, was not the only inadequate component of the *Pueblo*. The ship's complement, consisting of six officers, seventy-three navy enlisted men, two marine translators, and two civilian oceanographers, was far too inexperienced for such a mission. The youngest, Larry Marshall, was only nineteen years old, and the average age was a mere twenty-eight.[102] Furthermore, the *Pueblo*'s maiden voyage would also be the first for approximately half the crewmen.[103] Normally, such a crew would attend precommissioning school before launch to receive basic skills relevant to running and organizing the ship. Citing constraints of time, however, COMSERVPAC denied Bucher's request for this training.[104] Since the ship's many problems delayed her launch, Bucher was eventually able to send some men to firefighting and damage control training sessions in San Diego, but many more important aspects of their preparation went overlooked.[105] Those crew members who were reservists were prepared with a two-week boot camp and a two-week cruise. "We were not trained for anything," recalled Seaman Stu Russell, "except for knowing how to march (poorly), salute (even worse) and how to put on the uniform."[106]

A number of areas specifically warranted more training before departure. Precise navigation was required to avoid transgressing into enemy waters, but the ship carried only three experienced navigators: Bucher and Murphy, whose many other duties limited their available time, and Quartermaster First Class

Charles Law. Others were forced to assume these crucial duties despite their lack of training. "I shouldn't have been up there," recalled Photographer's Mate Lawrence Mack. "I didn't function the way a navigator should."[107] This problem was especially dangerous in the Sea of Japan, where atmospheric and weather conditions were known to play havoc with loran readings. Murphy, in charge of the navigating team, believed them all to be "well-qualified," yet, recalled Mack, "if I got two good fixes in a four-hour watch I was doing good."[108] Mack's recollections seem more accurate than Murphy's, especially since the ship's navigation log contained at least eleven erroneous entries from their eleven days at sea.[109]

The inexperience of the navigation team was dwarfed by the incapability of the ship's two translators, marine sergeants Robert Hammond and Robert Chicca. The two men came aboard a mere three days before the departure for Yokosuka, leaving Bucher little time to assess their qualifications. Their task of monitoring and translating Korean communications was crucial for the ship's safety, since they were relied on to warn the officers of any impending danger. In fact, by alleviating much of the risk involved in the mission, this job, if properly performed, might have compensated to some extent for the crew's inexperience and the ship's physical shortcomings. Yet neither Hammond nor Chicca was qualified for this critical position. Their training consisted of a nine-month course in Korean at the Defense Language Institute in 1965, as well as brief tours of duty in South Korea. Neither had used the language for years, and their skills had deteriorated to such an extent that upon arrival at the *Pueblo,* neither could read Korean without a dictionary. In fact, Hammond's fluency was so poor that while in captivity the North Koreans beat him repeatedly because his personnel file stated that he spoke Korean, but he was so inept at it that they believed he was trying to conceal this ability.[110] The men, Stephen Harris would later lament, "knew about ten words of Korean between the two of them."[111] Upon receiving their assignments, both men informed the navy of their shortcomings. Not only were their warnings ignored, but they were never even passed along to the ship's captain.[112] Accordingly, Bucher left port comforted by the belief that in case of trouble, he would have ample time to respond; had he thought otherwise, he recalled, "*I would have refused to undertake the operation until they had been replaced by personnel who could handle their assignment. If they had been competent interpreters, it is probable that I would have had sufficient warning of North Korean intentions on January 23, 1968, to have avoided capture, or at the very least, to have better prepared to carry out classified document and equipment destruction.*"[113]

The crew had other deficiencies that, though less perilous, still impaired their overall abilities. SIGINT, the ship's most critical function, was assigned to the segment of the crew with the least shipboard experience. Only four CTs had ever been to sea, only one had served aboard a SIGINT ship, and the senior chief CT, Ralph Bouden, had no shipboard experience at all. Many of them had not done any SIGINT intercept work for over a year.[114] Making things even harder was the lack of information they received regarding North Korean naval communications. "I had three days to familiarize myself with everything at Kamiseya on KORCOM [Korean Communists] naval activities," recalled CT Ralph McClintock. "In the files for KORCOM naval manual Morse code activity, there was nothing . . . the file was empty."[115] Yeoman First Class Armando Canales was responsible for the ship's paperwork, including mail delivery, obtaining security clearances, and filing evaluations. Overwhelmed with work yet refusing offers of help, he finally fell so far behind that important material went ignored. On one occasion, security clearances for the navigation teams sat on his desk for months, typed but not mailed for approval until they were finally found by Bucher. Other crewmen worked hard but simply lacked the training to be thorough in their jobs. "We had people aboard that ship who didn't know the front end from the back," recalled one officer. "There were just too many men," echoed a crewmen, "who didn't know what they were doing."[116]

Inexperience was a problem not only with the crew but with the officers as well. Commander Bucher had a strong background in submarines but had not served on a surface vessel for thirteen years and had never before had his own command. His performance as an executive officer had been solid but not strong enough to warrant his own submarine; he had always been, explained one admiral, "found wanting in one way or another."[117] Even the Navy Board of Inquiry admitted that "A review of Commander Bucher's fitness report file raises some doubts as to his qualifications for command."[118] The navy's logic is hard to understand. Despite thirteen years of training, Bucher was not considered command material for a submarine, so he was instead given control of a surface spy ship making her maiden voyage against a dangerous enemy. Considering the obstacles against him, including his own lack of experience, Bucher actually performed well during and after the attack. Still, the possibility exists that a more experienced captain would have achieved different results. Bucher recalled accepting the ship with "a number of reservations and as much protest as I dared make . . . [But] after giving the good fight to obtain the best available for his own command, the conscientious naval officer must know when to quit protesting and start doing."[119] Had the protests come from a more accomplished veteran, however, they might have carried greater weight with the navy hierarchy, or perhaps a more experienced captain might even have refused to set sail on such an unqualified vessel.

Bucher's inexperience aboard a surface ship was apparent to all. He often referred to the signal bridge as the "conning tower" and the mess decks as the "afterbattery."[120] More significantly, he treated the crew as if they were on a submarine, where the narrow confines sometimes require a commanding officer to overlook minor infractions as a way for the men to reduce tension. Reveille was not enforced, and the morning routine of cleaning topside areas, standard on a surface vessel, disappeared. Unaccustomed to the security required on a SIGINT ship, Bucher occasionally brought unauthorized guests into the SOD-Hut; at one point, the situation was so bad that Lieutenant Harris considered revoking his security clearance.[121] Although navy regulations required that a training board composed of department heads be established on all ships to supervise training, the *Pueblo* did not have one; instead, Bucher left the responsibility to his executive officer, as was common in submarines. The crew took liberties with Bucher's lenience. Drunken clashes with local authorities occurred on shore leaves, and small-stakes gambling on the ship was common. The officers looked the other way when one crewman was arrested for drunk driving with a fake identification after a serious accident in a stolen car. While docked in San Francisco, a crew member even had sex in the captain's chair with a woman he had met at a local bar, despite the fact that even sitting in the chair was technically a court-martialable offense.[122]

Executive Officer Edward Murphy was also experienced, but personal problems had consigned him to shore duty since 1965 and left him with a focus on family obligations that sometimes interfered with his job. He had never served as an "XO," and his last assignment had put him in charge of the motor pool for an inland navy installation. Lacking experience as an executive officer, he adopted a by-the-book attitude that clashed with Bucher's more lenient ways and alienated most of the crew. The two men fought constantly, usually because of Murphy's failure to complete assigned tasks. Murphy's fitness reports reflected this animosity. His XO, wrote Bucher, "was not professionally prepared to assume the responsibility of executive officer of a small, independently operated ship. He rarely completed any assigned tasks in a timely or satisfactory manner. . . . Procrastination and disorganization together with weak leadership qualities contribute to his inability to get the job done. He was unable to provide any constructive assistance to this command." Murphy, Bucher concluded, "is most competent when making excuses for his procrastinations and other shortcomings."[123]

Other officers also lacked relevant experience. Supply Officer Tim Harris was just out of supply school in San Diego, without any previous naval billets. Lieutenant (jg) Schumacher had only one prior assignment, as communications officer aboard the supply ship USS *Vega*.[124] Of the *Pueblo*'s six officers, only Lieutenant Stephen Harris had extensive preparation for his job. Despite their inexperience, most of the officers performed well during the difficult events. Nevertheless, the possibility remains that a more experienced group, although unlikely to avoid capture under the same circumstances, might not have been operating under the same circumstances to begin with.

The ship's chain of command was also muddled. While on a mission, the *Pueblo* was under operational control of Rear Admiral Johnson at COMNAVFORJAPAN. While in port, however, she was under the command of Vice Admiral William Bringle, commander of the Seventh Fleet. Administrative control fell to Rear Admiral Norvell Ward, commander of Service Group Three in Sasebo, who reported to COMSERVPAC.[125] Since COMNAVFORJAPAN lacked its own forces, Johnson had to turn elsewhere for support of the AGER missions, usually COMSEVENTHFLT and the Fifth Air Force. Had the *Pueblo* been assigned directly to the Seventh Fleet, Bringle could have easily integrated her support into his command, instead of providing last-minute backup to accommodate Johnson's requests. But COMNAVFORJAPAN barely even talked to the Seventh Fleet. "Our intelligence people," lamented one of the fleet's admirals, "didn't even know [about the missions]."[126] In fact, the navy had earlier considered placing the ship under COMSEVENTHFLT's operational control but rejected the idea because the intelligence component of the mission, especially the aspects involving the NSA, required that the command be more closely affiliated with Washington, D.C.[127]

The internal chain of command had problems as well. The twenty-nine members of the intelligence detachment spent much of their time in the SOD-Hut, virtually isolated from the rest of the crew. The navy was so afraid of the prospect of a nonapproved crewman observing these classified areas that it refused to provide the research spaces with portholes and required the door to be triple-locked at all times. The areas themselves had never been inspected by Naval Security or any other authority, and even Bucher was denied access to certain aspects of their work.[128] In fact, since all external communications came in through the SOD-Hut, the ship's captain could not even receive his own messages; he had to wait for Lieutenant Harris to approve them before they could be brought to his attention.

This isolation was not just physical; it also existed with regard to the ship's internal chain of command. Despite Bucher's status as captain, the twenty-eight-man CT unit reported to the Naval Security Group (NAVSECGRP) detachment in Hawaii, through the liaison of Stephen Harris. This arrangement essentially made Harris the highest shipboard authority for the research staff, a situation Bucher especially resented when Harris resisted his orders to put the CTs to work in capacities such as cleaning and cooking.[129] Bucher's frequent complaints were ignored until late September, when Captain Everett Gladding of NAVSECGRP, Pacific, ordered him to accept the situation. "The fact," Bucher lamented, "that it left me, the captain, with less control over my own ship (for which I was ultimately totally responsible) did not bother them."[130] Although this command arrangement was unusual, it was not unprecedented; in fact, the *Banner*'s first commander, Lieutenant Bob Bishop, had actually been outranked by the commander of his CT detachment. Bishop, as unhappy about the arrangement as Bucher would be, had complained to the Naval Security Station about the situation. After some study, the station agreed with Bishop's assessment and advocated a change, but CINCPACFLT denied the request because it was reluctant to abandon its direct control of the CTs.[131] The objections of the only two commanders forced to deal with the confused situation seemed of little importance. All that mattered to the navy—in this case, as in all other aspects of the conversion—was getting the *Pueblo* out to sea as soon as possible. Her condition when she got there was apparently considered of lesser importance.

CHAPTER THREE

A Minimal Risk

From "Venus" to "Mars,"
Charley shootin' the stars,
Songjin, Chongjin, and Wonson.
The PUEBLO a'bobbin',
Our receivers a'throbbin',
Us sly secret agents sailed along.

In an article in the journal *Naval History* twenty years after the *Pueblo* Incident, CINCPACFLT Admiral John Hyland assigned Bucher "a failing grade" in his performance as captain. "He didn't do anything," explained Hyland. "It was absolutely inexcusable not to have done something about it." Bucher responded: "I wonder what grade is assigned to the naval and air forces, close at hand who did not respond to our plight. What grade can be given to the many commanders, such as himself, who were not prepared for our emergency? What grade for the intelligence community that performed so miserably?"[1] This debate has remained central to subsequent discussions of the incident. To what extent did mistakes by Bucher and his officers lead to the tragedy? Or, as they claimed, had they been largely irrelevant, helpless pawns rendered powerless by the failings of their superiors? A close look at the ship's conversion has demonstrated the accuracy of Bucher's contention, at least in the realm of physical preparation. In almost all vital areas—navigation, defense, communication, maneuverability, emergency destruction—higher authorities ignored or dismissed the *Pueblo*'s obvious shortcomings. However, the navy's role in Clickbeetle operations extended beyond mere material preparation. Since every mission involved some risk, the navy was expected to examine each proposal thoroughly to ensure that the potential danger correlated to the value of the expected results. Hence, each one underwent an extensive evaluation by numerous military, intelligence, and civilian leaders, and a mission was approved only if all agreed that it was not inordinately risky. This process, at least in theory, ensured that no ship would embark on an assignment that was beyond its capabilities.

The planning of Clickbeetle missions began at periodic meetings of the relevant intelligence and navy command departments, which selected general areas for observation and then forwarded them to the appropriate naval intelligence branch for the assignment of priorities. These general plans were then sent to COMNAVFORJAPAN, where the operations department and the intelligence department collaborated to develop specific mission programs in accordance with these guidelines. Part of this task included compiling detailed reports that spelled out each mission's objectives, rules of engagement, operational control and support information, and, most important, risk assessment. If COMNAVFORJAPAN deemed the mission risk "minimal," it sent the report for approval to CINCPACFLT, CINCPAC, the Joint Chiefs of Staff, numerous intelligence agencies, and the 303 Committee, an interdepartmental panel overseeing the nation's high-risk covert operations (which was named after room 303 of the old Executive Office Building, where it originally met). No mission that COMNAVFORJAPAN decided was more than "minimal" risk was submitted for further consideration. Each higher authority was expected to perform an independent risk assessment, and approval was granted only if all branches reached a "minimal" risk designation. After each level had endorsed the assignment, a detailed sailing order specific to the mission was transmitted to COMNAVFORJAPAN, giving it clearance for launch.[2]

The origins of the *Pueblo*'s ill-fated journey came at a planning conference in March 1967, which selected general objectives along the Korean-Soviet border for future Clickbeetle missions. CINCPACFLT intelligence set priorities for the targets and then delivered them to COMNAVFORJAPAN, which organized them into six-month schedules for the *Pueblo* and *Banner,* beginning in early 1968. The *Pueblo*'s itinerary contained one visit to North Korea in January, one off the Soviet port of Petropavlovsk in April, and two others to the Sea of Japan in February and May.[3] On November 28, COMNAVFORJAPAN forwarded this schedule up the chain of command, with information on the objectives, support program, and risk assessments to follow. These details did not arrive at CINCPACFLT until December 16, about three weeks before launch. After each level declared it a "minimal" risk, official approval reached Admiral Johnson on January 3, 1968.[4] The proposal had passed all of the navy's tests. After many months of waiting, Captain Bucher and his crew were finally authorized for action.

By performing risk assessments at numerous levels, the system was designed to weed out overly dangerous missions. The inclusion of the 303 Committee ensured civilian participation, and Central Intelligence Agency (CIA), NSA, and Defense Intelligence Agency (DIA) involvement guaranteed that plans were considered in conjunction with the latest intelligence information. At higher levels, the operations were grouped with other classified proposals into monthly summaries, in the hope of avoiding unnecessary duplication. In reality, however, the process was much less thorough. Risk assessments were sloppy and incomplete, interdepartmental communication was poor, and high-level briefings were severely inadequate. For eighteen months, navy officials had handled the *Pueblo* poorly because they refused to recognize the risks inherent in her mission; now, during the last few months before departure, the intelligence community would do the same.

The primary responsibility for risk assessment fell to Admiral Frank Johnson's staff at COMNAVFORJAPAN, which was expected to conduct the most thorough analysis. The operations department, led by Captain William Everett, and the intelligence department, led by Captain Thomas Dwyer, determined the risk involved in particular missions by testing them against a standard set of criteria, including the results of previous missions, the sensitivity of the location and political climate at the time of operation, the scope of the intelligence tasks, the presence of international waters, the ship's overall abilities, the anticipated weather, and the navy's ability to provide support forces.[5] Although COMNAVFORJAPAN claimed to have considered all these factors thoroughly, its conclusion suggests otherwise. A serious examination of previous missions could not have justified a "minimal" risk determination, since the *Banner* had conducted only two operations in the area, neither for longer than thirty-six hours, neither armed, and neither since early 1967.[6] *Banner* commander Charles Clark, noting the brevity of these stays, had expressed particular concern about future assignments in this region, and Lieutenant General Seth McKee of the Fifth Air Force, who had placed support planes on alert for an earlier *Banner* operation in the region, still worried about Democratic People's Republic of Korea (DPRK) belligerence and believed that such preparation was again merited.[7] Others with knowledge of the area had similar anxieties; the head of the Korean division of the Air Force Security Service in Japan, charged with overseeing aerial interception operations, kept all the messages he received regarding the *Pueblo*'s mission in a folder that he designated "Operation Suicide."

Other criteria should have demonstrated the inadequacy of the "minimal" risk designation as well. North Korean hatred for the United States was well established, as was its penchant for secrecy. The weather in the Sea of Japan was almost always terrible in the winter, and the *Pueblo* had never experienced the snow and freezing rains that she would surely encounter. The expected intelligence collection was not vital and, in fact, could have been more easily obtained by other means.[8] The ship's abilities had already proved substandard; at about the same time that Dwyer and Everett were meeting, the *Pueblo* was being towed into Yokosuka harbor after her steering system had failed yet again. Although support forces were theoretically available, the policy of placing planes and a destroyer on alert in case of trouble had already proved futile. Three times, COMNAVFORJAPAN had requested strip alerts for *Banner* missions, and twice the ship had requested this assistance under conditions of severe harassment. Yet on neither occasion did the support arrive quickly enough to help, and once, a destroyer had actually taken sixteen hours to appear.[9] Overall, the *Pueblo* mission failed to satisfy almost every one of COMNAVFORJAPAN's stated criteria, yet it still received the designation of "minimal" risk. To understand how such a decision was possible, it is necessary to examine the inherent flaws of the navy's risk assessment system.

The process's most obvious problem was the fact that the authorities who created the mission proposals outranked those who evaluated them. Objectives came to COMNAVFORJAPAN from its direct superior, CINCPACFLT, and had therefore already been selected by a higher authority. Since labeling an operation anything other than "minimal" risk caused its cancellation, the COMNAVFORJAPAN intelligence and operations departments, composed mostly of career navy officers, had to consider the ramifications of such conclusions. This unspoken pressure even affected their decisions regarding the placement of support forces on strip alert; since such a request would likely have caused the mission's risk to be reassessed, possibly threatening the mission itself, such requests were not made lightly.[10]

A more significant problem was the lack of specific guidelines for weighing the relative importance of the stated criteria. COMNAVFORJAPAN claimed to examine many factors in determining risk, but there was no quantitative means of judging the significance of each one, nor was there a systematic formula indicating what combination of factors merited the cancellation of a mission. Instead, all was subjective; COMNAVFORJAPAN could weigh the results as it saw fit and thus arrive at whatever conclusions it wanted by stressing the positives over the negatives. The *Pueblo* case clearly demonstrates this problem. Of the seven main criteria used to evaluate risk, six (past missions, expected weather, ship's abilities, scope of intelligence collections, target sensitivity, and availability of support forces) should have warned against a "minimal" risk designation. Only one, the ship's expected presence in international waters, could reasonably be considered a sign of "minimal" risk. Yet COMNAVFORJAPAN placed this one factor above all others and gave the ship the necessary approval, despite warning signs from the other six categories. "Minimal risk," explained Johnson, "means to me that because the ship had the safety which was afforded to it by the right to operate on the high seas in international waters, there was minimal risk overall."[11] CINCPACFLT and CINCPAC agreed, concluding that there was little risk as long as the ship remained in international waters.[12] Even Johnson's predecessor at COMNAVFORJAPAN, Vice Admiral John Chew, shared this perspective: "The feeling was that [this] particular ship was a merchant type in international waters and it would be relatively, if not completely, safe. I think this was the prevalent feeling of everybody at the time."[13]

Other problems existed at the initial stage of the assessment process.[14] COMNAVFORJAPAN could draw only two possible conclusions about the missions, labeling them either "minimal" risk or "not minimal" risk. There was no scale to indicate distinctions within these two categories, nor was the term "risk" ever specifically defined. The navy simply left it to Admiral Johnson and his staff to use common sense to determine the extent of the danger. Higher levels on the command chain could assign a slightly more specific categorization, as they had four choices of risk assessment ranging from "minimal" to "highly improbable." Again, however, no specific definitions existed for the four categories, leaving each department to decide on its own which description was most appropriate. These different categories were not even defined for the intelligence communities, which were often unfamiliar with the military's classification system. One of the reasons the CIA rarely objected to a mission proposal, explained one former agent, "was that we didn't understand the computer language in which it was prepared. Under the risk category, there would be one of four letters—A, B, C, or D. Nowhere was there an explanation of what they meant."[15]

Because of these numerous flaws, COMNAVFORJAPAN's conclusion of "minimal" risk was not as revealing as it should have been. The evaluation process relied too heavily on personal opinion, used a subjective weighting of results, and did not allow for any expression of doubt. The inadequacy of the system is made apparent by the results prior to the *Pueblo;* overall, COMNAVFORJAPAN had analyzed nineteen proposals and had arrived at nineteen "minimal" risk classifications.[16] Higher authorities, however, canceled three of them, suggesting that the COMNAVFORJAPAN staff had not been as sensitive to the risks as they should have been. Further discrediting their conclusions was the fact that although these nineteen missions were all placed within the same risk category, even those at COMNAVFORJAPAN did not consider them all of equal risk. On three *Banner* operations, they requested that support forces be placed on alert, and on thirteen others they did not; yet all sixteen had been labeled "minimal" risk. "In certain areas," Johnson later explained in language reminiscent of George Orwell's *Animal Farm,* "there was a greater degree of minimal risk."[17]

Problems also existed in the way these evaluations progressed along the chain of command. The COMNAVFORJAPAN staff prepared the first risk assessments and then briefed Admiral Johnson on their conclusions.[18] Johnson would send the written evaluation upward, but the details of the briefing never left the room. Hence, specific concerns brought to his attention were not passed on to higher authorities; all that went was the report justifying the favorable recommendation. This was standard procedure at all levels, so a particular concern might be heard at one level but would be filtered out as the approval passed up the command chain. Theoretically, the JCS could thus receive a report whose approval at the lower ranks suggested unanimous agreement with the "minimal" risk appraisal, even though specific concerns about this conclusion may have been voiced at every stage. The failure to present a more complete picture of the assessments was especially problematic when the proposals reached the JCS and the intelligence communities, since they might have information that was unavailable elsewhere, perhaps providing greater validity to these concerns than could have been foreseen at the lower levels.

Other problems arose as the proposals advanced through the higher ranks. Perhaps most striking was the lack of attention they received. After COMNAV-FORJAPAN provided its study, each level of the command chain was expected to perform its own assessment. Instead, almost every one quickly accepted COMNAVFORJAPAN's conclusions and passed the evaluation upward. A quick look at the timetable of the *Pueblo* proposal demonstrates this problem. CINC-PACFLT, the first step in the command chain, approved the mission and sent the report to CINCPAC in less than thirty-six hours, all of which came over a weekend. "It took me about as long to approve it," recalled the CINCPACFLT assistant chief of staff for intelligence, "as it did to read it."[19] CINCPAC's approval took six days, coming only two days before Christmas.[20] On December 23, CINCPAC sent the request to the Joint Reconnaissance Center (JRC), which combined it with proposals from other branches into the monthly Joint Reconnaissance Schedule (JRS), a massive book containing hundreds of intelligence operations under consideration for the upcoming month. On December 26, the JRC sent the January 1968 schedule to all relevant intelligence agencies for their approval, which was granted by the afternoon of the twenty-seventh.[21] Again, the brevity indicates the lack of scrutiny these missions received. Typically, a former CIA agent recalled, the schedule would be dropped off at 9:00 A.M. and picked up by 10:30. "We'd normally leaf through it," he explained, "remark about how nice the cover was, and sign off on the memorandum attached to it. The man would return from collection guidance, and we'd say we had no problems with it. . . . Pressed by our other duties, we'd give the recon schedule as little time as possible and get on with our work."[22]

The Joint Chiefs of Staff continued this rapid assessment, evaluating and approving the JRS on December 29, less than a week before the *Pueblo* launch. The

JCS endorsement came while three members were away, including the chairman, General Earle Wheeler, forcing lower-level staff members to give consent in their place.[23] The JCS meeting was brief, consisting mainly of a summary of the schedule's highlights by the Joint Reconnaissance Center. Since the *Pueblo* was considered a standard operation, it is unlikely that it was even mentioned; Admiral Waldemar Wendt, operations deputy for the navy, recalled that the mission was considered "routine and would not therefore have been brought to my specific attention."[24] After being approved by the JCS that morning, the schedule went to the Defense Department, where Deputy Secretary Paul Nitze endorsed it in the afternoon. That evening the 303 Committee gave its approval, after a meeting where once again the *Pueblo* mission went unmentioned.[25]

Testifying before the House Subcommittee on the *Pueblo* Incident, Admiral Moorer tried to prevent the inadequacy of these examinations from becoming public knowledge:

> MR. SLATINSHEK (assistant chief counsel for the subcommittee): Was this mission properly considered in all its ramifications by the people who we charge with this responsibility all the way up the ladder of command?
>
> MOORER: I will give you the details in closed session, but I assure you, Mr. Slatinshek, the attention given to this type of mission is not perfunctory at all.
>
> MR. PIKE (D-N.Y.): You can tell us in open session, can't you, Admiral, how much time the Joint Chiefs spent in evaluating this mission?
>
> MOORER: Well, this is not the only mission.
>
> PIKE: I understand that these missions come up in a package. . . . How much time did you spend on the package that came up including this and other missions?
>
> MOORER: Well, this is a progressive proposition, and as I say, I really would like to go into this in great detail with you in closed session.
>
> PIKE: Is there any reason you can't tell us how much time the Joint Chiefs of Staff placed on this?
>
> MOORER: Well, I will tell you, sir, that there is a package, and that once a month this is given the closest scrutiny by the Joint Chiefs of Staff. To answer your question about time, it might take an hour.
>
> PIKE: Now, how many missions would be involved in this package?
>
> MOORER: Well, sir, I think it would be better if I didn't say exactly how many. It would be a very large number.[26]

Moorer's tactics did not fool anyone. "It is obvious from the volume of missions involved and the very short time spent in their approval that regardless of the amount of staff work done," concluded Pike, "the review given any individual mission by the high authorities responsible for that review and approval was necessarily cursory and perfunctory."[27] Despite his reluctance, even Moorer finally concurred, admitting, "As the request goes up the chain of command, of course, they don't get into the details."[28]

Evidence suggests not only that the various authorities spent inadequate time on the proposal but also that they failed to perform independent risk analyses. Such a conclusion is suggested by the brief amount of time the mission assessments spent in each department, as well as the fact that the various levels of navy hierarchy all produced remarkably similar evaluations. "Estimate of risk: minimal, since *Pueblo* will be operating in international waters," wrote COMNAVFORJAPAN. CINCPACFLT's staff agreed, concluding, "Estimate of risk: minimal, since *Pueblo* will be operating in international waters for entire deployment," and CINCPAC echoed, "Risk to *Pueblo* is estimated to be minimal since operations will be conducted in international waters."[29] Although it is possible that all three branches performed independent evaluations and arrived at these similar conclusions, the resemblances in phraseology, the brief time the reports were in each locale, and the fact that each branch ignored the many factors suggesting danger and isolated the same positive factor all suggest that the intelligence support staffs at these higher levels had merely parroted COMNAVFORJAPAN's conclusions. "Once a mission is proposed," wrote former CIA agent Patrick McGarvey, "and given a 'minimal risk' evaluation, no one up the chain of command questions it. . . . The attitude common to all levels is, 'the guy who proposed it must have done his homework.' "[30]

Not only was discussion of the mission brief, but it was likely based on incomplete information. Reports in the Joint Reconnaissance Schedule are provided by the agencies requesting the mission and are thus presented in the most favorable light. Information challenging their conclusions is typically omitted in an effort to justify their decisions to higher authorities. The result is a report more closely resembling a sales brochure than an analytical piece of research. Descriptions are usually brief and sometimes obscured by technical data or complex maps, and security classifications prevent many JRC staff members from obtaining specific details. "To a non-scientist," wrote one former CIA officer, "it is a truly incomprehensible collection of papers. . . . Under these conditions," he concluded, "[the] Committee usually passes the schedule with little or no discussion."[31] Nor did higher authorities often contact those close to the target areas for their expertise. "The people who were responsible," lamented an unasked but very on-the-spot General Charles Bonesteel in Korea, "were totally out of touch with what the situation was in North Korea."[32]

Having failed to assess the likelihood of involved risk correctly, the naval and intelligence communities proceeded to make even more egregious errors regarding specific danger signs that arose late in the evaluation process. One such signal came from the National Security Agency itself. After conducting their own investigation, NSA experts decided that COMNAVFORJAPAN had underestimated the risks involved in the *Pueblo*'s operation. On December 29, NSA director Marshall Carter sent a message elucidating these conclusions:

> The following information is provided to aid in your assessment of CINCPAC's estimate of risk. . . . The North Korean Air Force has been extremely sensitive to peripheral reconnaissance flights in the area since early 1965 . . . [and] has assumed an additional role of naval support since late 1966. The North Korean Navy reacts to any ROK [Republic of Korea] Naval vessel or ROK fishing vessel near the North Korean coast line. . . . Internationally recognized boundaries as they relate to airborne activities are generally not honored by the North Koreans on the East coast of North Korea. The above is provided to aid in evaluating the requirements for ship protective measures.[33]

Although NSA officials could likely have scuttled the mission if they had pushed, they were reluctant to do so on a navy operation. "It was a navy patrol proposed by navy people in response to navy tasking," explained the NSA official who oversaw these mobile platforms, "and we were an outsider saying, 'You really ought to look at that again guys. If that's what you really want, think about it.'"[34]

Carter directed the warning to the chief of naval operations, but it was improperly addressed by the DIA Signal Office in the Pentagon, delaying its arrival for thirty days. Another copy went to Brigadier General Richard Steakley, the chief of the Joint Reconnaissance Center, who ignored it for three days and then forwarded it to CINCPAC headquarters under the low-level priority heading of "information" rather than its deserved classification as "action."[35] The note reached CINCPAC a few hours after the arrival of the message that granted JCS approval for the mission. This timing, along with the message heading, led CINCPAC staff to the erroneous conclusion that higher authorities had already considered the warning. Another copy was passed along through back channels to the Naval Security Group in Washington, but it failed to persuade anyone that the mission might not be a "minimal risk."[36] Thus, despite the fact that the NSA had not issued such cautions for prior Clickbeetle missions, despite the fact that ignoring similar NSA concerns prior to the *Liberty* assault had proved costly, and despite the brevity with which the navy's own intelligence community had conducted its assessments, this message was never seen by the JCS, the 303 Committee, the CINCPAC commander or assistant chief of staff, or Admiral Johnson of COMNAVFORJAPAN.[37] Nor was it even sent to Commander Bucher, waiting in Japan for departure. General Joseph Carroll of the DIA explained the failure as the result of unfortunate timing; "I think," the director explained, "one would have to take into consideration when it occurred. . . . The fact that it transpired at night over a holiday is about all I can think of."[38]

Again, the navy tried to obscure its mistakes. On January 29, CINCPAC issued a statement claiming to have used the warning in making its assessment. The fact that it made this pronouncement a full week after the seizure, and even then only in response to a JCS inquiry, and the fact that the CINCPAC leadership had elsewhere admitted to not having seen the warning, suggest otherwise.[39] Even if the message had been delivered earlier, however, both CINCPACFLT and COMNAVFORJAPAN indicated that their decisions would likely have been unchanged.[40] The similarities with the *Liberty* are striking. Both intelligence ships had been ordered into dangerous waters despite their physical shortcomings. Both were assured by the navy of their safety. Both times the NSA expressed concerns about their security by sending messages to various levels of navy hierarchy, and both times, bureaucratic failures prevented the messages from being delivered in time to prevent disaster.

Other warning signs also were ignored. Although much was made of the *Banner*'s previous operations in this region, the climate around North Korea had changed dramatically in the year since they had been conducted. In 1967, DPRK foreign policy entered a more aggressive phase. Violations of the 1953 Military Armistice Agreement, for example, increased from 50 in 1966 to 543 in 1967, and ambushes of Republic of Korea (ROK) and American troops by DPRK patrols grew common by late 1967.[41] This aggressiveness was particularly acute toward the end of 1967. During the first nine months of the year, DPRK forces seized twenty ROK vessels operating off their coast; the same number were captured over the last three months, despite the worsening weather that made such ships more scarce.[42] In October, North Korean forces used artillery against ROK ground forces for the first time since the Korean War, attacking the Seventh ROK Division just south of the demarcation line.[43] Early 1968 saw no lessening of this bellicosity. Between January 1 and January 25, 1968, North Korea was involved in over forty military incidents on the peninsula. In fact, at about the same time that the *Pueblo* mission was being evaluated, the Joint Chiefs of Staff classified Korea as a hostile fire zone, making American troops stationed in the area eligible for combat medals and awards.[44] Clearly, evidence suggested that North Korea in January 1968 was much more dangerous than it had been during the *Banner* missions of late 1966 and early 1967, yet American intelligence and naval authorities failed to consider this changing situation in conjunction with the impending *Pueblo* mission.

Even if these North Korean actions could have been dismissed as random events, unreflective of an organized plot, one event shortly before the seizure should have suggested otherwise. On January 17, thirty-one North Korean army officers disguised as members of the ROK Twenty-sixth Army Division crossed through the demilitarized zone (DMZ), on a mission to assassinate ROK President Park Chung Hee. They reached the "Blue House," the official presidential residence in Seoul, four days later. Shortly before they launched their attack, a suspicious ROK policeman stopped them, and the ensuing fire-fight left eight South Koreans and five members of the commando team dead. The rest of the guerrillas fled, all but two of whom were captured or killed within the next two weeks.[45] An infuriated ROK population demanded retaliation, and only extreme American pressure prevented North Korean President Kim Il Sung from sparking a second Korean War. "Few people," recalled an American general, "realize how close we came to war on January 21."[46]

Kim's willingness to risk reopening the Korean War should have alarmed those overseeing the *Pueblo* operation, especially since it was quickly ascertained that the commandos' secondary objective had been the American embassy in Seoul. Yet no one associated the *Pueblo* mission with this clear indication that the United States was now a target for increased DPRK belligerence. Not only did the navy allow the ship to remain in the area without support forces on alert, but COMNAVFORJAPAN even decided not to send the *Pueblo* a specific warning about the attack, since it expected that news of the raid would be transmitted in the daily intelligence reports forwarded to the whole fleet. However, Lieutenant Stephen Harris was too busy to read the many general information documents the ship received and instead looked only at those specifically directed to the *Pueblo*.[47] "This story," Bucher later lamented, "made headlines around the world, but its significance was apparently lost on the people sending me daily intelligence reports, since I was never informed of it. . . . Had I been informed of the Blue House raid, I would have operated *Pueblo* much further out from Wonsan."[48]

Subsequently, the navy defended this decision by claiming that DPRK actions were typical of Kim's reign, and therefore this assault constituted "no new pattern."[49] Such a justification is difficult to accept. Although DPRK aggression had increased over the past twelve months, this was the first direct assassination attempt launched in the two decades of Kim's reign. Further, Kim's willingness to attack the U.S. embassy, the ultimate symbol of America's presence in Korea, should have demonstrated the dangers emerging in this region. Such a dramatic step clearly merited at least a warning to the captain of an unprotected ship operating in the area.

Nor could American military and intelligence leaders in Washington claim to be unaware of this new phase in DPRK policy. The United Nations (UN) Command Headquarters in Korea commented on the increased offensive in numerous messages and personal briefings.[50] Secretary of Defense Robert McNamara admitted that the Defense Department and the navy commanders involved with the mission were cognizant of the North Korean moves but had decided that the risks did not merit any cancellations.[51] While planning the mission, COMNAVFORJAPAN was made aware of the DPRK's increased naval activity in the Sea of Japan, including a recent sinking of an ROK ship operating off the eastern coast, yet it also refused to cancel the mission.[52] Ironically, North Korea's increasing belligerence had been one of the reasons that this area was selected for Clickbeetle operations, but no one recognized that this reason itself suggested increased danger incongruent with a "minimal" risk evaluation.[53]

Other warnings came from the North Koreans themselves. DPRK officials had spent months complaining loudly about American "espionage boats," which had forced them to begin taking defensive actions. On January 6, 1968, Radio Pyongyang warned that "the U.S. imperialist aggressor army, which has been incessantly committing provocative acts lately on the sea off the eastern coast . . . this morning again dispatched many armed boats . . . into the coastal waters of our side."[54] The following week, *Sankei Shimbun*, a Japanese paper, printed a North Korean statement warning that it would take action against the *Pueblo* if it remained in the area for longer than two weeks.[55] Radio Pyongyang issued another warning on January 11: "The U.S. imperialist aggressor troops dispatched from early this morning, hundreds of fishing boats and spy boats disguised as fishing boats into the coastal waters off the eastern coast. . . . As long as the U.S. imperialist aggressor troops conduct reconnaissance by sending spy boats, our naval ships will continue to take determined countermeasures."[56] On January 20, 1968, at the 260th meeting of the Military Armistice Commission (MAC), the North Korean representative directly warned the American delegates, "It is quite obvious that if one continues, as you have done, the provocative act of dispatching spy boats and espionage bandits to the coastal waters of the other side under the cover of naval craft, it will only result in disrupting the armistice and inducing another war. . . . We have the due right to make a due response to your thoughtless play with fire. We will fully exercise our rights."[57]

These warnings received little attention from those overseeing the *Pueblo* mission. The January 6 message was radioed to the American embassy in Seoul and then on to the United States, where COMNAVFORJAPAN Intelligence dismissed it as routine; the January 11 and 20 statements never even made it that far.[58] Despite the fact that both of the Radio Pyongyang statements were transmitted to the United States by the Foreign Information Broadcast Service and were carried on the English language service of the North Korean Central News Agency, they never reached CINCPACFLT or CINCPAC.[59] In fact, American representatives at the MAC talks considered their face-to-face warning so mundane that they had not even filed a report of the meeting with Washington by the time of the seizure.[60] Again, however, the navy admitted that even if these warnings had reached the appropriate locations, they likely would not have affected the assessment of the mission.[61] The presence of the ship in international waters, and the belief that the North Koreans, like the Soviets, would respect this right, outweighed all signs of danger. Subsequently recognizing its mistakes, the navy tried to minimize this failure to Congress. When Pentagon representatives briefed congressional leaders in early 1968, they made no mention of the North Korean warnings. "As a matter of fact," concluded a 1969 congressional report, "there appeared to be a deliberate effort to bury or obfuscate the fact."[62]

In the end, the navy and intelligence departments ignored ample evidence that their "minimal" risk operation was not as safe as they claimed. The House Subcommittee concluded:

> No level of authority in either the intelligence chain of command or the operating chain of command was sensitive to the abundant evidence indicating the development of a progressively more aggressive and hostile attitude by the North Koreans. The tremendously increased number of border incidents with South Korea, the attempted assassination of the South Korean President, and the North Korean broadcast with respect to ships entering claimed territorial waters were all discounted or ignored by responsible authorities, with the exception of the National Security Agency.[63]

Despite the ship's physical problems, despite her inexperienced crew, despite the growing signs of North Korean aggression, despite the NSA concerns, despite the problems that had enveloped the *Liberty,* the *Maddox,* and the *Banner,* the navy hierarchy consistently refused to recognize the possibility that the *Pueblo* might encounter difficulties. "If you were a betting man," claimed Admiral Johnson, "the odds a bookmaker would have given you on that [the seizure] happening . . . would have been so fantastic that not even a man as rich as Howard Hughes could pay off."[64] "We just never anticipated," echoed Admiral Hyland of CINCPACFLT, "that anyone would actually board and capture a vessel out on the high seas. . . . It is not reasonable in my opinion to hold, even from hindsight, that the illegal and reckless act by the North Koreans could or should have been anticipated."[65] "Nobody took action," recalled Rear Admiral Kemp Tolley. "In fact, they weren't prepared for action. Nobody . . . had conceivably foreseen such a thing."[66]

Such views dominated the American military's perception of the *Pueblo* mission. Superficially, they reflected the inability to realize that communist North Korea might not react in the same manner as the communist Soviet Union. In reality, however, these errors stemmed from a more fundamental precept that underlay the operations of the American military during the Cold War. As World War II began to fade, and the Soviet Union moved from hot-war ally to Cold War rival, most of the American military embraced the belief that emerging communist nations, despite their claims of independence, were in fact part of a unified global threat directed by Moscow. Hence, they grouped all communist nations under one all-encompassing rubric, which failed to acknowledge the individual differences among members. "We held," admitted General Omar Bradley, "the rather simplistic belief that all communist moves worldwide were dictated from Moscow." "The same compulsion," warned National Security Council Document #68, "which demands total power over all men within the Soviet state without a single exception demands total power over all Communist Parties and all states under Soviet domination." "The Communist parties outside of the Soviet Union," echoed *Infantry Journal*, "are junior partners or auxiliaries."[67] This myopia would have severe ramifications for American troops worldwide, whether they were fighting in the jungles of Vietnam, keeping the peace in Lebanon, or operating a small intelligence boat off the North Korean coast.

The Vietnam War represented the most dramatic manifestation of this belief. Determined to stop communism, American leaders failed to recognize that their opponents, despite communist leanings, were primarily nationalists fighting for independence rather than to advance the agenda of a greater communist movement.[68] "It is recognized," the Joint Chiefs of Staff wrote in 1962, "that the military and political effort of Communist China in South Vietnam . . . is part of a major campaign to extend communist control beyond the periphery of the Sino-Soviet bloc and overseas to both island and continental areas in the Free World. . . . It is, in fact, a planned phase in the communist timetable for world domination."[69] The war, in this view, was not about Vietnam; it was part of an international communist conspiracy threatening American interests on a global scale. In 1961, General Maxwell Taylor worried about the effects of the growing U.S. involvement in Southeast Asia on the anticommunist struggle in Berlin, and three years later, National Security Action Memorandum 288 warned that if South Vietnam fell, almost all of Southeast Asia will probably fall under Communist dominance (all of Vietnam, Laos, and Cambodia), accommodate to Communism so as to remove effective U.S. and anti-Communist influence (Burma), or fall under the domination of forces not now explicitly Communist but likely then to become so (Indonesia taking over Malaysia). Thailand might hold for a period without help, but would be under grave pressure. Even the Philippines would become shaky, and the threat to India on the West, Australia and New Zealand to the South, and Taiwan, Korea, and Japan to the North and East would be greatly increased.[70]

Yet Vietnam was not the only consequence of this misperception. For over four decades, the American military and intelligence apparatus conducted operations throughout the world, often sacrificing principle and idealism to contain this perceived international conspiracy. In 1953, the CIA worked with a Nazi collaborator in Iran to overthrow a popular government that was considered pro-communist, despite the fact that its leader, Mohammed Mossadeq, had led the opposition to making oil concessions to the Soviet Union after World War II.[71] The following year saw the ouster of Guatemala's popular and democratically elected President Jacobo Arbenz Guzman. Despite Guzman's promise to turn Guatemala "from a country bound by a predominantly feudal economy into a modern capitalist one," and despite a legislative record suggesting that he was more of a progressive than a radical, President Dwight Eisenhower perceived communist leanings and covertly arranged Guzman's replacement by a military dictator. "We cannot permit," explained Ambassador John Peurifoy, "a Soviet Republic to be established between Texas and the Panama Canal."[72] The internal struggles of smaller nations were thus seen not as local conflicts devoid of global ramifications but as part of the zero-sum battle between good and evil.

This same guiding principle that spearheaded global American involvement underlay the tragedy of the USS *Pueblo*. Although the 1960s saw a growing awareness within diplomatic circles of an emerging split between different factions of the supposed communist monolith, these ideas had not filtered down to the military leadership, especially to those within their intelligence branches. In December 1967, NSA officials briefed members of the Air Force Security Service on intelligence operations involving North Korea and concluded that there were no significant risks because the Soviets and Chinese accepted such missions. "I couldn't believe my ears," recalled one listener. "How could these 'experts' not know that of the Sino-Soviet bloc, two nations, namely Albania and North Korea, were not part of the communist monolith, and wrote their own rules concerning international behavior." Perceiving different members of the communist bloc as smaller, but identical, parts of a greater whole, navy leaders assumed that all communist nations would react in the same manner to American policies, as they had been assuming for over twenty years. Repeatedly, the American naval and intelligence communities prepared and assessed the *Pueblo* mission as if it were going to the Soviet Union, despite their knowledge of its true target. The ship's operational and sailing orders frequently alluded to anticipated Soviet reactions but made far fewer references to a possible Korean response; in fact, the text of the sailing orders mentioned Korea only twice, while naming the Soviet Union seven times.[73] The first sentence of the top-secret Special Instructions section stated, "The success of this intelligence collection operation depends upon the reaction of Soviet/Bloc forces to the assigned unit's presence."[74] Admiral Moorer justified the "minimal" risk assessment by pointing out that "the Soviets, of course, were doing the identical thing with their trawlers . . . so this was a routine collection of intelligence that we had been pursuing for some time."[75] "I don't regard this [AGER missions] as provocation," echoed a high-ranking American general, "unless you want to take it as a provocation that we have a Soviet intelligence collector that sits right off the port of Charleston all the time."[76]

Such sentiments were constantly expressed during the eighteen-month conversion process. Almost everyone involved in preparing the mission acted on the assumption that Soviet acceptance of these ships virtually eliminated the risk of the operations. Even the importance placed on the ship's presence in international waters reveals this fundamental misperception. North Korea had never publicly recognized the existence of such waters, nor had it signed the 1958 Convention on the Territorial Seas that guaranteed the right of free transit to those within them. Yet naval intelligence relied on the ship's presence in these waters as the most important assurance of safety, since, from its perspective, the Soviet Union's willingness to abide by the agreement indicated that other communist nations would do the same. Such, it was assumed, was the nature of the relationship between puppet states and the puppet master. The reality of the USSR-DPRK relationship, however, was not a simple matter of a master pulling lifeless strings but one more reminiscent of that between Pinocchio and Geppetto; the "father" may have played a formative role in the creation of the "child," but once given life, the child exercised his faculties of independent thought. Had the American military and intelligence leaders recognized the real nature of the North Korean "puppet," perhaps the tragedy of the *Pueblo* Incident might have been avoided. Instead, they clung to this simplistic perception of a uniform enemy and launched a ship that, like Pinocchio, was destined to be swallowed at sea.

On the morning of January 11, 1968, the USS *Pueblo* finally set sail from Sasebo, destined for the coast of North Korea. Despite the many danger signs, the navy was confident. "There was," insisted Admiral Johnson, "a very excellent precedent on which to base the safety of any one individual ship."[77] Resigning himself to the situation, Bucher hoped for the best. "Overcome those [problems] you can with ingenuity, resourcefulness, and training," he decided, "otherwise live with them and trust to luck." While Bucher relied on luck, the navy leadership clung to its faith in international waters and the implied agreement with the Soviet Union. Within two weeks, they would learn that their confidence had been sorely mistaken.

CHAPTER FOUR

We Are Being Boarded

We sailed quite free
until Jan. 23,
When out of nowhere there came,
Six boats from the west.
The KPA's best,
Six hunters, and PUEBLO fair game.

January 11, 1968, was a bad day for travel. A transport plane crashed in Nevada, killing nineteen marines. In Jersey City, New Jersey, a collision between two commuter trains left five dead and over 200 injured. Snow and ice blanketed America's upper Midwest, and temperatures approached thirty degrees below zero in New York. Protesting students at the University of Madrid set fire to a bus and then threw stones at firemen who tried to extinguish it. NASA announced that the Apollo spacecraft had failed five flammability tests, delaying the launch of the world's first three-man space vessel, and the Virginia State Corporation Commission abruptly closed fourteen automobile insurance companies. Even nonmechanical forms of transport joined the deluge; in the second race at Santa Anita in California, Sharp Tack II tossed and then rolled over his jockey, sending the unfortunate rider to the hospital with assorted internal injuries, and leaving a collection of unhappy bettors in the grandstand. These omens, however, seemed unlikely to penetrate the optimism in Sasebo, Japan, where only cheerful signs surrounded the USS *Pueblo* as she prepared to depart on her first mission.[1]

A better sailing day could hardly have been imagined. The weather was perfect, crisp and clear with excellent visibility. Most of the crewmen had recovered from a farewell night of carousing in Sasebo's bar district (affectionately known among sailors as "Saki Town"), and they now prepared their ship for departure with excitement and precision. The *Pueblo* responded well, pulling away from the dock without even a hint of the troubles that had plagued her conversion. The Tsushima Strait seemed empty, as even the Soviet ships that often lingered in the area were nowhere to be seen. Only one thing marred the departure: the

1MC speaker on the bridge malfunctioned, preventing Bucher from playing the *Pueblo*'s theme song, Herb Alpert's "The Lonely Bull," as they left.

The promising omens proved fleeting. Quickly, the skies darkened and freezing winds descended from the north. Within hours, one of the ship's two generators failed. Snow and ice rained from the heavens, and the vessel tottered perilously close to capsizing. So it always seemed to be for the *Pueblo:* a brief moment of sunshine followed by a downpour. It was a trend that would continue.

Officially, the *Pueblo* was an oceanographic research vessel designed for "technical research operations to support oceanographic, electromagnetic, and related research projects . . . to help the navy and mankind toward the complete understanding of the oceans."[2] She even carried two civilian oceanographers, Dunnie Tuck and Harry Iredale III, charged with conducting actual tests of water depth, temperature, and salinity. The ship's assignment would actually take her into a region where such inquiries were long overdue. The Naval Oceanographic Office had extremely limited information regarding North Korean waters, most of which came from incomplete surveys conducted by the Japanese three decades earlier. However, even a cursory glimpse of the *Pueblo* suggested that her research involved material far more sensitive than water temperature. Among other distinguishing features, she sported eight prominent antennae protruding toward the heavens. Trying to disguise her true purpose, recalled Executive Officer Murphy, "was wishful thinking at best. With all her rounded domes, multiple antennae, direction finders, and other protuberances, the *Pueblo* was about as inconspicuous as a billowy maternity dress. From even a good distance, you could see that she was pregnant with electronic gear."[3]

The ship's sailing orders arrived in January, directing her to conduct SIGINT operations off four of the DPRK's largest ports. Specifically, the *Pueblo* was instructed to "determine [the] nature and extent of naval activity [in the] vicinity of North Korean ports of Chongjin, Songjin, Mayang Do, and Wonsan . . . sample [the] electronic environment of [the] East Coast [of] North Korea, with emphasis on intercept/fixing of coastal radars, [and] intercept and conduct surveillance of Soviet Naval Units operating [in] Tsushima Straits in [an] effort to determine [the] purpose of Soviet presence."[4] The ship was ordered to stay thirteen miles from North Korea at all times and at least 200 yards from any Soviet naval vessels encountered at sea. Communications silence was to be strictly maintained unless "firm contact" was made with enemy units, in which case Bucher was to send daily reports to COMNAVFORJAPAN through the communications relay station in Kamiseya.[5] Secondary assignments included testing North Korean and Soviet reactions to her presence, evaluating the ship's overall intelligence-collection abilities, and monitoring any communist actions that could be considered threatening to the United States.[6]

The mission to the Korean coast was one that both the NSA and Naval Intelligence desired. The NSA originally recommended the target and specifically requested surveillance of the northern part of the peninsula, but the navy, which desired information from the central and southern ports, designed the operation to accommodate both objectives.[7] The navy's primary goal was to obtain any details on the North Korean submarine fleet thought to be stationed near Mayang-do, and there was also some hope of encountering one of a new class of Soviet submarines believed to be operating along Korea's east coast. The NSA's motives were less clear. Recent intelligence had suggested that the DPRK had strengthened its coastal defenses with surface-to-air missiles and cruise missiles; the *Pueblo*, the NSA believed, might intercept signals revealing their location. Information on the specifications of the DPRK fleet would also be useful, as would any intercepted messages, even routine ones, since they might help break secret North Korean codes. Should all these goals prove unreachable, the *Pueblo* was always equipped to obtain information on the nature, location, and frequency of DPRK radar, which would be especially helpful in responding to another North Korean attack on the South.[8]

Evidence suggests that other motives may have existed. Signals from radar and missile installations could have been more easily obtained by NSA intercept stations in South Korea and Japan, whose daily reports of the area already included detailed information regarding activity along North Korean ports. The National Reconnaissance Office, which managed satellite reconnaissance for the entire American intelligence community, regularly operated photo satellites over the Soviet Union and China, as well as SIGINT satellites specifically configured to intercept telephone signals, radio waves, and other forms of communication. American Corona satellites, which frequently occupied the skies in this region, had photographed virtually all Soviet intercontinental ballistic missile (ICBM) complexes by the mid-1960s, in addition to providing detailed information about Soviet air defense and antiballistic missile sites, submarine bases, and air bases. The air force operated approximately sixty aerial intelligence-collection missions in this region each month, sometimes using SR-71 spy planes, whose three high-powered cameras could get close pictures of a mailbox from 85,000 feet. The CIA was similarly active, in 1966 developing a new model of spy plane to succeed the U-2, code-named Oxcart. Oxcart planes carried sophisticated camera systems that used high-frequency sound waves to prevent picture distortion from even the highest ranges, and in 1967 they were approved for use from Okinawa, Japan. In May 1967, American A-12s and SR-71s began running Oxcart missions over Vietnam, successfully completing twenty-two of them by the end of the year. Not only were these other means of intelligence gathering safer and more reliable than nautical missions, but they were also more promising with regard to non-SIGINT collection, especially during the winter, when the Sea of Japan was so cold and dismal that significant naval activity was unlikely.[9]

Those closest to the assignment also questioned its value. Despite being thrilled at finally going to sea, Bucher was unhappy with the specific task. "I was a little disappointed at having to go up there at that time of year," he lamented. "It'd be so Goddamn cold, and I figured unproductive."[10] Events later proved him correct; despite operating near four of the largest North Korean ports, the *Pueblo* unearthed little signs of activity beyond routine shipping traffic. General Charles Bonesteel, commander of the UN Command in Korea, also had his doubts: "The risk, the degree of risk was totally unnecessary. . . . This was the intelligence tail wagging the dog. I mean, this kind of action and peripheral flights and all this stuff with regard to the Soviet Union, or even to some degree China, where there is some faint threat of intercontinental action, or threat to the United States is one thing, but North Korea wasn't a very serious threat to the continental United States."[11]

The redundancy of the operation encourages speculation that there was more to the objectives than the NSA claimed. One possibility is suggested by considering the assignment in conjunction with intelligence information regarding the Soviet Union. Shortly before the *Pueblo*'s departure, American intelligence suspected that the USSR would launch its version of the American MIRV in early 1968. Accordingly, American photo satellites maintained a steady presence over the Soviet Union in this period, including forty-one consecutive days between January 18 and February 27. By sending the *Pueblo* to Chongjin, in the northern part of the Sea of Japan, the NSA placed the SIGINT ship a mere 50 miles from the Soviet border and, perhaps more importantly, less than 150 miles from Vladivostok, the Soviet's foremost Pacific seaport and military facility. Because of its prominence, Vladivostok could be expected to be informed of any MIRV developments and might even have been the site of the test itself; in fact, the Russian Pacific Fleet stationed there was one of two major targets for the NSA's First Intercept Division stationed at Kamiseya.[12] Since the *Pueblo*'s mission would occur during the period in which these trials were expected, and since the NSA's stated objectives were easily obtainable by other means, the possibility certainly exists that obtaining information regarding these tests was the true aim of the mission.

Other aspects of the mission support the idea that the ship's target might have been Vladivostok. NSA training focused on the Soviet Union, rather than on North Korea. "North Korea," recalled CT John Grant, "was a surprise, since nothing had been mentioned about it in my training."[13] Although Bucher's orders did not specifically mention Soviet targets, they did authorize him to collect intelligence on any maneuvers that "may be indicative of pending hostilities or offensive action."[14] Information on a Soviet MIRV test certainly fit this definition and would likely have enticed him to pursue it at all reasonable costs. The ship's orders required stops at four naval bases on the east coast of North Korea, but rather than beginning at the closest target, Wonsan Harbor, the *Pueblo* went first to Chongjin, the northernmost port, and then doubled back toward the others. Such a course seems illogical, especially because it put a ship with a history of mechanical problems as far from help as possible before being given a chance to perform, but it did place the *Pueblo* close to Vladivostok immediately.[15]

Whatever the intelligence objective, the initial step remained the same; the *Pueblo* needed to reach the Korean coast as unobtrusively as possible.[16] Upon leaving Sasebo, Bucher swung his ship northward, clinging to the shore of the Japanese island of Kyushu in the hope of avoiding detection by the Soviet vessels that often operated in the Tsushima Strait.[17] After passing through the Korean Strait, he plowed northwest through the Sea of Japan until reaching Chongjin on January 16, within the region the navy had dubbed Operation Area Pluto. Bucher's plan was to remain in the area as long as the findings warranted and then descend slowly along the peninsula toward their other objectives. After a final stop off Wonsan, he envisioned a week spent observing Soviet vessels in the Tsushima Strait and then a mid–February return to Yokosuka.

Arriving off Chongjin was a welcome event for the men, many of whom had spent months hoping for some real activity. The CTs sprang to life, eager for the opportunity to demonstrate their abilities, and the SOD-Hut bristled with enthusiasm. Yet, as Bucher had feared, there was little for them to find. Some routine Morse code and voice transmissions were obtained, and signals were intercepted from a number of radar stations that the navy was already aware of, but overall, the intelligence collection was meager.[18] The non-SIGINT findings were equally disappointing. Some common shipping and fishing activity was noted, a few torpedo boats could be seen through binoculars, and Photographer's Mate Lawrence Mack snapped pictures of some Chinese and Japanese trawlers, but nothing of real interest was visible. There was one exciting piece of news. Shortly after arrival, Steve Harris reported that they had been spotted by North Korean coastal radar, but Bucher, convinced that the long-range radar sweep was routine, saw no reason to believe that they had been identified. Other problems actually seemed more pressing; the freezing temperatures, for example, had caused a dangerous amount of ice to collect on the ship's superstructure. In fact, the weather was so bad that steam from the steam hoses simply froze on the deck before the ice could melt, forcing the crew to chisel it off with wooden mallets. Bucher had the authority to remain in the specific target areas as long as he deemed it productive, but Chongjin clearly did not merit an extensive stay. Late at night on the seventeenth, the *Pueblo* began her trek southward toward Operation Area Venus.

The ship arrived near Songjin the next morning and once more found the intelligence activity disappointing. "The CTs," Bucher recalled, "were bored to death."[19] Again, several radar stations were spotted and some routine message traffic obtained, but overall, the results were paltry, and Bucher saw little reason to remain. On the evening of the nineteenth, the *Pueblo* resumed her southern course, arriving later that night off Mayang-do, an island about forty miles below Songjin, where intelligence suggested that the DPRK docked its fleet of four W-class Soviet-made submarines.[20]

The *Pueblo*'s first brush with danger occurred while she loitered off Mayang-do on the afternoon of the twenty-first. A DPRK SO-1-class subchaser appeared, apparently on routine patrol. At 138 feet long, the SO-1 was smaller than the *Pueblo* but faster and more maneuverable, with a speed of up to forty knots, and it carried vastly superior armaments, including a twin 57-mm cannon and a 25-mm antiaircraft gun. The ship closed to within 500 yards of the *Pueblo*'s port bow, close enough for those on the bridge to discern the number "26" beaded into her hull, but she never broke course or gave any other sign of noticing her American counterpart. Bucher now faced a dilemma. He had been ordered to contact Kamiseya and apprise COMNAVFORJAPAN if his ship was spotted, but there were no clear signs that this had occurred. Bucher consulted his officers, who almost unanimously agreed that they had not been recognized. The subchaser had never changed course or displayed any interest in them, and the CTs had detected no signals suggesting that they had been recognized.[21] Most likely, they concluded, the SO-1 had been in a hurry to complete her patrol and had decided that the *Pueblo* was a routine fishing boat, if it had spotted her at all. Accordingly, Bucher decided to continue the mission and ordered the ship south toward Wonsan. "It was a call on our part," Schumacher later lamented. "In hindsight, a bad call."[22]

On the morning of the twenty-second, the *Pueblo* arrived at Operation Area Mars, just outside Wonsan Harbor. Overall, the trip could only be considered a failure. "We had been twelve days out of Sasebo now," Schumacher recalled, "and had picked up nothing new or interesting."[23] Frustrated, Bucher resolved to spend two more days along Wonsan and then head toward the Tsushima Strait to study the Soviets. To an old submariner like the captain, a week spent maneuvering around enemy ships on the open seas offered the perfect antidote to the last two weeks of monotony. And, he thought, it might yield some productive results before the trip ended.[24]

That afternoon the *Pueblo* lay dead in the water approximately twenty miles off Wonsan. The sea was calm, the CTs were getting some good signals, and the oceanographers had just dropped a Nansen cast to test the waters, when suddenly the starboard lookout reported the approach of two North Korean trawlers. In the pilothouse, a worried Lawrence Mack was unable to ascertain their exact location and called for Murphy to help. "I'm not sure of our position," he told the XO, "and it would be most unfortunate if we got into that red area and they came out and threw a line on us and said 'You're our prisoners.'" "I wouldn't worry about that," responded Murphy. "We'll pull off and tell them to go suck eggs."[25]

The two DPRK ships, Soviet-built Lentra-class trawlers converted for military use, circled the *Pueblo* at a distance of less than 500 yards. After making a complete revolution, they fled northeast at about ten knots, then stopped three miles away, apparently to discuss the nature of their find. Hoping to hide the size of the ship's complement, Bucher ordered the crew to stay below deck and then began preparing a situation report (SITREP-1) for transmission to Kamiseya describing the encounter and including all significant intelligence materials collected on the mission. He also checked with the SOD-Hut to see if the CTs had intercepted any helpful information. The response was discouraging. They had picked up the communications between the two trawlers, but neither Chicca nor Hammond was proficient enough to translate them. After a brief wait, the two Korean vessels sprang to life and again closed on the American ship. This time they came within twenty-five yards, close enough for Sergeant Chicca (after consulting a Korean dictionary) to make out their names: *Rice Paddy* and *Rice Paddy I*. The *Pueblo* crewmen could also discern their North Korean counterparts staring back from the two ships and counted nineteen men on each. "They looked," thought Stu Russell, "like they wanted to eat our livers."[26] After a few more laps, the trawlers suddenly fled, heading directly toward Wonsan. This time there was no doubt that the *Pueblo* had been spotted.[27]

Once again, Bucher saw no reason to panic. His ship had been flying the international flag of a hydrographer when the trawlers arrived and had even been conducting legitimate hydrographic tests. Other than the "GER-1" beaded into her hull, no evidence of her nationality was visible. The *Pueblo* was in international waters, the Koreans had displayed no hostile intent, and besides, Bucher comforted himself, the mission was almost over. In accordance with his orders, he finished the SITREP notifying COMNAVFORJAPAN of the encounter, including the information about yesterday's sighting, but minimized the danger. "No attempt made at surveillance/harassment," it concluded. "Intentions: Remain in present area."[28]

At 4:45 P.M., Radioman Second Class Lee Roy Hayes retired to the radio shack to transmit the report. For the *Pueblo* to send a message, she had to contact Kamiseya and request the opening of circuit 21P. This signaled the communications base to respond with a specific frequency over which the *Pueblo* could deliver the information, which was then sent over an electronically coded 100-words-per-minute teletype. But, to Hayes's dismay, the ship's power proved too weak. Other vessels with higher antennae and more forceful transmitters were inadvertently drowning him out. Hayes could hear Kamiseya, but Kamiseya could not hear him, and the SITREP was too highly classified to be sent by manual Morse code. He worked throughout the night, which was more than could be said for the ship's best transmitter, which overheated shortly after dawn. At 9:00 the next morning, CT Second Class Donald McClarren, working with the inferior transmitter, finally linked up with Kamiseya and requested the opening of a teletype line. Overall, it had taken sixteen hours and thirteen different frequencies before the *Pueblo* had contacted its communications station; accordingly, CT Don Bailey, operating the teletype in the crypto room adjacent to the SOD-Hut, decided to keep the link open for a while.[29]

Dusk approached quickly, and Bucher saw no reason to deviate from his evening routine. As he did every night, he ordered the ship away from the coast, retreating to a point approximately twenty miles east of Korean territory. Overnight, the ship continued her drift to the east, and on the morning of the twenty-third, the crew awoke to find themselves approximately twenty-five miles from the Korean shore. After ordering a course back toward Wonsan, Bucher hurried to breakfast, anticipating another routine day of eavesdropping. The only good sign, the captain thought, was that the harsh weather appeared to be breaking.[30]

A few hours later, the *Pueblo* arrived at her destination, a point approximately sixteen miles from Ung-do, a small island at the mouth of Wonsan Harbor.[31] She remained in the area throughout an uneventful morning, although the CTs reported a significant increase in the amount of message traffic. It seemed possible, even likely, that these transmissions were related to yesterday's encounter, but Chicca and Hammond's inability to read them without a dictionary had considerably slowed the deciphering process. To Bucher's dismay, there was already a four- or five-hour backlog for message translation. Still, there seemed no reason for alarm, as there was virtually no activity within sight. The only sign of life visible to the naked eye was a faint trace of smoke rising from the direction of Wonsan. The isolation actually left Bucher and the crew a bit disappointed; yesterday's encounter, it appeared, might be the trip's only excitement.

The tranquillity was shattered just as the men sat down to a lunch of meat loaf, potatoes, and succotash.[32] From the bridge, Quartermaster First Class Charles Law called down to the mess hall, informing Bucher that a ship had been spotted about eight miles south, heading directly toward them. The captain ordered a position check and told Law to inform him if the ship closed to within five miles. In minutes, Law's voice again interrupted lunchtime conversation. The ship was already within five miles, indicating a speed well in excess of their own capability, and the *Pueblo*'s location, Law concluded, had been confirmed as fifteen miles off Korean territory. As Bucher hurried to the bridge, Gene Lacy's prophetic voice filled the mess hall. "Maybe," he cracked, "this won't be another dull day after all."[33]

Bucher arrived on the bridge just in time to observe the approach of a North Korean SO-1 subchaser, her bow bearing the number "35." Surprised to note that the ship was at general quarters and the crew at battle stations, Bucher briefly considered making the same move himself, but rejected the idea. An attack seemed highly unlikely; instead, it appeared that the *Pueblo* would finally experience the harassment that had marked the *Banner*'s journeys. Not wanting to provoke an international incident, Bucher ordered his crew to remain below and sent Harris to the SOD-Hut to try to intercept the subchaser's communications. Needing a steady hand on the bridge, he also replaced Charles Law with the more experienced Gene Lacy, and then waited for the North Koreans to make the first move.

He did not have to wait long. The subchaser approached along the *Pueblo*'s port side and began circling in a clockwise direction at a distance of about 500 yards. Soon, a North Korean shore station would begin passing along details of the encounter to higher commands; "subchaser number 35," it reported, "has approached a 300-ton vessel which is used for radar operation. . . . It is believed the vessel was not armed and that it was an American vessel."[34] Just after noon, the North Korean ship raised international signal flags asking "WHAT NATIONALITY?" Bucher ignored the query and sent Schumacher to prepare an updated report for COMNAVFORJAPAN. The standoff continued for fifteen minutes, until three more DPRK ships approached at high speeds, all Soviet-made P-4 torpedo boats, bearing the numbers 601, 604, and 606.[35] All three were capable of speeds exceeding fifty knots and carried 12.7-mm machine guns and two single 18-inch torpedo tubes. Despite the formidable array of firepower, the *Pueblo*'s officers remained calm. Multiple ship harassment was hardly unprecedented in these missions, and there seemed no reason to expect anything worse. "If the atmosphere aboard *Pueblo* had changed," Bucher recalled, "it was one of bracing for a test of nerves, not battle."[36] Again, Bucher checked their location, and again the response was reassuring; his ship was over fifteen miles off the Korean coast.

In the midst of a third circle around the *Pueblo*, the SO-1 suddenly raised another flag: "HEAVE TO OR I WILL OPEN FIRE." It was not totally unexpected. Soviet ships had flown the same flag at the *Banner* during a recent operation. Bucher ordered a third position check and again was gratified by the response, which placed them in international waters, 15.8 miles from the nearest Korean territory. Emboldened, he directed a reply: "I AM IN INTERNATIONAL WATERS. INTEND TO REMAIN IN THE AREA UNTIL TOMORROW." Still, he explored his options as the P-4s quickly assumed positions around his vessel. "Could we scuttle the ship quickly if we had to?" he asked Gene Lacy. "Not quickly," came the reply. "About two hours to flood the main engineroom after unbolting and disconnecting the saltwater cooling intakes. Then she would not sink without breaching the bulkhead to the auxiliary engineroom. Another tough long job."[37] A check of the water's depth placed them in less than thirty-five fathoms, further discouraging this maneuver, since the North Koreans could easily salvage much of the classified materials. The only likely result would be the death of the crewmen, who would have survived less than twenty minutes in the freezing water.

While Bucher contemplated his next move, the DPRK boats moved into closer positions around the ship. Quickly, Lieutenant Schumacher made his way to the message center with a new transmission for Kamiseya. Labeled PINNACLE 1/JOPREP 3 (Joint Operations Report), the message summarized the day's events and described Bucher's intended response. The *Pueblo*, PINNACLE 1 informed naval authorities, was going to remain in the area as long as possible and would withdraw slowly toward the northeast if necessary.[38] Reflecting the fact that the ship's officers still considered the situation fairly routine, the message received the "FLASH" designation, requiring that it be handled as a high priority, not given the emergency status of a "CRITIC" heading, which instructed readers to relay it to all echelons of high command immediately, including the NSA, the Pentagon, and the White House. All subsequent messages were sent under the CRITIC label. At the teletype, Don Bailey was "talking" to Richard Haizlip, a CT at Kamiseya, when Schumacher handed him the message. "Got company outside," Bailey typed, and then commenced transmitting the report at 12:50 P.M.[39] "How's it feel to be threatened?" asked Haizlip. "Not doing so good with them," replied Bailey, in what would soon become an understatement. "Roger, roger, know what you mean."[40]

The *Pueblo* was not the only ship keeping in touch with its commanders. A few minutes after the transmission of PINNACLE 1, the SO-1 radioed an update to North Korea; "We have approached the target," the subchaser reported, "and the name of the target is GER-1-2. I judge it to be a reconnaissance ship. It is Americans. It does not appear that there are weapons." The captain then broadcast his position, confirming the *Pueblo*'s contention that it was still in international waters by placing his own ship almost eighteen miles offshore.[41]

Quickly, the odds grew even worse. A roar of engines overhead alerted the crew to the arrival of two Soviet-built MiG planes. Off in the distance, another subchaser and torpedo boat could be seen coming from the Wonsan area; the subchaser, the crew realized as it drew closer, was number "26," the one that had passed them on patrol two days earlier. "Do you want to go to general quarters?" asked Lacy.[42] Bucher hesitated, but again rejected the temptation. Although leaving them in the best defensive position, general quarters might also provoke a more aggressive response—hardly wise, considering Bucher had been warned to expect harassment of this nature. He also wanted to test his ship's ability as an intelligence collector, as his operational orders demanded. Besides, it was clear that the *Pueblo* was already far outgunned; even at general quarters, she was unlikely to put up significant resistance. Instead, he sent Schumacher below to prepare an updated PINNACLE message and, just in case, ordered the crew to prepare for emergency destruction.

At 1:06 P.M., the leading SO-1 radioed North Korea of its intent: "According to present instructions, we will close down the radio, tie up the personnel, tow it, and enter port at Wonsan. At present, we are on our way to boarding."[43] Within ten minutes, a dozen armed soldiers from the DPRK's 661st Army unit, complete with helmets, rifles, and fixed bayonets, hopped from the subchaser onto one of the torpedo boats.[44] After tying rubber tires over the side to act as bumpers, the P-4 began backing down toward the stern of the American ship, drawing so close that the *Pueblo* crewmen could actually hear the soldiers cock their assault rifles. As the torpedo boat closed within five yards, Bucher's voice rang out: "All ahead one-third."[45] The *Pueblo*'s engines slipped into gear moments before the boarding party was within leaping distance, and the ship suddenly lurched forward toward the open sea and freedom. Pulling away, Bucher raised a new flag: "THANK YOU FOR YOUR CONSIDERATION," he signaled. "AM DEPARTING THE AREA."[46] "It looks like we're out of it," Law muttered anxiously.[47]

Secluded from the excitement, Don Bailey remained at his teletype in the crypto room. Unable to communicate directly with the bridge, he relied on passing comments to keep abreast of the situation, and, hearing mention of a boarding party, he assumed the worst. A new message went out to Kamiseya: "WE ARE BEING BOARDED . . . WE ARE BEING BOARDED. SOS, SOS, SOS, SOS."[48] Although unable to observe the events himself, Bailey proved to be the *Pueblo*'s best link with the outside world. Voice circuits were too difficult to establish, especially under these conditions. The ship's hi-comm, a high-frequency tele-phone link to Japan and Hawaii, had been designed for use in such emergen-cies, but the *Pueblo*'s usual bad luck surfaced when Murphy tried to use it. Pick-ing up the receiver while the ship leaped away from the boarding party, the XO found that the hi-comm operator in Japan was in the process of switching fre-quencies, a short task done only twice daily. Murphy interrupted to explain the situation, but no one was listening. "Stand by to change frequencies," a voice on the other end babbled incessantly.[49]

Bucher quickly increased to full speed, but the *Pueblo*'s engines were easily outclassed. Their pursuers closed the gap within minutes. Two torpedo boats followed in their wake, while the other two zigzagged across the bow at a dis-tance of less than twenty yards, blocking the path of escape. Evasive maneuvers were futile; the *Pueblo* was simply overmatched at every turn. At 1:18, Bailey sent out a second PINNACLE message, reporting the increased number of ships and the boarding attempt. "Departing area," it concluded, "under es-cort."[50] At the same time, the lead subchaser was sending a message of its own, ordering the torpedo boats to retreat from the *Pueblo* so she could open fire.[51] As the P-4s withdrew, the SO-1 began backing away to obtain a horizontal tar-get. Recognizing the maneuver, Chicca burst into the forward berthing com-partment. "Hit the deck," he yelled. "They're going to open fire." Fireman Mi-chael O'Bannon would not believe it. "They wouldn't dare. We're in open waters. And we're an American ship."[52]

Suddenly, the SO-1 rang out with her 57-mm automatic cannons, raining shrapnel over the bridge. Within seconds, the P-4's machine guns opened fire from each side. Lasting less than six seconds, the barrage reduced the bridge to shambles. Among its casualties was the antenna coupler on the mast that linked the hi-comm with the outside world. Down in the berthing compartments, CT Frank Ginther's voice could be heard over the din. "If you guys know any prayers," he advised, "now is the time to say them."[53] Another salvo quickly fol-lowed, shattering the windows in the pilothouse and leaving Tim Harris and CT Michael Barrett sporting small cuts from flying glass. Others were more seri-ously injured. Signalman Wendell Leach had taken some shrapnel in his leg; CT Stephen Robin, manning the bridge phone, was bleeding from his neck and left elbow; and Bucher had a small wound in his rectum. Recognizing that anyone on the bridge was an easy target, Bucher ordered a modified general quarters, sending those below deck to battle positions but denying permission for crew-men to come up top. It was a trick he had learned from the *Banner,* which had used such a modification during an earlier case of harassment.[54] Boatswain's Mate Second Class Ronald Berens, a veteran of navy operations in Vietnam, re-mained at the wheel. "Jesus Christ," he declared, "I'll take Vietnam over this."[55]

The scene was chaos throughout the ship. Bucher ordered the destruction of classified materials immediately after the first salvo, but complications hindered the crew's ability to comply.[56] According to naval regulations, the weighted bags constituting the ship's primary method of paper destruction could not be used in such shallow waters. The incinerator was too small for the enormous volume of classified papers and was located at an exposed position on the starboard deck. As a result, the crewmen, most of whom had never been in a combat situation, were forced to improvise an emergency destruction while under attack by six faster and more heavily armed vessels. Some tried to burn individual papers with cigarette lighters, while others started fires in wastebaskets. Small blazes sprang up in the passageways, filling the corridors with blinding smoke and leaving the men coughing and wheezing for air as they struggled to complete their assigned tasks. The heat grew so intense that the paint on the walls began to peel, and in some cases, the fires even ignited the deck itself. On the starboard deck, Robin, Schumacher, and Barrett tried to tear reports apart by hand for the incinerator, but they spent more time dodging bullets and shrapnel than destroying materials. Murphy was trying to flush classified materials down the toilet in his stateroom, forgetting that it stopped working when general quarters was declared; when Law and Steve Harris found him later, he was sitting on the toilet staring blankly into space.

Conditions were especially bad in the SOD-Hut, where the lack of direct communication with the rest of the ship prevented a coordinated destruct effort. One CT even recalled that he first became aware of trouble when he "heard the clatter of machine gun fire against the port side of the ship."[57] The modified general quarters made things worse by preventing anyone from coming topside to help with the destruction. Those already inside did the best they could under the circumstances, but the results were meager. Since the weighted bags were useless, the men started small fires in their chamber, hardly an adequate means of disposing of thousands of pages of paper. Because of the lack of ventilation, the main consequence was to fill the SOD-Hut with thick smoke and waves of heat, turning a difficult task into an impossible one. Some CTs tried to shatter the intelligence equipment with sledgehammers and fire axes but found their targets too well protected; Ralph Bouden directed a strike against one machine only to see the hammer fall apart while the equipment remained unaffected. Even the ship's tape recorders, first on the SOD-Hut's destruct list, were firmly encased in metal and thus impervious to the blows. Other machines were screwed into place, but no one had provided screwdrivers for their removal. The process, Harris recalled, was "painfully slow" and would, he estimated, have taken between nine and twelve hours to complete.[58]

Contrary to subsequent navy claims, the officers and crew cannot be blamed for the slow material destruction.[59] The ship relied on what the navy deemed an adequate system for emergency destruction, yet while the men worked feverishly, the system was letting them down. The navy's failure to anticipate these problems could be understood if such a system had never before been tested, but similar procedures had proved wanting less than a year earlier on the USS *Liberty*. After the attack on the *Liberty*, one crew member described the obstacles hindering the emergency destruction of material:

> Now, defenseless and under attack, everything classified but not actually in use was to be destroyed. The bags proved useless, as they were too large and heavy to carry, and the water wasn't deep enough for safe disposal anyway. The ship's incinerator couldn't be used, as it was on the 03 level within easy reach of the airplanes. As a last resort, Lieutenant Jim Pierce, the ship's communications officer, ordered his men to destroy everything by hand. Acrid smoke soon filled the room as he and Joe Lentini dropped code lists, a handful at a time, into a flaming wastepaper basket; nearby, Richard Keene and Duane Marggraf attacked delicate crypto equipment with wire cutters and a sledge hammer.[60]

The resemblance between the two destruction attempts is striking: inadequate incineration equipment, excessive dependence on weighted bags, poor ventilation, and ineffective defense provisions, all creating a disorderly and hectic destruction attempt that flooded the ship with smoke and heat while falling far short of its overall objectives. It is understandable that these shortcomings occurred once. Such deficiencies are usually uncovered only in combat situations, as no amount of testing under manufactured conditions can ever duplicate the real thing. However, after these failings were so clearly demonstrated the first time, their reoccurrence on the *Pueblo* is much harder to accept.

The DPRK ships maintained their positions around the *Pueblo* while destruction continued. A second volley of shots was launched, and unlike the first round, this time the firing continued intermittently. Before the day was done, the P-4s would expend more than a thousand rounds of ammunition.[61] Above the din, Gene Lacy's voice could be heard in the pilothouse, "Are you going to stop this goddamned ship?" he demanded of Bucher.[62] The captain hesitated. His vessel was covered with smoke and flames, slowly spreading throughout the passageways. Try as she might, the *Pueblo* could not outrun or outmaneuver her attackers. Her guns were unreachable and were inadequate even if they were not. The flying bridge had been reduced to rubble, and most of the antennae had been shot down. Eight 57-mm cannon shells had penetrated the ship, leaving the superstructure damaged and leaking. Translation problems had rendered the CTs useless; communications had been intercepted, but they were, as Chicca told Bucher, "Nothing but a lot of fast gibberish which we can only identify as Korean."[63] Despite Don Bailey's continued pleas over the teletype, no American support could be seen on the horizon. Looking around him, Bucher made a decision. Turning to Lacy with a nod, he authorized his chief warrant officer to ring up "ALL STOP" on the annunciator.[64] It was time for the *Pueblo* to surrender.

The shooting paused as the ship coasted to a halt. Bucher emerged on the bridge just as the leading subchaser closed to 800 yards and raised a new flag: "FOLLOW IN MY WAKE—I HAVE PILOT ABOARD."[65] Bucher nodded and ordered the ship "ahead one-third."[66] The *Pueblo* turned east, following the subchaser's path toward Korea at five knots. Below deck, Bailey kept Kamiseya apprised of recent events. "WE ARE BEING ESCORTED INTO WONSAN. WE ARE BEING ESCORTED INTO PROB WONSAN REPEAT WONSAN," he sent at 1:45; "ARE YOU SENDING ASSISTANCE?" The answer was only slightly encouraging: "WORD HAS GONE OUT TO ALL AUTHORITIES."[67]

Meanwhile, emergency destruction continued. "We will stall as long as we can," Bucher told his men. "What can't be burned goes over the side."[68] Surveying the ship left him dismayed, as he quickly recognized the extent of the task that remained. Classified materials littered the deck of the SOD-Hut, and much of the intelligence equipment remained intact. Secret publications had also collected around the incinerator and in the pilothouse. "Just as soon as we thought we had found all the classified materials," recalled Murphy, "someone would uncover another hoard."[69] Still, Bucher hoped that a slow trip into Wonsan would buy them some badly needed time.

Unfortunately for the captain and his crew, this hope was short-lived. Recognizing the paucity of the destruction, Bucher decided to gamble. At 2:00 P.M., he picked up the 1MC microphone and ordered the engines stopped, hoping to feign mechanical breakdown. Quickly, the leading subchaser turned and opened fire from off the *Pueblo*'s starboard bow. One shell landed near the laundry room, another hit the mainmast, and a third exploded inside the starboard passageway near the electronics room. The torpedo boats also joined in, raking the ship with machine gun fire from as close as 100 yards. Injuries were numerous, but two were especially severe. Fireman Stephen Woelk was struck in his leg and abdomen, opening a serious, but not life-threatening, wound. Fireman Duane Hodges was not so lucky. A shell struck his right hip as he carried a bag of papers to the starboard deck, tearing off his right leg and testicles and shredding his abdomen and urinary tract. He would be dead within an hour. His last words, spoken shortly after the North Koreans boarded the ship, expressed his gratitude for having had the privilege of serving in the American navy.[70]

The North Koreans had made their point. Bucher ordered the ship ahead at one-third speed, and again the *Pueblo* inched forward. Emergency destruction continued for a few minutes until the leading subchaser sent up a new flag, this time ordering the *Pueblo* to stop. Bucher's stalling had clearly exhausted their patience, and now the North Koreans had decided to take direct control of the ship. With few options available, a despondent Bucher complied. Gene Lacy's voice crackled over the 1MC, reminding the crew that the military Code of Conduct required that they provide no information beyond their name, rank, and serial number. Down in the crypto room, Don Bailey continued his correspondence with Kamiseya. "DESTRUCTION OF PUBS HAS BEEN INEFFECTIVE," he typed. "SUSPECT SEVERAL WILL BE COMPROMISED."[71] Within minutes a torpedo boat approached the fantail, throwing a line onto the *Pueblo*'s deck. As soon as a crewman mechanically tied it to a bit, ten DPRK soldiers followed, leaping on board with weapons drawn and bayonets fixed, and a second group quickly followed. Now officially in enemy hands, Don Bailey sent a final message: "FOUR MEN INJURED AND ONE CRITICALLY AND GOING OFF THE AIR NOW AND DESTROYING THIS GEAR."[72] It was 2:33 P.M.

The intruders easily took control of the ship, forcing Bucher to give them a tour at gunpoint, and gathering the men in the exposed well deck. The crew was quickly bound, blindfolded, and searched, with valuables disappearing into their captors' eager hands; Murphy's sunglasses, Ron Berens's pocketknife, Steve Harris's Bible, and a number of *Playboy* magazines were never to be seen again. Resistance was met with force, and after a few well-placed gun butts to the head, the stunned crew accepted their fate. Soon they were moved to the forward berthing compartment, remaining there for what seemed an eternity. Finally, the unmistakable crash of the ship's hull into a pier signaled their arrival. The USS *Pueblo* had reached her destination, the naval yard at Chojikan, near Wonsan Harbor, North Korea.[73]

The seizure left the United States stunned. No American ship had been captured in international waters since 1815, when the British navy had apprehended the USS *President*. It is therefore not surprising that some aspects of the event have long been steeped in controversy. The lack of definitive information made the incident especially contentious. The ship had been in emissions silence for two weeks prior to the seizure, few in the military and intelligence communities had been cleared to know anything about the mission, and the North Koreans could hardly be considered a reliable source of information. Even thirty years after the seizure, some important questions remain difficult to answer.

One unresolved issue concerns the extent of the intelligence loss. Immediately after the seizure, the Johnson administration ordered a special investigation of the ramifications for American intelligence, which concluded that the damage was "not vital."[74] "We do know," echoed Secretary of Defense McNamara, "that our worldwide communications were not compromised."[75] Others disagreed. "When the final reckoning is made," predicted columnist Drew Pearson, "it will be found that the North Koreans made a haul more important than the theft of atom bomb secrets."[76] Although many details remain clouded, evidence suggests that the reality of the intelligence loss was much closer to Pearson's claim than the administration's more optimistic pronouncements.

There is no doubt that the North Koreans captured extensive classified materials, which they quickly shared with the Soviet Union. Shortly after the seizure, in fact, a North Korean aircraft flew to Moscow carrying 792 pounds of cargo, presumably the salvage from the *Pueblo,* and U.S. intelligence intercepted a North Korean fax sending American cryptographic guidebooks to the Soviet Union. "The Soviets," KGB Chief Oleg Kalugin acknowledged, "had been allowed to inspect the captured material because they were the only ones who knew how to make use of it."[77] A number of crewmen estimated that complete destruction would have taken approximately ten hours, yet less than sixty-five minutes passed between the time Bucher ordered emergency destruction and the boarding of the ship. Radioman Third Class Charles Crandell carried a large stack of highly classified materials to the aft deck for destruction but was injured by a shell on the way and was never able to complete the task. After boarding the ship, DPRK troops took Murphy downstairs; "to my horror," he recalled, "I also saw that I was walking on a carpet of classified documents." Hundreds of pounds of documents, he later estimated, had been lost. Much of the paperwork in the pilothouse was destroyed, but less success was achieved elsewhere. An eight-drawer file cabinet in the ship's electronics office stored hundreds of classified publications, including a detailed account of top-secret American intelligence objectives for the Pacific; seven of the drawers remained intact for the North Koreans. The ship also carried classified U.S. communications manuals, including the ACP (Allied Communications Publication) and the JANAPS (Joint Army, Navy, Air Force Publication System). The *Pueblo* lost so much, recalled Schumacher, that when his captors showed him a small sample, he felt "lightheaded and sick. . . . They had so much, I felt I would fall out of my chair and off into space."[78]

Especially damaging was the loss from the SOD-Hut. Some of the SIGINT equipment was destroyed, but much remained, including a number of the most vital NSA encryption and decryption machines and the manuals that detailed their repair and operation.[79] Other classified communications machines also fell into DPRK hands, including eight R390A radio receivers, one of the intelligence community's leading communications interceptors. The receivers proved impervious to the crew's hurried destruction attempt; direct blows with fire axes, recalled one CT, barely chipped the paint.[80] Other equipment was thrown overboard and was easily fished from the Sea of Japan by DPRK frogmen.[81] The paper destruction was even less efficient. While showing his captors the ship, Bucher was stunned at the SOD-Hut's condition: "Large amounts of unburned papers blocked the open steel door and inside it a mattress cover stuffed full of what must have been classified publications had been left lying in plain view on the deck. . . . My heart sank when I saw how much Steve and his men had not been able to destroy."[82] Only one weighted bag of papers was tossed overboard, by CT Peter Langenberg; approximately ten others were filled but never removed.[83] Two or three naval mattress covers, at least six feet by three feet, were also filled with classified materials and then left in the SOD-Hut.[84] Unsurprising, then, was the NSA assessment shortly after the seizure that the loss was "a major intelligence coup without parallel in modern history."[85]

The most damaging loss may have been the Specific Information Collection Requirements (SICRs) the ship carried. SICRs spelled out in detail the information gaps that American intelligence wanted filled for specific areas. Despite the fact that the *Pueblo* was incapable of finding much of this information, COMNAVFORJAPAN had loaded her with all 128 SICRs for North Korea. Now American intelligence had to assume that they had all fallen into North Korean hands, thereby alerting them to future targets and to areas that had been compromised. Perhaps equally significant was the loss of the Electronic Order of Battle for the Far East, which spelled out the frequencies and operational details of the Russian, Chinese, and Korean radar sites and transmitters that American intelligence had located in the area. This provided a critical advantage to the United States in case of war. But with this map, it would now be a relatively simple matter for other nations to change these operational systems and nullify the American edge.[86] Other information presumed lost included the findings from the *Banner*'s earlier missions; the classified call signs for American ships; and information on American electronic countermeasures, radar classification instructions, and various secret codes and navy transmission procedures. Overall, the navy estimated that only 10 percent of the material in the SOD-Hut spaces had been destroyed.[87] The extent of the damage was revealed within a week at an NSA listening station in Wakkanai, Japan. The staff was routinely monitoring a fax link between Moscow and Pyongyang when suddenly, one NSA operative recalled, "There was this special transmission, and all of these secret code-word documents were coming across. All of the *Pueblo* stuff was coming across. Everything was captured."[88]

The loss of intelligence materials hurt in other ways. About ten weeks after the seizure, North Korean radio communications suddenly plummeted, likely reflecting the Koreans' realization of how easily they were being intercepted.[89] The capture also affected American SIGINT collection abilities worldwide, as North Korea quickly published detailed descriptions and photographs of the ship's electronic gear and intelligence systems in DPRK journals, thus articulating for other nations the specific abilities and limitations of American equipment.[90]

Only a few high-ranking intelligence officials actually understood the extent of the loss. A couple of those "in the know" wanted to destroy the ship before it reached Wonsan, even if it meant killing American crew members. Even House Minority Leader Gerald Ford (R-Mich.), who knew only the ship's general nature, told LBJ shortly after the capture, "I would have gotten rid of all that equipment, even if it required sinking our own vessel. . . . I might have blown it out [of] the water myself." One intelligence official estimated that the Soviets gained between three and five years on the United States in the race for intelligence technology. In private, LBJ drew an even gloomier picture, admitting to a select group of Democratic congressmen shortly after the seizure that the loss was "a severely damaging blow" to American security. The ship, Johnson added, carried the nation's most sophisticated intelligence devices, which were approximately fifteen years ahead of anything the Soviets had. "Now that the Russians have the model," he concluded grimly, "they may be able to catch up with us within a year."[91]

In fact, it would be many years before the full extent of the damage became clear. The *Pueblo* carried five of America's most advanced cryptographic machines—the KW-7 code radio, the KWR-37 crypto receiver, the WLR-1 intercept receiver, the KG-14 code radio, and the KL-7 off-line crypto unit. During the attack, Don McClarren destroyed the KL-7, smashing its rotors and crushing the interior components with a fire ax. The other machines, however, survived with only minimal damage and ended up in Soviet hands.[92] The loss of any secret cryptographic machine had ramifications, but those stemming from the loss of the KW-7 code radio were especially severe. The KW-7 was an online, send-and-receive unit that handled both ship-to-shore and intership radio communications and was used by over 80 percent of the Atlantic Fleet ships and all its submarines.[93] To encrypt a message, the operator typed on a keyboard as if he was working on a traditional typewriter. However, the rotors were aligned so that when a letter was punched, a different letter appeared on the message. To prevent anyone from breaking the code, the machine produced different letters even when the same letter was typed repeatedly; hence the word "ESTEEMED" might appear as "PCKQDMRA." Deciphering the message required specific NSA key lists that provided the daily settings necessary to produce the correct message. Thus, the American intelligence community believed that although the loss of the machine was significant, it did not appear to be vital without the key lists. In fact, following the *Pueblo* capture, the NSA merely modified the KW-7 and sent out new technical manuals and key lists to those using it.

It took two decades to discover that the United States had drastically underestimated the loss. In 1985, the Federal Bureau of Investigation arrested John Walker, Jr., a navy officer and one of the Soviet Union's most successful spies. Walker, who had volunteered to transmit classified information to the Soviets for financial inducements, had begun revealing American secrets to Moscow in late 1967, shortly before the capture of the *Pueblo*. Among his early prizes had been copies of the key lists and the new operational manuals for the KW-7. Now, with the machine from the *Pueblo* and the lists from Walker, the Soviets had easy access to critical American communications.[94] Meanwhile, Jerry Whitworth, another member of Walker's spy ring, had access to critical materials for the KW-37 and the KG-14, which were also delivered to the Soviets.[95] The consequences were devastating. Overall, Walker's espionage enabled the Soviet Union to decrypt an estimated 1 million American messages. Since the KW-7 was used extensively in Vietnam, the Soviet Union now knew about planned American bombing raids in advance, thus giving the North Vietnamese time to prepare their air defenses. The same was true for American naval operations. Lamented one navy commander at the time, it was almost as if "the Vietcong knew when we were coming and were waiting for us."[96] The Soviets also received advance notice of American naval exercises, often sending their own ships into the area just as the top-secret maneuvers began. Among other valuable information they obtained were details of American troop movements worldwide; the locations of Trident-class nuclear submarines, which they had found difficult to track; and the battle plans for the U.S. Atlantic Fleet.

Another controversial issue concerned the ship's location, both before and during the seizure. The navy and the Johnson administration insisted that the *Pueblo* had been in international waters for the entire mission. "There is no proof whatsoever," insisted Admiral Moorer, "that she did intrude." The Special House Subcommittee on the *Pueblo* Incident agreed, unanimously concluding that "at no time during its mission did the USS *Pueblo* ever penetrate North Korean territorial waters." All of the crew's accounts support this claim. "There was not even the remotest possibility that we were inside their claimed territorial waters," recalled Murphy. "There was," agreed Bucher, "never any question about our position."[97]

Despite Bucher's assurance, there were actually numerous questions about the ship's position, many of which originated in the United States. Within a week of the seizure, Senator William Fulbright (D-Ark.) declared that the ship was "within territorial waters of North Korea at [the] time of the incident." Connecticut Senator Abraham Ribicoff claimed to have conducted an independent investigation that convinced him that the *Pueblo* had violated North Korean waters. An administration official, Ribicoff added, privately confirmed this conclusion. *Newsweek* recognized that "there was even some doubt as to what exactly had happened; most important, whether the *Pueblo*'s skipper, Lloyd M. Bucher, had strayed across North Korea's 12 mile territorial limit and thus provoked the predicament himself." Newspapers observed similar doubts. The *Kansas City Star* noted, "Some are asking where the boat was. They question the validity of government pronouncements that it was in international waters." The *Minneapolis Tribune* reported, "There also appears to be considerable skepticism about our position." Telegrams poured into the White House, demanding that Johnson reveal the truth about the ship's location. "You well know," wrote a registered nurse from Grosse Pointe, Michigan, "that the *Pueblo* was probably transgressing into North Korean waters." Even the seventh-grade class of Hopeville Junior High School in Connecticut urged the president to get the men released quickly, "since there is a doubt about whether or not our ship was inside North Korean territorial limits." Privately, even the Johnson administration was not so convinced. "It is important to remember," cautioned McNamara the day after the seizure, "that we did not know where the ship was prior to the time of this incident." "I do not think," agreed Clark Clifford, "our case with reference to the ship is a strong one. The North Koreans have a better case on where the ship was. They were there. We weren't."[98]

North Korea helped to encourage this speculation. Within a month of the capture, the DPRK government released evidence of six specific violations of its territorial waters; more would follow at random intervals. The original six positions were as follows:

January 15, 7:45 A.M., *Pueblo* reported at 41–25N/130–03E, 11.2 nautical miles from Orang Dan.

January 16, 1:41 P.M., *Pueblo* reported at 41–51N/130–10E, 9.8 nautical miles from Kai Tan.

January 18, 3:25 A.M., *Pueblo* reported at 40–28.1N/129–36.7 E, 10.75 nautical miles from Nam do.

January 18, 4:32 A.M., *Pueblo* reported at 40–27.3N/129–30.0E, 11.3 nautical miles from Nam do.

January 21, 6:30 P.M., *Pueblo* reported at 39–48.9N/128.01.9E, 8.2 nautical miles from unnamed DPRK territory.

January 23 (the time of the seizure), *Pueblo* reported at 39–17.4N/127–46.9E, 7.6 nautical miles from Yo do.[99]

The DPRK released three forms of evidence to corroborate these claims. Most numerous were a series of confessions by the crewmen, admitting to these violations. North Korea provided more objective evidence by releasing three photographs of a *Pueblo* navigation chart displaying the ship's course throughout her journey, with the intrusions clearly marked. Finally, the North Koreans produced a picture of the ship's official position log, created by the navigator, which recorded two of the violations, and another photograph of a few pages of the "visual sightings log" confirming them.[100]

In reality, the administration had little to fear from these specific DPRK allegations. The intercepted communications between the SO-1 and shore confirmed the *Pueblo*'s presence well beyond DPRK waters at the time of the seizure. The North Korean navy's coastal watch radar reporting network also placed the ship thirteen miles outside of territorial waters. These findings, which were transmitted to Pyongyang by Morse code, were intercepted by South Korean intelligence at Kangnung. American radio direction finders throughout the Pacific, including one at Kamiseya, recorded the ship's position as well beyond North Korean waters, and in February, the Soviet ambassador to England admitted privately to a British official that the *Pueblo* had indeed been outside the twelve-mile barrier when attacked.[101] The DPRK evidence itself also falls apart under even the simplest scrutiny. The crew's confessions came only after severe beatings and torture. Virtually every crew member later repudiated them and described the frightening physical and emotional torment they endured before confessing. Bucher, the first to "confess," suffered thirty-six hours of severe physical and mental abuse, capitulating only when his captors threatened to shoot his crew in front of him, starting with the youngest member. After admitting to the intrusions, the captain was forced to repeat them to a DPRK press conference, where his exhaustion was so apparent that, upon hearing a tape of the conference, neither his wife nor an old friend identified the voice as his.[102] Nor was the ship's position log reliable, since Bucher required that all recorded locations be entered even if they were obviously incorrect. Considering the ship's poor equipment and inexperienced navigators, it is hardly surprising that the North Koreans were able to find a few erroneous points that indicated violations of their waters.

A more specific look at the alleged intrusions definitively refutes the DPRK claims. The first intrusion, dated January 15, was listed on the position log as having occurred at 7:45 A.M. This intrusion appeared in the log in the middle of a sequence of other recorded positions; the preceding entry was taken at 6:40, and the subsequent one at 8:10. The distance between the alleged violation and the position recorded at 8:10 is 7.4 nautical miles. For the *Pueblo* to have traversed this distance in this time would have required a speed of 17.6 knots, faster than she was capable of traveling. In fact, just looking at this series of positions suggests the North Korean subterfuge. The entries for the morning of the fifteenth appear as follows:

6:05 A.M.: 41–10N/130–06.5E
6:40 A.M.: 41–14.5N/130–07E
7:45 A.M.: 41–25N/130–03E (alleged intrusion)
8:10 A.M.: 41–22.9N/130–12.2E
10:02 A.M.: 41–36N/130–10E

Clearly, the 41–25N latitude is out of logical sequence, since it breaks the steady progression north indicated by all other entries. Such a position would thus have required not only unreachable speeds but also a radical and illogical course change that is incongruent with the mundane nature of the day's work. A closer look at the photograph of the captured chart suggests that the "5" in 41–25N had been written over; most likely, it was originally 41–20N, which would follow more logically in this course.[103]

The second intrusion, occurring on the sixteenth at 9.8 miles from North Korea, does not appear on the position log or the visual sighting log, existing only on the picture of the track chart. *Pueblo* crew members later claimed that this chart was not the one used on the ship, but had been fabricated by the North Koreans, who then forced Executive Officer Murphy to sign it. Evidence suggests that these claims were accurate. The chart that served as the backdrop for the plotted course in the picture was a U.S. hydrographic chart, which, because it covered such a large area, was not the type the navy used for navigation. On the bottom right-hand corner, a notation reads, "Drawn by Edward Renz Murphy, Jr., Executive Officer/Navigator." Although navigators do make such footnotes, the term "plotted by" is commonly used, rather than "drawn by," and Murphy had never before failed to use the correct term.[104]

Similar problems exist with the other alleged violations. The first of the two intrusions claimed on January 18, supposedly at 3:25 A.M., was 33 nautical miles from the position claimed at 5:17 A.M., requiring a speed of 17.8 knots. The second, at 4:32 A.M., is 7.2 nautical miles from the spot listed at 5:17 A.M., requiring a speed of 49.5 knots to make the distance in the allotted time, almost 400 percent faster than the *Pueblo* could travel.[105] For the January 21 claim, putting the ship 8.2 miles from DPRK territory at 6:30 A.M., the ship would have had to travel 18 knots from its 6:00 A.M. position, and 25.7 knots to have reached its 7:05 A.M. location. Again, the logbook numbers appear altered, with the latitude entry for 6:30 A.M. likely having been changed from 40.9 degrees to 48.9 degrees.[106]

Other problems existed. Bucher had ordered a position check on the twenty-second, as required before sending SITREP-1, yet the result does not appear on the photographed chart, as it should have by navy regulations. Nor is the *Pueblo*'s position recorded on the morning of the attack, despite the fact that all accounts indicated that the ship's oceanographers were running hydrographic tests at the time, and thus that position would have been specifically recorded.[107] These omissions give further support to the notion that these charts were created by the North Koreans and thus fail to offer any substantive proof for their claims.

The North Koreans continued to fabricate violations throughout the crew's detention, although their skill in plotting them did not improve. In August, they claimed to have discovered another eleven violations, raising the total to seventeen. The perfidy of these allegations is well demonstrated by noting that two of them placed the ship in rather unlikely places: one located the *Pueblo* thirty-two miles inland in North Korea, and another placed her in downtown Wonsan. If such information was accurate, it seems surprising that the DPRK waited until the ship was back at sea to capture it, when local police officers could simply have intercepted it while stopped at a Wonsan traffic light.

Although there is no question that North Korea had fabricated these specific intrusions, there still exists the possibility that the ship had inadvertently violated DPRK territory on other occasions. The skill of the *Pueblo* navigation team was hardly reassuring. Bucher was well qualified but was usually too busy to get involved. Murphy inherited most of the work, but his experience as lead navigator consisted of eight months aboard the USS *Robinson* in 1965, before he spent the next three years on shore duty. His performance prior to the seizure raises some questions about his ability; plotting a course to Sasebo from about 100 miles south, he took the ship on a direct collision course with a large rock in the Pacific. Only Tim Harris's sharp eyes saved the *Pueblo* from serious keel damage.[108]

Making the task of avoiding Korean territory even more difficult was the order to maintain emission control silence, thereby forbidding the use of radar and depth readings unless absolutely necessary. Accordingly, the ship utilized the radar only five or six times during the entire trip, and even then it was not always accurate.[109] Besides the mechanical problems typical of the *Pueblo*'s equipment, the radar also had to overcome North Korea's low and jagged coastline, which often caused signals to bounce off mountain peaks rather than off the shore. Unable to rely on their radar, the navigators used the Raytheon CA 400 loran system for most position fixes. The loran had functioned poorly since installation, failing so frequently that Murphy described its malfunctions as "commonplace," and even the navy later acknowledged that it had a margin of error of up to five miles. On one occasion, Bucher used it to obtain a reading while off the coast of Songjin; after forty-five minutes, it finally placed them five miles from their true position, as determined by visual sightings and celestial navigation. Three days before the seizure, it functioned so poorly that it could not determine their distance from Mayang-do, and even the night before the seizure, it placed them within thirteen miles of Wonsan, despite visual signs locating them seven miles farther out.[110]

Although the navigators used other techniques, particularly celestial navigation and visual sightings, these were of limited use. Overcast conditions often prevented celestial navigation. There were few visual landmarks, since the region lacked typical markings such as lighthouses and coastal installations. In the end, even the navy showed some skepticism. "It was known," concluded the Board of Inquiry, "that because of the infrequent use of radar, LORAN errors, uncertain weather conditions, and the uncertainty of bottom contour information, PUEBLO's calculated position could have been in error by as much as 5 miles, particularly at night."[111]

Other evidence suggests that the *Pueblo* was not always where it claimed to be. It is common knowledge within the intelligence community that these missions, even with top-flight navigation, routinely stray closer to their subject than ordered. Even the navy's legal specialists thought that such an intrusion was a strong possibility in the *Pueblo* case. NSA COMINT (communications intelligence) stations watching North Korean coastal defense systems indicated that the *Pueblo* had violated DPRK waters four times in the three days prior to the seizure. After the seizure, LBJ appointed a special panel to investigate the matter, headed by Undersecretary of State George Ball and three prominent military figures. After studying the evidence, the committee unanimously approved a report expressing "serious doubts as to the exact position of the *Pueblo*." Although specific violations cannot be proved at this time, it appears likely that the ship may have strayed into DPRK waters, although not at the positions claimed by the North Koreans.[112]

Perhaps the most controversial aspect of the incident remains the performance of Captain Bucher himself. Over the years, the navy encouraged a picture of the seizure that placed the blame squarely on his shoulders. Bucher, according to this argument, failed to recognize the threat quickly enough and thus reacted too late to avoid capture. Having lost any chance at escape, he did not even put up a token resistance, instead meekly surrendering without testing the North Koreans' reaction to force. Had Bucher "headed out to sea at maximum speed," claimed Admiral U. S. Grant Sharp, "these patrol boats would never have gotten alongside." Instead, Sharp concluded, "This guy just gave up his ship."[113] One of the intelligence officers involved in planning Clickbeetle operations questioned Bucher's "preparedness for the adversity he encountered at sea," and Admiral Daniel Gallery called the capture "a shameful milestone in the decline and fall of the United States . . . [when] the USS *Pueblo*, without firing a shot, was boarded, captured, and surrendered to a rabble of gooks off the coast of Korea."[114] Bucher's most serious criticism came from the Naval Board of Inquiry, which faulted him on many grounds, including not recognizing the threat quickly enough, failing to develop and utilize the ship's defensive capabilities, and not scuttling or disabling the ship. "Prior to the *Pueblo* being boarded," the board concluded, "she still had the power to resist. . . . Her ability to maneuver and head toward the open sea had not been impaired. The commanding officer never knew what success he could have achieved through using any or all weapons available to him because he simple [*sic*] never tried to use them. He capitulated without firing a shot. . . . He decided to surrender his ship when it was completely operational without offering any resistance."[115]

The evidence, however, does not support this avalanche of blame. The reality of the situation justified Bucher's original decision to remain in the area despite the DPRK harassment. Prior to departure, the navy had made it clear that the ship might encounter opposition and made it just as clear that Bucher should not overreact. "We had been told in our briefings," wrote Operations Officer Schumacher, "to expect harassment. . . . We were supposed to stand fast in any seagoing game of chicken. . . . The sense of our orders were that we should stay put, brazen it out, find out as much as we could."[116] In fact, the ship's operations orders specifically demanded that in the case of any "hostile, harassing, or embarrassing tactics . . . no action shall be taken that would give the impression that the United States acknowledges the authority of any nation to control international waters." If withdrawal were deemed necessary, it was to be "slow and gradual, and at a significant variance with any course prescribed by the non friendly unit."[117] Thus, rather than being negligent in recognizing DPRK aggression, Bucher had actually followed his instructions to the letter, remaining in the area while the North Korean ships circled, and fleeing only when they tried to board. To have withdrawn earlier would actually have been a direct violation of his orders.

Even if he had fled earlier, there seems little reason to think that the seizure could have been avoided. Approximately twenty minutes passed between the approach of the first subchaser and the arrival of the rest of the DPRK ships.

At top speed, the *Pueblo* was almost half as fast as the subchaser, and not even a quarter of the speed of the torpedo boats. Since the North Koreans' intent, as demonstrated by subsequent events and their own ship-to-shore communications, was to capture her rather than just scare her away, and since they were not intimidated by the ship's position in international waters, the likelihood of escape was negligible. Bucher thus faced a no-win situation. Had he headed toward open seas more rapidly, he most likely still would have been caught, but he would have faced navy censure for violating orders to hold his ground. Instead, he followed instructions and tried to brazen his way out and was subjected to navy criticism anyway.

Further, charges that Bucher failed to recognize the danger of the situation quickly enough are undercut by the fact that navy leaders did the same thing. When PINNACLE 1 arrived, the navy interpreted the events just as Bucher had: an exercise in routine harassment. "If you recall the text of that first message," explained Admiral Horace Epes, "it really doesn't inform you that there is any serious crisis. The appearance is that he is being harassed and so forth."[118] Accordingly, the navy responded to the situation with little alacrity. PINNACLE 1 arrived at COMNAVFORJAPAN twenty-three minutes after being sent to Kamiseya, but it waited there for over forty minutes before being sent to the message center relay in Fuchu, Japan, for retransmission to other naval commands. CINCPAC received it seventy-eight minutes after the original transmission, and the Fifth Air Force, which was supposed to provide support in case of trouble, was not notified for over two hours.[119]

This slow reaction continued throughout the crisis. At approximately 1:18 P.M., the *Pueblo* sent her second PINNACLE message, indicating the North Korean boarding attempt. It arrived at COMNAVFORJAPAN seven minutes after transmission but was not sent to CINCPACFLT and the Fifth Air Force for over an hour, or to the Joint Chiefs of Staff for over ninety minutes. The *Pueblo*'s 1:45 P.M. message declaring, "We are now being escorted into prob Wonsan" did not reach CINCPAC until 3:03 and CINCPACFLT until 3:20.[120] Considering that COMNAVFORJAPAN had no support forces of its own and relied on these other commands for assistance, these delays in communication reflected a dangerous laxity.

Even if the navy had reacted more quickly, it is doubtful that it could have assisted the *Pueblo*. Since COMNAVFORJAPAN was so convinced of the mission's "minimal" risk, and since the rest of the command chain had concurred, there had been no strip alerts requested. "The evaluation of the risk by the Commander U.S. Naval Forces Japan," explained Admiral Sharp, "as well as by me and my own staff, did not justify, in my view, such an allocation of forces."[121] The lack of such preparations dramatically hindered the American response. The Fifth Air Force, for example, had four planes stationed at Osan, South Korea, less than thirty minutes' flying time from the *Pueblo*. However, they were configured to carry atomic weapons and could not be prepared for conventional weapons in time to reach the ship, especially because the bomb racks necessary for such a rescue were stored at bases in Japan.[122] Had a strip alert been requested, a number of planes could have launched immediately; two, in fact, would have been fully prepared with pilots waiting in the cockpits in case of emergency. The Eighteenth Tactical Fighter Wing at Kadena Air Force Base in Okinawa, Japan, launched twelve F-105 Thunderchief fighter-bombers in support of the ship, but their takeoff was delayed because the planes needed to be fueled and armed, and some actually had to be recalled from training missions. Had the base been on alert, the planes could have departed in less than forty minutes and would have reached the *Pueblo* in about an hour; instead, two launched one hour and twenty-three minutes after receiving their orders, and the rest followed slowly over the next hour. With darkness arriving and their fuel dwindling, the planes were unable to arrive in time and landed in South Korea to await further orders.

Similar problems occurred elsewhere. At Yokota Air Base, Japan, Captain Paul Hanson of the 347th Tactical Fighter Wing received a phone call shortly after the attack. On the other end of the line was Don Wiedman, the duty officer at Fifth Air Force headquarters in Yokosuka, relaying orders to prepare his planes for an attack on Wonsan. However, the American base was in the middle of transitioning from F-105s, which were being sent to Thailand, to the newer F-4Cs. Only two F-4Cs were capable of launch, and both were configured to carry nuclear weapons. Immediately, Hanson ordered the planes be readied for combat, only to discover that the arming cables that connected the bombs to the bomb racks had not yet arrived. It would be almost a week before six planes could be readied for an assault. "We could not react," Hanson explained in frustration. "They picked a very good time." At Misawa Air Base in Japan, less than an hour from Wonsan, the 356th Tactical Fighter Squadron had five F-4Cs ready to launch, but it too was transitioning from older models, and the new aircraft had not yet passed their operational readiness inspection (ORI), scheduled for sometime before January 31. By 3:30, the five Phantoms were ready to launch, but without an ORI, they were not officially considered combat ready. Had they been ordered to launch, they would likely have arrived within striking distance of Wonsan by approximately 4:00 P.M., well before the ship reached her final destination.

The response everywhere was similar. Aerial combat forces could have been available if they had been readied in advance, but under the circumstances of the attack and the lack of prior warning, they were virtually useless. The Marine Corps maintained four F-4s and four A-4s at Iwakuni, Japan, less than fifty minutes from the attack, but the unprepared planes would take almost three hours to launch.[123] Overall, the United States had six fully operational air bases in Japan, each within ninety minutes' flying time of the *Pueblo*, but none had any planes that could be readied for launch in less than three hours, largely because of agreements with the Japanese government that prohibited the United States from using Japanese territory for offensive missions. A number of South Korean fighters and interceptors were also available, and possibly within range of the ship. American military officials in the area, however, refused to allow them to launch, partly because of a lack of information surrounding the incident, and partly out of fear that their response would be excessive, leading to a second Korean War. The navy also had three destroyers in port in Japan, approximately twenty hours from the *Pueblo*, yet none had been assigned to patrol near the ship's mission route. The world's most powerful aircraft carrier, the USS *Enterprise*, was only 470 miles away at the time of the attack and could have had planes there within two hours.[124] Yet, since no one had alerted the *Enterprise*, its F-4B Phantoms needed at least ninety minutes for conversion. Even then, they would have been armed only with Sidewinders and Sparrows, guided missiles designed for air-to-air combat and of little use against surface targets. "Number one," recalled the *Enterprise*'s commander, "we didn't know that there was such a ship as *Pueblo*, number two, we didn't know the *Pueblo* was up in the Sea of Japan. . . . By the time we waited for clarification . . . it was too late to launch."[125]

Navy leaders tried to minimize their role in this failure. Testifying before the House Committee, Admiral Johnson admitted that he had not requested strip alerts but claimed to have ensured "on call" support in case of an emergency. When pressed for a definition of "on call," however, Johnson's response suggested that this designation was a facade. "When I say 'on call' forces," he explained, "I mean those forces which I would call for in an emergency and for which no prior arrangements had been made." "Then is it not true," queried Representative Durward Hall of Missouri, "that literally speaking, nothing was on call?" Johnson disagreed, citing the F-105s in Okinawa as his "on call" forces, and he doggedly stuck to his explanation during the examination:

HALL: But you also knew that if an interception or harassing attack occurred after midday, that they could not respond.

JOHNSON: I knew they would not be helpful.

HALL: Then they were not on call, were they?

JOHNSON: Yes sir, in my definition they were on call.[126]

In the end, however, even Johnson was forced to admit that "there were never any forces available that could reach the scene in time to prevent unlawful seizure."[127]

Similar criticism of Bucher's failure to resist was also unjustified. The ship's operations orders specifically warned against appearing hostile. The late addition of guns led Admiral Johnson to emphasize this point; Bucher was to keep his weapons covered and minimize the threat that he presented. Even the *Pueblo*'s sailing orders demanded that "defensive armaments should be stowed or covered in such a manner as to not elicit unusual interest."[128] Accordingly, Bucher did not go to battle stations when the North Koreans first approached. To have done so would have been a violation of his orders.

Even if he had chosen to fight, little would have been accomplished beyond killing more of his crew. The *Pueblo* was so badly outgunned that there was no chance for military success. Even Admiral Moorer admitted that the vessel "was not nor could she be considered a combatant ship." It was highly unlikely that Bucher could have fired his .50-caliber guns even if he had wanted to, since getting to the mounts would have exposed the gunners to DPRK machine gun fire. "If I sent people to those guns," he recalled, "they would be shot. I saw no point in senselessly sending people to their deaths." The ship also carried ten Thompson submachine guns, each with about two magazines of ammunition but with an effective range of less than 100 yards. Resistance was thus impossible; some of the *Pueblo*'s guns could not reach their targets, and the others could not be reached themselves. While the navy was bashing Bucher for not shooting back, the State Department was secretly disagreeing. "If the ship's light weapons and small arms were not used," concluded a memo for the Senate Foreign Relations Committee, "this would be very understandable." In private, even General Wheeler agreed. An attempt to fight back, he told a meeting of Democratic leaders, "would have been suicidal."[129]

Once it was clear that the *Pueblo* could not escape her pursuers, Bucher put a primacy on destroying classified materials. "To accomplish this," he concluded, "we had to stay alive."[130] With material destruction as the paramount goal, he acted simply to buy time. Disabling the engines would have hindered the North Koreans' ability to guide the ship into Wonsan, but it also would have given them an earlier reason to board her, as well as depriving Bucher of the chance to escape should American support arrive.[131] Putting up more of a fight only invited the enemy to disable his ship and then quickly board it or tow it to North Korea. Although the destruction went poorly overall, Bucher's actions in delaying the seizure of his vessel played a crucial role in what little success was achieved.

Bucher also believed that by delaying he had the best chance of being rescued. On November 14, he had been briefed on the mission by Captain Charles

Cassel, the assistant chief of staff for operations, COMNAVFORJAPAN, and was told that although he would be beyond the range of immediate assistance in case of attack, "you can count on everything being done as quickly as possible to come to your assistance."[132] On January 4, Bucher and Captain Clark of the *Banner* met with the staff at COMNAVFORJAPAN for final instructions. Bucher asked about support in case of emergency and was told that there would be no immediate assistance available. However, he was also informed that the Fifth Air Force would be kept apprised of the situation and could provide help in approximately two hours if necessary.[133] "Obviously," Bucher concluded, "they had plans for some form of help in case the unexpected happened. This was good enough for me."[134] Other signs hinted that an appropriate response had been prepared; his operations orders included emergency instructions regarding ship-to-ship communications if a surface unit were dispatched to help in case of a crisis, clearly suggesting that the navy had support plans ready.[135]

Convinced that help could arrive at any minute, Bucher continued to stall for time. Communications with Kamiseya encouraged this tactic, since a number of messages suggested that assistance was indeed on its way. "Last I got," radioed the naval facility at 2:07, "was Air Force going to help you with some aircraft . . . this unofficial but I think that what will happen." "We still with you and doing all we can," came a message at 2:12. "Everyone really turning to and figure by now Air Force got some birds winging your way." Two minutes later, Kamiseya told them, "Sure process already being initiated for some immediate relief," and at 2:19 promised, "We be right there."[136] Thus, Bucher's decision to stall, ensuring a better destruction result while hoping that help was on its way, reflects not cowardice or incompetence but a logical choice that was the best one available among the limited options he had left.

In the end, the specifics made little difference. After extensive hearings into the seizure, the navy's Board of Inquiry still singled out Bucher for censure. He had failed, it concluded, to "condition his mind or adequately prepare himself and his crew for such contingencies."[137] Yet, while Bucher was not above reproach for certain decisions, such criticism obscured the deeper roots of the incident. The largest contributing factor in the seizure of the USS *Pueblo* was not any individual performance but the failure of the entire chain of command to overcome the narrow assumptions that dominated its perception of the Cold War. The many deficiencies in preparing the mission—physical conversion, risk assessment, support preparation—all stemmed from an inability to accept the idea that the North Korean response might derive from purely indigenous circumstances. Had anyone considered the mission for what it was—a dangerous foray into hazardous waters during a tumultuous period—

perhaps the inherent risks would have been recognized and steps taken to address them. Instead, however, the American military and intelligence communities clung to their preconceptions of a monolithic and uniform communist bloc and ignored the more complex reality of international relations. The consequences of this failure would be borne by the eighty-three members of the USS *Pueblo*.

CHAPTER FIVE

The Key Question

We had men 83,
But Duane was set free,
When PUEBLO took her dealt lashes.
But more likely than not,
He'll not be forgot,
Till this country is buried in ashes.

"The key question," wrote the *New York Times* on January 28, was "why did they do it?"[1] Why would DPRK President Kim Il Sung risk national annihilation to capture a ship that posed no immediate threat? Most of the architects of the *Pueblo* operation answered by linking the attack to a larger Cold War conspiracy: North Korea acted on behalf of the Soviet Union; North Korea hoped to aid North Vietnam by diverting American attention and resources prior to the Tet Offensive; North Korea was part of a communist plot to expel the United States from Asia by opening, as Che Guevara demanded, "Two, three, many Vietnams."[2] CIA director Richard Helms summed up this attitude: "This appears to be an effort by North Korea to support the North Vietnamese in their efforts. . . . It looks at this time like collusion between the North Koreans and the Soviets. It also appears to be another attempt to divert us from our efforts in Vietnam."[3] General Maxwell Taylor advised President Johnson to view the seizure "within the pattern of events taking place in the Far East" and concluded, "I feel deeply that this PUEBLO incident is linked to South Vietnam."[4] LBJ accepted the counsel. "You look at *Pueblo,* Khe Sanh, Saigon," he told his cabinet, "and you see them as all part of the communist effort to defeat us out there."[5]

A common shortcoming, however, renders such explanations inadequate. They are all rooted in a "great power" worldview that evaluates international events only from within the larger framework of the Cold War. In this weltanschauung, all foreign crises were connected to the perceived global struggle between the "free" and "unfree" blocs. Accordingly, there seemed to be no need to consider the importance of indigenous circumstances in these situations, since it was assumed that there was always an external force directing the actions of communist nations. Yet a thorough examination of the circumstances surrounding the *Pueblo* Incident demonstrates the problems with applying this internationalist explanation to North Korean actions. Since the Soviet Union operated similar SIGINT missions in American waters, the Soviets' complicity would have established a precedent as potentially damaging to themselves as to the United States. At the same time that the *Pueblo* was seized, a number of Soviet intelligence ships were within easy capture of American or American-allied forces; in fact, the powerful USS *Enterprise* was at that very moment being closely shadowed by the Soviet AGI *Gidrolog* in the Sea of Japan.[6] The unspoken quid pro quo permitting the use of these ships had provided both sides with profitable intelligence without risking nuclear war. There was thus little reason for Moscow to violate it because of a ship that had never even approached the Soviet coast. Soviet complicity might also have threatened the superpower rapprochement that emerged toward the end of the Johnson years, marked by such events as the 1967 Glassboro Summit, the 1967 Consular Convention, the 1968 Civil Air Agreement, and especially the 1968 Treaty on the Nonproliferation of Nuclear Weapons. With all this at stake, it seems unlikely that the Soviets, especially considering their growing rivalry with China, would have risked a major international incident over such a relatively insignificant ship, a fact subsequently confirmed by Soviet intelligence officers. "This was simply not something we would do," explained former KGB Major General Oleg Kalugin.[7]

The relationship between the Soviet Union and North Korea also argues against such coordination. Since Kim Il Sung had never been easy to control, it seems unlikely that the USSR would have chosen his nation for such a delicate task. "North Korea," recalled one member of the Central Committee of the Soviet Communist Party in the 1960s, "was an independent country. . . . They would down a plane, capture a ship, join the nonaligned countries, and we would only learn of it from the newspapers."[8] "The North Koreans," echoed Kalugin, "they have their own agenda."[9] Furthermore, the relationship between the intelligence services of the two nations at this time was badly strained, resulting in an almost complete cessation of joint operations.[10] The Soviets, all signs suggest, were as stunned by the attack as was the United States.

Connections between the *Pueblo* Incident and the Vietnam War were more commonly suggested, especially after the North Vietnamese launched the Tet Offensive on January 31. Reflecting a view shared by many military figures, General Maxwell Taylor expressed "a strong suspicion . . . that it [the *Pueblo* seizure] was related to the Tet Offensive which occurred about the same time." National Security Adviser Walt Rostow described the operation as "the contribution of the North Koreans to the Tet Offensive, a diversion of resources . . .

[an attempt to] see if they could divert our attention." Again, however, these international attributions are problematic. The eight-day window between the capture of the ship and the launching of Tet was hardly enough time to affect America's ability to respond in Vietnam in any significant manner. Had Kim's objective truly been to spur the redeployment of troops and resources, he would likely have seized the ship earlier, especially since radar had located it seven days before the actual seizure, fifteen days before Tet. Eight days were simply unlikely to make a substantial impact.[11]

Other evidence suggests a lack of collaboration between the DPRK and North Vietnam. North Korean threats against American spy ships off their coast seem unlikely in this context, since Kim would have been foolish to alert the United States to the increased danger if he had already agreed to the seizure. Further, the *Pueblo* moved to twenty to twenty-five miles off the Korean coast at night. It seems likely that Kim, knowing that the ship might depart for other waters at any time, and undoubtedly aware that such operations were usually run near China or the USSR, would have interpreted this as a prelude to leaving Korean waters and would have moved to capture the ship immediately so as not to forsake his allies. Instead, he waited over a week before acting.

Such a connection also seems out of character for Vo Nguyen Giap, the skilled North Vietnamese military commander. Giap depended on the element of surprise in the Tet Offensive and had already diverted American attention by a successful feint at Khe Sahn, a small outpost located just south of the DMZ and east of the Laotian border. As Tet approached, Giap was confident that American arrogance would lead U.S. troops right into his trap. "The US Generals" he wrote, "are subjective and haughty, and have always been caught by surprise and defeated."[12] His trickery worked. Although American intelligence officials had some idea of the impending invasion, they largely considered it a decoy from the real battle at Khe Sahn. "Even had I known exactly what was to take place," recalled Major General Philip Paulson, intelligence adviser to General William Westmoreland, "it was so preposterous that I probably would have been unable to sell it to anybody."[13] The *Pueblo* seizure thus risked increasing the military's attention on Asia at the precise moment that Giap needed it to be unaware. It also risked sparking an increase of American forces in the area by providing the administration with an excuse to enlarge its commitment; in fact, following the seizure, President Johnson called up 15,000 reservists and increased the number of American B-52s reinforcing the bomber fleet in the Far East. Although ostensibly dedicated to the Korean crisis, the proximity of these forces to Vietnam allowed the B-52s to be used during the month-long Tet Offensive, a situation that the prescient Giap surely would have sought to avoid.[14]

Not only did the seizure threaten the American military's complacency, but it also chanced stabilizing Johnson's relationship with the American public by adding credence to his warnings of an Asian communist conspiracy. Aware of the importance of American public opinion in conducting a war, Giap had used tactics designed to drive a wedge between the people and the war effort. This strategy worked. As U.S. involvement increased, the relationship between the government and the populace declined. Giap recognized this division, writing in late 1967, "In the United States itself, the Johnson administration is faced with a conflict between the ruling clique and the growing protests of the American people. The widespread rebellion of the American Negro is a fierce aggressive blow at the Johnson clique's domestic and foreign policies. Never before has Johnson been at such an impasse as he is now. . . . The White House is suddenly like a building whose roof is about to fall in."[15] Giap was thus unlikely to risk strengthening Johnson's position by giving him more evidence to support his policies. The North Korean action might also have ignited "rally-round-the flag" sentiments, the tendency of the American people to unite behind their president when foreign crises suddenly emerge. With LBJ's approval rating below 40 percent in 1967, the Vietnamese general seems unlikely to have risked increasing it by taking actions that might stimulate a sudden burst of American patriotism.[16]

Finally, the *Pueblo* seizure risked strengthening the position of American "hawks" such as Senators Strom Thurmond (R-S.C.) and John Stennis (D-Miss.), Representative Mendell Rivers (D-S.C.), and Governor Ronald Reagan (R-Calif.), who had long demanded more forceful military actions in Vietnam. This faction, largely conservative Republicans and southern Democrats, viewed the war as a critical aspect of the global struggle against international communism and advocated such measures as expanding the war into Laos and Cambodia, removing the restrictions on attacks against Hanoi and Haiphong, and possibly even using the atomic bomb. Anti-American actions by another Asian communist nation risked strengthening these calls for increased involvement by demonstrating the futility of Johnson's more moderate course. Partly to placate these critics, LBJ had significantly expanded the list of military targets in 1967, even approving attacks on barracks inside formerly restricted areas along the Chinese border; in 1968, the possibility that the *Pueblo* seizure might steer him even closer to these views is something that Giap seems unlikely to have overlooked.

Considering the many possible negative consequences the *Pueblo* seizure presented for the Tet Offensive, and the fact that a diversion had already been accomplished, the perception of a larger communist conspiracy motivating Kim's actions seems inadequate. Such explanations fail to consider the incident from within a strictly North Korean context, clinging instead to a belief in international communist bogeymen who directed DPRK actions. This attribution is perhaps unsurprising, as it is easier to ascribe all adversity to one omnipresent factor than to recognize and evaluate the complexities of disparate international events. Blaming global communism thus allowed American policy makers to cling to a comfortable Cold War paradigm in which the world's problems could be laid at a single doorstep; what it did not permit was a realistic understanding of what happened off the North Korean coast on January 23, 1968.

The *Pueblo* seizure can best be understood by considering it in conjunction with the realities of DPRK life in the 1960s. Specifically, it requires knowledge of *juche,* the ideological construct that dominated the nation during and after the 1960s.[17] Literally translated as "self-identity" or "self-reliance," *juche* was (and still is) the almost ubiquitous principle directing DPRK life. On a basic level, it can be defined as a state of mind in which actors, both individually and collectively, advance their interests without external influence. In the words of its formulator, Kim Il Sung, *juche* consists of "having an attitude of a master toward the revolution and construction of one's own country."[18] Rooted in the idea that man must determine his fate, and that of his nation, based solely on his indigenous experiences, *juche* demanded that North Koreans embrace a purely Korean way of life. As Kim explained:

> We are making the Korean revolution. As far as the Korean revolution is concerned, Koreans know about it better than anyone else. The masters of the Korean revolution are the Korean people and our own strength is the decisive factor in its victory. . . . In order to ensure that the Korean revolution is a success, its masters, the Korean people themselves, must use their brains, solve all problems that arise through their own efforts and settle them in conformity with the interests of the Korean revolution.[19]

Although remaining true to Marxist-Leninist precepts by perceiving working-class man as history's determining force, *juche* rejected the traditional Leninist emphasis on the primacy of the vanguard party in the revolutionary struggle, as well as Marx's stress on the leadership of the working class itself. Instead, it advanced the idea of the *suryong,* an individual leader without whose guidance the masses would be unable to act collectively, develop revolutionary consciousness, or discern the correct path toward their socialist destiny.

Kim first promulgated *juche* in a speech to party propaganda and agitation workers in 1955. Laying the foundations for his emphasis on Korean exceptionalism, he suggested that the ideological underpinnings of other socialist nations would not be dominant principles in North Korea, which would instead follow its own path toward socialism based on native experiences and values.

> What is juche in our Party's ideological work? What are we doing? We are not engaged in any other country's revolution, but solely in the Korean revolution. Devotion to the Korean revolution is juche in the ideological work of our party. Therefore, all ideological work must be subordinated to the interest of the Korean revolution. When we study the history of the Communist party of the Soviet Union, the history of the Chinese revolution, or the universal truth of Marxism-Leninism, it is entirely for the purpose of correctly carrying our own revolution.[20]

Increased permissiveness from Moscow following Joseph Stalin's death in 1953 undoubtedly aided Kim's quest to stress Korean exceptionalism over the Soviet model of development. At the Twentieth Congress of the Soviet Communist Party in February 1956, Soviet Premier Nikita Khrushchev even condemned Stalin's brutalities against party members and acknowledged the existence of "different roads to socialism." Moscow enunciated this early glasnost even more clearly in a 1960 statement declaring that "Marxism-Leninism demands creative application of the general principles of socialist revolution and socialist construction depending on the specific historical conditions in the country concerned, and does not permit of a mechanical copying of the policies and tactics of the Communist parties of other countries."[21]

Kim capitalized on this benevolence by steadily pushing *juche* to the forefront of Korean society, even at the expense of Marxism-Leninism. In February 1960, Kim declared at a local party meeting, "juche means doing everything in accordance with the actual conditions of our country and creatively applying the general principles of Marxism-Leninism and the experience of other countries to suit our realities."[22] Two years later, the Fifth Plenary Session of the Fourth Korean Workers Party (KWP) Central Committee hailed Kim for having "creatively applied Marxism-Leninism into the unique and specific conditions of North Korea."[23]

By the mid-1960s, *juche* had become the dominant precept of North Korean ideology. In 1964, Kim demanded that Korean encyclopedias conform to "the principle of juche and give information mainly on our country to meet the requirements of our revolution."[24] On August 12, 1966, *Nodong Sinmun,* the official party paper, demanded the end of "big-nation chauvinism" and advocated *juche* as the leading guide in all aspects of DPRK life.[25] Less than one month before the *Pueblo* seizure, Kim clearly proclaimed *juche*'s dominant role before the Fourth Supreme Peoples Assembly of the DPRK:

The government of the republic will thoroughly implement the line of independence, self-sustenance, and self-defense to consolidate the political independence of the country, further strengthen the foundations of an independent national economy . . . and increase the defense capabilities of the country . . . by excellently materializing our Party's idea of juche in all fields. Our Party's idea of juche represents the most correct Marxist-Leninist idea of leadership for the successful accomplishment of our revolution and construction and is the invariable guiding principle of the government of the republic in all its policies and activities.[26]

Official pronouncements, of course, do not necessarily reflect national ideology, since their ideas may not be shared by those outside the policy-making clique. In fact, the ability of elites to force a selected value system on the whole of society is extremely limited. Even in the antebellum American South, plantation owners were unable to impose their chosen philosophy on society without some concessions; instead, a relationship of mutual interaction limited the planters' hegemony and afforded certain advantages to both sides. Such is the reality of interaction and mutual dependence in a complex world. Elites, whether American slaveholders, Prussian Junkers, or Russian lords, have traditionally found their ability to exert complete ideological dominance limited by the reciprocal nature of the master-servant relationship. However, in terms of elite hegemony, North Korea is the proverbial exception that proves the rule. Here, in the most fundamentally closed and repressive nation of the twentieth century, Kim was able to spread his ideological construct throughout society far more successfully than could elites elsewhere. This construct utilized *juche* as the glue holding the nation together; without it to justify the *suryong* and unite the masses behind him, North Korean life would likely have followed a very different path.

Kim's unparalleled success in forcing these tenets on society derived from a number of sources, foremost of which was the personality cult developed during his early years in power. Although communist dictators have often created such cults, Kim's was unequaled. He appeared at the center of Korean society to an unrivaled extent, his face visible in every school, home, public office, factory, street, bus, train, and subway station, as well as on the pin that all North Korean citizens were required to wear on their left breasts. Children called him "our father," brides and grooms swore allegiance to him at their weddings, and a daily loyalty oath was demanded of all citizens. Every room he visited for inspection received a red plaque engraved with the date of his presence, and objects he touched at official functions, even ashtrays and pencils, were covered with white veils to mark their distinctiveness. His birthplace at Mankyongdae remains a national shrine, called "the cradle of world revolution," and his birthday is the nation's foremost holiday. Decades of spreading this image of Kim the omniscient, omnificent, and omnipresent elevated him to the status of demigod, a role that he played with the utmost precision and that provided his teachings with an aura of infallibility.[27]

This personality cult could not ensure *juche*'s dominance, however, if even the slightest remnant of a competing vision existed. Slaves in the American South might accept their master's pronouncements to his face, but they could discern challenges to his authority in the example of escaped slaves and free blacks or could take mental, if not physical, solace in the existence of the North. Slaves also preserved some of their African heritage by sustaining their cultural traditions in areas such as religion, cooking, and song. No such alternative reality existed in North Korea, where Kim's complete dominion ensured the promulgation of only his ideas. The DPRK controlled all media, even to the extent of altering radio dials to receive only government broadcasts. The KWP disseminated foreign news based on a "need-to-know" basis, and rarely did anyone not closely affiliated with Kim "need to know." Emigration and immigration were sparse, and foreign visitors, even those from China and the Soviet Union, were rarely allowed to converse freely with the common people. Almost every village received libraries, propaganda rooms, and broadcasting networks, all devoted to spreading Kim's ideas. Bookstores not only excluded the bourgeois works of Western authors but often even omitted Marx and Lenin because of their occasional disagreement with the *suryong*, whose writings were always present. All citizens, even those abroad, were expected to devote at least two hours per day, and four hours on Saturday, to the study of Kim's political thought. Pronouncements on *juche* or Kim himself dominated virtually all sources of information; a 745-page political dictionary published in 1970 included 2,604 references to Kim Il Sung (over three per entry), and elementary school textbooks published the same year devoted 65 percent of their space to Kim.[28]

Kim's hegemony was further enhanced by the fact that the *juche* ideology reflected indigenous Korean values. As is common in new states, the Korean population was awash in nationalism following its 1948 "independence," determined, as anthropologist Clifford Geertz wrote of such emerging nations, "to become a people, rather than a population."[29] Korean nationalism was especially pronounced, deriving from centuries of opposition to expansionist neighbors, a shared ancestral origin, and a native culture and language. This spirit deepened in the late nineteenth and early twentieth centuries, when an educated elite of antimonarchists collaborated with foreign powers against the Yi dynasty, in the hope of advancing their own power. Most North Koreans regarded this sycophancy, labeled *sadaejuui,* with utter contempt, seeing it as the symbol of decades of repression and betrayal. Thus, by the time the independent state of North Korea emerged in 1948, there already existed powerful feelings of exceptionalism and a desire for self-rule that needed to be placated.

Accordingly, Kim portrayed his philosophy as ensuring the advance of such sentiments. "Independence," he insisted, "is what keeps man alive."[30] At every opportunity, he denigrated foreign influences and competing ideas as not being "Korean" enough. Everything from language to books to songs to art to education stressed the importance of Korean society to the exclusion of all else. "Our music," announced Kim in 1964, "must be Korean in essence . . . our people do not like the pure European music which is alien to their sentiments."[31] The result was a demonization of foreign elements and a continuing sense of Korean exceptionalism that unified the nation by appealing to the desire for indigenous leadership and examples of self-reliance, while at the same time offering Kim a means of discrediting his opposition as non-Korean.

These factors combined to give Kim's teachings an unparalleled position in North Korean life. His speeches were commonly referred to as "immortal classical works of creation," or simply "the teachings," and were accepted, as one historian concluded, "as cardinal truth."[32] Fragments of his past utterances filled most public essays and speeches. Even more tellingly, personal conversations among North Korean citizens bore the same trait. Most songs, dances, films, books, and operas were based on Kim and his teachings, and the word *juche* regularly appeared in common DPRK colloquialisms. *Juche* was so firmly ingrained in North Korean life that its influence dominated well into the century; in 1982, the DPRK built the *juche* tower, a 170-meter monument honoring *juche* and its ideas, complete with 25,550 blocks of white granite, one for each day of Kim's life from birth to his seventieth birthday.

Juche's position as the key to DPRK society did not deny North Koreans the faculty of independent thought; on the contrary, it relied on it by using the connection between such thought and the need for a model from which it derives. The process of "thinking" requires the act of evaluating the unfamiliar in terms of the familiar. "Every conscious perception," explains Geertz, "is . . . an act of recognition, a pairing in which an object (or an event, an act, an emotion) is identified by placing it against the background of an appropriate symbol."[33] Because Kim was so successful in advancing *juche* thought throughout the nation, it ascended to the constant role of the "familiar" through which society evaluated all "unfamiliars." *Juche* thus created a unifying lens, one that united the North Korean people at the same time that it enslaved them, and through which they judged everything that touched their lives.

Although originating as a general call for self-reliance, *juche* was soon defined more specifically. Kim consistently articulated three realms in which its application was vital, demanding "independence in politics, self-reliance in the economy, and self-defense in national defense."[34] In each of these realms, *juche* demanded an assertion of North Korean exceptionalism and a rejection of all external forces. Only through such behavior could the DPRK advance its socialist revolution toward the promised utopia.

In the political realm, *juche* demanded *chaju* (independence), the freedom of North Korea to govern itself without outside influence. This ability to act independently, Kim claimed, was "the prime criterion of any sovereign state."[35] A government that acted under pressure from another power, he warned, "cannot be called a genuine peoples government responsible for the destiny of the people."[36] *Chaju* not only united the population by appealing to nationalist sentiments; it also gave Kim a weapon against his rivals, since opposition could be dismissed as the tool of foreign powers. Kim utilized this strategy in the early 1950s, successfully discrediting the KWP's pro-Soviet and pro-Chinese factions as great power "flunkies," and thus threats to the cherished *chaju* of the Korean people.

Economically, *juche* called for *charip* (self-sustenance), which required a largely self-contained economy based on domestic workers using domestic resources to satisfy domestic needs. The labor of North Korean workers, Kim claimed, could "produce all the material riches of society, and bring about social renovation and progress."[37] Although not forbidding all imports and assistance, *charip* did demand that the nation develop the ability to survive on its own when necessary, eradicating the threat of economic dependence and thus subordination. Hence, by developing indigenous resources geared primarily toward heavy industry, this domestically organized economy would provide the "material basis of political independence," ensuring the perpetuation of North Korean independence under the rule of Kim Il Sung.[38]

In defense matters, *juche* advocated *chawi* (self-defense), a foreign policy based on complete equality and mutual respect among nations, as well as the right of self-determination and independent policy making. The DPRK, Kim insisted, "formulates its foreign policy on the basis of the juche idea and is guided by this idea in carrying out its external activities. In a word, our republic firmly maintains its independence in its foreign activities."[39] Accordingly, North Korea would refuse to depend on others, even communist allies, for protection, instead relying on its own strength to protect its interests, especially against the bourgeois powers that would inevitably threaten North Korea's socialist advancement.

By justifying the position of the *suryong* and uniting the people behind him,

Kim was successful in using *juche* to advance his interests. Yet there were risks in so thoroughly embedding this belief into the fabric of national self-identity. By closely associating the government's legitimacy with its successful pursuit of *juche*, Kim had created a Janus-faced monster. When *juche* was triumphantly achieved, his rule would be perpetuated and even embraced, but if the pursuit was unsuccessful, the most fundamental justification for his rule would appear violated. Aware of this danger, Kim constantly emphasized the ways his leadership had advanced the nation along *juche* lines. His speeches at party functions, for example, regularly attributed national accomplishments to independent Korean actions and ideas.[40] Occasionally, he took autonomous actions that risked the wrath of the communist superpowers but demonstrated his independence; one scholar has calculated that of twenty-seven key international events between 1956 and 1990, North Korea openly supported the Soviet position on only ten and the Chinese on just six.[41] Kim's refusal to support his allies more consistently may have raised tempers in Moscow and Peking, but by demonstrating his commitment to *juche*, it was a necessary component of preserving his rule.

In the 1950s and early 1960s, Kim was able to claim a number of successes in all three *juche* realms, especially economics, thus reducing any threat of ideological reevaluation. The Five-Year Plan established in 1957 actually achieved its targets in four years, despite Soviet professions that the goals were "fantasy."[42] The average annual growth rate in industrial output during these four years was 36.6 percent, and income rose at an annual rate of 21 percent. In 1962, North Korea had a trade surplus of $95.5 million (U.S.), while military spending remained low, accounting for only 2.2 percent of all government expenditures. The benefits of this economic growth were apparent: in 1945, North Korea had over 2.3 million illiterates, and not a single college or scientific research institution; by 1960, one-quarter of the population was enrolled in the over 8,500 schools in North Korea, and by 1961, over 100,000 students attended its seventy-eight colleges and universities.[43]

Kim also demonstrated *juche* in politics and foreign affairs. In 1961, he refused Soviet demands to denounce the Albanian Communist Party at the Twenty-second Congress of the Communist Party of the Soviet Union. He also criticized the Soviets for compromising in the 1962 Cuban Missile Crisis and concluded treaties on commerce and navigation with both China and the Soviet Union, despite the growing tension between the two. Politically, Kim's rule was virtually unchallenged, especially with the employment of almost a quarter of a million government operatives to oversee the direct implementation of his program among the masses. Almost all of these "administrative cadres," as one historian called them, were selected because of their class background and government loyalty, rather than their education or training, and thus could be trusted to advance the government line.[44] Foreign pressures were also minimal, especially as China and the Soviet Union competed for the loyalty of smaller nations.

Accordingly, North Korea entered the early 1960s with *juche* appearing undeniable and unstoppable. In 1961, Kim informed the Fourth Party Conference that "the historic revolutionary tasks of completing socialist transformation in town and country, and building the foundation of socialism have been triumphantly carried out."[45] Then, introducing his Seven-Year Economic Plan, he predicted that by the middle of the decade his people would have "a rich life, living in tile-roofed houses, eating rice and much meat, and wearing fine clothes . . . all aspects of our people's life will become bountiful, modern, and more enjoyable."[46] Over the next seven years, the plan predicted an increase in national income of 270 percent, a rise in real income of 170 percent, an increase in factory and office workers of 150 percent, and an annual industrial production growth rate of 18 percent.[47] Taxes would be abolished, since sufficient income would be derived from state-controlled enterprises, and spending would be dramatically increased on schools, hospitals, housing construction, and social welfare programs.[48] North Korea seemed on the brink of utopia, one that would be achieved by the continuous application of *juche* in all three of its crucial areas. However, by the middle of the decade, unexpected difficulties forced Kim to adapt his tactics to meet emerging circumstances.

In the 1950s, signs of Kim's successful quest for *juche* had been most apparent in economics; in the 1960s, signs of trouble were most pronounced in the same realm. Not only did economic conditions fail to meet Kim's predictions, but in many areas they steadily declined. Evidence of stagnation was ubiquitous; in 1966, the Seven-Year Plan was extended to ten years to meet its targets, and still objectives went unrealized in important industrial areas such as steel, cement, chemical fertilizers, and machinery.[49] The 36.6 percent annual growth rate in industrial output achieved during the preceding Five-Year Plan fell to 12.8 percent during the Seven-Year Plan, and in both 1966 and 1969, industrial production actually declined from the previous year. Agricultural production rates also slowed, increasing at an estimated annual average of 3.5 percent between 1961 and 1967. Conditions were so bad that after 1966 the government even discontinued its practice of publishing comprehensive economic statistics, a clear indication of Kim's desire to hide the severity of these problems from his own people.[50]

Signs of the declining economy were plentiful, especially since the government set wages and prices. Low salaries in all but the most dangerous professions left most families suffering, while the cost of consumer goods remained inordinately high. The average monthly stipend for unskilled workers in 1967 was between 35 and 42 won, while skilled laborers and engineers earned 40 to 45 won and 70 to 85 won, respectively. Anyone trying to survive on such wages could recognize that despite Kim's promises of *charip,* a functional domestic economy had not been achieved; one kilogram (2.2 pounds) of chicken, for example, cost 5 won, approximately three days' work for unskilled laborers. A dozen eggs were 3 won, cotton underwear was almost 20 won, and radios exceeded 150 won. Less essential goods were even more exorbitant. An unskilled worker forsaking food, clothing, and any other form of spending might save enough money in eighteen months to purchase an accordion. Even for those with the ability to pay, many items were simply unavailable; beef, for example, was virtually unobtainable, and pork could be purchased only a few times each year, usually on holidays. Food was not the only scarce commodity, as housing shortages also dotted the North Korean landscape. Despite Kim's promise of 1 million new family units by 1970, home construction was halted in 1966, leaving such a dearth of shelter that most small families were considered lucky to get two rooms.[51]

A heavy reliance on imports further demonstrated the failure to achieve *charip.* A trade deficit of almost $25 million in 1965 replaced the 1962 trade surplus, and after a brief rally, it swelled to $50 million by 1968 and $110 million by 1969.[52] Soviet imports were extensive in the production of such crucial industrial items as steel, iron ore, and oil products.[53] Even the *Pueblo* crewmen, largely isolated from society, noticed, among other things, Mercedes and Plymouth automobiles, Toyota trucks, Zeiss movie projectors, Nikon cameras, Sony tape recorders, RCA televisions, Czechoslovakian buses, and Japanese watches; even some of their confessions were written with Bic pens.[54]

Kim's willingness to admit these shortcomings in public settings demonstrated the extent to which they were recognized by the DPRK population. There can be little doubt that the man who denied China's role in the Korean War would have denied this economic reality if he had the power to do so; the fact that he did not illustrates the extent to which this crisis was a public concern. Kim commented on the economic decline as early as 1963, in a New Year's address that acknowledged economic problems in the crucial areas of coal and steel and ordered the mobilization of 1 million women into the labor force.[55] The following year, he admitted that production was "not abundant as to meet all the requirements of the people," and in 1966, he told the Second Korean Workers Party Conference, "We must . . . radically improve the material and cultural life of the people."[56] At the Supreme People's Assembly in May 1967, Kim demanded that the party "wage a resolute struggle to expand the varieties of goods and improve their lives," and even in 1970, when announcing the completion of the goals established in the Seven-Year Plan, he admitted that the last nine years had been "a period of harsh trial, in which very complex and difficult circumstances were created."[57]

A number of factors produced the North Korean economic decline, including an increased defense burden, the high percentage of males in military service, poor infrastructure systems, the low rate of return on industrial investment, a decline in foreign aid, and the relatively uneducated workforce. Planning errors by the Party Central Committee also contributed, such as the decision in the early 1960s to divert huge sums of money and manpower to relocate important military and industrial centers underground in case of war, and the decision to emphasize the development of heavy industry over light industry and agriculture. It is also worth noting that North Korean production was not wholly unimpressive; its 1970 production in coal (1,975 kilograms), electricity (1,184 kilowatt hours), and steel (158 kilograms) was all solid, if unspectacular.[58]

In reality, some of the failures to achieve production goals stemmed not from planning or implementation problems but from the selection of overambitious targets in 1961. Still, the economic situation failed on its most important level—as a sign of the government's ability to maintain *juche* in economic relations. The inability to reach widely publicized objectives, the public admissions of shortcomings, the inadequacy of shelter and sustenance, and the obvious cancellation of many major industrial and social projects fostered problems that transcended simple economic need. Since North Korean society evaluated everything from within a construct that demanded economic stability and independence *(charip)*, the failure to achieve these results was a violation of the most sacred precepts of North Korean life. By demonstrating a dearth of *juche* in the economic realm, these conditions called into question Kim's ability to guide the nation down that sacred *juche* path, and by Kim's own admission, a government without that ability could not be considered a true government of the people. Kim's rule was thus in danger of losing its raison d'être.

Perhaps the poor performance in *charip* would have been less threatening had Kim's pursuit of *juche* in its other two realms been more successful, but circumstances beyond his control dictated otherwise. At the same time that the outlook for economic self-sufficiency worsened, prospects for independence in the political realm *(chaju)* came under assault as well. DPRK relations with both communist superpowers had been generally stable throughout the 1950s, leaving Kim's ability to make policy largely unchallenged. North Korea's commitment to remain within the communist orbit, its willingness to refrain from another attack on South Korea, and the loosening of Soviet controls following

Stalin's death enabled Kim to express differences with the leadership while still maintaining good standing. In 1957, for example, he rejected without significant retaliation a Soviet request to concentrate on developing light industry and instead focused the Five-Year Plan on heavy industry and defense.

As the decade closed, however, strains emerged in DPRK-Soviet relations. Nikita Khrushchev's policy of peaceful coexistence with the United States upset Kim by limiting his ability to demand the removal of American troops from the South. Kim refused to join the Soviet-sponsored Council for Mutual Economic Assistance (COMECON), seeing in it the roots of a collective economic system that offered the great powers a means of controlling the Korean economy; instead, he accepted only observer status in 1957 and withdrew completely in 1964. The emerging Sino-Soviet split further exacerbated tensions, especially since Kim's early sentiments favored China, which was in a stage of economic and political development comparable to that of the DPRK. China, like North Korea, had accepted the revisionist thrust of recent Soviet pronouncements with little enthusiasm, and Chinese endorsement of a DPRK policy of heavy industrial development also helped win Kim's allegiance.[59] Soviet actions in the early 1960s further strained this alliance, as Kim perceived "revisionism" in such policies as Albania's expulsion from COMECON in 1962, the Cuban Missile Crisis compromise, and Moscow's pro-Indian position in the 1962 Sino-Indian conflict.[60]

This course provided North Korea with certain benefits, especially in the economic arena. China dramatically increased DPRK aid in 1960, loaning $105 million (U.S.), with promises of more to follow. However, it also provoked Soviet hostility. Khrushchev abruptly canceled a North Korean visit in 1960, and foreign leaders at the 1962 Congress of Eastern European Communist Parties treated the KWP representatives with great contempt. In January 1963, *Nodong Sinmun* publicly defended the Chinese Communist Party against its Soviet rivals for the first time, and by September, it was openly accusing the Soviet Union of both "big power chauvinism" and the economic exploitation of North Korea. In 1963, the Soviets retaliated by suspending aid to North Korea. Kim had thus acted with true *juche* principles, pursuing an independent policy line even at the risk of alienating a great power.[61] Quickly, however, it became clear that serious ramifications would follow such a vigorous expression of *chaju*.

The loss of Soviet aid was economically devastating. Major components of the Seven-Year Plan had to be canceled, including expanding the Kimchaek iron and steel facilities, building a thermopower plant in Pukchang, and constructing a new oil refinery; without these steps, Kim's dream of advancing North Korea militarily and industrially was virtually impossible. The Soviets also cut the DPRK off from their latest military equipment and technology, an especially damaging loss following Kim's 1964 decision to increase assaults on the South. Even already obtained Soviet MiGs were grounded due to shortages of jet fuel and spare parts. Accordingly, Kim reversed himself and sought to mend fences with the Soviets, a task aided by Khrushchev's 1964 fall from power and the American escalation of the Vietnam War in 1965. Rapprochement officially began in early 1965, when Soviet Premier Aleksei Kosygin visited North Korea. In May 1965, Kim sent his chief of staff, Choe Kwang, to Moscow to develop an aid agreement, and the Soviets began restoring funds the following year. Over the next two years, Moscow also supplied Kim with more advanced weapons, including T-54 and T-55 tanks, Komar missile ships, and MiG-21 jet fighters. Although this reconciliation provided important military and economic assistance, it clearly demonstrated that political *juche* could not be pursued at the expense of Soviet aid.[62]

Forced to moderate his stance toward the Soviets, Kim pursued *chaju* in other directions. He now adopted an independent policy line at the expense of China, especially after its curtailment of economic aid in the midst of the chaotic Great Proletarian Cultural Revolution. With relations deteriorating, Kim again seized the opportunity to demonstrate his independence by chastising a great power for its "revisionism," specifically criticizing China's refusal to participate in united action in Vietnam and its interference in the internal affairs of the North Korean and Japanese Communist Parties.[63] Rather than try to settle the dispute at a political level, Kim turned it into a public test of *juche*, repeatedly blasting China for challenging North Korea's independent policy making. A *Nodong Sinmun* editorial in August 1966, for example, denounced those "big-power oriented flunkies who . . . vigorously opposed our party's independent policy" and who demanded that Kim "emulate mechanically the policy position of a certain fraternal party, and likewise conduct our foreign and domestic affairs."[64] Later that year, Kim's Report to the Conference of the KWP pledged not to yield this Korean right, instead promising to continue "criticizing their [China's] negative aspects and helping them to rectify them."[65]

Tensions grew as the Chinese claimed 100 square miles of sacred Korean territory along the Korean-Chinese border near Mount Paektu as a price for their aid in the Korean War. In 1967, China stationed several army divisions just north of the Yalu River, igniting border clashes between the two sides in 1967 and 1968. In meetings and messages, leaders refused to address each other by party titles, and a Chinese publication called Kim "an out and out counter revolutionary revisionist, as well as a millionaire, an aristocrat, and a leading member of the bourgeoisie."[66] Near the Yalu River, Chinese guards with loudspeakers lambasted Kim as a Soviet puppet, and the situation grew so hostile toward the end of the decade that Kim even tried to build a wall along the border.[67]

Once again, Kim's ability to antagonize a superpower proved limited. China's strength, even during such turbulent times, still dwarfed the DPRK's. North Korea's internal economic problems made the lost interaction especially painful, particularly as the Cultural Revolution wound down toward the end of the decade. The situation began to improve in 1969, when Kim sent a North Korean delegation to the twentieth anniversary celebration of the founding of the People's Republic of China, and the PRC placed it at the head of a parade for foreign representatives. Premier Chou En-lai visited North Korea in April 1970, and later that year he dispatched a Chinese trade delegation to Pyong-yang.[68] Once again, Kim had been forced to make a difficult choice. The pursuit of *chaju* in DPRK-Chinese relations allowed for strong expressions of *juche,* but it also risked war and lost economic assistance. Just as had happened in the economic realm, Kim's need to apply *juche* in policy making ran headlong into the contradictory realities of modern life, and once again, *juche* was sacrificed to avoid dire consequences. Though Kim had demanded equality in his international relations, his pursuit of *chaju* had instead proved the truth of the old Korean proverb: "A shrimp is crushed in the battle of the whales."

Kim faced not only external threats to his policy-making authority but domestic ones as well. Following some party disputes in the late 1950s, the KWP remained largely united until a split emerged in the mid-1960s. The conflict revolved around an emerging group of moderates who demanded greater spending on light and consumer industry and more balanced industrial development. Some members of this faction also supported the idea of economic incentives, and others advocated ending the extensive application of resources toward fomenting rebellion in South Korea. The more hard-line wing, represented mostly by military leaders, supported greater emphasis on military and defense spending and a focus on heavy industrial growth at the expense of consumer products.[69]

The split emerged most clearly following the Conference of Party Representatives in October 1966, in which the party leadership sided with the militant faction and endorsed a policy of expanded defense fortifications. Following the fifteenth plenum of the KWP's Central Committee in March 1967, Kim purged many of the moderate wing's leaders, including such prominent figures and longtime allies as Pak Kum-ch'ol, vice chairman of the Party Central Committee, and Yi Hyo-sun, whose position as director of Southern strategy for the KWP's Central Committee placed him fifth within the party hierarchy.[70] The strength of the moderate program, however, was demonstrated by the fact that even after the purge, Kim felt it necessary to address these ideas publicly. In a speech in March 1969, he criticized the moderates for their "opportunist theory" and argued that higher domestic productivity would arise from "the people's high revolutionary zeal" rather than from "individual selfishness."[71] More important than the specifics was the fact that he gave an answer at all, suggesting that he considered this challenge to his authority serious enough to warrant a public rebuttal.

Although Kim purged the moderates, he returned to their side by the end of the decade. In 1969, he replaced the leaders of the more militant faction, including the vice premier of the Defense Ministry, Kim Ch'ang-Bong, and Ho Bong-Hak, director of the party's Liaison Bureau, filling both positions with moderates. He also dismissed several top military officers, including Army Chief of Staff Choe Kwang. These three figures, Kim, Ho, and Choe, held positions that ranked them sixth, fourteenth, and sixteenth in the party hierarchy. Overall, these two purges had dramatic ramifications. Of the eighteen members of the party's Political Committee holding office in 1964 (twelve full members, six alternate members), only five were reappointed at the Fifth Party Congress in 1970. Three of those purged simply moved to lesser party positions, but nine others vanished from the party completely.[72] In the end, almost two-thirds of key local government and party posts were left vacant by 1968; this, combined with the various conflicts with China and the Soviet Union, offered clear evidence that Kim's ability to exert unchallenged political authority was under assault.[73] By the mid-1960s, *chaju*, like *charip*, was no longer the easy avenue for *juche* expression it had been earlier. These changing circumstances would have dramatic ramifications in *chawi*, the field of international relations.

From the mid-1950s to the early 1960s, Kim had successfully achieved evidence of *juche* in all three realms. He was thus able to exert some moderation in each, since there was no reason for a more reckless approach in any specific area, as long as signs of success could be demonstrated in all three. Hence, Kim was content during this period to follow a largely restrained course in *chawi*. Although he still took opportunities to demonstrate his independence, he appears to have recognized that taking significant risks to achieve significant gains was not necessary. Relations with South Korea reflected his relative tranquillity; between 1960 and 1961, for example, he offered a series of proposals for "peaceful unification," including cultural and economic exchanges, resumption of postal services, and even a North-South confederation.[74] By the mid-1960s, however, emerging obstacles limited his pursuit of *charip* and *chaju*. Without other means of obtaining clear signs of *juche*, Kim was forced to adopt a more aggressive pursuit in *chawi*, the only avenue still available.

Kim's relations with South Korea most clearly demonstrated this renewed belligerence in international affairs. In 1964, he created an underground revolutionary party in the South (the Revolutionary Party for Unification) that aided various front organizations in subverting Park Chung Hee's administration. In 1966, he increased direct action, sending guerrillas into the South for the first time since the Korean War. As late as 1965, Southern territory had seen only 17 significant military incidents between the two rivals, 6 of which involved the exchange of fire; in 1967, there were 121 incidents, with 96 exchanges of fire. That year also saw two ship-to-shore firefights along the Southern coast, a North Korean attack on an ROK army barracks, and continued large-scale guerrilla infiltration. In 1968, DPRK commandos even seized control of a small village near Ulchin, South Korea, before being driven out by ROK police and military forces.[75]

This more aggressive foreign policy affected nations beyond the Korean peninsula. In 1966, Kim increased DPRK involvement in the Vietnam War, sending approximately fifty pilots, increased material support, and almost 300 advisers. That same year, he provided economic aid to the Forces for National Liberation in Venezuela, which were fighting to overthrow the Venezuelan government. Military spending exploded, jumping from 12.5 percent of total government expenditures in 1966 to 32.4 percent by 1968. Kim also sought a more assertive role in the Third World, frequently appealing to smaller communist nations to support the North Vietnamese, and encouraging them to exert more independence in international affairs. He also redoubled efforts to establish diplomatic ties abroad; in the fourteen years between 1950 and 1964, North Korea had opened ambassadorial-level relations with just twelve nations, one less than was established between 1965 and 1970.[76]

Only by placing North Korean actions in the context of these changing circumstances does the motivation for the *Pueblo* seizure become clear. Through Kim's own efforts, *juche* had become the defining principle of North Korean society. The system's existence was predicated on the *suryong*'s ability to lead his people to a socialist utopia by successfully pursuing *juche;* failure to demonstrate such ability threatened not only Kim's government but also the very essence of North Korean society. As long as all three paths toward *juche* were open, as they had been in the late 1950s, Kim could balance his aggressive maneuvers among the three, but as two paths closed in the mid-1960s, he had little alternative but to redouble his efforts along the remaining one, spurring a more bellicose phase in DPRK international relations. The *Pueblo* seizure thus makes sense only when it is removed from the context of the global superpower struggle and is considered instead as the product of indigenous North Korean circumstances affecting relations not only with the United States but with most of the world. As much as the exigencies of the Cold War dominated attention in Moscow, Peking, and Washington, in Pyongyang they were secondary to the need to conform to the ideological program that virtually defined the society.

North Korean actions after the capture support the idea that the *Pueblo* was seized for domestic ideological purposes rather than as part of the Cold War. The ship's intelligence value was staggering, as it carried top-secret SIGINT equipment, thousands of pages of classified documents, and a number of American intelligence specialists and their personnel files. Yet the DPRK largely ignored this aspect of its catch and instead sought to use the incident only for domestic propaganda. Beatings of the crew were frequent, but their purpose was almost always to obtain "confessions" of espionage and statements of repentance, rather than to extract any valuable military or intelligence information. "My torture was given for one reason," recalled Murphy, "to admit the intrasion [*sic*] or espionage."[77] "The interrogations," he later recalled, "continued at regular intervals. Yet the hard questions still went unasked . . . all we knew for sure was that the right questions weren't being asked."[78] Other crew members expressed similar surprise. His captors, Schumacher recalled, "were unaware of the vast knowledge and experience some of the members of the crew had; or else they had no further interest in our intelligence operations. Our value to them was apparently as propaganda pawns only."[79] Even while seizing the ship, the North Koreans made no effort to hinder the crew's attempts to burn classified materials. Instead, they watched as numerous crewmen exposed themselves to fire while carrying papers to the incinerator, but made no effort to stop them.

On the unusual occasion that they expressed interest beyond propaganda, the captors rarely ventured toward the ship's obvious military and intelligence value. Supply was studied carefully, including an effort to determine how many rolls of toilet paper the ship carried. Great interest in American society was also evidenced. Civil rights and material possessions were common topics, and one crew member speculated that if the North Koreans had questioned them as closely on military matters as they did on American women, the entire American communications system would have been in jeopardy.[80] When military information was sought, the questions were simple and the answers rarely classified. How many men were in the U.S. Navy? How many in the National Guard? Where was the Central Intelligence Agency? Where was the Naval Academy?[81] The DPRK administered beatings to get such information, which most encyclopedias could have provided. Yet, while they focused on what American women wore to the beach, they almost never sought material on American attack plans in Vietnam, defense capabilities in South Korea, naval weapons and technology, or any other significant topic.

The North Koreans even ignored intelligence information that was literally staring them in the face. During one interrogation session, Schumacher observed on the table in front of him a number of secret documents captured from the ship, yet, he recalled, his tormentor "asked me no questions about them. He showed not the slightest interest in the technical gold mine spread out on his table. He just wanted abjectness and a confession."[82] During a similar incident, Murphy noticed a copy of his personnel file in the room, indicating his past service aboard the guided-missile destroyer USS *Robinson;* like Schumacher, he was stunned when the guards asked nothing about her equipment, training, or missions.[83] Even the CTs, whose files clearly indicated some expertise in American methods of intelligence collection, received the same treatment. The interrogation, recalled one:

> was about my life up to that time. "What did you study in school before the navy," "what schools did you go to in the navy," "what does your family consist of," and my favorite, "what does the National Guard do with its tanks when they are not using them?" I was never asked one question about what I did at Kamiseya or anything else about my job or our operations. Most of these Q&A sessions consisted of them spieling off how I was a spy and deserved to be shot if I was not "sincere." . . . By the way, the answer to the National Guard question is: "Oh, the tank drivers take them home and keep them in their garages so the hub caps won't be stolen." They wrote all that down and were very pleased.[84]

Kim's domestic presentation of the incident also demonstrated this concern with public perception. The DPRK government made every effort to ensure that popular attention remained focused on this bold maneuver. Most of the crew's actions were recorded and disseminated for public consumption. In fact, within hours of being towed into Wonsan, the men were photographed disembarking a train in Pyongyang, and the pictures were quickly released to the domestic press. Kim must have expected the photos to reach the United States, perhaps inflaming a situation that already threatened war; yet he still elected to release them. This was not an isolated event. The men were frequently on camera over the next eleven months (usually filmed by one omnipresent photographer nicknamed "Jack Warner"), and the results were commonly disseminated to the public. Further reflecting the importance of these public appearances, DPRK interrogators took care not to leave bruises on the crewmen's faces before photo sessions.[85]

These efforts to keep the men at the center of attention went beyond pictures. The crew was occasionally taken into public, including trips to a theater, a circus, a concert, and the "Museum of American Atrocities." Copies of confessions and letters home frequently appeared in the *Pyongyang Times*.[86] Confessions were also noteworthy for their content, which focused almost exclusively on admitting American transgressions and praising North Korean strength but were devoid of international references. Their structure was almost formulaic: first the "confessor" provided personal background and described his role on the ship, then admitted to spying and other transgressions, and finally repented and acknowledged the evil of his ways.[87] Flattering references to North Korea and Kim were common, but mentions of the Soviet Union, China, capitalism, or communism were almost nonexistent. In fact, most confessions read as if the outside world did not exist; a thirty-five-paragraph "Joint Letter of Apology" signed by the entire crew in February failed to make even one reference beyond the Korean peninsula.[88] Had Kim been driven by the Cold War, it seems reasonable to expect at least an occasional mention of countries beyond his borders, but none existed. Instead, the focus was simply on the "greatness" of North Korea and its *suryong*.

The domestic focus was also apparent in the occasional press conference, in which the crew gave prearranged answers to prearranged questions. Again, the exchanges reflected little interest in the global situation, instead emphasizing North Korea's power and wisdom. At his first press conference in February, Commander Bucher recalled the ship's capture: "We had intruded into the coastal waters of a number of socialist countries and carried out espionage activities, but we felt very uneasy and much hesitation as we were approaching the coast of the Democratic People's Republic of Korea, because we knew that the coastal defenses of the Korean People's Army were quite strong."[89] He added that the crew operated off North Korea "with unease and fear," and he lauded the North Koreans for their fair treatment. Other conferences echoed the same themes: North Korea was strong; North Korea was fair; North Korea was wise. Crewmen praised their captors for their exercise programs, their living conditions, and even the movies they were allowed to watch, yet they almost never mentioned (or were even asked) anything bearing on global rivalries, international communism, or the Vietnam War. On September 12, a special press conference marking the DPRK's twentieth anniversary was held. This five-hour spectacle welcomed many international reporters, yet only one question addressed American aggression against other socialist nations, and none specifically mentioned China, the Soviet Union, or Vietnam. Instead, the focus was on North Korean greatness. Bucher commended the ability of the North Korean navy, Hospital Corpsman First Class Herman Baldridge applauded the North Korean medical facilities, and others thanked the DPRK for its wisdom and generosity.[90] The Cold War, it seemed, might not have even existed.

Specific propaganda statements also suggested the importance of *juche* in

Kim's actions. On February 8, a *Pyongyang Times* headline charged, "United Nations has no right to meddle in *Pueblo* case," despite the fact that the UN had made no effort to become involved since late January. The article, however, reminded readers of Kim's strength in preventing outsiders from intervening in this affront to DPRK sovereignty.[91] After releasing the confessions of Bucher and Schumacher, which admitted to other American and ROK plots against the North, Kim publicly delivered two long statements to the army, demanding that it prepare with "revolutionary alertness, militant vigilance, and ... full preparedness for shattering any vicious provocative machinations."[92] A few days later, Kim demanded that the North Korean people accept austerity so that he could increase defense expenditures. "Only when each country strengthens its self-defense capabilities in every possible way," he explained, "is it possible to strengthen the overall might of the socialist camp, overwhelm the imperialist aggressive force, accelerate world revolution, and successfully prepare defenses against the aggressive machinations of the imperialists."[93] Such exhortations—by demonstrating the courage of Kim's government in standing up to the powerful capitalist imperialists, uniting the nation in a quest to protect its revolution against outside forces, and justifying economic shortages as a necessity to preserve the DPRK revolution—reveal Kim's determination to milk the incident for evidence of *juche*. The same message dominated most of Kim's propaganda releases during the ordeal. In the twelve months following the seizure, he released ninety-one *Pueblo*-related propaganda statements of over 300 words. Tellingly, none of these took the Cold War or international competition as a main theme; instead, they usually had a domestic focus, with fifty-two of them stressing the need to remain strong against future American espionage.[94] One study that analyzed all such statements concluded that they demonstrated "an increasingly insecure North Korean regime" and reflected "a DPRK fear of isolation, but at the same time a strong sense of national pride used to justify a continued Stalinist political and economic program and to insulate the country from outside influence."[95]

Other actions demonstrated the domestic sources of DPRK conduct. While detaining the ship and crew, Kim publicly stressed the danger of American retaliation and praised North Korean unity and resistance in the face of this threat. He even created fictitious American attacks and their equally fictitious defeats, always attributed to courageous North Korean resistance. In February, he described a failed American attack on a sentry post in the western section of the DMZ, and in March, he claimed two American defeats near Mount Osongsan and west of Soan-ni. Other U.S. spy ships were reported to be launching raids on North Korea; one on February 16, for example, supposedly attacked Surido before being repulsed. Although DPRK propaganda had often made such claims, they became more pronounced following the *Pueblo* seizure, thus keeping the incident in the public eye while at the same time providing examples of DPRK strength for public consumption.[96]*

By placing Kim's actions within their ideological context, they take on a more intelligible picture. The gains of seizing the *Pueblo* were vast, as it provided the DPRK ruler with a wealth of *juche* at a time when it was otherwise hard to achieve. "In this particular case," noted Oleg Kalugin, "he raised his own stature to a level unthinkable before. He challenged the United States. He kept Americans in prison. He kept the *Pueblo* in the hands of the North Koreans and never let it go."[97] The American military and intelligence communities, by failing to consider the possibility that Kim might act in accordance with his domestic needs, rather than as the subservient junior partner of a larger conspiracy, had launched an unprepared ship on a risky mission near a dangerous enemy at the worst possible time. In doing so, they had doomed eighty-two American sailors to North Korean prison camps. Now, the responsibility for getting them home fell to Lyndon Johnson.

*In fact, recent evidence from former communist bloc nations indicates that Kim had acted alone. The night after the attack, the North hosted a meeting of all socialist ambassadors, in which the Deputy Foreign Minister declared his intention to "inform your governments [about the] invading armed American ship seized by our navy." The attack, he noted, was one "of which you might already have read in the newspapers." The guests, including the Soviet Ambassador, were clearly in the dark about the attack. "The North Korean authorities," the Romanian delegate explained, "were aware of the fact that Romania did not welcome the terrorist actions that might have extremely serious effects and, therefore, North Korea avoided consulting and even informing Romania in detail." A week later, DPRK Charge D'Affaires Kan Cher Gyn met with Soviet Foreign Minister Gromyko to request support for Kim's actions, and in April when the North Korean Ambassador to the USSR met with Kosygin, the Soviet leader lectured him on their failure to better inform his government. "The difficulty of the situation on the Korean peninsula is understood in the Soviet Union, and developments are closely watched," noted Kosygin. "However, we are not aware of the considerations and plans of the DPRK government with regard to the further development of events. This makes it difficult for the Soviet Union to provide the DPRK with support in the international sphere." Kosygin concluded with a message for Kim: "We would like full trust and frankness in our relations." Even the East German Ambassador noted the Soviet surprise at Kim's aggressive maneuvers, writing that "Such an aggravation of the situation ... had not been expected." Nor was Moscow pleased by Kim's handling of the crisis. A typical report from the Hungarian Embassy observed that, "In the Soviet's view, the North Koreans interpreted the Korean situation quite incorrectly." Moscow saw the attack as "a dangerous miscalculation," and "sheer adventurism." "These actions such as the capture of the *Pueblo*," it concluded, "actually reinforced the position of the South Korean dictatorship, providing it with a pretext to resort to repressive measures and ask for military aid from the USA."

The USS Pueblo *(AGER-2) during training exercises in 1967. It should be noted that, because of steering problems, the ship is going backward. (National Archives II, still picture unit)*

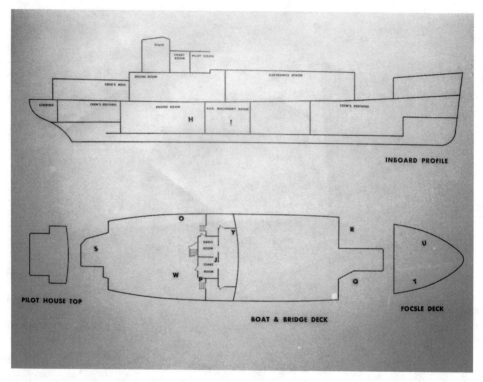

Outline of the USS Pueblo *boat and bridge deck, side and top views. (National Archives II, still picture unit)*

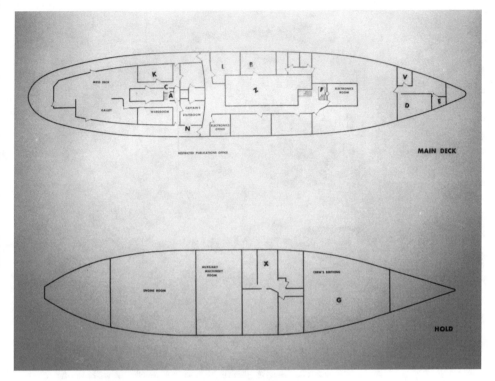

Outline of the USS Pueblo *main deck and hold, top view. (National Archives II, still picture unit)*

The crew's mess area. (Naval Historical Center, photo services branch)

Soviet SO-1–class patrol boat, the type used to seize the USS Pueblo. *(Naval Historical Center, photo services branch)*

North Korean propaganda photo of the crew of the USS Pueblo *holding a press conference. Commander Lloyd Bucher is standing in the center. (Naval Historical Center, photo services branch)*

North Korean propaganda photo of eight Pueblo *crewmen in captivity. Seated, left to right, are Howard Bland, Don Peppard, Jim Layton, and Monroe Goldman. Standing, left to right, are Ron Berens, Harry Iredale, Doug Scarborough, and Charles Law. Note the extended middle fingers of Jim Layton. (National Archives II, still picture unit)*

North Korean propaganda photo of charts and logbooks showing the Pueblo's *alleged violations of DPRK territory. (National Archives II, still picture unit)*

American Major General Gilbert Woodward signs the "three A's" letter (apologize, admit, assure) as written by the North Koreans, on December 23, 1968. (National Archives II, still picture unit)

The Pueblo *crewmen march across the Bridge of No Return. (National Archives II, still picture unit)*

North Koreans load the body of Duane Hodges onto a jeep for transport over the Bridge of No Return. (National Archives II, still picture unit)

Duane Hodges's body is honored at a memorial service shortly after the return to the United States. (National Archives II, still picture unit)

Monroe Goldman (above) and Ralph Bouden (left) celebrate their return with their families. (National Archives II, still picture unit)

WELCOME, BRAVE CREW

Such patient suffering—how little we knew
Of the "captured" PUEBLO and her brave crew.
From the long, dark days 'neath the Communist yoke,
With morale still high and their spirits unbroke,
They sped o'er the ocean without wake or foam
To a joyful reunion with loved ones at home.
Time will heal bruises and make them all well—
But they'll remember a prison of hell.

Presented in Honor of the Crew of the U.S.S. PUEBLO
on the occasion of its release from a prison camp in North Korea
by the
AMERICAN BATTLESHIP ASSOCIATION

The American Battleship Association honors the return of the men. (National Archives II, still picture unit)

The navy's Board of Inquiry investigates the seizure. Left to right are Admirals Richard Pratt, Marshall White, Harold Bowen, Edward Grimm, and Allen Bergner. (National Archives II, still picture unit)

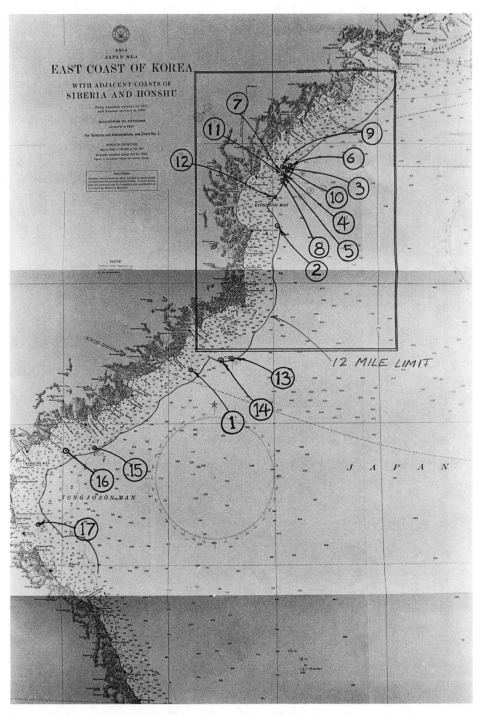

A chart prepared for the Board of Inquiry detailing some of the Pueblo's alleged intrusions into DPRK waters. (National Archives II, still picture unit)

Commander Lloyd Bucher. (National Archives II, still picture unit)

Executive Officer Lieutenant Edward Murphy. (National Archives II, still picture unit)

Commander Bucher receives the Purple Heart in 1969. (Naval Historical Center, photo services branch)

The eighty-two surviving crewmen of the USS Pueblo *at the Balboa Naval Hospital, January 1969. (National Archives II, still picture unit)*

Jaw to Jaw

To Pyongyang we were taken,
All comforts forsaken,
When into the "Barn" we were led.
All set for the winter,
Cords of bread you could splinter,
A rat ate my turnips, now he's dead.

Rear Admiral John Smith hated his job. As senior member of the United Nations delegation to the Korean Military Armistice Commission (MAC), Smith had the unpleasant task of representing the UN at commission talks held sporadically in a small camp near Panmunjom. The MAC had been created by the 1953 armistice agreement that ended the Korean War and was envisioned as a peaceful forum for representatives from the United States and North Korea to discuss their differences, especially those relating to the agreement itself. However, the commission rarely approached its creators' aspirations. Instead, it emerged primarily as a place to exchange insults, allegations, and blame. "In open meetings," Admiral Smith complained, "it was just screaming at each other for the benefit of whomever was interested." Meetings were so antagonistic that Smith refused to drink anything beforehand, afraid that any request for a bathroom break would give his North Korean counterpart, Major General Pak Chung Kuk, ammunition in his never-ending quest to criticize the United States for not taking the talks seriously. Since meetings occasionally lasted as long as eleven hours, the admiral lamented, one of the most important assets for a MAC negotiator was "a good bladder."[1]

At the time of the *Pueblo* seizure, Smith had represented the UN forces for only three months, but it was long enough for him to develop a dislike of his job and his DPRK opponents. "These people," he complained, "are mad dogs. ... [They] just don't have any feelings. They are completely without scruples or conscience."[2] The tour, however, had not been a complete waste. Smith had taken to amusing himself by blowing cigar smoke in Pak's face from across the table. The admiral had grown so proficient that he could direct it into his opponent's ear with some accuracy. Pak, a cigarette smoker, tried to respond in kind, but in an interesting Cold War metaphor, the small North Korean cigarettes lacked the range of the larger American cigars. These exchanges, Smith admitted, "gave me fiendish delight."[3]

On January 23, 1968, the two men met to discuss North Korea's recent attack across the 38th parallel. Although the details of the *Pueblo* Incident were still emerging, the State Department ordered Smith to demand the release of the ship and crew, along with an apology. Pak and his staff responded with laughter and ignored the demands. "They had no knowledge," Smith decided, "that it [the *Pueblo*] had been operating or that it had been seized. . . . Apparently the North Korean headquarters forgot to tell them."[4] The same participants met again the next day, and this time Pak had a response. "I cannot but pity you," he began, "who are compelled to behave like a hooligan, disregarding even your age and honor to accomplish the crazy intentions of the war maniac Johnson for the sake of bread and dollars to keep your life." The *Pueblo*, he announced, was "a link in the chain of your US imperialist aggressive policy for provoking [and] perpetrating a new war of aggression"; another part of that chain, he added, was the 4,670 bullets UN forces had fired from the DMZ into North Korea in the last three days.[5] His government, Pak continued, would consider returning the hostages only after the Johnson administration agreed to "admit the violations, provocations, and aggressive acts committed by your side in the DMZ and in our coastal waters, to apologize to our side for them, to severely punish as required by the armistice agreement the mad main culprits who organized and commanded the incidents and all the criminals involved in them, and to assure at this table your side will not commit again such provocations and aggressive acts." A few minutes later he reiterated these conditions, declaring, "all you have to do is admit military provocations and aggressive acts committed by your side, apologize for them and assure this table that you will not recommit such criminal acts."[6]

Despite the fact that this exchange was the first between the two sides regarding the *Pueblo*, it received little attention in Washington, D.C. Fifteen years of combative meetings had demonstrated the MAC's ineffectiveness in dealing with substantive issues, and there seemed little reason to expect this situation to be different. Even Smith questioned the wisdom of holding further debate in this forum. "What do you say," he wondered, "to a Mongolian savage who holds 82 of your countrymen hostage?"[7] Accordingly, the administration turned its attention to more traditional avenues of international diplomacy, including the United Nations, the World Court, and other forms of third-party mediation. Yet, in a few weeks their focus would return to the MAC, where it would remain for the next eleven months. It was not an about-face they made happily; in fact, ROK opposition to private American–North Korean talks made Panmunjom one of LBJ's last choices for such a dialogue. Kim Il Sung, however, refused to negotiate anywhere else, and in the end, the president realized that he had no option but to yield. The fact that Kim's wishes triumphed over Johnson's reflected a crucial reality that would guide the *Pueblo* negotiations. The United States, despite its greater economic, military, and political power, despite the support of most of the international community, and despite the rightness of its position, had little control over the situation. For the next eleven months, Kim Il Sung pulled the strings, and Lyndon Johnson had no choice but to dance.

News of the *Pueblo* seizure reached the administration just before midnight on January 22, when a ringing phone jarred National Security Adviser Walt Rostow from a deep sleep. Jim Brown, chief of the watch at the White House Situation Room, was on the other end of the line with troubling news. A CRITIC message from a ship named *Pueblo* had arrived less than an hour ago, and although brief and confused, it suggested that she might be under attack. Attempts by Watch Officer Andrew Denner to collect more information, or even to find someone at the Pentagon who had heard of the *Pueblo*, had been unsuccessful. Never one to sit idly in times of crisis, Rostow made brief phone calls to inform Secretary of State Dean Rusk, Secretary of Defense Robert McNamara, and Assistant Secretary of State William Bundy, then climbed into his Volkswagen and headed for the White House.[8]

He arrived at the Situation Room just after 1:00 A.M. Messages from the *Pueblo* continued to arrive, but they were vague and unhelpful. Rostow decided not to wake the president without more specific information and instead began preparing the intelligence report that LBJ would undoubtedly want the next morning. It proved to be a difficult task. No one could establish the ship's specific location at the time of the seizure. Pentagon aides insisted that the *Pueblo* carried emergency destruct devices for classified materials, yet messages indicated that the destruction process had been "ineffective" and some would be "compromised."[9] No one knew why the ship had surrendered, nor why no assistance had been available. Even William Porter, the usually well-informed American ambassador in South Korea, lamented the "general dearth of hard info" that made it difficult to evaluate the situation.[10] Shortly before 3:00 A.M., Rostow decided to wake the president. All they knew for sure, he explained, was that an electronic intelligence ship operating outside Korean waters had been captured sometime between 10:52 P.M. and 12:32 A.M. Four men had been injured, one perhaps fatally. Assured that nothing could be done at the moment, Johnson asked a few questions and then, after demanding a fuller accounting in the morning, went back to sleep.[11]

The next day, the president awoke to find a haze of chaos and confusion still hanging over the incident. As he did almost every Tuesday, Johnson lunched with a group of senior foreign policy advisers. Robert McNamara opened the meeting with a wry comment directed at Clark Clifford, who was scheduled to replace him shortly as secretary of defense. "This is what it is like on a typical day. We had an inadvertent intrusion into Cambodia. We lost a B-52 with 4 H-bombs aboard. We had an intelligence ship captured by the North Koreans." Clifford did not miss a beat. "Mr. President," he asked, turning toward his new boss, "may I leave now?"[12] Since information was still coming in, the luncheon group made no decisions regarding the American response. Instead, Johnson ordered the creation of a *Pueblo* Advisory Group to develop an overall strategy for resolving the crisis.

The Advisory Group included Rostow, Rusk, McNamara, and a number of other leading officials, including Undersecretary of State George Ball, Undersecretary of State Nicholas Katzenbach, and CIA Director Richard Helms. After six days of deliberations, they presented their findings. The best approach, they concluded, required the administration to pursue three specific goals. First, they must arrange the speedy return of the eighty-two American prisoners. Second, they needed to placate South Korea, which was already displaying signs of unease at the DPRK aggression, in order to prevent ROK President Park Chung Hee from withdrawing his forces from Vietnam. Third, they needed to avoid being drawn into a larger military conflict on the Korean peninsula.[13] All the goals seemed possible, but as Johnson soon learned, the last two undermined the first. By choosing to forgo the option of a military response, and hindered by the need to appease South Korea, the president had no way to convince Kim to meet his first demand—the speedy repatriation of the crew. For the next eleven months, LBJ would struggle to find a solution to this contradiction, but his best efforts would fail. In the end, there was simply no way for him to achieve his immediate goal—the swift return of the crew— without sacrificing his long-term ones.

Of these three objectives, the one Johnson needed to address first was the issue of a military response. Cries for retaliation quickly arose throughout the nation. The Joint Chiefs of Staff, recalled Admiral Moorer, were "in favor of giving them an ultimatum to turn the ship loose or else."[14] CINCPACFLT recommended sending an American destroyer into Wonsan to do "whatever was necessary" to retrieve the ship and crew, and General Charles Bonesteel, commander of the UN Forces in Korea, advocated giving Kim a nuclear ultimatum.[15] Within hours of the attack, the navy directed a number of destroyers to the area at top speed, and CINCPAC began planning a number of photo reconnaissance missions to determine the *Pueblo*'s exact position. Plans for a rescue attempt were also passed down the chain of command. The operation called for at least three destroyers to charge into Wonsan Harbor at first light, while others laid down a suppressing fire, and planes from the *Enterprise* provided continuous air coverage. One destroyer, likely the USS *Osbourn,* would carry a detachment of marines who would climb aboard the *Pueblo,* kill or drive off any Korean troops, cut the ship loose from the pier, and then fit her to be towed out.[16]

Such a response would have pleased the majority of the American people, who demanded swift retribution. Senator Jack Miller (R-Iowa) called for "some kind of a more positive response . . . than just a protest up there at Panmunjom, so that if these people get the idea that by continuing to do this they are going to pay the penalty for it, then maybe they won't be so anxious to carry it on." Senator Strom Thurmond (R-S.C.) demanded that the United States "fight if necessary to obtain the immediate release of this ship and all of its personnel."[17] "The Big Stick," lamented Congressman Albert Watson (R-S.C.), "has been replaced by nothing more than a wet noodle."[18] Americans outside the government echoed these sentiments. The Reverend Paul Lindstrom of the National Remember the *Pueblo* Committee insisted that "the big stick is necessary. We will only get the olive branch of peace by using the sword of power."[19] Telegrams demanding military action flooded the White House. One from Los Angeles asked Johnson to "drop a juicy bomb on their capital," and another from Philadelphia demanded, "drop the hydrogen bomb and let's end it."[20] Even after the initial rush of anger subsided, many Americans still wanted action; in a February Gallup poll, those choosing force as their preferred response outnumbered those choosing diplomacy by an almost two-to-one margin.[21]

Despite the outcry, a number of factors discouraged Johnson from choosing a military response. Most important, any retaliation would likely have resulted in the immediate death of the crew, since the strong DPRK air defenses made any simultaneous rescue attempt virtually impossible. Although the Joint Chiefs had shown him twenty different plans, LBJ lamented, "None of them will get [the] men home alive." "If you just strike out and bomb somebody," echoed Rusk, "well, that might make you feel a little better, but it doesn't get your people back . . . as a matter of fact, it almost guarantees their death." Not everyone agreed. Former CIA director Allen Dulles argued that the nature of intelligence collection required this type of risk-taking and sacrifice. The possibility of North Korea executing the crew did not change his mind. "I am afraid," he concluded, "that is inherent in the business." Despite the critique, however, Johnson and his staff refused to sentence the crew to death; after all, Rusk admitted, "We ourselves had ordered the *Pueblo,* an undefended vessel, on that mission."[22] Secretly, the administration did prepare a plan to send twelve F-105s into Wonsan to destroy the ship before the communists had a chance to give it a full inspection, but President Johnson never gave the final approval to launch. John Wright, the army colonel charged with leading the attack, was briefed about the operation and then readied his men for what appeared to be a suicide mission. Calling them together, Wright realized that he had thirteen pilots and only twelve planes. They should, he told the squad, decide among themselves which pilot would remain home. One man raised his hand, and Wright gently excused him from the mission. "No, that's not it," the man replied. "One of the ships is a two-seater, and I'll ride in the back."

Even if the administration had been willing to sacrifice the men, other factors argued against a rescue or retaliation. Every military option had serious drawbacks. Capturing a North Korean ship and crew seemed an appropriate response, but it appeared unlikely that Kim would exchange the *Pueblo* crew for the hostages. Furthermore, the DPRK had only a few large naval vessels, which generally clung to the Korean coast. Most of those that did cruise international waters were owned jointly by North Korea and Poland and were operated by predominantly Polish crews. Should such ships be seized, warned the Polish ambassador to the United States, the communist-bloc nations would lose all incentive to assist with the crisis. Accordingly, only the bellicose Rostow endorsed this risky alternative.[23]

More significant forms of retaliation had even greater possible ramifications. Blockading the major North Korean ports risked conflict with the Soviets and Chinese, who used them for trade. The possibility also existed that the Soviets might respond by improving North Korea's aerial capabilities, which were already strong enough to inflict significant damage on the American forces executing the blockade. The DPRK had docked the *Pueblo* in the well-defended port of Wonsan and surrounded it with seven KOMAR-class guided-missile patrol boats, making it virtually impossible to reach without significant American casualties.[24] Air strikes against North Korea would likely face fierce opposition from its powerful air force, which included approximately 500 fighter planes, several hundred of which were Soviet-made tactical light fighters like the MiG-15, MiG-17, and MiG-21.[25] The planes were also well dispersed, many of them hidden in caves and other enclosures for protection, as were their fuel storage facilities. Although strikes could undoubtedly be accomplished, a task force charged with evaluating military options warned that their impact "would not substantially reduce or disrupt North Korea[n] military capabilities," and they would undoubtedly be condemned by international public opinion.[26] The task force drew similar conclusions about an assault across the DMZ, which would not only violate the 1953 armistice agreement but also face the difficult opposition of North Korea's ground forces, which had begun mobilizing shortly after the seizure and were armed with the formidable PPS-43 Soviet-made submachine gun, Soviet-made T-54 and T-55 tanks, and an extensive array of surface-to-air missiles.[27] The price struck Clark Clifford as too steep. "I am deeply sorry about the ship and the 83 men," he told the president, "but I do not think it is worth a resumption of the Korean War."[28]

In addition to these obstacles, any offensive move risked North Korean retaliation across the 38th parallel. The ROK armed forces were no match for their rivals. In contrast to the DPRK's 500 planes, for example, the South Korean air force numbered approximately 300, mostly F-86 Sabre jets that were almost twenty years old, and some F-5s that lacked air-to-ground capability. Accordingly, any such attack would likely necessitate a significant American military commitment to defend South Korea. With its growing difficulties in Vietnam, the administration desperately sought to avoid the prospect of another Asian front. "A renewal of the Korean War," Rusk explained, "would be something that we would look upon with the greatest dismay because we had enough of a struggle going on in Southeast Asia." "One war at a time," echoed Nicholas Katzenbach, "is enough."[29]

Despite their frustration with the slow pace of negotiations, the administration wisely stuck to the diplomatic path, even in the face of public criticism. The *St. Louis Globe-Democrat* called the response "weak-kneed" and lamented, "What a miserable pass has the United States come to when its president begs before a tinpot nation, which has pirated our ship on the high seas in an overt act of aggression."[30] A San Juan man telegrammed LBJ with the order to "forget diplomacy. Demand release of men and ship immediately or declare war," and a group of Indiana residents wrote that "48 hours warning should be long enough. Restore gunboat diplomacy and American pride."[31] Still, the president stood firm. "I do not want to win the argument and lose the sale," he told his advisers.[32] Johnson had reacted quickly to the alleged attacks in the Gulf of Tonkin in 1964, launching a military response without ascertaining all the facts or exhausting the opportunities for a peaceful dialogue; in doing so, he took a critical step toward escalating American involvement in Vietnam. Four years later, he adopted a more patient approach. By resisting pressure to launch a retaliatory strike and clinging to the unpopular decision to seek a diplomatic solution, LBJ not only saved the lives of the eighty-two hostages but may well have saved the thousands of others who would have been lost in another Korean War.

Johnson did order some military maneuvers, primarily to create an implied threat in support of his diplomacy. He dispatched a naval task force to the Sea of Japan that included three aircraft carriers and eighteen destroyers, approved the delivery of seven tactical fighter and two tactical reconnaissance units to South Korea, ordered the *Banner* to take the *Pueblo*'s place in the Sea of Japan, and deployed twenty-six B-52s and ten KC-135s to Okinawa and Guam.[33] Between January 26 and February 7, the number of U.S. Air Force planes in Korea jumped from 214 to 395, with 308 of them combat ready, backed by millions of pounds of bombs and ammunition.[34] Overall, Operation Combat Fox would become the largest strategic airlift in air force history. Two submarines, a fast-attack nuclear submarine already operating in the region and the diesel-electric USS *Volador* (SS-490), usually used for intelligence and reconnaissance, were also dispatched. The *Volador* carried CTs and linguists from Kamiseya, who were quickly summoned to the wardroom by the captain for a briefing about their mission. Should capture be imminent, he informed them, the sub carried three explosive charges that would be detonated, although not before the ship "took some of them with us." LBJ also activated almost 15,000 reservists from the Air National Guard, the Air Force Reserves, and the Navy Reserves, the first such call-up since the 1962 Cuban Missile Crisis. The president also approved Black Shield reconnaissance flights over North Korea, starting on January 25. The flights were conducted by CIA A-12s and SR-71 Blackbirds, charged with making three quick passes over North Korea, and were supplemented by "Bumble Bug" drone reconnaissance missions.[35] Although Soviet, Chinese, and North Korean radar tracked these flights, no action was taken to intercept them.[36] Overall, it was a restrained but firm American response. Should more force prove necessary, Secretary McNamara suggested, "We could move the USS *Kitty Hawk* into the area without public knowledge. She is only two days' steaming time away."[37]

The United States was not the only nation strengthening its forces in the area. By early February, the Soviets had sixteen ships operating in the Sea of Japan, including a number of Krupny-, Kotlin-, and Kashin-class guided-missile destroyers; two intelligence collectors; and a few submarines.[38] LBJ's decisions won the support of American military leaders, who, after their initial bellicosity, recognized the need for restraint. Quickly, CINCPACFLT directed its arriving forces to make no show of force in the area, and the planned rescue and towing operation was scrapped.[39] "[I] agree fully with our present moves to get the prisoners returned by diplomatic means," wrote Admiral Sharp. "I do not believe there is any military move we can make that will assist us in getting the *Pueblo* crew returned." Just in case diplomacy failed, however, Sharp did promise the Joint Chiefs that his forces would be prepared to take such steps as mining Wonsan Harbor and sending the *Banner* into the area under armed escort. "We also will be ready with various nuclear options," he concluded ominously. "I am not sure any of these military moves will assist in getting the *Pueblo* crew back," he added, "but they would teach North Korea a lesson."[40] Despite the difficult obstacles facing the rescue mission, many Americans in the Sea of Japan were disappointed. "Everything was being handled diplomatically," recalled a frustrated crewman on the USS *Ranger,* "much to the displeasure of everyone onboard."[41]

Johnson's decision to reject military action complicated his second objective—keeping South Korea under control and fighting in Vietnam. To most South Koreans, the Blue House attack and the *Pueblo* seizure were part of Kim Il Sung's larger plan to conquer the South, first through guerrilla attacks designed to erode their confidence, then with a conventional assault across the 38th parallel. Refusing to take a stronger stand now, they feared, only encouraged more aggressive action later. Accordingly, many took to the streets to protest LBJ's peaceful response. On January 31, the Korean People's Anti-Communist League sponsored a rally in Seoul; despite twenty-degree weather, 100,000 people showed up to march three miles and burn a ten-foot straw effigy of the North Korean dictator.[42] On February 7, American soldiers fired warning shots to turn back demonstrators marching near Panmunjom, and the next day over 1,000 ROK high school students protested in front of U.S. Information Service Centers at Taegu and Kwangju, demanding, "Away with boot-licking conferences."[43] South Korean newspapers threw more fuel on the fire. On February 6, the *Independent Chungang* attacked the "humiliating appeasement posture of the United States," and two days later, the *Korean Herald* concluded, "Instead of dealing a severe blow of retaliation against a series of barbarous acts of bellicosity committed by the North Korean communist aggressors, the world's biggest power seems to have started dancing to the communist propaganda tune."[44] Some South Koreans took even more dramatic steps; on February 20, Pak Chae-Sok, the secretary of the ROK's Blind Cooperative Association, sent a petition to the American embassy in Seoul demanding action against Kim Il Sung. Pak had written the petition in blood and attached the severed first joint of a human finger. Still, Ambassador Porter concluded, "Despite sanguineous aspects, letter is friendly in tone."[45]

The South Korean government, especially President Park, was at the forefront of this uproar. The day after the seizure, Park warned Ambassador Porter that if the North continued its aggression, a military response was "inevitable," and he suggested a joint U.S.–South Korean assault that would first bomb DPRK airfields and then attack North Korean ships off the east coast; two days later, he ordered the ROK First Army into full combat status.[46] At a January 26 press conference for all major American media representatives in South Korea, Park did not even wait for a question before launching into an extended diatribe on the need for American military action if diplomacy did not quickly resolve the situation.[47] The following week, he insisted that "the communists should be taught a lesson that any aggressive action cannot escape due punitive action."[48] Other officials followed his lead. In February, the ROK National Assembly passed a resolution expressing "national indignation" at Johnson's decision to seek a solution through MAC talks.[49] Meanwhile, Prime Minister Chung-Il Kwon called for teaching the communists a lesson "without delay" and warned that "a lukewarm US response would encourage the communists to engage in another Korean War."[50]

Although concern about DPRK aggression was certainly an important factor in Park's reaction, it seems likely that he also viewed the crisis as an opportunity to counteract declining American economic and military assistance. Aid from the United States, which had been an integral part of ROK development for two decades, appeared to be waning by the mid-1960s. Between 1956 and 1961, American economic assistance averaged $232 million annually, but budgetary concerns and the ROK's impressive economic growth sparked a reassessment. By 1964, U.S. aid had fallen to $124 million, and military assistance seemed likely to follow. "We're so overinsured in Korea," advised Robert Komer of the National Security Council in 1963, "that we'd better bite the bullet while the time is ripe."[51] In 1964, McNamara recommended removing one of the two American Army Infantry Divisions from the South, and the following year, the administration began considering a decrease in the amount of material sent through the Military Assistance Program (MAP), a Defense Department program through which the United States purchased military supplies for use by allied nations.[52]

Park's struggles against these reductions had seen little success until 1965, when Johnson dispatched 40,000 American combat troops to Vietnam. Hoping to avoid domestic criticism for acting unilaterally, the American government pressured its allies to provide troops, and South Korea quickly responded. "No Asian nation," Clark Clifford would later write, "had contributed more to the war effort."[53] The first South Korean combat division arrived in 1965, and by 1967, the ROK had provided 45,000 combat troops and over 20,000 technical support personnel, a higher per capita percentage than even the United States. This assistance, however, did not come cheaply, as it forced the administration to abandon any hope of decreasing aid to South Korea. "Our flexibility to accelerate this [economic] reduction," lamented one adviser in 1967, "is politically limited by the Korean commitment of 45,000 troops in Vietnam."[54] American aid to South Korea suddenly reversed its downward spiral, and the administration was frank about the reciprocal nature of this arrangement. In 1966, McGeorge Bundy asked LBJ for "final approval of a commitment to make a $15 million program loan to Korea during FY [Fiscal Year] 1967, as part of the deal to get another Korean division and brigade into Vietnam."[55] Two years later, Johnson informed his staff that "Park has agreed to give 5,000 military or 6,000 civilians. I told him we would get him an additional $100 mil over the $300 mil we had already given him."[56]

In 1967, Park had agreed to provide a third combat division to Vietnam in exchange for additional military and financial assistance. Before he dispatched the troops, however, the Blue House raid and the *Pueblo* crisis offered him a chance to obtain these inducements without fulfilling his commitment. After the seizure, Park began hinting that the increased DPRK threat might force him to retain the troops in South Korea and might even require a recall of the two divisions already committed to Vietnam. Perhaps, he suggested, the two divisions could remain if the United States would "take measures to further strengthen the defense capabilities of the Republic of Korea's forces."[57] Park supported his threats with actions; in late January, the ROK Joint Chiefs of Staff requested that General Bonesteel begin planning for the return of South Korean forces from Vietnam, and a few days later, the National Assembly debated a resolution calling for a withdrawal of ROK forces from Vietnam if the United States did not satisfy ROK demands.[58]

Park's hints had their intended effect. Johnson and his staff were already worried about Park's reluctance to deliver the third division, especially after a 1967 mission by Clifford and Taylor to solicit more troops from American allies had been rebuffed at every stop.[59] In the immediate wake of the Tet Offensive, the prospect of losing the two divisions currently engaged left them aghast; such a loss, warned General Westmoreland, was "militarily unacceptable."[60] Nor could LBJ permit Park to bring his troops home in order to launch a retaliatory attack across the 38th parallel. "We certainly did not want them to start another Korean War," recalled Rusk, "by launching an attack against North Korea. After all, we were heavily involved in Vietnam."[61] Accordingly, the administration had little choice but to satisfy Park's demands.

Johnson used a number of approaches to mollify the South Korean leader. Immediately, LBJ appealed to his vanity, issuing flattering public statements and overt promises to remain committed to the ROK. "I have great respect for the President of South Korea and his judgments," he declared at a press conference shortly after the seizure. "They are being received, considered, and acted upon every day."[62] The following week, Johnson sent Park a personal letter, promising to keep him "fully informed" of the *Pueblo* talks and praising his "courageous leadership" and faithfulness as a "trusted friend and ally."[63] The sentiments had some impact. Park, wrote Ambassador Porter, was "clearly moved. . . . I have not seen him affected in this way before. . . . One may occasionally make him smile and even laugh but it is a very rare thing to see his emotions stirred as they were by the president's message."[64] Despite the demonstrative response, however, Park managed to compose himself sufficiently to subject Porter to a two-hour lecture on the threat of Kim Il Sung and the ROK's need for American assistance. Recognizing the hint, the ambassador informed the State Department after the meeting that it would "help us greatly if you could arrange early delivery to Kimpo airport by largest airplanes available of substantial amount of counterinsurgency items."[65]

Like Porter, President Johnson recognized that the key to placating Park lay not in flattering letters but in material goods. Within days of the seizure, he ordered Porter to tell the South Korean president that the United States was considering a substantial increase in its MAP allocation; this information, he warned, was "for Park alone and not to be published in any way."[66] In early February, LBJ asked Congress to add $100 million in military supplies to South Korea's already approved aid package for 1968, which totaled over $220 million.[67] Although admitting that the money would help fortify the ROK against DPRK aggression, Johnson also stressed the need to keep the South Koreans fighting in America's larger Asian crisis; the request was warranted, he insisted, "in view of their troop contributions in South Vietnam."[68] "We need to give whatever aid is necessary to South Korea," he told congressional leaders a few days later. "They are among our best allies."[69]

While Congress debated, Johnson turned to Cyrus Vance, one of his favorite troubleshooters, to keep Park under control. Vance arrived in South Korea on February 11, with orders to dissuade the South Korean leader from launching attacks against the North, to win his public acceptance of MAC talks, and, most important, to fortify his willingness to maintain troops in Vietnam.[70] To win these concessions, Johnson authorized Vance to discuss the details of the proposed MAP increase. Vance also carried a stick to accompany his $100 million carrot. Prior to departure, Johnson had told him that if Park resisted, Vance should tell him that "the whole package" was contingent on the ROK staying in Vietnam. Any troop disengagement, he warned, would not only jeopardize the MAP funding but also cause "a reduced US participation in Korea."[71]

Vance arrived in South Korea to find the situation "fragile and serious . . . pockmarked with tension, suspicion, and distrust."[72] Park, Vance reported to Johnson, "is moody, volatile, and has been drinking heavily."[73] Early meetings with ROK military and political leaders accomplished little. "They were convinced," recalled one of Vance's aides, "that Kim Il-Sung was a bully. The only way to teach him a lesson was to belt him hard."[74] Vance and Porter sat down with the ROK foreign minister on February 14 to compose an acceptable agreement. A "torturous" ten-hour meeting produced a statement pledging both sides to seek a peaceful resolution to the crisis and to consult the other before taking any military action. The communiqué left vague the price the United

States would pay for this promise, noting only that America agreed to take "extra-ordinary measures" to strengthen ROK defenses.[75]

Although the Foreign Ministry accepted the agreement, Vance still had to obtain Park's approval, which appeared unlikely when the two met the next day. Park dismissed the statement as "not strong enough" and demanded that the United States make a more explicit guarantee of a military response in case of future DPRK aggression. Vance, using the type of skillful diplomacy that had won him his reputation, patiently walked the ROK president through the agreement. The lack of a promised military retaliation, he explained, did not indicate a lessening of the American commitment to South Korea. It merely reflected the reality that no decision should be fixed in advance, since each crisis needed to be evaluated on its own merits. It took hours of debate and all of Vance's ability to change Park's mind, but in the end, he succeeded. Park signed and further promised not to impede the MAC talks, provided they were concluded within a reasonable time.[76] "I believe," Vance wrote to LBJ, "that [our] objectives were essentially realized."[77]

Relations between the two sides stabilized after the Vance mission. ROK criticism of the MAC talks declined, and plans for a retaliatory strike were abandoned, although Park did continue tantalizing American officials with the prospect of additional soldiers for Vietnam.[78] In March, he promised to send the third combat division if the United States would provide its equipment and supplies, as well as "additional assistance," including destroyers and helicopters. The troops, he added, had already been readied for departure but had been delayed because of the DPRK situation.[79] He also requested that the United States pay the men an annual stipend of at least $4,000, despite the fact that their salary at home would have been about $600.[80] In April, Park submitted an additional list of desired military items, even though, as General Wheeler complained, he had not "shown any inclination to send additional light division to [South Vietnam]."[81] That same month, Prime Minister Chung privately suggested to Porter that two additional divisions might be sent in return for "additional US assistance," including a significant increase in equipment for the ROK reserves and the creation of a large air base on Cheju Island.[82] Having recognized that future ROK troop commitments were unlikely, the administration wisely chose not to pursue these offers. Nevertheless, it was clear that Park had not exhausted his attempts to extract the last drop of support from his American benefactors; in fact, his requests grew so large by the end of 1968 that Rusk sent Porter to advise Park to tone down his "ambitious shopping list," which might scare the incoming Nixon administration.[83]

Over the next six months, the administration put the final touches on the aid program. The ROK had submitted a "wish list" of items, which LBJ wanted followed as closely as possible, despite the fact that it sometimes contradicted the suggestions of American military advisers. On these disagreements, Johnson endeavored to honor the ROK requests. The primary goal of the equipment, he reminded the military, was not to improve combat effectiveness but to have "the maximum political and psychological impact on South Korea."[84] Congress approved the request on July 8, authorizing transfer to South Korea of an F-4E jet squadron worth over $58 million, small arms for its Homeland Reserve Force, air-field improvements, four fast patrol cutters, 10,000 new M-16 rifles, and over $15 million in various counterinsurgency and police funds, which included a self-propelled eight-inch howitzer battalion and a company of helicopters.[85] Johnson also arranged an additional $32 million counterinfiltration package that included patrol boats, surveillance planes, electronic detection systems, and chemical defoliants and was funded by a MAP allocation intended only for Vietnam-related purchases.[86] Reflecting the high priority that he placed on keeping Park satisfied, Johnson demanded that the military rush the supplies to South Korea, ordering that the transfer be given "the same priority as we give Vietnam."[87]

Although military and economic assistance was the primary inducement, LBJ took other steps to ensure ROK cooperation. Some were minor, such as his pledge to appoint a South Korean as deputy commander of the UN military forces in Korea, and his offer to provide training for Park's Presidential Protective Force.[88] Others were more substantial, such as his promise to increase ROK access to business opportunities in Vietnam. In some cases, Johnson even forced Agency for International Development (AID) administrators to purchase substandard ROK products for use in Vietnam. Rutherford Poats, assistant administrator for AID's Far East branch, recalled the president using "rather colorful language" with AID personnel, demanding that they keep Park happy until he agreed to send additional troops. Accordingly, Poats, who had been about to suspend purchases of ROK-produced galvanized steel, continued to buy it, despite the fact that he considered it "not up to snuff." "We clearly leaned over backwards," he recalled, "to find a way to avoid a permanent preclusion of Korea from the Vietnam market . . . because of the fact that the decision came along at a time when Korea was going to make a yes or no decision on President Johnson's request for additional troops."[89] ROK personnel also received increased access to nonmilitary jobs in Vietnam. By 1969, South Koreans constituted more than half of the foreign civilian employees in Vietnam, and 20 percent of Seoul's foreign currency derived from Vietnam-related enterprises.[90]

Although the deal appeared to be one-sided, it actually benefited both nations. Park had the ability to wreak havoc with American foreign policy; one military strike over the 38th parallel could have sparked a war, with disastrous ramifications for the United States. Even just a few properly timed public comments might have ruined, or at least delayed, the MAC talks. By providing Park with economic aid, military assistance, and public adulation, Johnson kept alive his best possibility for retrieving the men while reducing the chances of another Korean War. Nor did he yield to Park's demands on crucial issues. The State Department, for example, refused to allow ROK representatives to attend the closed MAC sessions, nor would it send transcripts of the conversations to the ROK, despite the fact that they were sent to Japan and the Soviet Union.[91] This pattern of giving in on the smaller issues in order to win the larger ones marked U.S.-ROK relations throughout the crisis. Johnson was willing to sacrifice money, equipment, and time to placate his South Korean ally, but he would not allow the ROK to hinder negotiations for the prisoners, impede his efforts in Vietnam, or drag America into another Korean War. For these larger goals, millions of dollars in equipment seemed a small price to pay.

Johnson's final objective—the speedy return of the men—would be the most difficult to achieve. He had avoided war, mollified Park, and ensured allied unity in Vietnam, but in doing so, he had sacrificed his only means of forcing Kim Il Sung to meet him halfway in negotiations. As a result, LBJ's efforts to find a compromise solution were doomed before they began. In the end, his only path to freeing the crew lay in yielding to the demands Pak had made at the January 24 MAC meeting, calling for the United States to admit that the ship had intruded into DPRK territory, apologize, and assure North Korea that it would not happen again. For the next eleven months, Johnson sought other options, but Kim refused to budge from what quickly became known as the "three A's demand": admit, apologize, and assure. Until the United States acquiesced, Kim would be content to continue holding unproductive MAC meetings, since their mere existence could be disseminated at home as evidence of how his bold foreign policy had forced the enemy to meet with him— on his soil and without the ROK—to plead for his magnanimity. Since Johnson had ruled out military force, and since Kim was not easily influenced by world opinion, international organizations, or the communist superpowers, the administration could do little to alter his agenda. In this sense, LBJ was as much a prisoner of Kim's need for *juche* as were the eighty-two survivors of the USS *Pueblo*.

Initially, the Johnson administration acted in accordance with the same Cold War tenets that had guided the navy and the intelligence communities and refused to believe that Kim had acted out of solely indigenous motives. Instead, LBJ blamed the global communist conspiracy, headed by Moscow. "He was convinced," recalled Clifford, "it was part of a worldwide challenge to him and to the nation, a coordinated communist plan to smash our will and stretch our resources to the breaking point."[92] Others shared this belief. Rostow insisted that the seizure was connected to "other Soviet actions in the Pacific" and suggested that the United States order the South Koreans to capture a Soviet ship, an action he termed "symmetrical."[93] Although rejecting this proposal, McNamara pointed his finger in the same direction. The seizure, he concluded, "had been pre-planned. The Soviets knew of it in advance."[94]

Although this belief in an international communist plot dominated thinking at the higher levels, some in the lower echelons of the policy-making bureaucracy suggested otherwise. Especially prominent was the State Department's Bureau of Intelligence and Research, which repeatedly suggested that the North Koreans were more than Soviet puppets and speculated that the Soviets were unlikely to have played a role in the operation. The USSR, reported the director of the bureau on January 24, "appears to have been caught unawares by the *Pueblo* incident. . . . There is no indication that Moscow instigated the North Korean seizure of the *Pueblo* or that Moscow even knew in advance the incident would take place."[95] LBJ and his advisers, however, rejected this assessment. Accordingly, Johnson's first diplomatic move was to order Llewyllen Thompson, the American ambassador to the Soviet Union, to confront Soviet leaders as soon as possible.[96] As quickly as he could arrange it, Thompson met with Deputy Foreign Minister Vasily Kuznetsov to discuss the incident, but received little satisfaction. Kuznetsov informed him that the United States should contact North Korea directly and expressed surprise that the Americans had even approached Moscow.[97] Instead of taking the advice, the administration became even more convinced that its rival was involved, especially since the deputy foreign minister seemed to have a prearranged answer. "The Soviets," concluded Johnson, "could scarcely have obtained the necessary information regarding the incident from the North Koreans, conferred about it, and taken a position so quickly without prior information."[98]

For the first few days of the crisis, the belief that Moscow had orchestrated the seizure dominated the discussion. Dissent was quickly dismissed. "Isn't the most plausible conclusion," asked Katzenbach at a State Department meeting, "that this is simply a North Korean action?" "For any Red country to go after the US, [I] don't think so," Rostow replied. "They were going for a vessel in which the Russians are much interested."[99] This belief reflected the administration's predisposition to see international communist plots at the root of all foreign crises. Six weeks after LBJ assumed office, Panamanians had rioted over American control of the Canal Zone. The president had refused to believe that the crisis derived solely from native forces. "Castro," he wrote, "working closely with the Panamanian Communist Party, had been sending guns, money, and agents into Panama."[100] He viewed the Vietnam War the same way, warning in

1964, "Let no one think for a moment that retreat from Vietnam would bring an end to conflict. The battle would be renewed in one country and then another."[101] "I knew," he reiterated after he left office, "that if the aggression succeeded in South Vietnam, then the aggressors would simply keep on going until all of Southeast Asia fell into their hands, slowly or quickly, but inevitably at least down to Singapore, and almost certainly to Djakarta. . . . Moscow and Peking would be moving to expand their control and soon we'd be fighting in Berlin or elsewhere."[102] In 1965, Johnson had placed much of the blame for a Dominican uprising on "the three major Communist parties in the Dominican Republic—one oriented towards Moscow, another linked to Castro, and a third loyal to Peking"—and had responded by sending 22,000 American troops after an adviser warned him that the choice was "Castro in the Dominican Republic or U.S. intervention."[103]

In the *Pueblo* Incident, these assumptions appear erroneous, as evidence strongly suggested that Kim had acted alone. Such an action did not fit with the general tenor of Soviet foreign policy during this period, which sought to improve relations with the United States while at the same time continuing to use similar intelligence platforms for its own purposes. In the late 1960s, the Soviets were also negotiating with Japan about the possibility of joint economic development in Siberia; a conflict in Korea would only complicate this situation. As for the Thompson-Kuznetsov meeting, the administration had allowed its predispositions to overcome the facts. Although the American ambassador had been ordered to meet with Kuznetsov immediately, it took almost ten hours to arrange a conference, more than ample time for the Soviets to develop a basic position. Furthermore, Kuznetsov's reply, which essentially provided no comment except to direct the United States toward Pyongyang, hardly suggested that extensive time had been spent in preparation. The "evidence" that Kuznetsov had not needed approval from above before making a rejoinder was also undercut by the fact that he approached Thompson the day after the meeting to inform him that he had discussed the matter with his superiors, who had concurred with his response.[104]

In fact, it appears that not only were the Soviets uninvolved in the DPRK action, but the seizure played a significant role in alienating the two nations. Although information from Soviet archives is unavailable, evidence suggests that the Soviets resented Kim's handling of the incident. Moscow requested detailed information on the crisis a few days after it occurred, but Kim Il Sung did not reply, and in February he ignored the Soviets again when they advised him to return the ship and crew without waiting for an apology.[105] Later that month, the CIA reported that the Soviet Union "has been quite cool towards the North Koreans since the *Pueblo* seizure," an attitude that was apparent in

Moscow's unenthusiastic public support of Kim's position.[106] In late February, a Soviet delegation led by Communist Party secretary Boris Ponomarev arrived in North Korea to evaluate the situation and recommend appropriate military aid; although the advisers approved some assistance, including new surface-to-air missiles, they refused to send many of their most recent weapons.[107] In April, Kim declined to send a representative to a Conference of Communist Parties held in Budapest, and the following year, the Soviets openly helped the United States search for lost crewmen after North Korea shot down an American EC-121 reconnaissance plane.[108] Although many factors undoubtedly contributed to this emerging rift, it appears likely that the *Pueblo* Incident played a part in convincing Moscow that the dangers of supporting Kim's regime might outweigh the benefits.

The Johnson administration made no secret of its belief that the Soviets had been involved and publicly criticized their apparent unwillingness to help resolve the situation.[109] Although openly ridiculing such statements, Moscow privately used back channels to pass along the truth. At a luncheon on January 26, a member of the Soviet Foreign Ministry informed Senator Walter Mondale that his government had played no role in the seizure and would work for a peaceful resolution. The next day, while Soviet President Aleksei Kosygin visited India, a Soviet embassy officer in New Delhi approached American correspondents from the *Baltimore Sun* and the *Washington Post* to provide the same assurances. Similar comments went to other diplomats and writers, leading Adam Clymer, the *Baltimore Sun* correspondent in New Delhi, to conclude that the Soviets were "obviously seeking to get this version to the U.S." Other sources reported similar conversations; the Soviet delegation to the UN, for example, informed Canadian officials that its government had not been involved, and Soviet ambassadors in Burkina Faso and Colombia also denied any involvement to local officials.[110]

As these reports trickled in, the administration reassessed its conclusions. Within a week of the seizure, State Department officials suggested that the Soviets might not have played a role after all; "North Korea," they concluded, "appears to have acted without consulting with either of the two communist powers beforehand."[111] Ambassador Thompson agreed, citing Kosygin's willingness to forward American messages to North Korea, and by the end of January, the consensus among Johnson's advisers was that Moscow was acting with a "distinct tone of restraint."[112] Accordingly, the administration lessened its public criticism. State Department spokesman Bob McCloskey, who had declared on January 24 that the "response of the Soviet government has not been satisfactory," had a different message six days later. "If you're trying to get another government to assist in a case like this," he announced, "one of the ways we are not going to do it is if we start publicly saying what other governments will or will not do. I think they prefer to work quietly, and I think we should give them the opportunity to do so."[113]

Still, the initial reaction may have had ramifications. Less overt criticism would have left Kosygin in a better position to exert his influence; the Soviets, American Ambassador Thompson noted, "were more inclined to be helpful if they are not exposed to the charge of collusion with us or of twisting the arms of their little brothers."[114] Public remonstrance, however, coming while the Soviets competed with China for leadership of the communist bloc, left them wary of appearing to have been intimidated by American criticism. Putting them in this position, lamented a Soviet official, had been a "tactical blunder."[115] For the next eleven months, the Soviets worked quietly to keep the *Pueblo* crisis from turning into a military confrontation, but they seem to have always been constrained by this fear.[116] Still, their influence in North Korea was limited, and even without this handicap, they may not have had any greater success. Johnson's response, however, had denied the United States of a potential ally in a difficult situation. Now, the administration would have to defuse the crisis on its own.

Although quickly recognizing that the Soviets had not been involved, Johnson and his staff still refused to believe that Kim had acted for indigenous reasons. Instead, they sought other ties between the *Pueblo* Incident and international communism and believed that they had found them when North Vietnam launched the Tet Offensive in late January. "Practically every expert I have talked to on Korea and North Vietnam and the Communist operation," President Johnson announced, "all of them, I think without exception, believe there is a definite connection."[117] "[It is] very obvious," he told congressional leaders, "that they want to put some pressure on us. We think to try to divert us from Vietnam."[118] Time never dimmed LBJ's conviction. "The North Koreans," Johnson wrote three years after leaving office, "were aware of the Tet Offensive in Vietnam, which was scheduled to take place eight days later. They were trying to divert US military resources from Vietnam and pressure the South Koreans into recalling their two divisions from the area."[119]

His advisers concurred. Rusk concluded that the DPRK "may be trying to put additional pressure on us with reference to Vietnam. They may be trying to open up a second front. I do not see much in it unless they had either one of these two objectives in mind." Clifford agreed that "possibly there is some planning behind it so that the North Koreans are going to cause enough difficulty in Korea to force us to withdraw naval and ground units from Vietnam to come over and face the new threat that exists in North Korea."[120] From Vietnam, General William Westmoreland concluded that there was "a relationship" between the *Pueblo* and the Tet Offensive, and from Seoul, Ambassador Porter speculated that the action was designed to "create a diversion in [the] Korean Peninsula and force us to divert military resources from [our] Vietnam effort and stimulate additional domestic and overseas pressures against US Asian policy."[121] McNamara not only agreed that the real target had been the Vietnam War but also lamented the fact that the ploy had apparently succeeded, since the administration could not move in South Vietnam until the *Pueblo* issue had been resolved.[122] This assessment was virtually unanimous. "We all agreed it was a diversionary effort," recalled Rostow. "We did not wish to be diverted."[123] Convinced that international conflicts were always started by wolves in sheep's clothing, the Johnson administration refused to believe that a sheep in sheep's clothing could actually exist.

Reflecting their belief that this was part of an international struggle, members of the administration instinctively turned toward international solutions. At Johnson's command, United Nations Ambassador Arthur Goldberg sought UN intervention, asking the Security Council to act "with the greatest urgency and decisiveness" to help obtain the release of the crew and ship and to end North Korean aggression against the South.[124] The council considered a number of avenues—inviting the ROK and DPRK to present their cases, creating a select committee to arbitrate, sending a secret Romanian delegation to mediate—but they all collapsed when Kim refused to participate in any UN-sponsored initiative.[125] On January 26, LBJ sent Roger Tubby, the American ambassador to Geneva, to ask the International Red Cross (IRC) to make an "urgent approach to [the] North Korean Government and Red Cross to inquire about the welfare and physical condition of the captured personnel, [and] to request their prompt release and good offices in arrangements for their return."[126] The IRC requested information from Kim that afternoon, again the next day, and once more on February 15; finally, the DPRK made its only response by sending a copy of a newspaper editorial attacking American imperialism.[127] The administration also launched a global demarche shortly after the seizure, contacting every nation with ties to either the Soviet Union or North Korea in order to request their intercession. American representatives were dispatched to hundreds of nations from Australia to Uruguay, none of which could convince Kim to listen.[128] Other plans involving the International Court of Justice, secret talks at a neutral site, or any other form of third-party mediation reached the same fate. Kim simply refused to discuss the issue with anyone other than the United States and at anyplace not of his choosing.

Although rejecting American advances, Kim did send signals indicating where he might be more accessible. On January 27, Major General Pak sent a secret message to the American MAC staff, informing them that the crew was being well treated and suggesting that the *Pueblo* crisis could be solved if the United States would "show [a] willingness to negotiate or discuss in a normal way when one side would like to have prisoners back."[129] Clearly, "the normal way," if the men were prisoners of war, would involve the commission charged with handling problems related to the 1953 armistice agreement. At the same time, the Hungarian representative to the UN informed Ambassador Goldberg that Kim would negotiate for the release of the crew, but only at Panmunjom.[130] The clearest sign came on January 31, when Kim Kwang-Hyop, a member of the North Korean Communist Party Central Committee, publicly commented on American attempts to involve the United Nations. "That the US imperialists," he declared, "have illegally brought the *Pueblo* case to the United Nations—although there is a precedent for the treatment of similar cases at the Korean Military Armistice Commission—is a premeditated intrigue for covering up their criminal acts and misleading world public opinion. . . . It will be a different story if they want to solve this question by the method of previous practice."[131]

Desperate for an opening, the administration welcomed these hints with some enthusiasm. "This is the break," Rostow told LBJ. "The problem is how to do it with maximum dignity."[132] An optimistic State Department telegram predicted that "the first round of [MAC] talks will produce the release of the crew," and Rusk described the meetings to congressional leaders as "the most promising," although he privately estimated the chances of success at "about 50–50."[133] On January 28, Rusk ordered Admiral Smith to arrange a MAC conference as soon as possible, and after some haggling over details, the two sides agreed to meet in early February.[134] Accordingly, the administration had all other attempts to break the impasse placed on hold, leaving Ambassador Goldberg, who had recently convinced the UN Security Council to intervene in the crisis, in the awkward position of now having to convince the UN not to act while the United States explored the MAC channel.[135]

On February 2, Smith and Pak returned to their familiar positions in a MAC conference room, glaring at each other across a rectangular table that straddled the Military Demarcation Line. Again, Pak rejected claims of American innocence. The ship's mission, he declared, was "the most flagrant violation of the armistice agreement," and the crewmen were "aggressors and criminals." Pak made no reference to possible solutions, except to warn Smith that there would be no progress unless the U.S. government "change[d] your stand and attitude in addressing the subject."[136] Still, he refrained from the usual personal insults and appeared generally cooperative. The administration was somewhat encouraged. "We believe," concluded Assistant Secretary of State Sam Berger, "the meeting went about as well as could be expected."[137] This restrained behavior held throughout the next week, as the two sides met four times over the next eight days.[138] Meetings were brief and businesslike, and although Pak still refused to discuss a specific formula for a settlement, he did encourage the United States by providing the names of the dead and wounded and by his overall behavior, which Porter described as "polite, soft-spoken, and cooperative."[139]

Pak's changed attitude likely stemmed from Kim's desire for the United States to make the MAC the sole focus of its diplomatic efforts. The plan succeeded, as the administration quickly turned its full attention to this forum and abandoned any other means of negotiation. These early meetings also helped Kim accumulate evidence of *juche*. At almost every conference, Pak sought a statement indicating that the American government had accepted this forum for face-to-face communications with the North Korean government, thus admitting that the Americans were sitting down as equals with a regime whose validity they denied. "May I understand," Pak asked at the February 4 meeting, "that . . . you are proposing that this issue be treated as a matter between both sides, that is between the Democratic People's Republic of Korea and the United States?"[140] After numerous similar comments, Ambassador Porter recognized Pak's purpose. "His goal," Porter concluded, was "the full panoply of formal government-to-government negotiations."[141] Kim also used these meetings to gain *juche* by publicly claiming that the United States had come crawling to him in desperation; on February 4, for example, Radio Pyongyang announced that the DPRK delegation to the MAC, "at many requests made by senior member of the US side, John V. Smith, met with him in Panmunjom on 2 and 4 February."[142] The DPRK government vehemently denied any hint that Kim had sought the talks. After receiving Pak's secret message on January 27, Smith responded with a letter requesting a MAC meeting, in accordance with the general's suggestion. Pak's reply came swiftly. "I have sent no message to you," he wrote. "Nor did I await any reply from you. I cannot meet you on the basis of such a fabricated document." Instead, he requested that "you retransmit the aforesaid letter with the above mentioned sentences deleted."[143] Despite noting the "obvious propaganda implications" of the request, the United States complied, redoing the letter in such a way that Kim could present it at home as an example of his assertiveness in foreign policy.[144]

Only after LBJ demonstrated a commitment to future MAC negotiations did Pak formally present his conditions for releasing the crew. On February 15, he repeated the three A's demand. "We will be able to consider," he told Smith, "the issue of returning the crew members only when your side apologizes for the fact that the US government dispatched the armed spy ship *Pueblo* to the territorial waters of the Democratic People's Republic of Korea, conducted espionage activities, and perpetrated hostile acts, and assure that it will not commit such criminal acts again." Johnson quickly rejected the proposal.[145] Instead, the administration spent February advancing other suggestions, none of which included an American confession. In early February, the United States dropped its demand for a North Korean apology and even expressed a willingness to sign a receipt for the prisoners, as long as it did not contain either an apology or an admission of guilt.[146] On February 10, the United States offered to "conduct a full and impartial inquiry" and to "express regrets" if it found evidence that the ship had violated DPRK waters; the offer was contingent, however, on Kim first returning the ship and crew.[147] Pak rejected the proposal at the next meeting and returned the dialogue to the three A's. "If you really want to solve promptly the issue of the crew members of the *Pueblo*," he advised, "you should . . . apologize for the espionage activities and hostile acts committed by the armed spy ship which intruded into the territorial waters of the Democratic People's Republic of Korea under the instructions given by the United States government, and you must assure that you will not commit such criminal acts in the future."[148] While the two sides argued over the ship's future, American officials noticed that it was moving; on February 12, American intelligence indicated that the North Koreans had moved the *Pueblo* from Chojikan to the nearby Munp'yong-ni Naval Base in Wonsan Harbor.[149] Two months later, it would be moved again, this time to Najin, a port near the Soviet border.[150]

Still, LBJ sought other alternatives. In the middle of February, the United States offered to abide by the findings of an impartial fact-finding body and pledged to apologize if it ruled in North Korea's favor, but it again demanded that Kim first release the men. "We do not see," concluded the State Department, "how we can go any further."[151] After Kim rejected the idea, the administration suggested that the men be released to a neutral nation that would hold them while the charges were investigated. Pak called the idea "nonsense . . . an insult to [DPRK] sovereignty."[152] Another suggestion, this time to try the case before a three-member investigatory panel, was similarly dismissed as an "absurd example of Washington's brigandish logic."[153] The administration continued to work with the Soviets as well, hoping to convince them to pressure North Korea, but this channel offered little reason for optimism. Kosygin clung to the line that the matter needed to be resolved between the United States and North Korea at Pyongyang, and third-party intercession would just complicate matters. The American military buildup in the area, he noted, "indicated that there were many hotheads in the Pentagon who needed tranquilizers."[154]

As February drew to a close, the crisis seemed no closer to resolution than it had been a month earlier. Although it had achieved two of its main objectives, the administration had made little progress toward the most obvious one, largely because the decisions on the other two had sacrificed control of the debate to Kim. Rostow continued to push for action, as much to impress the Soviets as to help the crewmen, since, he concluded, "Nothing would damage our credibility with the Russians more than if, having put forces in the area and stated to Kosygin the urgency of the matter, we did nothing." Since North Korea offered such dim military options, Rostow suggested that the administration mine the ports of North Vietnam, in order to "maintain our credibility with Kosygin & Company."[155] Still, Johnson overruled all such proposals and clung to the diplomatic path, despite his growing frustration. "The nights are very long," LBJ told the annual Presidential Prayer Breakfast in early February. "The winds are very chill[ed]. Our spirits grow weary and restive as the springtime of man seems farther and farther away. . . . I can, and I do, tell you that in these long nights your president prays."[156] Two days later, a reporter asked if he was confident that the United States could get the ship and crew back. "No, I am not," Johnson answered glumly.[157] Despite his temptation to end the talks, however, LBJ recognized his lack of options. Without the ability to exert diplomatic, political, or economic pressure on Kim, the president's only means of forcing him to settle for less than the three A's was to use military power, which meant abandoning his other two goals. Wisely, he refused to make this exchange, thus keeping peace in Korea while sentencing the *Pueblo* crew to extended captivity and condemning himself to eleven months of frustration. Ambassador Goldberg best summed up the administration's attitude in a telegram to the president in late February: "I see no alternative," he lamented, "to painstakingly continuing discussions on the hope that we can wear the North Koreans down before they wear us down. It is better," he concluded, "to Jaw-Jaw than War-War."[158]

CHAPTER SEVEN

Forgotten Men

So this would be home,
For how long was unknown.
Our future was filled with deep ditches.
Each day would bring fun,
Loads of laughs, sun-to-sun.
But the laughter was measured in stitches.

While the Johnson administration sought peaceful solutions to the *Pueblo* crisis, the American people sought revenge. "There should be no word mincing in our demand for the swift and safe return of both ship and crew," wrote the *Buffalo Daily News,* "nor should North Korea be deprived for long of the measured dose of retribution her sudden belligerency has so emphatically asked for."[1] Telegrams calling for action flooded the White House. One Georgia resident ordered the president to "get off your complacent rear and get the ship and its crew back," and a Florida man demanded, "Release, retaliation, or your resignation."[2] Different solutions were offered—economic sanctions, seizing DPRK ships, attacking Pyongyang, dropping an atomic bomb—but the one thing most Americans agreed on was the need for a swift and decisive response to North Korean aggression.

Nowhere were such sentiments articulated with more fervor than on Capitol Hill. Senator Bourke Hickenlooper, the ranking Republican on the Senate Foreign Relations Committee, called on LBJ to "send a fleet into that area, level our guns on the shore and serve an ultimatum of release of the ship and the men." Senator William Bennett (R-Utah) advocated "steaming into the port city of Wonsan, tossing a towline aboard the *Pueblo,* and bringing it out," and an even more pugnacious Mendell Rivers (D-S.C.) told the press, "I'd select a target. I'd do like Truman did—let one of them disappear." Senator Russell Long (D-La.) suggested that the United States begin sinking North Korean gunboats and holding their merchant ships hostage. "If the Soviets want to deal itself in on it," Long trumpeted, "they can get in on it, too."[3]

The administration's failure to take immediate action sparked howls of protest. "Once," wrote the *Lynchburg (Va.) News,* "the American nation was led by men of courage and integrity. Now it is led by appeasers, liars, and cowards, who sneer at honor and truth as luxuries we can no longer afford." "Our official bird is not an eagle, hawk or dove," echoed the *Milwaukee Sentinel.* "It is chicken." Governor Ronald Reagan (R-Calif.) described the situation as "the most disgraceful thing to happen in my memory of America," and House Minority Leader Everett Dirksen (R-Ill.) lamented the "clammy spirit of fear and timidity [that] surrounds our efforts to regain the ship and her crew." The American public released a similar torrent of frustration. "Our government's handling of the *Pueblo* seizure," wrote a Wisconsin man to President Johnson, "is the most gutless unpatriotic act this government has ever perpetrated. Why don't you publicly have the Pentagon haul down the flag and be done with it?"[4]

Such bellicosity was unsurprising in Cold War America. Since the collapse of the U.S.-USSR alliance at the end of World War II, Americans both in and out of government had consistently demanded a strong response to any perceived communist aggression. Isolationist sentiment faded, to be replaced by a new foreign policy paradigm that suggested that American security and prosperity could be guaranteed only by a determined opposition to the spread of communism on every front, and a concomitant resolve to spread American values in its place. This "liberal internationalism" did not extinguish all foreign policy debate, as conflict frequently emerged over tactics, timing, and priorities. Still, this general consensus was firmly entrenched in the collective American mind by the end of the 1940s.

The rise of the liberal international perspective could be seen as early as 1946, when George Kennan, America's foremost authority on the Soviet Union, warned that the Russians "had learned to seek security only in patient but deadly struggle for total destruction of rival power."[5] It was therefore necessary, he wrote the following year, to "confront the Russians with unalterable counterforce at every point where they show signs of encroaching."[6] Agreeing with the diagnosis, the Truman administration acted against perceived Soviet aggression in Iran, Turkey, and Greece, and in 1947, it pledged to "support free people who are resisting attempted subjugation by armed minorities or outside pressures."[7] The following year, the Marshall Plan gave $17 billion in aid to Europe, in order, explained Dean Acheson, "to call an effective halt to the Soviet Union's expansionism and political infiltration, and to create a basis for political stability and economic well-being."[8] In 1950, the National Security Council called for a 300 percent increase in defense spending. Communism, the council explained, was "a new fanatic faith," determined to achieve "absolute authority over the rest of the world."[9] For American policy makers, the world had become a simple place defined by a struggle between the forces of light and darkness. "The cleavage that exists is not between the Soviet Union and the United States," explained Truman. "It is between the Soviet Union and the rest of the world."[10]

Repeatedly, the American public rallied in support of such sentiments. Between 1945 and 1947, the number of Americans who viewed Russia as "aggressive" rose from 38 to 66 percent. In 1948, a *Newsweek* poll found that a growing number of Americans favored a preventive nuclear first strike on the Soviet Union, an idea echoed the following year by Senator Brien McMahon (D-Conn.), head of the Joint Congressional Committee on Atomic Energy. A 1949 Gallup poll reported that 70 percent of the nation opposed a government pledge of no first use of the atomic bomb, and 73 percent favored universal military training. "We must clearly assume a militant attitude if we are to survive," explained the president of the American Historical Association in 1949.[11]

Domestic society also reflected this determination to resist the spread of the communist menace and to celebrate the American way of life. "What is the new loyalty?" asked historian Henry Steele Commager. "It is, above all, conformity. It is the uncritical and unquestioning acceptance of America as it is." Loyalty oaths were required not only to teach in public schools but also to obtain a New York fishing license or be a professional wrestler in Indiana. The 1950 Internal Security Act required communist groups to register with the attorney general and led to the establishment of prison camps for their members in five states. Foes of civil rights won support by pointing out that communists advocated equality of the races, while adherents won support by arguing that desegregation was necessary if the United States was to win international loyalties in the struggle against communism. In 1954, President Eisenhower's State of the Union Address suggested revoking the citizenship of American communists, and seven months later, the Communist Control Act deprived the party and all related organizations of "any rights, privileges, and immunities normally granted under American laws."[12]

Americans showed little tolerance for challenges to this belief system. The extent to which the liberal internationalist consensus had become ingrained in the fabric of domestic life became clear in the election of 1948. Former vice president Henry Wallace sought the White House as the standard-bearer of the Progressive Party and criticized America's increasing hard line toward the Soviet Union. His party, Wallace bragged, had "stopped the Cold War in its tracks." The election revealed how little appeal these ideas had to American voters. Wallace won no electoral votes, and his approximately 1 million popular votes came overwhelmingly from Jewish Americans who approved of his public support of Israel, or from African Americans who were encouraged by his stance on civil rights (half his votes came from New York alone). On foreign policy, Americans overwhelmingly rejected the Progressives' anti–Cold War platform. The results, wrote one historian of this election, "meant the end of meaningful dissent on foreign policy, as the two major parties imposed a Cold War consensus which was destined to prevail for nearly two decades."[13]

Although the sense of immediate crisis had dimmed by the 1960s, most Americans still clung to the ideals of liberal internationalism. President Kennedy justified his decision to launch the Bay of Pigs invasion with rhetoric echoing the open-ended commitment of the Truman Doctrine. "It is clearer than ever," he told the American Society of Newspaper Editors, "that we face a relentless struggle in every corner of the globe. . . . We dare not fail to realize that this struggle is taking place every day, without fanfare, in thousands of villages and markets—day and night—in classrooms throughout the globe. The message of Cuba, of Laos, of the rising din of Communist voices in Asia and Latin America, these messages are all the same: the complacent, the self-indulgent, the soft societies are about to be swept away." Despite the tragic consequences of the Cuban operation, Kennedy's willingness to stand up to communism sparked a 10 percent jump in his approval rating. Similar sentiments surfaced three years later when 72 percent of Americans supported their nation's involvement in Vietnam. "The debate on Vietnam," concluded a leading history of the war, "could virtually be called a nondebate. . . . The main theme, that the United States could not afford to lose, was echoed over and over again by congress, the press, and later, the man on the street. . . . There was no need to doubt the importance of the United States preventing the forced communist domination of Vietnam. It was self-evident."[14]

Bellicose public reactions to perceived leftist activities were the inevitable by-product of the liberal internationalist consensus. In 1979, Iranian protesters captured the American embassy in Tehran and held fifty-three Americans hostage for over a year, sparking a huge uproar. "The nation," recalled President Carter's chief of staff Hamilton Jordan, "was gripped by outrage and emotion. . . . From the first day, the hostage crisis dominated the news." The country followed the developments on the daily television news show *Nightline,* which began in response to the seizure, and Walter Cronkite usually ended his CBS news broadcasts by reminding viewers how many days had elapsed since the crisis began. The anti-Iranian fervor reached such heights that the state legislatures of Louisiana and New Mexico barred Iranian students from attending state universities. Considering the values that underlay America's views of foreign policy, the reaction was unsurprising. Yet, despite the similarities between the Iranian crisis and the *Pueblo* Incident, the passionate American response in 1979 would prove to be very different from the one eleven years earlier.[15]

In late January, the *Pueblo* was the lead story on the news, the front page of the local paper, and the topic of happy-hour conversation. "These men," promised the State Department, "are not, nor will they ever become, forgotten men."[16] Many Americans—including a group of World War II veterans in Buena Park, California, some high school students in Dallas, and an elderly Massachusetts veteran—offered to assist in rescue attempts.[17] Cars soon sported "Remember the *Pueblo*" bumper stickers, and songs about the *Pueblo* graced the airwaves ("In the land of North Korea, over the ocean far away / There's a godless band of pirates who would rule the world some day / But I know the Yanks are coming with a great and mighty roar / to retrieve the USS *Pueblo* from this communistic shore").[18] The public outcry, however, proved to be as fleeting as it was vehement, and the men quickly faded from the national consciousness. Nine days after the seizure, the *New York Times* relegated the story to page thirteen—just beneath an article about Princess Margaret's tonsillectomy—while the editors found space on the front page to analyze a bond request from the local air pollution control commissioner.[19] Later that month, Philadelphia Congressman John Dent sent questionnaires to every home in his district, soliciting opinions on important national issues. The survey covered seventeen topics, including the Panama Canal, automotive safety regulation, and meat inspection laws, but it failed to mention the *Pueblo,* despite the fact that four crewmen hailed from Pennsylvania.[20]

By spring, the crisis had almost completely vanished from America's memory. "When was the last time," asked a Florida television newscaster in March, "you heard anything about the USS *Pueblo* and its crew?"[21] Later that month, the brother of CT Bradley Crowe complained to President Johnson that "already the *Pueblo* is taking the back pages in the paper," and two weeks later, the sister of another crewman lamented, "It seems that this incident has almost been forgotten by the general public."[22] In April, the North Koreans released more fabricated "proof" of American border violations, a crucial and hotly disputed issue that the *New York Times* ran on page three, leaving the front page clear for articles about a sanitation strike in Memphis and the mayor's position on the possible sale of Long Island University. Page two even discussed a meeting between Yugoslavian Premier Josef Tito and Mongolian Premier Yumzhagin Tsedenbal.[23] Such priorities were not unusual. The *Times* discussed the *Pueblo* on May 23 and then found no reason to mention it again for eighteen days, although the editors did find room in the international news section to discuss a Greek policeman's attempt to retrace Odysseus's route on a three-month sailboat excursion.[24] The *Times*'s coverage was hardly exceptional. The *New Republic* carried three articles about the *Pueblo* during the entire eleven-month crisis, all in the first three weeks of February, while *Newsweek* discussed it ten times in February but only four times between May and September. This short American attention span shocked even the North Koreans, who, Murphy recalled, "could not understand how a story could dominate the front page one day, and on the following slip to page thirty-two or disappear entirely."[25] Despite the State Department's promise, forgotten men were exactly what the *Pueblo* survivors had become.

This public apathy marked the eleven-month ordeal. In June, Congresswoman Charlotte Reid bemoaned the "disturbing commentary that today—150 days later—many Americans have seemingly already forgotten that the USS *Pueblo* and its eighty-three valiant crewmen are still captives of North Korea." *Time* magazine's October 18 issue carried a picture of eight *Pueblo* crewmen gathered around a table in their prison with middle fingers extended in a gesture of contempt familiar to most Americans. No article accompanied it, no commentary, nothing except a brief caption. Yet *Time* found space elsewhere for five paragraphs about Rhodesia, four about Panama, and four about the Congo. Six weeks later, *Time* examined the international crises awaiting the incoming Nixon administration but (amazingly) neglected to mention the *Pueblo*. Even the December 27 issue, which referred to the crew's possible release for the first time, did so only in a footnote to an article about Vietnam.[26]

One could easily conclude that this lack of interest stemmed from the chaos of the times, since the late 1960s produced many issues of urgent public concern. Most distracting was the nation's growing role in the Vietnam War. Draft calls in the summer of 1967 enlisted over 30,000 men per month, and by the time of the *Pueblo* seizure, American troop strength in Vietnam approached 500,000. In the summer of 1968, the military requested 206,000 additional soldiers, which sparked public outrage when the *New York Times* broke the story. With U.S. combat fatalities rising dramatically, it seems plausible to assume, as many have, that the American public simply lost sight of the *Pueblo* in its concern for what appeared to be a more pressing crisis.[27]

The distractions of the exploding civil rights movement present another possible explanation. After 100 years of freedom but inequality, African Americans began rejecting the peaceful protests of the past. "The days of the free head-whipping are over," wrote Stokely Carmichael in 1967. "Black people should and must fight back." Riots exploded in 126 cities following Martin Luther King's 1968 assassination, including one in Washington, D.C., that lasted three days and required federal troops to surround the White House. Again, it seems reasonable to surmise that Americans focused on this more immediate crisis at home rather than on those on the other side of the world. "Go . . . into any home, any bar, any barber shop," explained Chicago Congressman Roman Pucinski, "and you will find people are not talking about Vietnam or rising prices or prosperity. They are talking about Martin Luther King and how they are moving in on us and what's going to happen to our neighborhoods."[28]

Other possible diversions existed. In March 1968, President Lyndon Johnson stunned the nation by deciding not to run for reelection, and in June, Robert Kennedy was assassinated shortly after a victory in the California primary seemed to assure him the Democratic nomination. The summer saw a heated congressional battle over a proposed tax increase, culminating with the June passage of a 10 percent tax surcharge. That same month, Chief Justice Earl Warren resigned from the Supreme Court, igniting a long struggle over his replacement that would remain unresolved until the Nixon presidency. In August, Soviet armed forces entered Czechoslovakia to oust rebellious President Alexander Dubcek. Thus the *Pueblo* Incident, which appears so significant when viewed in isolation, assumed a secondary position within the complex mosaic of the times.

Despite the appeal of this explanation, however, a closer look calls it into question. Civil rights and the Vietnam War were certainly pressing issues, but they had been developing in the United States for years. By 1968, most Americans already held strong opinions about both, so it is hard to accept the contention that the public was too mentally saturated for the *Pueblo* Incident, which had exploded onto the national consciousness with an incomparable suddenness. North Korea's steady release of photographs, transcripts of press conferences, and the crew's confessions should have kept the crisis in the public eye. Furthermore, evidence suggests that the problems of the period did not sate the public but instead increased people's involvement in the political system. The 1968 presidential election saw approximately 3 million more voters cast ballots than had done so in 1964, and 2 million more than would do so in 1972. Almost 61 percent of eligible voters cast ballots in the election; twelve years later, with the Iranian hostages still in captivity, voter turnout was just 52 percent.[29] Hence, it seems unlikely that millions of Americans would have entered the political system in the late 1960s only to concern themselves with a few crises that had existed for years. Explaining this apparent contradiction requires moving beyond the *Pueblo* Incident itself and examining the changing values and beliefs that directed American society in this period.

Just as North Korean actions make sense only when viewed within a *juche* framework, so too is it necessary to identify the principles that directed American life in order to grasp the nation's response. Americans made sense of the "unfamiliar" (the *Pueblo* seizure) by evaluating it in terms of the "familiar" (their central convictions about America's conduct in foreign affairs). Since the end of World War II, Americans had perceived, and thus reacted to, international events based on the ideals of liberal internationalism. The late 1960s, however, were unique in American Cold War history in the extent to which this consensus began to collapse. For a few years, new elements had been penetrating the dialogue concerning America and its position in the world, shattering ideological constraints and steering debate on international issues into unprecedented terrain. Recognizing these new components of the nation's worldview is therefore vital to understanding the reaction of the American public to the *Pueblo* Incident.

One critical element of the liberal international consensus was the belief that the leaders of the American political system could be trusted to handle national affairs with honesty and principle. This conviction was in stark contrast to the perception most Americans had of Soviet leaders, who were largely regarded as immoral and untrustworthy dictators using the conflict with the United States to justify the enslavement of their own people. However, many Americans in the late 1960s had begun to develop doubts about the veracity of their own leadership, and for the first time since the onset of the Cold War, a significant number of citizens began to accept the possibility that American political and military figures were taking unwise or immoral actions and then concealing them from the public.

This emerging sentiment helped steer the public reaction to the *Pueblo* seizure in virtually unprecedented directions. Although outraged by the news, many Americans soon began questioning the government's explanation rather than accepting the usual contention that blame should be placed on the Moscow-directed communist conspiracy. Americans, wrote the *Chicago Tribune,* were "a bit hesitant about coming to verbal defense of the nation in this newest crisis because they could not be sure that they had been fed the right facts."[30] "I don't find it such an incredible possibility," echoed one letter to the *Los Angeles Times,* "that an American ship would be spying within their territorial waters."[31] The administration's early reaction to the news of the seizure encouraged these sentiments. Initially, Johnson's press secretary informed the public that the ship had been 25 miles from North Korean territory when it was captured; within a few days, the distance shrank to 16.3 miles. "Are we ruling out the possibility," asked one reporter, "that this ship did cross into territorial waters?" "I'm not going to get into fine lines on this thing," snapped Press Secretary George Christian.[32]

This willingness to doubt the president's honesty was a relatively new phenomenon in American foreign policy, whose roots lay chiefly in President Eisenhower's falsehoods regarding the 1960 U-2 Affair. However, if Eisenhower planted the seeds of distrust, Lyndon Johnson turned them into a forest. In August 1965, LBJ ordered the marines to the Dominican Republic during a civil war, explaining the decision as necessary to protect American lives. A few days later, administration spokesmen released a new justification, this time claiming that they had acted to prevent the nation from falling to communist aggression.[33]

Recognizing the public confusion over these disparate motives, Johnson released a list of fifty-eight communists supposedly active in the uprising. The list, however, fell apart under scrutiny. Some of those named were in prison, others were out of the country, and a few were dead.[34] In making his case to the American public, LBJ had also overdramatized the immediate threat, describing a horrific scene where blood flowed in the streets, radicals beheaded conservatives, and stray bullets forced the American ambassador to take refuge under his desk.[35] The extent of this exaggeration quickly became clear, as did its ramifications for the nation's trust in its president. Within a week of the intervention, newspapers warned of a "breakdown in communication between the White House and the American people."[36] Johnson himself recognized the danger of the situation. "I don't like people calling me a liar," he told the ambassador to the Dominican Republic. "I want you to go down there and see if you can find some of those people who were beheaded."[37]

Subsequent events reinforced what many had already labeled the "credibility gap." In 1966, two American bombers collided near Cartagena, Spain, resulting in the loss of four hydrogen bombs, yet the government made no official admission of the accident for forty-five days. At the time of the Gulf of Tonkin Incident, the Johnson administration had presented the public with a less-than-candid explanation of American involvement, claiming that the *Maddox* had only been in international waters, had been engaged in a routine patrol, had not been involved in the coastal attacks, had not fired the first shots, and had not pursued the enemy ships toward Vietnam. In 1968, the Senate Foreign Relations Committee began nationally televised hearings on Vietnam, with the Tonkin Incident playing a central role. Although evidence had slowly accumulated indicating the truth about the event, the hearings brought the administration's duplicity into focus. "In England," concluded the *New Republic,* "the government would have fallen that made such a disingenuous presentation as that on Tonkin." Even little things contributed. On a trip to South Korea in 1966, Johnson informed American troops that his great-grandfather had been killed at the Alamo; what he meant to say, his press office later explained, was that a great-uncle had been killed in the Battle of San Jacinto. Accordingly, it seems unsurprising that some Americans doubted the version of the *Pueblo* Incident presented by the government. "We have been misled by information that has too often been repudiated," noted a Wyoming woman. "Can the people be criticized for doubting, or for not always listening?"[38]

The greatest impetus for these doubts, however, came from Johnson's duplicitous handling of the Vietnam War. At a July 1965 press conference, the president revealed his decision to send 50,000 "combat support troops" to

South Vietnam but neglected to mention that he had also decided to deliver another 50,000 later in the year. He had scheduled the conference for noon, rather than prime time, and lumped the announcement together with a number of other items in order to hide the true extent of the commitment. "It was," recalled General Westmoreland, "a masterpiece of obliquity. To my mind the American people had a right to know forthrightly, within the actual limits of military security, what we were calling on their sons to do, and to presume that it could be concealed despite the open eyes of press and television was folly." Other efforts to mislead American public opinion existed, including a stream of deceptively optimistic pronouncements that, despite many gloomy intelligence reports, encouraged the belief that the war was being won. In 1967, LBJ spoke of "progress in the war itself, steady progress . . . rather dramatic progress," and Army Chief of Staff General Harold Johnson predicted that troops could probably start home in about eighteen months, since, he explained, "We are very definitely winning."[39]

Although such statements undoubtedly helped to mute early antiwar sentiments, they also promoted popular distrust of the administration as the war continued. In 1966, Richard Goodwin, a former Johnson aide, wrote in the *New Yorker*, "There has never been such intense and widespread deception and confusion as that which surrounds this war. The continual downpour of contradiction, misstatements, and kaleidoscopically shifting attitudes has been so torrential that it almost numbs the capacity to separate truth from conjecture and falsehood." By the summer of 1967, 65 percent of Americans believed that the administration was "not telling the public all they should know about the Vietnam War," and a Harris survey that same year concluded that "perhaps the most serious criticism focuses on his [Johnson's] credibility: that he has too often raised false hopes that the war would be ended and that he was not honest about sending troops to Vietnam."[40]

The 1968 Tet Offensive provided the final blow to LBJ's credibility just as the nation began evaluating the *Pueblo* crisis. "The sheer ability of the North Vietnamese and Vietcong to mount such a large scale offensive," recalled LBJ aide Joseph Califano, "had shattered the American people's confidence in the president's word."[41] An Iowa voter urged Senator Bourke Hickenlooper to take caution in the American response to the *Pueblo* seizure, because "our government has lied to us in many other incidents."[42] Criticism of LBJ's veracity flowed from all corners of the nation in 1968. "There is no infamy," wrote one American, "there is no treachery, there is no deception that would not instantly and unquestionably be believed about Lyndon Johnson."[43] "Government morality," echoed another in a letter to the president, "has sunk to the bottom when, as a teacher in New York City, I have to remind my students that they cannot take any of your administration's statements at face value."[44] Despite a lack of money, name recognition, and oratory skills, Senator Eugene McCarthy (D-Maine) received surprising support in the 1968 Democratic primaries, largely because he promised to "alleviate at least in some degree this sense of political helplessness and restore to many people a belief in the process of American politics and of American government."[45]

On February 4, McNamara and Rusk appeared on the television news show *Meet the Press.* Responding to a question about the ship's location, McNamara admitted that because radio silence had been maintained, "We can't say beyond the shadow of a doubt [that] at no time during its voyage did it enter Korean waters." Still, he expressed complete confidence that no intrusion had occurred and noted that "at the time of the seizure, we are quite positive it was in international waters." Rusk quickly supported him, adding, "This was a ship particularly qualified to navigate with accuracy. . . . We have not a single scrap of information from any source whatever that this vessel was inside the twelve-mile limit at any time during its voyage."[46] Other administration spokesmen made similar comments. William Bundy, appearing on the *Today* show the following morning, stated, "We have no slightest evidence [*sic*] that she didn't adhere to her orders which were to stay fairly in international waters, there's no evidence of that at all," and later that day, the State Department announced that there was "not a scrap of evidence that the vessel intruded into territorial waters." Yet the public ignored these statements and latched on to McNamara's comment as if it were a definitive admission of guilt. "First we were the innocent party attacked at sea," read one telegram to LBJ. "Now it comes out that we were in their waters to begin with. What next?" "Such a statement," concluded the *Washington Post,* "does not enhance the public's confidence in an administration with more than its share of trouble in that regard." This reaction is especially revealing when compared with the public response to the 1964 Gulf of Tonkin Incident, when almost the entire American nation accepted Johnson's version of events without hesitation.[47]

These doubts sent the nation in search of the "true" reasons for the crisis. "This smacks strongly of the Tonkin Gulf Incident which was used as a pretext for attacking North Vietnam," read one telegram to LBJ. "This *Pueblo* affair must not be used as an excuse for widening the war to North Korea." Oliver Schroeder, Jr., director of the Law-Medicine Center at Western Reserve University, wrote to his old friend Assistant Secretary of State Eugene Rostow and asked, "Did certain elements in our government really want to create the incident?" An Indiana resident accused Johnson of "arranging the ship incident to assure your re-election," and an Oregon man speculated that LBJ had intentionally provoked the crisis "to quiet those of us who feel the Vietnam fiasco has proceeded beyond moral boundaries." "The fact is," concluded the *Birmingham News*, "Americans by now don't know what to believe. And that's an even greater tragedy than the hijacking of an American ship."[48]

Thus, the *Pueblo* seizure left Americans outraged, but many found that changes in their fundamental beliefs about the government made them unsure where to direct that anger. North Korea was a bitter rival, and the communists were considered duplicitous by definition, but the Johnson administration had already proved its willingness to conceal the truth about international affairs. Was the ship really in international waters? Had its purpose been as harmless as authorities claimed? What else had the *Pueblo* done on its mission? Many discounted the administration's answers, including syndicated columnist Murray Kempton, who wrote that he could not believe "anything my government says about the *Pueblo*." Kempton admitted that he found North Korea's account more convincing, since, he concluded, "North Korea hasn't lied to me lately." "No intelligent thinking person," echoed one letter to LBJ, "believes the news reports on the North Korean situation. You know the truth and we know that you do."[49] No longer sure that their government was conducting foreign policy with honesty and virtue, many Americans were simply unable to demonstrate the moral outrage they would have displayed ten years earlier.

Another idea entered the nation's foreign policy discourse in the late 1960s, one that presented an even greater challenge to the principles of liberal internationalism. This view struck at the core of the Cold War consensus by questioning its fundamental tenet, the belief that the United States was a bastion of freedom and liberty, the last line of defense against the forces of evil. Instead, this view saw structural flaws in the American economic, social, and political systems, flaws that transcended the simple dishonesty of the present administration. These ideas were especially pronounced in their application to foreign policy, where they stood the liberal internationalist viewpoint on its head by defining America not as the defender of freedom and liberty but as an immoral predator driven only by rapacious self-interest. In 1967, historian Ronald Steel concluded that "intervention has been the dominant motif of American post-war foreign policy . . . involv[ing] ourselves in situations that have been morally compromising, militarily frustrating, and politically indecisive." Reflecting these changing beliefs, Americans began describing their nation's foreign policy in words they would not have used ten years earlier. Spokesmen warned of "corporate imperialism," denounced the American "war machine," and condemned a system that "lives by murdering people, [and] exploiting the world." Within this view, the *Pueblo* Incident became just another example of the larger problems inherent in the American system. Only by addressing the deeper problems of the American way of life, many believed, could specific shortcomings be alleviated. "If the system," wrote a Vermont resident, "has come to subvert the interest of the public by exploiting the machinery of democracy to defy the popular will and in fact constitute a new form of tyranny, then it is imperative that the system be radically altered."[50]

Again, the Vietnam War lay at the heart of this new perception, as it suggested to many that the nation was acting in ways inconsistent with the principles that it claimed to represent. On an immediate level, some Americans argued that the very act of intervening in Vietnam was immoral. Vietnam, they contended, was engaged in a war of independence, an attempt to throw off great-power imperialism just as the United States had done two centuries earlier. Others saw it as a civil war, an internal matter between the Vietnamese that neither needed nor merited American involvement. Nor did those whom the United States was supporting conform to expectations of principled leadership. Corruption and repression were the hallmarks of South Vietnamese administrations from Ngo Dinh Diem to Nguyen Van Thieu; Air Vice Marshall Nguyen Cao Ky, for example, made few friends in the United States when he admitted that his childhood hero had been Adolf Hitler. Elections were fixed and opposition was silenced in the name of advancing the cause of freedom that the United States claimed to champion. For a growing number of Americans, this contradiction did not go unnoticed.

Other Americans challenged the war from a more legalistic perspective, pointing to the fact that American actions were in violation of numerous international laws and agreements. The United States had pledged to recognize the 1954 Geneva Accords, which called for unifying elections in 1956. Article 4 of this agreement specifically prohibited "the introduction into Viet Nam of foreign troops and military personnel as well as of all kinds of arms and munitions," and Article 5 proclaimed that "no military base under the control of a foreign state may be established." Yet, that was exactly what American officials had done. Similar arguments emerged regarding the charter of the United Nations, Article 2 of which pledged that "all members shall restrain in their international relations from the threat or use of force against the territorial integrity or political independence of any state, or in any other manner inconsistent with the purposes of the United Nations." Violating these agreements, some contended, reflected the dearth of moral principles in American foreign policy. "Some of my colleagues in the Senate and some members of the administration are not happy when I call my country an outlaw nation for its violations of international law in Southeast Asia," declared Senator Wayne Morse in 1966. "But we have convicted ourselves by our own illegal acts."[51]

The majority of the war's opponents, however, objected not to involvement per se but to the specific form it took. Massive aerial bombings limited

American casualties but inevitably caused a high number of civilian fatalities. American planes dropped over 100 million pounds of chemical agents, defoliating forests, ruining crops, and poisoning water supplies. Cluster bombs, napalm, and Agent Orange challenged the traditional American notion that the United States adhered to moral principles even during times of warfare. In 1968, an NBC photographer captured South Vietnamese General Nguyen Ngoc Loan shooting an alleged Vietcong in the head while the suspect stood motionless with his hands behind his back, and in 1969, details began to emerge about the murder and rape of hundreds of Vietnamese civilians in a village Americans came to know as My Lai. Such brutality flew in the face of traditional views of the nation as a moral leader. Senator William Fulbright (D-Ark.) noted in 1968 that "there was always something about this war that has gone against the American grain. The dissent was not born of something alien to American life and experience: it was born of traditional American ideas about decency and fair play and the sanctity of life."[52]

Although the American public's response to the Vietnam War offered the most obvious example of the growing doubts about the nation's innate goodness, domestic life provided evidence of similar feelings. Nowhere was this more apparent than in the dramatic transformation within the African American civil rights movement in the late 1960s. Throughout the 1950s and early 1960s, most of the members of the civil rights movement believed in the American way of life and sought integration as their primary goal. "First and foremost," explained Martin Luther King, Jr., in 1956, "we are American citizens—and we are determined to apply our citizenship—to the fullness of its means. . . . If we were trapped in the dungeon of a totalitarian regime," he concluded, "we couldn't do this. But the great glory of American democracy is the right to protest for right."[53] By the 1960s, however, changing sentiment had begun to divide the movement, as many African Americans rejected this belief in the fundamental goodness of the United States. King's leadership slowly became contested by Malcolm X (among others), who urged African Americans to find "a land of our own, where we can . . . lift up our moral standards."[54] The Black Panthers, who proclaimed themselves the defenders of the black community against the institutional forces of a racist society, were born in 1966. "Only with the power of the gun," wrote its founder, "can the black masses halt the terror and brutality perpetuated against them by the armed racist power structure."[55] Testifying to the strength of this more aggressive sentiment, the Black Panthers' New York chapter recruited nearly 800 members in June 1968 alone.[56] The Student Non-violent Coordinating Committee, which had been formed in 1960 as a peaceful, pro-integration group, embodied this change. By 1965, its chairman, John Lewis, described the fight as "a struggle against a vicious and evil system that is controlled and kept in order for and by a few white men throughout the world."[57] The following year, Lewis was replaced by the more militant Stokely Carmichael, whose position on American society was clear: "Integration," he wrote in 1966, "is a subterfuge for the maintenance of white supremacy."[58] What was needed, he insisted, was "an African ideology which speaks to our blackness—nothing else."[59]

African Americans were not the only group whose struggle for equality metamorphosed as it incorporated these new doubts about the United States. In 1961, an American Indian conference in Chicago resolved, "We believe in the future of a greater America . . . with Indians and all other Americans cooperating," an integrationist statement reflecting the fact that 35,000 Native Americans had left the reservations for life in the American city in the 1950s. By the end of the decade, however, emerging radicals rejected such calls. Clyde Bellecourt, who had founded a moderate Indian rights group in 1964, cofounded the American Indian Movement four years later, a more radical group whose symbol was an upside-down American flag. Later that year, American Indians seized the abandoned Alcatraz federal prison in San Francisco Bay, holding the territory for eighteen months. Again, the American way of life had been judged and found wanting. "I tried to work within the system," lamented Bellecourt. "They weren't interested."[60]

The women's movement underwent a similar transformation, with the emergence of a growing faction that blamed women's status on fundamental flaws within the American system. Reform groups after World War II had demanded change, but in traditionally American ways, advocating, for example, such reforms as a Bill of Rights for women and an Equal Rights Amendment. Again, however, calls for a more dramatic rejection of American society appeared as the 1960s progressed. More radical feminist organizations such as the Red Stockings, The Feminists, and the Women's International Terrorist Conspiracy from Hell, emerged, all of which advocated more fundamental change and rejected traditional American ways. Protesters at the 1968 Miss America pageant rebelled against the portrayal of women as beauty objects by burning brassieres, curlers, and girdles in "freedom trashcans," while poet Robin Morgan explained their objections to the contest in terms that offered a clear challenge to conventional American self-perceptions: "It has always been a lily-white racist contest; the winner tours Vietnam entertaining the troops as a murderer mascot. The whole gimmick is one commercial shell game to sell the sponsor's products. Where else could one find such a perfect combination of American values? Racism, militarism, and capitalism—all packaged in one 'ideal' symbol: a woman!"[61] The following year, women stormed the offices of *Ladies' Home Journal,* a magazine that celebrated women's traditional roles, and Kate Millet's *Sexual Politics*, which condemned America's male-dominated patriarchal society, reached the best-seller lists.

This was not a new struggle. The movement for women's rights was centuries old in the United States. What was changing, however, was the tone with which it was articulated. No longer a celebration of American society and a demand for inclusion, the movement, or at least factions of it, had slowly embraced views that questioned the nature of the American system itself. With the moral qualifications of the American way of life suddenly under suspicion as never before, the liberal internationalist consensus, which relied on this belief as the bedrock for its existence, began to crumble as well.

Presidential politics in 1968 revealed the extent to which the traditional principles of American life were under attack. Former Alabama governor George Wallace stunned many with his strong showing as a third-party candidate. Wallace was no spokesman for the new values; instead, he ran as the defender of the system, attacking those who would tear it down. A typical Wallace rally offered a celebration of America: denunciations of communism, hosannas to God and country, and promises to restore the nation to its days of glory. "Most of all," wrote the *Washington Post*'s political reporter, "there is the appeal for law and order, the demand for a return to domestic tranquillity." Wallace's candidacy had obvious limitations—he was a southerner and an avowed segregationist; had little national name recognition or organization and a small war chest; and was the choice of the Ku Klux Klan, the John Birch Society, and the American Nazi Party—yet he performed surprisingly well. A secret AFL-CIO survey in September 1968 named him as the choice of one-third of its members nationally, and a *Chicago Sun-Times* poll that same month showed him getting 40 percent of the white steelworkers' vote in Chicago. In the end, Wallace received fifty-eight electoral votes and over 14 percent of the popular vote. Certainly, people cast their ballots for Wallace for a variety of reasons, but his promise to return the country to traditional American values was clearly one of the most important. His supporters' unhappiness, wrote Wallace's biographer, "was with the anti-war protest movement, led by silver-spooned brats who rejected a whole constellation of American cultural and religious values, of which 'patriotism' was at the core."[62] Had there been no strong antitraditionalist movement, it seems unlikely that there would have been a strong Wallace candidacy.

Although political struggles offered the most overt challenges to the old self-perceptions, the new feelings were also manifested in everyday life. Americans who never marched in protest, sat in at a lunch counter, or burned a bra found other ways to reject what had once been accepted as basic national values. Quickly, American popular culture became infused with new styles that represented a fundamental rejection of traditional idioms yet were embraced by mainstream America. In April 1968, for example, the rock musical *Hair* opened on Broadway, complete with the first male-female nude scene the theater district had seen (at least on stage). The show was a staggering success, despite—or perhaps because of—its willingness to reject old norms. *Time*'s reviewer described it as "flower power, pot, and protest. . . . *Hair* is lavish in dispraise of all things American."[63] The late 1960s also saw the rise of "guerrilla theater," performances conducted on city street corners by troupes refusing to be limited by the confines of the traditional theater setting. "We try in our own humble way to destroy the United States," said the leader of a San Francisco group whose performance included skits protesting the Vietnam War, mocking the profit system, and satirizing the song "Yankee Doodle."[64] Rock and roll moved from the largely upbeat and optimistic songs of the 1950s to a new sound that reflected American disillusionment. The Beatles, who made their first impact on American ears in 1963 with lighthearted and romantic songs like "She Loves You" and "I Want to Hold Your Hand," won the 1967 Grammy Award for *Sergeant Pepper's Lonely Hearts Club Band,* an album that sang about getting "high with a little help from my friends," explored the world of "Lucy in the Sky with Diamonds" (LSD), and announced that the group would "love to turn you on." "In loyalty to their kind / They cannot tolerate our minds," sang the Jefferson Airplane in 1968. "In loyalty to our kind / We cannot tolerate their obstruction . . . You are the crown of creation / And you've got no place to go."

Mainstream America also began to accept underground films as a legitimate form of entertainment. Such independently produced pictures—art films, experimental films, pornographic films—had always been geared toward a specialized segment of American society, but they now began to achieve national popularity and were shown in traditional theaters for the first time.[65] Even mainstream movies adopted some of these controversial techniques, such as Joseph Stick's *Ulysses* (1967) and Peter Collinson's *The Penthouse* (1967), which were produced by Columbia and Paramount Pictures, respectively, despite their sexual overtones and graphic dialogue. The plots of the era's most popular films further reflected the collapse of traditional American values. In 1964, the *New York Times* film critic complained that the message of *Dr. Strangelove* was that "top-level scientists with their computers and their mechanical brains, the diplomats, the experts, the prime ministers and even the President of the United States are all fuddy duds or maniac monsters."[66] *Bonnie and Clyde* (1967) glamorized the antisocial behavior of its criminal heroes. "They're young, they're in love, they kill people," ran the ad copy. That same year, *The Graduate* became the third highest grossing film in Hollywood history to that point by warning that even the good young men of traditional American society would eventually rebel against the bland life they had inherited. Crowds across the nation cheered as the young Dustin Hoffman rescued the young Katharine Ross from a life of snobbery, predictability, and plastics.[67] *Easy Rider* grossed $60 million in 1969, while family-oriented films such as *Dr. Dolittle* (1967) were huge box-office disappointments and John Wayne's *The Green Berets* (1968), a patriotic portrayal of the Vietnam War, was met by protests at its opening.

These changing forms of cultural expression in the theater should not be taken too far. Clearly, most of the people who went to see *Hair* did not do so as a conscious means of rebelling against a repressive society. Nevertheless, the mere existence of such dramatic change in cultural expression, and the willingness of much of mainstream America to experience it, indicates the extent to which the once dominant values were under attack in ways more subtle than direct political protest. With traditional values crumbling on so many fronts, it is not surprising that cracks in the liberal international consensus that had guided the nation for decades appeared as well.

The merger of the *Pueblo* Incident, popular culture, and changing American self-perceptions appeared most clearly in an unlikely source, the television science-fiction show *Star Trek. Star Trek*'s producers aspired to create more than a simple futuristic adventure series; each episode carried a deeper message about American society. The show, explained David Gerrold, one of its top writers, "was designed as a set of contemporary morality fables against a science fiction background . . . the stories are about us." Accordingly, different episodes addressed such issues as overpopulation, conformity, and government repression, and the writers did not hesitate to draw unflattering conclusions. "If our heroes represented the American attitudes," concluded Gerrold, "then as such they could be thrust into a variety of situations which would test those attitudes. And once in a while, those attitudes would be wrong."[68] On September 27, 1968, *Star Trek* aired its fifty-ninth episode, entitled "The *Enterprise* Incident," whose story was based on the *Pueblo* seizure.[69]

The plot for "The *Enterprise* Incident" strayed far from the actual events in North Korea, largely because NBC demanded changes in the original script, which had followed the real story more closely.[70] The details of the rather convoluted plot are not relevant here; what matters are the larger themes and beliefs it revealed. The show made it clear that the producers had their doubts about the supposed American moral superiority that lay at the heart of the liberal international consensus, and it reflected the questions many had about the specific details of the incident as provided by the Johnson administration. The aggressor in "The *Enterprise* Incident" was not the traditional enemy but the

United Federation of Planets (symbol of the United States), whose callous violation of enemy territory for the purpose of theft undercut its claim to be the defender of peace and virtue. Similarly, the presentation of the enemy Romulans, symbolizing the communists, also deviated from traditional views. It was the Romulans who behaved with restraint, choosing merely to capture the *Enterprise* for violating their territory, rather than to destroy it as the crew had expected. In fact, their restraint was a courtesy that the Federation was unlikely to have displayed had the situation been reversed. "If a Romulan vessel ventured far into Federation territory without a good explanation," asks the capturing commander, "what would a star base commander do?" Knowing the answer, *Enterprise* Captain James Kirk makes no reply. "You see," his captor concludes, "it works both ways." The lesson was clear. "As presented in 'The *Enterprise* Incident,'" Gerrold wrote, "Starfleet was no better than the evil Romulans."[71]

Again, such conclusions should not be taken too far. Obviously, the vast majority of those who watched the show did so for reasons other than its political statements, and many more did not watch it at all. Nevertheless, the fact that such a popular show could even suggest images of American heroes and their rivals that reversed the defining perceptions of the previous two decades indicates the extent to which these new values had permeated the collective mindset of American society and shattered the consensus that had until so recently dominated American life. By the late 1960s, 28 percent of Americans reported feeling "substantially alienated" from mainstream society, and George Gallup concluded, "All the time we've been operating, thirty-two years now, I've never known a time like this—when people were so disillusioned and cynical." "Never in our history," echoed Richard Rovere in *Atlantic Monthly*, "has the individual seemed as wretched and despairing as he is today; and seldom have free men anywhere felt so thwarted and powerless in their relations to a government democratically chosen. . . . Never have disaffection, alienation, and frustration been more widespread."[72] Viewed in this light, the failure of American society to exhibit the expected outrage over the North Korean attack becomes more comprehensible. No longer did Americans rush to the defense of their country in any altercation with a communist power; instead, their changing perspectives forced many to view these crises with doubt and skepticism, and even as evidence of larger shortcomings and moral failures that needed to be addressed within the United States.

Although liberal internationalism was battered, it was not beaten. Despite the growing number of skeptics, the consensus still occupied a central position in the American worldview, and many, especially those in the mainstream political system, continued to cling to it as the defining paradigm for America's role in the world. Even here, however, circumstances directed attention away from the *Pueblo*. In most foreign crises, liberal internationalists were able to respond to both manifestations of their perceived enemy—the communist superpower that directed the aggression and the local forces that conducted it—but the nature of the *Pueblo* Incident encouraged a different response. Direct involvement in local conflicts typically came when the government was convinced that only American assistance could ensure a favorable resolution, or at least stave off a communist victory. Hence, American power had been used in Laos, in the Dominican Republic, in Lebanon, and in Guatemala *during* the crucial period when the outcomes of the crises were still in doubt. In Vietnam, Presidents Johnson and Nixon had used the military to resist what they believed to be communist aggression, while at the same time attempting to resolve the crisis diplomatically. The nature of the *Pueblo* Incident, however, produced a different response, since the seizure had occurred too quickly for American power to be brought to bear. The ship was in Wonsan and the men in prison camps so fast that preventing the capture through an American military response in Korea was not an option. Accordingly, the liberal international consensus directed the attention of many Americans not toward Korea but toward Moscow, where their ideological predilections led them to believe the true responsibility lay.

Republicans, free from concerns about embarrassing the president, were especially outspoken advocates of this view. "The Soviet Union and North Korea," explained Congressman William Bray (R-Ind.), "are certainly working together." Alabama Senator Jack Edwards warned of "a master hand" behind the crisis, whose ultimate objective was to "picture us as a paper tiger by showing that we cannot, or will not, protect our legitimate interests when we are challenged," and Congressman Edward Gurney (R-Fla.) compared asking the Soviets for help to "asking an arsonist to put out the fire he started, while he is standing there watching the building go up in flames." Although generally less belligerent, most Democrats concurred. Senator Stuart Symington (D-Mo.) called the seizure "only one of various Soviet activities in that area," and Senator Russell Long (D-La.) thought that the communist plan was "to bleed us as much as they can as long as they can, whether they win or not."[73]

In accordance with this belief, liberal internationalists demanded that a response be directed at Moscow rather than Pyongyang. Congressman Daniel Kuykendall (R-Tex.), for example, insisted that the administration "bring the Soviets to immediate responsibility for the provocative excesses not only of North Korea but of all Communist nations," and Ohio Senator Robert Taft went even further, insisting that Johnson "interrelate our entire foreign policy to the solution of this particular problem, specifically putting maximum pressure on the Russians and upon others involved." Like their GOP counterparts, many Democrats focused not on North Korea but on the perceived larger enemy. The president, demanded Congressman Roman Pucinski (D-Ill.), should "serve clear notice on the Soviet Union itself that this country is not going to tolerate this kind of communist aggression all over the world."[74]

Such principles not only attributed the seizure to the global communist conspiracy but also echoed the Johnson administration's belief that North Korea's ultimate objective was to aid its communist ally in North Vietnam. "The roots of that crisis," declared the *New York Times* shortly after the seizure, "are not in Korea but in Vietnam." "This is no fluke incident," agreed the *Richmond News Leader*. "It is a conscious effort to open another Asian front." *Newsweek* found it "difficult to reject the notion that the *Pueblo* Incident, at least indirectly, was related to the US's ever deepening involvement in the war in Vietnam," and a San Antonio radio station warned that "North Korea has begun a major campaign of provocation and harassment, a campaign apparently intended to divert US and South Korean attention from Vietnam and to create new tensions elsewhere in Asia." Some in Congress expressed similar thoughts. "There is no question in my mind," announced Strom Thurmond, "that the seizing of the *Pueblo* and its crew by the North Koreans was not an isolated incident but was closely tied in with the war in South Vietnam."[75]

Hence, for liberal internationalists, it mattered little that no evidence linked the Soviet Union with North Korea's action, since their deeply held beliefs saw the communist conspiracy at all times and for all matters as a unified and monolithic evil, a modern-day Hydra whose many indigenous heads protruded from a single body. Only by concentrating on the body, they concluded, could the enemy be defeated. Hence, it made little sense to focus on the *Pueblo* itself when a greater culprit in Moscow needed to be addressed. For many others, however, liberal internationalism itself had come into question. For a few years at the end of the 1960s, a number of Americans had rejected the accepted Cold War framework that demanded a forceful response to anything that smacked of communism. These Americans thus turned away from the *Pueblo* not because they were callous, not because they were bad people, not because other events distracted them, but because new elements had emerged to alter the ideological framework through which they understood their nation and their world. Ironically, these new ideas may have done a great service to the *Pueblo* survivors by restraining the response of the American public. American bellicosity flared up briefly when the news of the seizure reached the United States, but the fragmentation of the liberal international consensus introduced new elements into the dialogue of American foreign policy that served to suppress this response. Simply, the American people did not make the traditional demands for government action, the type of demands that would later help drive Jimmy Carter from the White House during a similar crisis. Free of pressure for a more dramatic reaction, the Johnson administration was thus able to cling to its three-point strategy to resolve the crisis and patiently wait for a diplomatic opportunity to bring the captives home. For the eighty-two men enduring the torture and squalor of DPRK prison camps, this patience may have saved their lives.

CHAPTER EIGHT

Hanging On

Imprisoned eight months,
A grand collection of lumps
We've gathered since the dawn of detention.
But do you think we're resentful?
Hell no! We're repentful!
How repentful it's safer not to mention.

"Dear Mr. President," the letter began, "we, the officers, crew, and civilian oceanographers of the U.S.S. *Pueblo*, are writing you jointly to explain the facts and those points we consider pertinent to our capture and our detention in the Democratic People's Republic of Korea, and to request your assistance in our repatriation." Acting in accordance with their orders, the men admitted that they had "intruded into the territorial waters of the Democratic People's Republic of Korea" and had been captured "while committing hostile acts 7.6 miles from Yo-do in the vicinity of Wonsan." Their crimes left them ashamed. "We have had many hours of solitude since our detention to reflect and consider the nature of our offense," they wrote, "and rather than harboring resentment toward the Korean people for our capture, we have a strong feeling of guilt for the act we committed." Accordingly, they had confessed and offered a public apology to the North Korean people; now, they suggested, their government should do the same. "Our future happiness and the well-being of the many hundreds of Americans in our families is in your hands," the message concluded. "We do not doubt that you will see us swiftly returned."[1]

Major General Pak handed the statement to Admiral Smith on March 4, 1968, at the tenth closed MAC meeting concerning the *Pueblo*. The letter, along with many subsequent confessions and apologies endorsed by the crew during their captivity, left many Americans stunned. "These men are being hailed as heroes," declared Senator Richard Russell (D-Ga.) after the crew returned to the United States. "They are heroes in the sense that they survived the imprisonment, but they did sign a great many statements that did not reflect any great heroism in my mind."[2] Between January 25, when Commander Bucher signed a personal letter of confession and apology, and December 23, when American

MAC representatives signed a similar one to end the standoff, the crew and officers of the USS *Pueblo* produced countless documents used by the DPRK government in a barrage of propaganda. The admissions took different forms—some men penned confessions, some wrote letters home, some spoke before press conferences—but the details rarely varied. Almost every one admitted to committing acts of aggression, apologized for them, praised North Korea, and begged the United States to comply with Kim's three-A's demand.

Their actions clearly violated the 1957 Armed Forces Code of Conduct, which established specific standards of behavior for American military personnel in captivity. Article 5 demanded that prisoners of war provide only their name, rank, date of birth, and serial number. "Oral or written confessions, true or false," it added, "questionnaires, personal history statements, propaganda recordings or broadcasts, appeals to other prisoners of war, signatures to peace or surrender appeals, self-criticism or any other oral or written communication on behalf of the enemy or critical or harmful to the United States, its allies, the armed forces or other prisoners are forbidden."[3] During their ordeal, the *Pueblo* men produced almost every form of propaganda forbidden by Article 5, opening the door for a rash of criticism from military leaders (and others) when they returned home. Yet a close examination of the crew's eleven months in North Korea suggests that the situation was not as clear-cut as it appeared.

The sailors' ordeal began as soon as the *Pueblo* reached North Korea.[4] While guards led the men from the forward crew's compartment to the deck, an unfamiliar voice cut through the silence: "You have violated the laws of our country, and you will be punished."[5] Blindfolded, and with fishing line binding their hands in front of them, the eighty-two survivors marched across makeshift gangplanks and onto one of two waiting buses. It was a difficult task made even more daunting by the actions of their captors, who spent their time poking the men with bayonets and showering them with kicks and punches. They also restrained the hundreds of North Korean civilians who had gathered on the shore to berate the hated Americans. If not for the presence of the soldiers, the crowd would likely have torn them apart. Rocks, saliva, and invective filled the air: "Kill Yankee," the onlookers shouted again and again, "Kill Yankee."[6] The guards almost complied. Rifle butts smashed into the prisoners' heads with such force that some men almost lost consciousness, and many soldiers used their American counterparts to demonstrate their karate skills, much to the delight of the cheering onlookers. Guards loaded the wounded Stephen Woelk onto a stretcher and carried him to the bus, repeatedly dropping him on his injured thigh and buttock along the way. Woelk moaned in pain each time he hit the ground, and each time his porters responded with a flurry of body blows;

after finishing their assault, they would carry him a few more feet before dropping him again and repeating the whole process.[7]

As the buses pulled away from the dock, soldiers forced the men to sit quietly in their seats with heads bowed in the manner of Korean criminals. The slightest movement brought swift retribution. For trying to peek under his blindfold, Don Bailey received a painful gun butt to the back of the head. Robert Hammond, whose tight restraints had cut off the circulation in his hands, wiggled his fingers in an attempt to restore some feeling; quickly a guard placed Hammond's hand on a metal bar in front of him and smashed it with his rifle. Hammond was not the only one whose restraints caused him problems. Earl Kisler's hands were blue when guards finally untied them, and Michael Alexander's wrists bore rope burn scars for months.[8] The violence outside the vehicles matched that on the inside, as the sounds of civilians screaming in rage and pounding on the windows filled the air whenever the buses slowed. It was a terrifying experience for even the strongest man. As the buses rolled on, the voice of an interpreter rang out over the din: "You have been trying to make infiltration of North Korea with South Korean spies. You are criminals who will be tried in our People's Court and shot." A horrified Bucher protested, insisting that as prisoners of war his men should receive the protections of the Geneva Convention. "You capitalist dogs and Korea are not at war," the voice replied, "so no Geneva Convention applies. You have no military rights at all. You will be treated as civilian espionage agents of CIA."[9]

After a short ride, the buses stopped in front of a train station. Guards led the men inside and onto a train, where the beatings continued. Soldiers pummeled Richard Rogala's testicles, others dragged Larry Strickland across the floor by his thumbs, and Tim Harris was knocked down by a blow to the face and then hauled across the ground while he struggled to regain his feet. The worst abuse was heaped on the Filipino and Mexican crewmen—Steward's Mate Rogelio Abelon, Steward's Mate Rizalino Aluague, Storekeeper First Class Policarpo Garcia, and Seaman Ramon Rosales—whose dark features suggested to their captors that they were South Koreans. "Filipino, Filipino," Garcia cried out, but the hands pulling his hair would not relent.[10] Beatings continued intermittently throughout the long train ride that finally ended at Pyongyang at 6:00 A.M.

Bucher and four of his officers led the men into the freezing North Korean morning, while the fifth officer, Ed Murphy, remained behind to help carry Woelk.[11] A swarm of DPRK photographers descended as the Americans stepped off the train, unleashing a torrent of flashbulbs that temporarily blinded their targets. Violence awaited those who moved too slowly, too swiftly, or in any other manner that attracted the guards' attention. A huge painting of

Kim Il Sung watched over the procession from a nearby clock tower. "I knew," Schumacher lamented, "I was in his hands now, and he did not look benevolent to me."[12] After the photographs, the men were loaded onto another bus for a short ride to their new home. Silently, the crew took in the foreboding structure, a dilapidated four-story building composed of faded bricks and a dark tile roof, with a heavy metal fence surrounding it. "It was what I always imagined any Asiatic-Siberian Communist concentration camp would look like," recalled Bucher. The captain led the men into the new residence, which they soon dubbed "The Barn."[13] Hundreds of jeering guards welcomed them. "The only simile that fits," Schumacher recalled, "is that of a racist lynching mob in a grade-B movie."[14]

Guards distributed room assignments as the men reached the third floor. Officers got their own quarters, while enlisted men shared rooms in groups of four. The new lodgings made the *Pueblo*'s dilapidated accommodations seem palatial. Rooms were twelve feet wide and seventeen feet long, each with a straight-backed wooden chair, rickety wooden beds, dirty blankets and pillows, and a single unshaded lightbulb hanging from the ceiling. Decaying plaster walls, unevenly fitted floorboards, and cracked windows covered with bed sheets provided little protection from the freezing North Korean winds, and the radiators were either broken or useless against the hostile environment.[15] Murphy, who briefly shared a room with three enlisted men, found the conditions deplorable. "By American standards, our one room apartment for four should have had a 'condemned' sign nailed to the door," he complained.[16] The Barn's condition, however, supports the idea that the seizure had not been part of a preplanned international conspiracy. There were ample signs that the North Koreans had hastily converted the building from its original purpose as a military academy to a jail for the *Pueblo* crew. There were no locks on the doors, no bars on the windows, and it took days for the guards to distribute prison garb. Had the DPRK planned the operation in advance as part of a coordinated communist plot, it seems likely that these basic aspects of penitentiary life would have been anticipated.

Upon arrival, most of the men collapsed in their rooms, overwhelmed by exhaustion, hunger, and fear. They had also been awaiting an American response and were confused and bitter by its failure to appear. "All the beatings that I and the rest of the crew took didn't hurt half as much as the fact that when we were pleading for help, we got none from the largest navy in the world," recalled Don Bailey.[17] While the crewmen contemplated their fate, guards gave Bucher a firsthand demonstration of what awaited them. The captain was quickly dragged into another room for a face-to-face meeting with his new landlord. The waiting North Korean major demanded that Bucher admit that the *Pueblo* was part of a larger American plot against North Korea. Bucher clung to the story he had been using since the capture, insisting that the ship was a research vessel conducting electromagnetic testing of sunspots. His heart sank when his inquisitor reached into a pile of documents on his desk and produced a copy of his service records. "You deny," the North Korean yelled angrily, "what is written here in your own official documentation?" "I deny your interpretation of it," the American responded. Suddenly, the guards swarmed over him with a series of kicks, punches, and karate chops that knocked him to the floor, while in the background an interpreter translated the major's running commentary: "Sonabitchy criminal! Goddamned liar! Spydog!"[18]

While Bucher was being beaten, guards brought the rest of the officers to a conference room at the end of the hall. The captain soon joined them, dragged in by two DPRK soldiers. The men took seats before a North Korean general, who quickly launched into an extended diatribe composed mostly of berating the United States for spying. When the harangue ended, he turned his full attention to the six American prisoners. "Will you admit you were spying?" he demanded suddenly. "That you violated our coastal waters?" "No," Bucher answered. "We were operating on the high seas." The rest of the officers echoed this response. After a tense pause, the general asked again, and received the same unanimous reply. With an ominous glare, the North Korean addressed them slowly and precisely. "If that is your persist [*sic*] then you will all be shot this afternoon. Would you like to be shot one at a time or all together?" Bucher leaped to his feet. "I demand that you shoot me and let the rest of the crew go back to the United States on their ship," he declared. "There was no question," Murphy recalled, "about the skipper's sincerity. He meant every word he said." Bucher's suggestion was lost on the general, who merely ordered him to sit down. "You will be shot," he repeated, "before sundown."[19]

Shaken, the officers returned to their rooms, where a small meal of hot water and an unidentifiable vegetable waited; Bucher even got a few cookies and a pitcher of milk. The food brought a glimmer of hope. The quality was wretched by American standards, but it seemed unlikely that the Koreans would feed them hours before they were to be shot. Once again, the men collected their thoughts while Bucher received all the attention. This time, guards delivered him to a North Korean colonel, who appeared to be in charge of the confinement. After delivering a lengthy lecture, the colonel, whom the men soon nicknamed "Super C," handed Bucher a typed confession admitting to espionage operations on behalf of the CIA. "You must sign confession now," Super C ordered through an interpreter. Bucher shoved it back, saying, "I will sign nothing." "Then," replied Super C, "[you] must take the consequence of refusing to cooperate." At the colonel's order, guards led Bucher to his room, where they took turns throwing him against the walls until he collapsed on the floor, bleeding and only semiconscious.

Such beatings continued throughout the day, until Bucher met with Super C again in the evening. "We have proof," the colonel screamed at him, "that you were spying on our country." He slammed down another confession. "Sign this," he ordered. Bucher refused. "You have exactly two minutes to decide to sign," the North Korean yelled, "or then be shot." Two guards wrenched Bucher from his chair and forced him to his knees. One unsheathed a pistol and placed it in the captain's ear. Tension filled the room. "I love you, Rose," Bucher muttered over and over in the ominous silence. Time elapsed quickly, and the North Korean again turned to his prisoner. "Are you ready to sign?" he asked. Bucher shook his head. Super C's voice exploded: "Kill the sonabitchi!" The guard pulled the trigger, and the metallic snap of an empty cartridge echoed in the American's ear. "Well," the colonel exclaimed, "that was a misfire. Very lucky. So then take another two minutes—a last chance to confess without trusting to luck again." Again, Bucher refused to sign, leaving his tormentor howling with rage, "You are not worth a good bullet!" Turning to the guards, he issued another order: "Beat him to death." "This one," Bucher recalled, "he came to within an inch of making good." Soldiers descended with a flurry of blows to his kidneys, stomach, testicles, and the small of his back until, mercifully, he lost consciousness.[20]

It was not long before he awoke in bed, unable to move. Guards soon took him by car to a nearby building. Once inside, Super C led him to the basement and then pointed toward a wall. "This is a South Korean spy we have caught," he exclaimed. "Look at his just punishment!" Instinctively, Bucher turned in the direction of the colonel's gesture. There, in a corner of the barren room, was a man hanging six feet above the floor, suspended by a leather strap around his chest that connected to an iron fixture in the wall. Three spotlights illuminated him as the alleged spy twitched, jerked, and frothed from his mouth, with one eyeball dangling from its socket and a lower lip hanging in shreds. Dark bruises covered his torso, and pieces of bone protruded through flesh where one of his arms had clearly been broken. Transfixed, Bucher stared at the man while his captors loudly boasted of their feat. It was too much to absorb, and once again the captain of the *Pueblo* felt consciousness slipping away from him. When he awoke, he was back in the Barn with Super C standing over him. "So now you have seen for yourself how we treat spies," the North Korean declared. "Perhaps you will reconsider your refusal to confess?" Bucher shook his head. The two sparred for a few minutes until the colonel lost his patience. "We will now begin to shoot your crew," he exclaimed angrily. "We will shoot them one at a time, right here in front of your eyes so that you can see them die. We will shoot them all, starting with the youngest one first and so on, sonabitchy, until you sign [the] confession. And if you have not signed it when they are all dead, then we still have ways of making you do it, and all your crew will be dead for nothing. So that's what we mean about you being responsible for their lives. You are not sincere. We now bring in the crew member Bland [Fireman Howard Bland] to be shot."[21]

While a guard fetched Bland, Bucher's dazed mind searched for answers. The crewmen were more to him than just subordinates; they were, a friend later wrote, "like sons to him and he was like a father, and the idea of giving them up, like he had been given up when he was a kid, was very hard."[22] No solutions were forthcoming. "This dilemma," he concluded, "was beyond my training as a naval officer, as captain of a ship, as a human being with deeply ingrained sensitivity for his fellow men." The image of the tortured South Korean remained burned in his mind; how could he condemn his men to a similar fate just to avoid signing an obviously fabricated document? The battle of wills was over. After thirty-six hours, the North Koreans had won. Bucher turned toward Super C. "All right," he muttered. "I will sign."[23]

The confession the North Koreans brought him was surprisingly restrained. It admitted that the ship had committed aggressive actions against North Korea on behalf of the CIA but made no mention of intelligence gathering, espionage, or violations of DPRK territorial waters. This was not an oversight but the standard interrogation technique of beginning with a relatively inoffensive demand, thus allowing the victim to rationalize his participation more easily. Then, once this mental hurdle was overcome, the captors could easily increase their demands until they obtained their real objective. After Bucher signed the first letter, Super C returned with another, slightly stronger in its criticism of the United States. Again Bucher signed. Shortly thereafter, Super C brought another, then another. After a few hours, Bucher endorsed the final version and then, at Super C's command, copied it over in his own handwriting. "I am Commander Lloyd Mark Bucher," it began, "Captain of the USS *Pueblo* . . . who was captured while carrying out espionage activities after intruding deep into the territorial waters of the Democratic People's Republic of Korea. . . . Having been captured now, I say frankly that our act was a criminal act which flagrantly violated the armistice agreement, and it was a sheer act of aggression. . . . Therefore, we only hope, and it is the greatest desire of myself and my crew, that we will be forgiven leniently by the government of the Democratic People's Republic of Korea."[24] Super C was pleased with the confession. So, it seems, were the North Korean authorities, who released it to the Korean Central News Agency and Radio Pyongyang for broadcast within a few days, and on February 1, it appeared in the *Pyongyang Times*.[25]

Bucher's confession was, on the most obvious level, a defeat for the American prisoners and a triumph for the propaganda efforts of their captors. Yet on a deeper level, it was also the first example of the *Pueblo* men finding a place for covert resistance within overt submission. Recognizing that eventually the DPRK torture would break him, the commander gave them the statement they wanted but tried to do so in a manner that undermined its credibility. Bucher could not change the content, since it had been written for him, but his captors demanded that he add some brief biographical information at the beginning. He complied but provided a false age and serial number, errors overlooked by the North Koreans but not by the Johnson administration, which recognized them as hints that he had not acted of his own free will.[26] On a practical level, such actions were almost meaningless; they did not help end the crew's captivity, improve the conditions of their imprisonment, or impair Super C's ability to obtain propaganda. Yet, by exercising some degree of control in an impossible situation, Bucher maintained a sense of pride and a belief in himself that not only helped him survive but also helped him lead the crew through the difficult months to come.

After Bucher signed the final confession, Super C gave him another task. "You will be present at a press conference exactly thirty minutes from now," he ordered. Thoughtfully, the colonel also provided the questions that Bucher would be asked and the responses that he should give. At the appointed time, guards returned him to the conference room, which was filled with Korean military officers and journalists. After Bucher admitted his crimes, his captors invited inquiries from the audience. On cue, journalists leaped from chairs and read questions from their scripts with righteous indignation. "Did the United States Central Intelligence Agency," read one journalist with a voice full of rage, "not promise that if this task was done successfully, a lot of dollars would be offered the crew members of your ship and particularly yourself would be much honored?" Bucher's reply came mechanically from his text: "The United States Central Intelligence Agency promised me that if this task was done successfully, a lot of dollars would be offered the crew members of my ship and particularly I myself would be much honored." Reporters muttered to each other and shook their heads in disgust. The obviously choreographed performance satisfied no international standards of journalism, but such standards were irrelevant to Kim, who wasted little time releasing the transcripts to numerous DPRK papers.[27]

Bucher's confession and press conference were merely the first in a long line of similar propaganda efforts orchestrated by the North Koreans. Guards started questioning Murphy on January 25, with physical attacks beginning two days later. They forced him to kneel with his arms elevated above his shoulders and square wooden sticks wedged behind his knees, and took turns beating him. "I chose death," he later recalled, "but quickly learned that Korcoms [Korean communists] were going to make me just wish I was dead." Guards revived him after he finally lost consciousness and then repeated the exercise while forcing him to hold a heavy wooden chair above his head. He wrote his first confession on January 29, which Super C rejected because it did not admit to any violations of DPRK waters. The colonel demanded a new version, and Murphy's refusal ignited another wave of beatings. Six times guards battered him into unconsciousness; six times they revived him and started anew. Finally he gave in and agreed to confess. After signing a few revised statements, he returned to his room, taking some satisfaction from the knowledge that the document was full of stilted English that he hoped would reveal how it had been derived. "Bad grammar, incorrect usage," he recalled, "I put it all down, hoping every word would get through and cast doubts on every bit of 'proof' offered by the North Koreans." This insight helped his mental state but not his physical pain; it would be two months before the executive officer could again bend his back.[28]

In the end, all the officers succumbed to North Korean brutality. Gene Lacy lasted the longest, agreeing to sign a statement in early February after guards stripped him naked and forced him to sit on a hot radiator. Tim Harris lasted almost as long, but eventually the same tactics persuaded him to cooperate. Working from an outline provided by his captors, Harris produced an innocuous four-page statement that Super C rejected and then wrote an eight-page one that received the same response. After two more hours of intense beatings, he agreed to provide whatever they wanted. "What I wanted to do," he later admitted, "was take my life."[29] Steve Harris signed a confession on January 30, which Radio Pyongyang broadcast three days later. His beatings had been relatively mild, but, combined with the threat to kill the CTs under his command, they had been enough.[30]

The confessions all followed a similar pattern, stressing the ship's intrusions, the brave capture by the DPRK, and the crew's repentance. Schumacher's, which came only after his attempt to commit suicide failed, was typical; the *Pueblo*, it admitted, was "carrying out military espionage activities, having intruded deep into the coastal waters of the Democratic People's Republic of Korea." After fourteen paragraphs detailing these activities, the statement asked for mercy. "What I have done . . . can never be tolerated. I humbly beg of you to forgive me my crime." Guards forced Schumacher to read the statement before a DPRK camera crew, and on February 1, it appeared in the *Pyongyang Times*.[31] The men did take some solace in the fact that they had not provided much top-secret information, which, in reality, reflected more a lack of interest by their tormentors than their own bravery. "The North Koreans," recalled Murphy, "seemed far more intent on getting us to agree to their version of the facts than digging to find the real truth. Propaganda, not intelligence, seemed their main interest."[32]

Once the officers had capitulated, the North Koreans turned their attention to the enlisted men. Guards brought personal history forms to every room, demanding that each man provide such basic information as name, hometown, education, background, and years of naval service. Since all these facts could be obtained from the prisoners' service records, it was clear that the exercise was intended as a test of wills. At first, the men resisted. Some refused to do them at all; a few provided only name, rank, and serial number; and others filled the forms with false information. Retribution for such acts was immediate. Dale Rigby, who declined to reveal any information, was beaten with a wooden table leg until it broke over his back, forcing the guards to use a block of wood two inches thick. After four hours, Rigby agreed to complete the form but filled it with lies until a few more hours of beatings persuaded him to cooperate. North Korean soldiers pummeled Charles Law with a four-foot-wide board and forced a naked Charles Ayling to crawl on his knees while they took turns kicking him; when he fell, they stomped on him with their heavy boots.[33] Lawrence Mack was beaten so badly that he asked his torturers to shoot him, and only after they refused did he agree to cooperate. "All I could see," he explained, "was unending torture."[34] Others received the same gun ploy that had been used on Bucher—a pistol placed near their heads that always misfired at the crucial moment (evidently, either the North Koreans thought that this was a particularly effective means of breaking someone's will, or they had only one broken gun that all the guards shared). Even the strongest crewman was no match for DPRK cruelty. Robert Hammond, a tough marine with training in resistance techniques, put up the fiercest struggle. Hammond had concealed his knowledge of the Korean language on the personal history forms, but his service record revealed the truth. Guards beat him unmercifully for six hours until he admitted it, and then, to make an example, they continued the torture for another eleven hours. When they finished, recalled one of Hammond's roommates, "I couldn't recognize him because his face was all swelled out of proportion. His face consisted of five colors: black, blue, yellow, red, and some patches of white. His eyes were so swollen that he could barely see out of them. The next day, when Hammond undressed, I saw the rest of his body, and his sides, back, underside of his arms, and parts of his leg were completely red, not like after a slap but red like blood underneath the skin and swollen to twice their size."[35]

Like the officers, the men broke under North Korean brutality, leaving most of them feeling guilty and ashamed. Yet they quickly put these thoughts behind them and turned to more practical matters of survival. Their ability to do so stemmed from the recognition that direct confrontation with their captors was futile and only postponed the inevitable. "What information they wanted," recalled Mack, "they were going to get from me one way or another, and they could get it from me hard or get it from me easy . . . but they were going to use torture or whatever was necessary to get it."[36] Having accepted this, the men had two options. They could either completely yield to the North Korean demands or adopt more subtle forms of resistance. They chose the latter. For the next eleven months, the *Pueblo* crewmen sustained themselves through surreptitious challenges to their captors' authority. Many of these actions were so subtle that they could be easily overlooked by anyone unwilling to accept the idea that resistance could exist on other than an overt level. Three psychological studies of the crew, for example, which were based on interviews conducted immediately after their release and again three months later, assumed that since the prisoners had acceded to DPRK demands, they had offered no resistance at all.[37] Instead, these analyses suggested, the men had survived only by using psychological defense mechanisms such as emotional isolation, denial, or rationalization. Had the authors considered the use of symbolic protest, however, the studies might have recognized that the crew's survival stemmed not from avoiding their subjugation but from challenging it on the only level available.

The prisoners' situation began to improve after the first few weeks of captivity. Beatings declined, and the guards distributed toothpaste, soap, cigarettes, and even some reading material, which generally consisted of DPRK propaganda such as the writings of Kim Il Sung and old copies of the *Pyongyang Times*. By mid-February, Barn life had settled into a routine. Guards woke the men each morning before dawn, usually by slamming doors, screaming threats, and dispensing random blows with their rifles. Each room received five minutes in the bathroom, where the three clogged sinks, four urinals, and three toilets were all badly cracked and leaking. After breakfast, soldiers took a few crewmen to the interrogation rooms at the end of the hallway while the rest remained seated in their rooms. Sleeping, talking, looking out the window, and lying on the bed were punishable offenses. The same schedule followed lunch and dinner, until the men went to bed at 10 P.M.

The monotony was almost unbearable. Lights remained on at all times, even at night, and doors and windows remained shut. All prisoners wore the same outfit, which consisted of dark blue uniforms, heavy pants, long underwear, and fur hats with earflaps; in honor of the caps, the men dubbed the attire "CBOs"—Charlie Brown outfits. Communication with other crewmen was strictly forbidden, and although a few words passed secretly, silence was an ever-present companion. Meals usually consisted of turnip soup or turnips with rice, sometimes complemented with bread or raw fish that the crew referred to as "filet of sewer trout." The provisions, estimated the ship's cook, contained roughly 500 calories per day, although that did not include the nutritional value of the occasional tooth, bug, or even eyeball that found its way onto their plates.

Still, the men would gladly have chosen the boredom over the beatings. "The loneliness was bad," recalled Murphy, "but the not knowing was worse. Not knowing whether the footsteps in the hall meant they were coming for you. Not knowing if an interrogation session might be the last."[38] Torture continued for a variety of reasons beyond the regular interrogations, especially for perceived violations of prison rules. For falling asleep, Earl Kisler was forced to stand at attention while a DPRK officer administered a ninety-minute beating, and for asking to go to the bathroom before it was officially time to awake, he received a kick to the groin that left him paralyzed for ten minutes. Even the smallest offenses—a wrinkled bed, a poorly timed smile, a torn article of clothing—could invoke a guard's wrath. Occasionally, guards beat prisoners simply for their own amusement. One soldier ordered Fireman Michael O'Bannon to read a book written in Korean and Russian, then pummeled him with the wooden handle of a flyswatter when he was unable to comply.

With confessions and personal history forms in hand, the North Koreans began issuing new propaganda demands. Press conferences, usually resembling the one Bucher had conducted in January, were not uncommon. The first one to involve numerous crewmen occurred on February 13, when Super C summoned the ship's officers and oceanographer Donnie Tuck to one of the interrogation rooms, where they faced an audience of North Korean journalists and photographers that included representatives from *Nodong Sinmun,* the Korean Central News Agency, and the Korean Central Broadcasting Committee. The men had received the questions in advance and were given time to devise acceptable responses. For five hours the *Pueblo* men droned on about the courage of the Korean government, the strength of the Korean military, and the greatness of the Korean people. "My impression, as commanding officer," declared Bucher, "has been that the Democratic People's Republic of Korea is very progressive and has a gentlemanly and understanding people." Radio Pyongyang broadcast the conference on February 15, and the *Pyongyang Times* reprinted it the following week under the heading "Officers of the US Imperialist Armed Spy Ship Reaffirm Brigandish Acts of Aggression of US Imperialists Bent on Preparation for Another War on Korea."[39]

Although the press conference helped Kim demonstrate his *juche,* it also helped his American prisoners. For the first time since the initial hours in the

Barn, the officers knew that the rest of the ship's wardroom was still alive. The press conference also offered them the first chance to engage in a collective act of symbolic resistance by exploiting their captors' inability to understand the nuances of the American language. Skip Schumacher delivered his answers in stilted English and a singsong voice that mocked the coaching of his North Korean trainer, and Bucher informed the audience that they had "committed a grave crime . . . for which we are deeply shy." Murphy intentionally missed a cue, and when praising his captors' "gentlemanliness," he moved his upper body as stiffly as possible, revealing his inability to bend his back. The North Koreans, satisfied that the officers were reading their scripts as ordered, paid no attention to these minor acts, but the men considered them evidence that they could still exert some control. "There was no doubt," Murphy recalled, "the North Koreans would get some propaganda mileage out of it. Yet, petty though our tricks were, for us they marked a new beginning. We were still alive, still capable of a united effort to thwart our captors. If nothing else, that alone was tremendously encouraging."[40]

The day after the press conference, Super C again called the officers together. This time, he demanded that they compose a letter of apology to the Korean people. The Americans formed a drafting committee, which produced a letter within a few days. The colonel approved it only after changing it so dramatically that it barely resembled the original product. "We, the whole crew of the USS *Pueblo*," it began, "frankly admit and truly repent our serious crimes. We hereby submit a joint letter of apology in order to request the government of the Democratic People's Republic of Korea to deal with us leniently." After following the standard format of admitting that they had been ordered to commit espionage, apologizing for their violations of DPRK territory, and calling for the American government to provide the three A's, the letter praised their captors. "The government of the Democratic People's Republic of Korea has treated us in such a humanitarian way that there is little difference between our present life and our life before our detention, except for our guilty consciences as criminals."[41] CT Elliot Wood, chosen because of his neat penmanship, copied Super C's version over in his own handwriting, and on February 16, guards dragged each crewman out of bed to sign the letter while DPRK cameras clicked furiously in the background. That evening, the statement reached a domestic audience by way of Radio Pyongyang, and the next day it went out to international audiences.[42]

A few days later, Super C announced a similar project: a personal letter to Lyndon Johnson. Again, he ordered the officers to compose it, and this time they produced a document that met his expectations, thus avoiding corrections. Subtly, however, they included hints and phrases intended to demonstrate that they had been coerced. "Our principal aim," Bucher recalled, "[was] to insert words which hopefully would get through to our own intelligence people."[43] The finished product contained various grammatical errors and used hyperbole to mock the Korean demands; in one dramatic moment, the letter described Bucher marching into the pilothouse and exclaiming to Schumacher, "All right, mister! Let's intrude and provocate!"[44] The linguistic tricks escaped Super C's attention but not that of his superiors, who ordered that another version be prepared. In late February, the officers completed a revised letter, largely devoid of subterfuge, which the North Koreans accepted. Again, Super C demanded that it be signed by the entire crew. Some declined but quickly reversed their positions when Earl Kisler, after his refusal, returned from an interrogation session "with his head," according to one roommate, "looking like hamburger and three times its normal size."[45] On March 4, General Pak handed the letter to Admiral Smith, along with another one from Bucher assuring its authenticity; that same day, it was broadcast over Radio Pyongyang.[46]

The crew's treatment improved in late February. With the men cooperating, the North Koreans had little need for extended torture sessions and instead began enforcing the rules with quick-strike discipline. "A swift kick in the shins or a rabbit punch," Kisler recalled, "became as natural to this crew as breakfast and the morning paper are to most Americans."[47] The solitude declined as well. On the night of February 24, guards herded the men into a nearby stadium, where, despite the snow and freezing winds, Charles Law led them in calisthenics. A few days later, they were granted thirty minutes for daily recreation, during which time they could gather in the third-floor lobby to play cards or Ping-Pong. Within weeks, a regular outdoor exercise period was added, during which the men could play volleyball, football, and basketball; baseball, however, was forbidden, because Japan had forced it on the Koreans during their years of occupation.

Conditions relaxed even further in March, when the crew was relocated to a new home closer to Pyongyang.[48] The facility, which the men dubbed "the Country Club," was a three-story marble building that had been constructed, according to the guards, "to last a hundred generations." A fifteen-foot wall ran the entire length of the courtyard, which was dominated by a billboard that portrayed a North Korean soldier standing over a cowering American prisoner. Inside, the floors were marble and pristine, with a spiral staircase and paintings of Kim Il Sung gracing the walls. The men were led to the upper two floors, where guards dispensed new room assignments. Enlisted men were divided into groups of four or eight, while the officers again lived by themselves. It was still a prison, but it was a more hospitable one whose rooms came equipped not only with beds, tables, and chairs but also with wash pans, closets, mirrors, large tables, night tables with drawers, and two light fixtures that could be extinguished at night. Jack Warner dutifully recorded the crew's pleasure with their new quarters, and Super C even ordered the officers to reenact their first press conference so that the films would display the more lavish facilities in the background.

The routine continued to improve throughout the spring and summer. A second outdoor exercise period was added, giving the crew a short one every morning and a longer one in the afternoon. A large room on the third floor served as a mess hall, bringing the men together for meals in one of two twenty-minute shifts. For recreation, they could choose among cards, chess, Ping-Pong, and any number of games they had invented using the chess boards and pieces. Various "classes" were offered: James Shepard and Don Peppard taught German, Peter Langenberg taught Japanese and Russian, Victor Escamilla taught Spanish, and Charles Ayling taught algebra. Aspiring card players could learn pinochle from Lacy or bridge from Bucher and Schumacher. Some men exchanged homemade crossword puzzles; others played shuffleboard with coins; still others carved figures with the small pocketknives the guards had distributed after the move. Tim Harris spent hours playing an imaginary guitar, and Seaman Stephen Ellis worked on his golf swing. The cooks mentally planned elaborate meals; Lacy built and disassembled cars in his head; and Schumacher designed a new home, although he had second thoughts after Bucher warned him about the high property taxes. Debate swirled around who would play them in the movie; general agreement was reached on Troy Donahue for Tim Harris and Lee Marvin for Commander Bucher.

Part of the routine was devoted to "reeducation." The men spent at least one hour each day in self-examination, during which time they were expected to contemplate the teachings of Kim Il Sung and the banality of their own society. Each room also had an assigned propaganda officer, who led group discussions usually twice weekly for four hours. North Korean officers imparted political lectures, almost always focusing on the flaws of American society. Among other topics, the commentaries addressed the treatment of American minorities, the vast power of the CIA, and the assassinations of Robert Kennedy and Martin Luther King (which, Super C explained, had been arranged by LBJ in order to "make sure wars and provocations against peace-loving peoples of Socialist Republics continue"). Friday night movies became a regular event, with plots almost always involving the triumph of North Korean peasants over American imperialists. The stories rarely varied: the girl fell in love with her job at the factory, the boy fell in love with his rifle and new farm equipment (usually played by a bright red tractor), both fell in love with Kim Il

Sung, and in the end they devoted themselves to the twin objectives of living in accordance with his teachings and killing as many Americans as possible.

The relaxed rules left the men with more opportunities for subtle forms of resistance. Perhaps most common were their struggles with the rubber tree plants that their captors had placed in each room. The guards considered these plants special signs of Kim's benevolence and demanded that the men provide them with the utmost care. In response, the *Pueblo* sailors declared war, using whatever means necessary to kill these symbols of North Korean control. Tim Harris and Gene Lacy drowned theirs in urine, while Schumacher killed three by tying knots in the vines. Guards brought one of Schumacher's victims to Bucher with an appeal for help; the captain agreed to try to save it and then, over the North Koreans' gasps of protest, quickly whittled it down to a stump with his penknife. "Now," he told them, "it will sleep and conserve its strength."[49]

Men pursued other avenues of symbolic protest. Since the North Koreans had banned baseball, crewmen played kickball with baseball rules and were thrilled to learn that the guards had begun playing it themselves. Obviously, there were few tangible benefits from such a symbolic statement; nevertheless, the mere act of playing their national pastime in direct defiance of their captors' wishes helped preserve the men's identities as Americans and bolstered their pride in the face of an overwhelming and dehumanizing enemy. Similarly, many crew members played an improvised version of Monopoly using cards and a chessboard. Uncomprehending guards watched as the men engaged in a contest, banned in many communist societies, that rewarded the blatant accumulation of capital at the expense of one's comrades. Had the game's true nature been exposed, the men would doubtless have faced severe retribution, but like those who played kick-baseball, the participants found that the psychological rewards of covert defiance outweighed the risks.

Others found different ways to resist. Seaman Richard Rogala used Morse code to spell out at the bottom of his confession, "This is a lie."[50] Many of the men, especially CTs Jerry Karnes, Wayne Anderson, and Peter Langenberg, argued with the guards over the propaganda films and lectures. During interrogations, CTs rambled on about unimportant details of their equipment, trusting that their questioners would be unable to distinguish between what was vital and what was not and would be too afraid of looking foolish to ask. In the fall, the crew's diet improved, with meals that occasionally included treats of apples, canned pork, or potatoes that they could bring to their rooms. One guard, nicknamed "The Fly" for his constant haranguing of the men to kill more flies, continually stole the apples, until the men decided to retaliate. Charles Sterling, Earl Kisler, and Michael Alexander selected a choice apple, pricked it full of tiny holes, then soaked it in urine before returning it to their tray. The next morning, both the apple and The Fly were gone. The Fly returned in a few days looking seriously ill, and the men lost no more apples.

The men also used more subtle forms of insubordination. Window shades that were required to be closed were "accidentally" left open. After Super C revealed a willingness to honor American holidays with better food and a relaxation of the rules, Bucher submitted a list of eighty such days, including Sadie Hawkins Day and Alf Landon Concession Day, some of which the men were allowed to celebrate. Crewmen resisted the guards' attempts to make them march in tandem by purposefully bumping into walls and one another in complete disarray. "Why," asked one exasperated DPRK soldier, "you not march like soldiers?" "We're Americans," replied Chicca. "We just don't walk like you."[51] Language offered other avenues for protest. A remarkable resemblance emerged between the phrases "thank you" and "fuck you." Men also reacted to orders given in clear English as if they were incomprehensible. "Whenever a guard said 'open the door' or 'close the window,'" Tim Harris recalled, "we'd shrug and pretend we didn't understand. . . . This used to drive them out of their skulls."[52] On one occasion, Bucher responded to a command by placing his chair on his table, then his night table on the chair, and then his washbasin on the night table; the exasperated guard finally fled when the captain reached for the bed. Again, such actions had little impact on a practical level. However, by allowing the men to feel that they had, for one fleeting moment, turned the tables against their oppressors, such maneuvers played a crucial role in helping them survive.

Once the crew had settled into the Country Club, Super C orchestrated a new propaganda barrage. This time, he demanded that the men write letters to family, friends, government officials, and media representatives in the United States. A steady stream of letters echoing their earlier confessions poured from the Country Club, offering apologies, admissions of guilt, praise for the DPRK, and appeals for the three A's. Since there was no mail exchange between the two nations, most letters went by diplomatic pouch to communist embassies in Western Europe and were then forwarded to the United States, although some were brought in by communist diplomats and mailed through the American postal system. Within three weeks, the men had sent twenty-four letters, and many more would follow.[53] Typical was one from Stephen Ellis to Congressman George Murphy (R-Calif.) that read, "I believe it is only when my government apologizes will the crew of the *Pueblo* be allowed to return," or another from Ralph Bouden that told his parents, "if our government would admit the intrusions into the territorial waters of the D.P.R.K. and the hostile acts, apologize for them and give the assurance that neither shall ever happen again, the Government of the Democratic People's Republic of Korea might act more favorably toward our repatriation."[54] As usual, Kim shared the statements with his domestic audience; Radio Pyongyang broadcast five letters on March 22, with the editorial comment that leniency would continue only "if the United States imperialists make [a] proper apology to us and give assurances that it will not repeat similar hostile acts."[55]

Refusing to participate was not permissible. To persuade Earl Kisler to write letters, guards beat him with a one-inch-thick wooden stick. After he collapsed on the floor bleeding, they kicked him in the lower back and legs for two hours. When the men were finally released in December, he still had only partial feeling in his right leg.[56] Others suffered similar fates for challenging their captors' directives. Again, the lesson was clear: direct resistance was futile. The crew's next best option was to embrace more subtle methods, giving Kim the propaganda he wanted, but doing so in ways that reflected their determination to assert themselves.

Again, the crew utilized their advantages regarding American language and culture to undercut the letters. Kisler told his parents to say hello to Aunt Jemima, Uncle Ben, and Jack Spratt and his wife. Engineman Rushel Blansett and Commissaryman Harry Lewis asked their wives to do the same to a number of their dead friends.[57] One writer sent greetings to Tom Swift, and another told his wife that the North Koreans were the nicest people he had encountered since his last visit to St. Elizabeth's; St. Elizabeth's, the North Koreans would have been surprised to learn, was a mental institution in Washington. Bucher asked Rose to give his regards to various family members and beseeched her, "don't forget Cythyssa Kroikashit [this is a crock of shit]."[58] Others used awkward phrases to indicate that they were not speaking freely. "Quite distasteful," wrote Murphy to his wife, "are the fruits of our imagination when pondering our plight, should immediate affirmative response not be proffered by the United States government."[59] The recipients usually recognized these hints. Radioman Lee Hayes's mother rejected the idea that her son would use words like "atone" and "gravity" in a letter, and Seaman Richard Rogala's parents confirmed that a letter from their son was written in his handwriting, but they concluded that "the wordings weren't his."[60]

Conditions in the Country Club began to decline as the weather grew warmer. In April, the guards embarked on a flurry of beatings that the crew called the "April Purge," with violence reminiscent of the first few weeks. Since the men offered little direct resistance, guards found other reasons to punish them, beating Schumacher for having a missing button on his shirt and Michael O'Bannon for dumping ashes onto his finished plate, and knocking James Kell unconscious for leaving the mess hall with rice in his mouth. The violence declined as suddenly as it had started, but the tension remained, especially since the guards enjoyed standing outside the men's rooms, loudly predicting which inhabitants would be called next and describing in painful detail what they planned for the interrogation.[61]

Hardships beyond the beatings also existed. The vast number of mosquitoes forced guards to distribute nets for the men to sleep under, and in July, they gave each room flyswatters and an order to kill fifty each day, a target few had difficulty reaching. Flies were so common that the men referred to them as the "National Bird of Korea," although their captors insisted that they were actually American flies dropped on North Korea by American biological warfare experts. The heat drove various animals to seek shelter inside, including a number of huge gray rats. The quality of meals also declined (to the extent that this was possible); in the summer, the men began receiving an unidentifiable green vegetable that vaguely resembled grass. Although no one knew what it was, they soon learned what it did, as most of those who ate it developed internal worms.

Health problems abounded, including diarrhea, fevers, urinary tract problems, skin infections, and pedal edema.[62] The North Koreans displayed little concern for those afflicted; Hayes, for example, received no treatment for a bad case of hepatitis, even when his skin turned a sickly shade of yellow, and Rigby went ignored despite a rash that left 90 percent of his body covered with sores. Dysentery left some of the men with stomach cramps so severe that they occasionally collapsed in the halls, defecating on themselves. When the North Koreans did provide medical attention, the cure was often worse than the disease. Doctors removed shrapnel from Stephen Woelk's wounds early in the confinement, but rather than use anesthesia, they tied his hands behind his head, blindfolded him, and had a nurse sit on his legs. After the operation, a helpless Woelk lay in bed, ignored by the medical staff while his blood soaked the sheets. Finally, guards took him to a nearby hospital, where improved food, changed bandages, and a series of antibiotics restored his health. After six weeks of treatment, Woelk returned to the prison in much better condition, to the delight of the DPRK cameramen who were on hand to film his joyous return.[63] Chicca also had surgery to remove shrapnel; minutes after it ended, doctors forced him to walk back to his room down the hallway. Law, whose eyesight had been better than 20/20 before the confinement, experienced vision problems as a result of an inflamed optic nerve. Doctors treated him by putting pins in his ears to free the evil spirits, but the spirits apparently stayed, since his vision continued to decline. Eventually Super C summoned another doctor, who gave Law thirteen injections into both eyeballs with a three-inch needle, again without the benefit of anesthesia.[64]

While the men suffered, the North Koreans continued to extract propaganda. Letters poured from the Country Club. "Unless the United States does admit and apologize to the Democratic People's Republic of Korea," wrote Boatswain's Mate First Class Robert Klepac to Texas Governor John Connally, "and guarantee that such espionage activities will not happen again, we will be detained here indefinitely and be severely punished."[65] In June, Kim Il Sung released a small book about the crisis entitled *Naked Act of Aggression by U.S. Imperialism against the North Korean People,* which included copies of confessions, ship's documents, and photographs. Unsurprisingly, considering the thoroughness of Kim's efforts to keep the seizure in the public eye, every one of the enclosures had been released previously.[66] In July, thousands of North Koreans flocked to theaters to watch a seventy-minute movie about the incident, which contained pictures of the ship, clips of Bucher reading the joint letter of apology, blurry photos of the *Pueblo*'s altered logbooks, and shots of various crew members happily engaged in their daily routine.[67]

Although they continued to cooperate, the crewmen maintained their pattern of subtle resistance. In June, they watched films of the DPRK soccer team playing in an international tournament in London. In one scene, British fans extended their middle fingers toward the North Korean players, who smiled and bowed in response. The men saw an opportunity. "Did you see that," Law whispered to Escamilla. "These guys don't know what the finger means."[68] When Jack Warner took his picture the next day, Boatswain's Mate Ronald Berens extended a middle finger toward the camera, receiving only a blank stare in return. With their hypothesis confirmed, the crew released a torrent of erect fingers, which, they explained to their confused captors, was a Hawaiian good luck symbol. In August, Warner took a series of photographs of each room; in almost 80 percent of them, the men later estimated, at least one person had an extended middle finger. The gesture became so common that even the Koreans began using it. Before an August press conference, Super C extended his finger toward the men, telling them, "Good luck. I wish you a very successful press conference."[69] The risks of such defiance were obvious. If the North Koreans ever found out what the gesture meant, Law told Bucher, "They'd literally beat the hell out of us." Bucher agreed but refused to stop. If they were discovered, he answered, "We'd lose the battle. But we'd win the war."[70] Both of these predictions eventually proved correct. The North Koreans soon discovered the truth, and as Law had anticipated, they retaliated with unprecedented violence. Yet such small victories inspired the men while at the same time discrediting DPRK propaganda. As Bucher had suggested, they may have lost the battle, but by surviving, they would win the war.

Bucher continued to encourage the men to "goof up the press conferences," which they did with language and gestures. In September, Super C (now also known as "Glorious General" or "GG" for a recent promotion), organized a conference to honor the DPRK's twentieth anniversary, which was attended by seventy members of the international press, including one American, Lionel Martin of the *National Guardian*. To ensure a good performance, the crewmen were given two weeks to compose and practice their answers, and beatings lessened dramatically to guarantee that they appeared healthy. Again, they gave the promised answers but did so in ways that discredited their presentation. Lawrence Mack described a longing for "the bosom of our fatherland," Michael Barrett reported that the only doctor he needed was one "to mend broken hearts," and Ralph McClintock promised that "if I am ever allowed to return to my beloved home and family, I will never commit such a naughty crime again."[71] The reporters, some of whom fell asleep, recognized the event for the sham that it was. "Let's get this suck-ass bullshit over with," groaned the East German representative.[72] The session ended in chaos, as an Afghanistani reporter began screaming that he could not hear, and another loudly demanded that the men be allowed to answer without scripts. When the guard presiding over the conference became confused and halted the event before all the questions had been answered, Bucher leaped to his feet and, as the crowd laughed, insisted that he be allowed to read his closing statement. Despite the many problems, Glorious General was so pleased with the performance that later that night he rewarded the men with a ration of beer. Ironically, while many of the reporters recognized Bucher's actions for what they were, many in the American government did not; Bucher's speech, wrote the CIA in a scathing memo to the White House, "seemed sincere, natural, and from the heart."[73]

Letters and confessions received similar treatment. When GG requested that the men suggest a list of public figures to whom they should send letters, they named Bill Bailey, Billy Sol Estes, Jimmy Hoffa, John Dillinger, and Reverend Dr. Hugh Hefner. In October, Bucher, Schumacher, McClintock, Mack, Steve Harris, and CT Wayne Anderson collaborated on a confession that quoted the Uniform Code of Military Justice's definition of rape, admitting that "neither the frequency nor the distances of these transgressions into the territorial waters of this sovereign peace-loving nation matter, because *penetration, however slight, is sufficient to complete the act.*"[74] They also assured their captors that the men wanted to "paean [pee-on] not just the Korean People's Army, not just the people of North Korea, but the Korean People's government, and most of all, Kim Il-Sung."[75] The following week, the same team produced another confession in which they claimed to have been trained by Buzz Sawyer and given orders by Fleet General Barney Google and intelligence operative Sol Loxfinger; if their mission failed, Google warned, Don Ho would likely give them the dreaded tiny bubbles treatment.

The crew's ordeal thus illuminates some important aspects of the *Pueblo* crisis. Although the men acquiesced to the North Korean demands, they did so only as a result of their captors' brutality, a brutality for which the navy had failed to prepare them. The Code of Conduct not only established guidelines for prisoners but also required that the service branches prepare their soldiers to comply with these rules. "To insure achievement of these standards," the code begins, "each member of the armed forces liable to capture shall be provided with specific training and instruction designed to better equip him to counter and withstand any enemy efforts against him."[76] Yet only one *Pueblo* crewman had received navy instruction in methods of interrogation resistance, and two others had been trained by the marines. This omission, which again reflected the navy's unwarranted belief that this was a minimal risk operation, may not have proved significant in the face of such extreme violence. "The harsh reality of this kind of captivity," wrote Schumacher, "is that pain can make you do anything."[77] Yet, one must wonder if the outcome would have been different had the entire crew been better prepared, especially considering that the three prisoners with resistance training proved to be among the best at opposing DPRK authority. It seems reasonable to assume that even if the torture had still broken the men, such preparation might at least have made it easier for them to survive. Hence, only by considering the brutality of their imprisonment and the navy's failure to live up to its own obligation can one achieve a balanced judgment about the crew's conduct.

Furthermore, a close study of the crew's behavior suggests that, despite their cooperation in the North Korean propaganda efforts, the men never fully capitulated to DPRK demands. The first few weeks of captivity convinced them of the futility of overt resistance; their captors were simply too powerful, too brutal, and too full of hate to be defied. To avoid total subjugation, the men adopted subtle forms of insubordination that were typical of repressed segments in societies. James Scott, in a study of Malaysian peasant resistance, explains these tactics in words that can apply equally to American slaves, Russian serfs, or navy sailors trapped in a North Korean prison camp. "Open subordination," he concludes, "in almost any context will provoke a more rapid and ferocious response than an insubordination that may be as pervasive but never ventures to contest the formal definitions of hierarchy and power. For most subordinate classes, which, as a matter of sheer history, have had little prospect of improving their status, this form of resistance has been the only option. What may be accomplished within this symbolic straitjacket is nonetheless something of a testament to human perseverance and inventiveness."[78] So it was for the *Pueblo* men. Direct challenges to DPRK authority left them near death, without helping to rebuff their captors' demands. Subtle forms of resistance, conversely, not only undercut the legitimacy of the North Korean propaganda but also preserved the crew's pride and self-confidence by demonstrating that they still maintained some control over their fate. By doing so, these seemingly minor actions proved crucial to their survival.

Finally, a close examination of the crew's ordeal reinforces the idea that *juche* was the driving force behind the seizure. Almost every aspect of their captivity seemed intended to demonstrate Kim's wisdom and strength to the North Korean people. Confessions, apologies, and letters were almost always released to a domestic audience. Jack Warner filmed virtually everything the men did—bathing, eating, reading, playing sports—except when such pictures would have reflected badly on their treatment. Despite the frequency and the fervor of the torture, guards took care not to leave visible marks on men who would soon be in the public eye. For eleven months, the *Pueblo* crewmen seemed to have only one function, to serve as public reminders of Kim's action. "Almost every day or every other day," recalled Bucher, "I was taken before cameras for one reason or another."[79]

In the end, nothing the men did hindered Kim's objective. In this sense, the North Korean leader triumphed by obtaining exactly what he wanted—evidence of *juche* for use in domestic propaganda. Yet on another level, the crewmen also won. In the face of a ubiquitous force bent on crushing their spirits and reducing them to propaganda machines, they offered a surreptitious resistance that allowed them to undercut DPRK propaganda abroad and, more important, fostered a pride and self-confidence that enabled them to survive eleven months of torment. Criticism for cooperating with the enemy seems somewhat unreasonable, considering that the crew had no training in resistance techniques, no means of escape, and no signs of the promised response coming from the United States. "None of us wanted to do what we had to do over there," explained Schumacher. "It became a question of what we could do in the form of resistance."[80]

Bucher led the insurgency. "We couldn't have asked for a better captain," recalled Fireman Michael O'Bannon. "He never gave the impression of being depressed."[81] Stu Russell agreed: "He alone, I think, pulled everybody through it. He was a giant, and we'd follow him anywhere."[82] It was Bucher who most often feigned incomprehension at orders, Bucher who led the barrage of double-talk and innuendo, Bucher who repeatedly delivered the Hawaiian good-luck symbol, Bucher who baffled the guards with his mysterious bouts of "lockjaw," which left him unable to open his mouth for days. Schumacher offered perhaps the best encomium: "I found depth and cunning and intelligence in his quick-wittedness. He used all this equipment, often at his own personal peril, to help his men. He pumped fight back into his beaten crew. By force of his own example, he restored their emotional life, their pride in being American navy men."[83]

However, leadership existed throughout the ranks. Many prisoners singled out Charles Law for his ability to lift his shipmates' spirits.[84] Law, along with Hammond, Escamilla, Berens, Hayes, and Chief Engineman Monroe Goldman, voluntarily took beatings for those who were injured or sick. Corpsman First Class Herman Baldridge defied DPRK orders by providing medical care to injured crewmen. Angelo Strano and Hayes risked certain beatings by attempting to build a radio from spare parts; Strano's first attempt to magnetize a nail to act as the voice coil in the speaker succeeded only in causing the prison's lights to flicker, sending guards searching for the faulty fuse. When finally confiscated in the winter, the radio needed only one more piece to be operational. Stilted English, urine-filled apples, and kick-baseball clearly could not equal the impact of belt buckles, clubs, and radiators, but they could do just enough to dissuade the men from complete collapse and inspire them to continue subtly undercutting the DPRK propaganda efforts. "We saw," recalled Schumacher, "the difference between having something or nothing to live for, between hanging on and giving up."[85] They chose to hang on.

CHAPTER NINE

At the Brink

A thousand "Go Minhs"
We gave for our sins;
Still here we sit and that's awful.
But if we get back,
No coins will we lack,
So beware all ye banks, bars, and brothels!

For Lyndon Johnson, 1968 was a year of hardship and frustration. The war in Vietnam raged on with no end in sight, while the War on Poverty drowned in a sea of political bickering and domestic unrest. "Together," noted Senator William Fulbright, "the two wars have set in motion a process of deterioration in American society." Summer race riots inflicted more damage on the District of Columbia than had the War of 1812, which saw the British burn the Capitol building and president's mansion to the ground. A serious balance-of-payments problem, complicated by a dangerous run on the gold market, threatened the stability of the dollar; in April, the chairman of the Federal Reserve Board raised the discount rate to its highest point in forty years, glumly commenting that "the nation is in the midst of the worst financial crisis since 1931." In Czechoslovakia, Soviet troops brutally crushed a growing independence movement, and in Guatemala, Ambassador John Gordon Mein became the first American ambassador assassinated in his host country. The turmoil dispirited even the usually optimistic President Johnson, especially as his approval rating dropped to 35 percent in September, the lowest of his tenure. "Americans looking back on 1968," he proclaimed at the annual Thanksgiving breakfast, "may be more inclined to ask God's mercy and guidance than to offer him thanks for his blessings."[1]

LBJ had first come to Washington in 1931 as the private secretary to Texas Congressman Richard Kleburg and had watched in admiration as a Democratic president addressed the problems of the depression with a flurry of activity and conviction. More than thirty years later, Johnson tackled the problems of the 1960s much as Franklin Roosevelt had tackled those of the 1930s, unleashing an unprecedented wave of legislation and social programs that reflected his confidence in the ability of the American government to solve the nation's woes. Despite his efforts, however, the problems not only refused to disappear but steadily worsened. Johnson had done more to advance the cause of civil rights for African Americans than any of his predecessors, yet the first nine months of 1967 saw 164 race riots resulting in 77 deaths, 4,000 arrests, and nearly half a billion dollars of damage. In 1965, LBJ had predicted that the war in Vietnam would be "like a filibuster—enormous resistance at first, then a steady whittling away, then Ho hurrying to get it over." Three years later, American troop strength in Vietnam had passed 500,000, yet barely a hint of a solution existed.[2]

Meanwhile, American congressmen slowly turned their backs on Johnson's domestic reforms. In the summer of 1968, the House of Representatives refused to even debate his request for $20 million to exterminate rats in poor neighborhoods throughout the country. These failures tormented the president's final year in the White House. "As I look back over the crowded diaries listing the telephone calls and meetings of 1968," he later wrote, "as I reread the daily headlines that jumped so steadily and forebodingly from one trouble spot to another, as I review the memos and the intelligence reports, I recall vividly the frustration and genuine anguish I experienced so often during the final year of my administration. I sometimes felt that I was living in a continuous nightmare."[3]

The *Pueblo* Incident both typified and contributed to this frustration. "If I had to pick a day that symbolized the turmoil we experienced throughout 1968," LBJ later wrote, "I think January 23 would be the day—the morning the USS *Pueblo* was seized."[4] Once again, Johnson found himself desperately seeking a solution to a crisis that seemed impervious to all his efforts. He was willing, the president told an aide, to "do anything to get those men back—including meeting naked in the middle of the street at high noon."[5] Yet his attempts to free the crew led down the same path as his attempts to solve the other problems—toward frustration, depression, and failure. By no traditional definition of power could North Korea be considered America's equal; in 1968, for example, the entire DPRK army numbered 345,000 men, almost 200,000 fewer than the United States had fighting in Vietnam. Yet Kim Il Sung continued to reject every American proposal while clinging to the three A's demand: admit, apologize, and assure. In accordance with the three-pronged strategy adopted on January 29—avoid another conflict in Asia, maintain South Korea's commitment to Vietnam, and obtain a speedy return of the men—the administration proved unable to force Kim toward any middle ground, as the commitment to the first two goals continued to undercut its ability to achieve the third. "In spite of every effort we could make," Johnson lamented, "in spite of our patient attempts to balance firmness with reason, and in spite of our innumerable diplomatic moves, eleven miserable months went by before the men of the *Pueblo* were given their freedom. Every day that passed during those eleven months, the plight of those men obsessed and haunted me."[6]

The administration's attempts to use international pressures to end the crisis continued but produced few reasons for optimism. Vice President Hubert Humphrey suggested including the incident in negotiations concerning the Vietnam War. "This [the *Pueblo*] is tied in with it," he explained. "It may be that it [release] will be part and parcel of the total negotiated settlement." The next day, a North Vietnamese spokesman rejected the idea, explaining that there was "no possible connection" between the two.[7] Suggestions trickled in from such international bodies as the United Nations and the World Court, but Kim had already rebuffed their involvement in any capacity. Accordingly, the American government pursued them more for the sake of public relations than from any real expectation of success.[8] Moscow continued to apply covert pressure but, despite LBJ's urging, declined to take any public position or coordinate its efforts with the United States; the Soviet Union, explained the Soviet ambassador, was "really in no position to give advice on the *Pueblo* problem."[9] By late February, the administration recognized that it had virtually no control over the negotiation process. The only solution Kim would accept involved lengthy MAC talks that culminated in the three A's. Unless LBJ abandoned the three-point plan that formed the basis of his negotiating strategy, there appeared to be little the United States could do to change the situation.

Throughout the winter, Smith continued to present compromises involving third-party mediation, which Pak continued to reject. The administration quickly recognized that despite the initial optimism about MAC talks, no easy solution would be forthcoming, since, complained Ambassador Porter, the DPRK showed "very little evidence of give [and] . . . no willingness to concede to US position."[10] Accordingly, the frequency of the meetings began to decline. The two sides met in Panmunjom nine times in the first month of the crisis but only twice in April, twice in May, and once each in June, July, and August. Thirteen meetings had occurred in the first 65 days; it would take another 263 days for the next thirteen. North Korean negotiator Pak's courtesy declined as well. "I cannot help asking you," he noted at a March meeting, "for what purpose on earth do you think we meet here? . . . The crew of the *Pueblo* are the criminals, caught in the very act while conducting espionage activities and committing hostile acts after illegally intruding into the territorial waters of the Democratic People's Republic of Korea. . . . Do you believe that you can compel us to accept such an unwarrantable claim? If you really believe it, it would be the height of folly of you."[11] Three days later, as the two sides adjourned from another bitter session, Pak glared across the room at Smith. "Just wait," he warned. "You'll find your head chopped off."[12]

Still, the administration could not abandon the MAC channel, regardless of North Korean obstinacy, since it was the only forum where Kim would negotiate. In late February, Pak sent Admiral Smith a secret message warning that the American proposals had been insufficient and that his government might place the crew on trial under DPRK law unless a better offer was tendered soon.[13] Pak reiterated this threat at a MAC meeting the following week, warning that if the United States did not provide a solution based on the three A's, his government "would have no alternative but to take another step."[14] Although publicly discounting such statements, the administration was concerned. "We fear," concluded a State Department report, "this means to place crewmembers on trial."[15]

This anxiety, combined with the frustration of being unable to force Kim into any form of compromise, motivated the American government to make new proposals in the spring. "Time has come," advised the State Department, "to go to the outer limits of our position."[16] On March 21, at the twelfth MAC meeting regarding the *Pueblo,* the administration took its first step toward satisfying the DPRK demands. Smith promised that simultaneous with the release of the men, the United States would "acknowledge that the *Pueblo* was on an intelligence gathering mission . . . provide assurances that ships of the United States Navy will continue to be ordered to remain more than twelve nautical miles from North Korea . . . [and] express regret for any violation of orders by the USS *Pueblo* which may have resulted in the ship's approaching closer than twelve nautical miles to North Korea."[17] The offer reflected the realization that some form of apology would be required to end the stalemate. It also represented a definitive break with the traditional methods of diplomacy. No longer would American representatives cling to ideas involving international mediation or impartial investigation; instead, the next nine months of debate would revolve around the specific details of an American apology.

If Kim appreciated this dramatic step, his response did not show it. The two sides met again on March 28, and Pak, after lambasting Smith with even more vitriol than usual, rejected the proposal. Specifically, he objected to the suggestion that there had been actions that "may have resulted" in transgressions into DPRK waters. This clause was "nothing else but a phrase-making, using slippery, ambiguous phrases," Pak declared. "A careful examination shows that you want to express regret for a certain unknown, hypothetical action. . . . How can you settle the matter with such an attitude?" The only way to resolve the incident, he reiterated, was for the United States to provide the three A's exactly as demanded.[18] The administration refused. "We have gone as far as we can go,"

Nicholas Katzenbach told a cabinet meeting a few days later.[19] While the *Pueblo* men struggled for survival, the two sides appeared to be at an impasse.

With this rejection, the administration prepared for a long wait. The time had come, Rusk advised the president, "to face the fact that it is unlikely that any course will lead to a quick return of the crew."[20] They also began considering other options. In March, the Korean Task Force (KTF) proposed a new plan, suggesting that Smith sign the letter of apology, but only after writing a phrase on the paper indicating that his endorsement was intended only to "acknowledge receipt" of the men.[21] This sentence would let the DPRK claim that the United States had apologized, while allowing the United States to argue that it had merely noted the crew's repatriation. However, there were some concerns about the impact of such an agreement on the rest of Asia. General Bonesteel argued that the solution would "irreparably damage" U.S.-ROK relations and would "gravely impeach our consistent statements that we will not let South Vietnam down."[22] Pak's frequent comments that it would be easy to arrange a release once the letter was signed also worried the Americans, since this implied that the men would not be released simultaneously. Accordingly, Johnson placed the plan, known as the "overwrite formula," on reserve and had the KTF draft nine possible apology letters, ranging from a simple, one-sentence expression of regret (#2) to a more elaborate, five-paragraph version (#8).[23] Still, patience seemed the best course, especially since the waning interest of the public limited the pressure for more drastic action. The early bellicosity of the American people continued to dissipate as the year progressed; in the summer, a "Remember the *Pueblo*" protest march at the State Department produced only a handful of demonstrators, and a prayer vigil in San Diego attracted only 800 people, despite the attendance of Rose Bucher.[24]

The pressure that did exist came from an unsurprising source: the family members of the *Pueblo* crew, who found little to praise in LBJ's policies. Their disenchantment began almost immediately, rooted in the belief that the administration had acted too slowly in informing them of the seizure. Rose Bucher first heard the news on the *Today* show while watching television at the Bahia Motor Hotel in San Diego. In the three hours it took for Captain Hap Hill, the navy's local public affairs officer, to phone her with official notification, she was inundated by calls from family, friends, and reporters. It took so long to reach her, Hill explained, because the navy had been searching for her in Lincoln, Nebraska, where she had not lived for fifteen years.[25] A friend notified Janice Ginther, the wife of CT Frank Ginther, at 10:00 on the morning after the capture, and Carol Murphy and Mary Ellen Lacy received hysterical phone calls from another *Pueblo* wife the same day.[26] Nor did the government seem very concerned about their immediate problems; for example, the day after the seizure, Japanese communists protested in front of Tim Harris's house in Yokosuka, but the navy sent his wife no assistance in dealing with them.[27] Official notification from Washington did not arrive for a few days, and when it did, it came as a mimeographed form letter, most of which was devoted to telling them what could and could not be said. "The USS *Pueblo*, to which your husband is assigned," began the one to Rose Bucher, "has been boarded by military forces of North Korea while the ship was operating in international waters. . . . Department of Defense has announced that the *Pueblo* is a Navy Intelligence Collection Auxiliary Ship. This is all that should be said about the mission of the ship or your husband's duties."[28] Not until late February did Rose receive a more personal letter from LBJ, which included the backhanded compliment that her husband had "handled himself to the best of his ability."[29] It was the only communication she would ever receive from the president.[30]

Over the next few months, neither the navy nor the Johnson administration made a significant effort to keep in touch with the families. In February, Rose replied to a letter from Senator Frank Church by noting, "You were the only senator that sent me any kind of communication—my only communication from Washington DC, in fact." Church forwarded the response to the White House and the navy, which then began preparing letters to the families.[31] Specific requests for information often proved unproductive; during one week, Rose called Captain James Mayo, an adviser in the Bureau of East Asian and Pacific Affairs, three times. "Mrs. Bucher," Mayo told her the last time, "you're harassing me. I don't know why I even bother to talk to you. If you were my wife and I was Pete Bucher," he added, "I'd like you to get yourself into a nice rocking chair by a quiet lake and stop asking questions."[32] In the spring, the administration provided the families with an address to use to write the men letters, but the information came one month after three other nations had not only provided the address but also volunteered to forward their mail.[33] In April, Rose asked the navy for the names and addresses of all the men's relatives, in order to write the reassuring letters expected of the captain's wife. Vice Admiral B. J. Semmes, Jr., chief of naval personnel, refused to give them to her, citing official policy to protect their privacy against "harassment from news media or agitators." Another request in May received a similar reply, this time from the assistant chief of morale services, who added, "We have found that it is difficult and not particularly useful to correspond with individuals who are not in sympathy with the administration or who are looking for a target on whom to vent their frustrations."[34]

Other family members kept up the pressure. In April, Steve Harris's mother wrote letters to every senator, asking them to provide an apology before it was too late. "We are dealing with an outlaw regime," she wrote. "Even outlaws can lose their patience."[35] Others wrote directly to the president. Bucher's thirteen-year-old nephew begged Johnson to arrange "the return of my uncle and its crew [sic]," and Stephen Ellis's father blamed LBJ for "abandoning our men to long months of abuse, hardship, and incarceration."[36] Janice Ginther marked her June 23 birthday with a telegram to the White House full of questions: "How do I know my husband is still alive? If there is progress, why does the State Department deny it? What do I tell my little girl when she cries for her father? What kind of future do we have? Aren't those eighty-two lives important? What about all the families that are involved? . . . I'm tired of hearing 'be patient,'" she concluded. "You can't possibly realize what a terrible nightmare this is."[37] A letter from the parents of Lee Roy Hayes went ignored until their congressman, Samuel Devine (R-Ohio), requested an explanation from the White House; in response, congressional liaison Barefoot Sanders sent him a brief note to forward to the family. Devine remained unsatisfied; the reply, he wrote back, was "appalling by your lack of sensitivity" and "an insult to send to the mother of Lee Roy Hayes."[38]

Pressure from the families continued throughout the summer, with Rose Bucher leading the way. The once-introverted girl from Nebraska suddenly appeared on talk shows, held press conferences, sent letters to congressmen, and maintained a steady barrage of criticism of the administration's failure to free the men. Her behavior became a source of concern to LBJ, who even considered a face-to-face meeting with her but decided against it after his advisers expressed misgivings. Sanders, among others, was opposed, explaining that Rose was "somewhat erratic."[39] In June, she gave a press conference on Capitol Hill to express her dissatisfaction with the government's response, especially its reluctance to communicate with the crew's relatives. In September, the family of Lee Roy Hayes picketed Dean Rusk's office, with his mother carrying a sign reading: "I want my son without an apology." Rusk, claiming a full schedule, refused to see them.[40] He did find time to meet with Bucher's sister, Angela Smedgard, and the Reverend Paul Lindstrom, the self-appointed head of the National Remember the *Pueblo* Committee and the proprietor of the Church of Christian Liberty in suburban Chicago, where six of the trustees were members of the John Birch Society. Lindstrom, who insisted that the scriptures demanded that the United States use force to save the men, asked Rusk why Johnson expressed such concern for the poor but not for the *Pueblo* crew and lectured him on the evils of appeasing communism. When the angry Rusk responded by abruptly ending their forty-minute meeting, Lindstrom handed him a "Remember the *Pueblo*" bumper sticker and a framed certificate of membership in the Remember the *Pueblo* Committee and departed, pausing outside the White House to tell reporters, "The State Department is guilty of un-Christian conduct. I would personally go to war."[41]

Republicans also tried to remind the voters of LBJ's inability to resolve the crisis. The GOP Congressional Committee newsletter carried a weekly reminder listing the number of days the men had been held, and Congressman William Scherle (R-Iowa) inserted a daily reminder into the *Congressional Record*. The six-month anniversary produced a particularly vehement blast from Republican ranks. Representative Bob Michel (R-Ill.) called it "still another failure of United States foreign policy during the past eight years," and Representative Louis Wyman (R-N.D.) publicly wondered when the administration would "get off its duff" and free the men.[42] In July, a House Republican Policy Committee statement on the seizure and detention of the *Pueblo* attacked the administration's unwillingness to stand up to North Korea and deplored the resulting loss of U.S. prestige.[43] Similar comments had marked the occasion of Independence Day a few weeks earlier. "How can we celebrate July 4 and hold our heads high," asked Scherle, "while these Americans languish in communist prisons? How can we look at our flag, the Statue of Liberty, or any of the various monuments to our nation's heroes, and not feel that our country is welching on its promise?"[44] Still, this criticism did not include examples of what LBJ should be doing differently. "When there is a Republican administration," announced the party leadership at a July press conference, "and we have access to all the facts, we will have an answer to that."[45]

Despite the actions of these two groups—the families and the Republicans—the overall indifference of the American public prevented the *Pueblo* from becoming a major policy problem for the administration. Although a September poll showed that only 2.3 percent of Americans surveyed chose "continue present conferences" as their favored solution to the crisis, there was little serious pressure on LBJ to adopt a new approach, simply because the nation did not seem to consider the incident worthy of much attention.[46] Ironically, the same could not be said of South Korea, where interest in the American ship never waned. Despite Johnson's munificence, ROK President Park continued to express his unhappiness with the limited response, thus keeping the administration alarmed by the prospect of another Korean War. Park, wrote Rusk in late February, had "become increasingly obsessed with the desire to strike back across the DMZ," and later that week, the State Department called the regime "a government with a total fixation on the threat of the North."[47] Although Park made few public comments, other members of his administration were more loquacious. "We urge the government," announced Kim Jai Sun, the official spokesman of Park's ruling Democratic Republican Party, "to change drastically the concept of our national defense to a self-reliant, independent posture."[48] Leaks from unnamed ROK officials also spoke of the "wide difference" between the two nations concerning the appropriate response to the DPRK and often hinted that South Korea might take unilateral action if the United States continued discussions with its enemy.[49]

Park continued to make demands behind the scenes, not only asking for more aid but also insisting that an ROK representative be included in even the most sensitive *Pueblo* discussions and demanding that the United States do nothing at the MAC talks that could be construed as granting recognition to the DPRK.[50] He also continued to threaten to take unilateral action against the North. In the spring, he sought reiterations of support from the sixteen nations that had aided the South during the Korean War. No one responded positively to what the British Foreign Office called a "somewhat half-baked approach," one that the Johnson administration had opposed the eight previous times the ROK had suggested it.[51] Other South Korean officials worked to keep the pressure on the United States as well. Shortly after Smith proposed to "express regrets" for any territorial violations, Pak Keun, director of the ROK International Affairs Bureau, sent a memo to the State Department insisting that the United States stand firm in the face of DPRK demands.[52] The same month, the ROK minister of national defense sent letters to American congressmen requesting enormous military support for his country in its struggle against "communist provocations." "I am confident," he concluded, "that after carefully considering all the facts, you will do what is necessary to prevent another VIETNAM from occurring here in Korea."[53] Ironically, by refusing to give in to ROK pressures for a more militant response, the administration was doing exactly that.

Once again, LBJ acted carefully to placate South Korea. In late February, the administration upgraded the communication network between Washington and Seoul. In April, Johnson and Park met in Honolulu for highly publicized talks concerning the Korean situation. Privately, the American president promised to continue supporting South Korea and pledged to expedite the already promised military and economic aid. Publicly, he agreed to a joint communiqué that "reaffirmed the readiness and determination of the United States to render prompt and effective assistance to repel armed attacks against the Republic of Korea . . . recognized the need for strengthening [the] security of the Republic of Korea . . . [and] recognized the need for continuing modernization of the armed forces of the Republic of Korea."[54] That same month, Johnson insisted that during MAC talks the American negotiating team "avoid terms such as 'your territory' or 'your coast' that might imply recognition of Pyongyang's sovereignty over part of Korea," and in July, he awarded the Presidential Unit Citation to the First Cavalry Regiment of the Ninth Company of the ROK army, the first non-American unit fighting in Vietnam to be so honored.[55] In May, the two nations held joint Defense Ministry talks, with such high-profile figures as Deputy Secretary Paul Nitze, Assistant Secretary Paul Warnke, and JCS Chairman Earle Wheeler representing the United States. Although it had little practical value, the meeting offered the South Koreans another chance to get a public commitment from the United States to defend them against DPRK aggression, provided an opportunity to harangue the United States about military assistance, and allowed Park to demonstrate to his nation the close ties between the two governments.

Perhaps the worst pressure to resolve the crisis, however, came from within the administration itself. Although Vietnam continued to claim American lives, LBJ and his advisers could take some comfort from the knowledge that these men went to battle armed with the finest weapons and supplies in the history of warfare; by late 1967, American ships were delivering over 1 million tons of supplies to Vietnam every month.[56] The *Pueblo* men, in contrast, had been sent on their mission virtually unarmed and unsupported, a fact that Johnson and his advisers never forgot. As negotiations dragged on, the inability to obtain even the slightest concession from Kim added to the president's overall frustration. "I never saw him so grim, serious, and curiously unfriendly," recalled one senator after a *Pueblo* briefing. "He didn't have the old self-confidence."[57] Still, LBJ wisely resisted the temptation to take military action. When, in March, Ambassador Porter asked if "there is still a steel fist inside that silken glove," Rusk responded that despite the appeal of such actions, the administration would take no steps that "might be counterproductive."[58] "The job of the president of the United States," Vice President Humphrey explained during the summer, "is not to pick a fight. Any damn fool can pick a fight. We've got one war right now and don't need another."[59]

In May, Smith's term as MAC representative expired. Despite some reluctance to change negotiators in the middle of the talks, the administration decided to replace him with Major General Gilbert Woodward. Porter and Rusk had actually contemplated replacing Smith a few months earlier. Although the admiral was "undoubtedly [an] excellent naval officer," wrote Porter, "he has suddenly been thrust into [a] strange field. We feel he is not psychologically suited nor does he have [the] temperament and mental agility for the job that has to be done at this time. I regret that I must recommend in the national interest that he be relieved."[60] The slowness of the bureaucratic wheels, however, derailed their attempts until Smith's term expired in May. The change seemed to make little difference, however, as Pak continued to reject anything short of the three A's. Yet, despite the lack of progress, he wanted to continue the meetings. "The North Koreans," noted Porter after an unsuccessful conference in May, "find it to their advantage to continue and prolong these sessions, and probably intend to do so."[61] "Pak," he concluded after another discussion the following month, "made clear he wishes to keep meetings going."[62]

On May 8, Pak provided a specific example of the apology letter Kim expected, handing Woodward a one-page document that echoed the demand he had been making since the first meeting. "The government of the United States of America," it began:

> acknowledging the validity of the confessions of the crew of the USS *Pueblo* and of the documents of evidence produced by the representative of the government of the Democratic People's Republic of Korea to the effect that the ship, which was seized by the self-defense measures of the naval vessels of the Korean People's Army in the territorial waters of the Democratic People's Republic of Korea on January 23, 1968, had illegally intruded into the territorial waters of the Democratic People's Republic of Korea on many occasions and conducted espionage activities of spying out important military and state secrets of the Democratic People's Republic of Korea,
>
> Shoulders full responsibility and solemnly apologizes for the grave acts of espionage committed by the US ship against the Democratic People's Republic of Korea after intruding into the territorial waters of the Democratic People's Republic of Korea.
>
> And gives firm assurance that no US ship will intrude again in the future into the territorial waters of the Democratic People's Republic of Korea.
>
> Meanwhile, the government of the United States of America earnestly requests that the government of the Democratic People's Republic of Korea, taking into consideration the fact that the former crew members of the USS *Pueblo* confiscated by the Democratic People's Republic of Korea side have confessed honestly to their crimes and petitioned the government of the Democratic People's Republic of Korea for leniency as well as the above mentioned apology and assurance of the government of the United States of America, deal leniently with the crew members.

If the United States would just sign this document, Pak promised, the details of returning the men could be settled easily.[63]

Johnson rejected the proposal, preferring to wait for further developments at the MAC.[64] Woodward officially declined at the next meeting and instead suggested that the DPRK reexamine the American offer made in March or one of the recommendations for impartial investigation. "Our proposal," he explained, "fully reflects the area of agreement reached in these talks and strikes a fair compromise on the points still in dispute." Pak's reply was discouraging. "Your side," he complained, "has not only failed to come with a properly written document as we have demanded but also has refused to do so, and once again persists in the draft receipt of your side, the injustice of which has already been fully repudiated by our side as a basis for the discussion of the question. This clearly shows that your side is not concerned about the fate of the crew of the *Pueblo* and has no intention of settling the question really at these meetings. . . . I advise your side to give up its unjust position and write and submit a proper document so that the question of the crew may be settled speedily." The meeting took only thirty-four minutes, which included a six-minute pause while Pak examined a written copy of Woodward's statement. After exchanging denunciations, the two sides agreed to a recess and left the room with little reason for optimism.[65]

While negotiations continued, Johnson also worked to quash rumors that he had secretly agreed to pay a ransom for the crew's release. Such speculation had existed for months but did not capture public attention until April, when Congressman John Anderson (R-Ill.) claimed that the United States had pledged to provide farm equipment, including twenty trailer-mowers purchased from the Avco New Idea Farm Implement manufacturing plant in Ohio, in exchange for the hostages. The American government, Anderson added, had already shipped the tractors to Texas by railroad flatcar in the dead of night, where they were then forwarded to North Korea on March 16 as a precursor to the crew's release. Despite the contention and the brief public outcry it generated, there was no truth to Anderson's claim that the United States was trading farms for hostages; in fact, a shipment of such equipment had recently been sent to Korea, but the recipient was on the southern half of the peninsula.[66] In July, Senator Stephen Young (D-Ohio), a member of the Armed Services Committee, brought similar allegations to public attention by predicting an August release in return for an American indemnity of $100 million. The administration quickly dismissed the claim. "We just don't know where Senator Young came by or obtained such information," insisted Bob McCloskey. "The matter of ransom has never entered the picture."[67] Still, to prevent any such chicanery, Congress passed an amendment to the 1968 Foreign Assistance Act specifically prohibiting Johnson from sending assistance to North Korea until Kim released the crew. Considering that the United States had not sent any aid to North Korea since its 1948 creation, such a measure was more of a political slap in the face than an important piece of legislation.

The standstill in negotiations left the American government with an ever-increasing sense of hopelessness. In August, LBJ decided to propose the overwrite formula, despite the skepticism of some of his advisers. "I can not see," said Clifford, "how they would take the 'acknowledged receipt.'" Even if they would, the secretary of defense still had reservations, since the crisis resulted from DPRK, not American, machinations. "It was an illegal act on their part," he explained. "I do not agree with the use of trickery."[68] Former ambassador to South Korea Winthrop Brown also worried that if the sentence were written in water-based ink, the North Koreans would simply erase it.[69] Johnson overrode the objections. "Let's try to jazz it up," he ordered, "and get the language so it suits them."[70] After much deliberation, it was decided that Woodward should offer to write a single sentence on the North Korean letter: "There have been turned over to me today at Panmunjom eighty-two surviving members of the crew of the USS *Pueblo* and the body of seaman Duane Hodges."[71] This solution was contingent on Pak agreeing to release the crewmen simultaneously, or at least, wrote Rusk, "a substantial majority, say more than sixty."[72]

Although Woodward was eager to deliver the proposal, circumstances forced him to wait. Custom decreed that the two nations alternated the right to call meetings, and the Americans had requested the last one. Frustrated, Woodward sent Pak a note on August 13, reminding him that it was his turn. The reply was noncommittal. "We understand," Pak wrote back, "that it is our turn to hold the next meeting in accordance with established practice."[73] On August 25, Woodward decided to break custom and requested a meeting for the twenty-seventh. Pak refused, but Woodward persevered. "I intend to be at [the] conference room . . . at 1100 today," he wrote on the twenty-seventh, "for a meeting of the senior members." When he arrived, the North Koreans were nowhere to be found, and a message left by Pak explained that they could not comply with a meeting "called by your side in disregard of the established practice." Later that day, however, Pak requested a meeting for the twenty-ninth. Woodward's persistence had lost the battle but won the war.[74]

On August 29, Woodward proposed the overwrite formula. "If I were to acknowledge receipt of the crew," he asked, "on a document whose language was satisfactory to you, would you then be willing simultaneously to release to my custody the entire crew?" Pak's interest was obvious. "May I understand," he asked, "that your last statement implies that your side is ready to sign the document of apology and assurance put forth by us?" "If you are willing," Woodward replied, "to simultaneously release to my custody the entire *Pueblo* crew, I would acknowledge receipt of the crew on a document whose language was satisfactory to you." An enthusiastic Pak promised to respond at the next meeting and proposed a hasty adjournment, but Woodward wanted to clarify the American offer. "I take note of your statement," he said before agreeing to the recess, "and only wish to reiterate that the language of my statement should be carefully studied since your last statement contains language that I did not use."[75]

The two sides met again on September 17, and Pak delivered his promised response. "If your side signs the document presented by our side at the meeting of May 8," he answered, "the crew of the *Pueblo* will be sent back." Yet, trouble lurked behind the apparent agreement. The representatives discussed the proposal in detail, but their dialogue suggested that neither was listening to what the other was saying. Pak interpreted Woodward's pledge to "acknowledge receipt of the crew on a document whose language is satisfactory to you" as the simple promise to sign the DPRK letter, and Woodward was not clear in describing his intentions. The two men talked past each other for four hours:

WOODWARD: Let me make certain that I understand your proposal . . . you will simultaneously release to my custody the entire crew of the *Pueblo* if I will acknowledge receipt of the crew on your document. . . . Is that correct?

PAK: I have clearly stated that our side will send back to your side only the crew of the *Pueblo* if your side signs the document. . . . Is your side ready to sign the document?

WOODWARD: You are using language I did not use. I said that if you will simultaneously release the entire crew to my custody, I would then be prepared to acknowledge receipt for the crew . . . and I asked you whether you accept this principle of simultaneous release?

PAK: I have already clearly told you that the crew of the *Pueblo* will be sent back if the government of the United States submits the document of apology and assurance. . . . Yet what can't you still understand? Is your side ready to sign the document?

WOODWARD: I speak of acknowledging receipt because I can only agree to an arrangement which involves the simultaneous receipt of the entire crew. Now can you agree to this principle of simultaneous release?

PAK: If your side signs the document . . . the crew of the *Pueblo* will be able to return. What can't you understand here? Is your side ready to sign the document?

WOODWARD: I said that if you will simultaneously release the entire crew to my custody, I would then be prepared to acknowledge receipt of the crew on a document whose language was satisfactory to you and I asked you whether you accept this principle of simultaneous release. Would you answer that question?

PAK: I have already clearly told you that if your side signs the document presented by our side on May 8, the crew will be returned.

When the meeting finally adjourned, both sides thought an agreement was at hand. "Progress at last meeting," wrote the State Department, "makes it appear at least possible that overwrite ploy will work."[76]

On September 30, the two men sat down again, and Pak gave the North Korean answer. If Woodward signed the letter, Pak promised, his government would release the crew simultaneously. Triumphantly, he handed Woodward the statement that the United States was expected to sign. It was the same letter he had given in May, with an additional sentence at the end: "Simultaneously with the signing of this document," it read, "the undersigned acknowledges receipt of eighty-two former crew members of the *Pueblo* and one corpse." This clause appears to have been added to accommodate the Americans' demand that they sign to "acknowledge receipt," and thus reinforces the idea that the DPRK had not really understood the overwrite proposal. At the bottom was a line for Woodward's signature: "On behalf of the Government of the USA, Gilbert H. Woodward, Major General, USA." Further details, the two sides agreed, would be resolved at the next meeting.[77]

On October 10, the MAC representatives met to discuss the *Pueblo* for the twenty-third time. Feelings of anticipation filled the room, a welcome change from the usually hostile atmosphere. Pak even brought photographers to take pictures of what he clearly expected to be a historic meeting, leaving Woodward scrambling to assemble the same number of American photographers.[78] The session started optimistically. "I am pleased to note," began Woodward, "that at our last meeting you agreed very clearly to the principle that the entire crew will be released at the same time that I acknowledge on your document that I am receiving them."[79] Quickly they moved on to the specific details of the exchange. Pak wanted Woodward to sign the letter at the MAC conference room, in front of DPRK photographers; the crew, he added, would be released two hours later at the Sachon Bridge—known to Americans as the Bridge of No Return—which traversed the Military Demarcation Line. Woodward promised to consult with his superiors and have an answer by the next meeting. Only these minor details, it appeared, blocked an end to the crew's long nightmare.

Suddenly, the promising mood collapsed. In order to avoid last-minute complications, the State Department had ordered Woodward to provide a specific demonstration of his intent before the end of this meeting. When Pak suggested that they adjourn, the American refused. "I want to make perfectly clear," he announced, "what I am prepared to do to solve the problem. . . . I do not want there to be any doubt in your mind or my mind about what the other intends to do. On May 8," he explained, "you presented a draft of what you would consider a suitable document of apology and assurance. . . . In order to reach a solution to this problem, in order to reduce tensions in the area, and in order to permit these eighty-two innocent men to return to their families, I am prepared to use the draft . . . as a basis for solving the problem by acknowledging on it that I am receiving the custody of the crew. I will write on the draft the words: quote; 'I hereby acknowledge receipt of the *Pueblo* crew' unquote, and I will sign my name and title." The comment left Pak stunned. "Your side," he exclaimed angrily, "agreed to the matter of principle for the solution of the question of the *Pueblo* crew, but has now taken the insincere and arrogant attitude frustrating the agreement. Whom are you fooling? . . . As our side already made it clear, your side should understand clearly that it cannot get its crew back forever unless it makes the apology and assurance as we have suggested." [80]

The positive mood collapsed, and the meeting closed with hard feelings apparent to all. Yet, despite the DPRK reaction, some optimism still existed on the American side. A resolution had seemed so close, wrote Rusk to Ambassador Porter, that perhaps it had "generated momentum favorable to the overwrite compromise."[81] In fact, the State Department remained so confident that on October 15, Colonel Willis Helmantoler was ordered to Seoul, "in connection with [the] physical arrangements for handling [the] press at such time as *Pueblo* crew [is] released."[82] These delusions were shattered when the MAC representatives met again two weeks later. Handing Woodward a copy of the apology letter, Pak demanded that the American demonstrate his intentions. Woodward complied, pretending to write the "acknowledge receipt" phrase diagonally across the text of the letter. "Ha!" Pak exclaimed sarcastically, while in the background his officers loudly declared that the American's intent was to cross out the text. Woodward then suggested adding the phrase at the bottom, under his typed name and title, a solution Pak called "shameless" and "absurd." "The so-called compromise," he declared, "cannot be interpreted other than as ridiculing the meeting and it cannot be even a subject to be discussed." The North Korean overrode Woodward's justifications with a clear threat. "Such attempts," he warned, "will eventually bring only unfavorable consequence to the crew. . . . I have already reminded your side that our patience too has its limits. As a matter of fact, our side has said all we wanted to say to your side. . . . Your side had better go back and study my statements carefully and come again to this meeting place when your side is prepared to sign the document we have presented as it is and get the crew back."[83] The overwrite formula, it appeared, was finished. Any future attempts along these lines, Katzenbach concluded, would likely be "a dead end."[84]

As the winter dragged on, the administration's frustration continued. Some officials even wondered if a solution was possible during their tenure. "They'll return the crew when they get good and ready to do it," Katzenbach lamented, "and maybe that'll be before the end of Mr. Johnson's office and maybe it won't."[85] "There is really no hope," agreed a Pentagon source, "that anything is going to happen before January."[86] On the 300th day of captivity, Johnson received a petition with over a thousand signatures, including Rose Bucher's, demanding action on the *Pueblo:* "what in god's name," it asked, "are you doing about it?"[87] Still, the president clung to his larger goals—to keep South Korea in check and avoid a disruption of American efforts in Vietnam—and refused to take more aggressive action. "If you went and bombed one of their cities or something like this," Katzenbach explained, "you wouldn't help get the eighty-two men back and you run the risk of starting a war. So there's not much we've been able to do except talk."[88] It was a difficult and frustrating course, but better options did not exist. Any more extreme action would likely have had disastrous consequences for the crew, the administration, and the United States.

As 1968 drew to a close, the Johnson team decided to make one more effort to end the standoff. At Porter's suggestion, they launched "a review at the highest levels," exploring options new and old in a last-ditch effort to find a solution.[89] One particular proposal caught the eye of those on the job. In late November, James Leonard, the State Department's country director for Korea, had discussed the *Pueblo* standoff with his wife, Eleanor.[90] He saw no solution other than providing the apology, Leonard admitted, but wondered how to do it in such a way as to minimize the American humiliation. Eleanor had an answer: have Woodward agree to sign the letter only if North Korea would allow him to make a statement publicly repudiating it before doing so. Leonard brought the idea to the administration, where it found some supporters, particularly within the Korean Task Force. It also had its opponents, including many in the State Department who suggested reissuing the conditional apology proposed in May as a final offer. Deputy Assistant Secretary of Defense Richard Steadman disagreed. "I do not share State's agony," he wrote to Paul Warnke, "at the repercussions of our signing a document we believe to be false, if we repudiate it both before and after it is made."[91]

In late November, LBJ approved the plan, which had become known as the "Leonard proposal." Rusk ordered the MAC staff to call another meeting "to present what will be in effect [the] final offer from [the] present administration."[92] Since this would be their last offer, he advised Woodward to be forceful with the North Koreans, as there was little to be lost should talks collapse. Rusk also instructed him to stress Richard Nixon's impending assumption of the presidency. "Our hope," the secretary of state wrote, "is North Korea will calculate that they are not likely to get more from President-elect Nixon than from President Johnson."[93] Woodward loved the idea. "I said right then and there," he remembered, "they'll buy it. . . . It satisfied their one condition, a signature on a piece of paper. . . . The North Korean people would never hear about the repudiation. Their propaganda boys would take care of that. And as for the rest of the world, well, they just didn't care."[94]

The administration took other steps to encourage Kim to accept the offer. Ambassador Goldberg made a final appeal to U Thant at the United Nations, who promised to use his limited influence to help arrange a deal.[95] Johnson also sent word to the Soviet leadership, informing them that this would be his final overture. Typically, the Soviets took no public position but appear to have quietly encouraged the DPRK to accept the Leonard proposal. "United States officials," wrote the *New York Times*, "say Moscow has urged North Korea to come to terms. The Soviet Union, which operates a large fleet of eavesdropping ships all over the world, is said to be uncomfortable about the *Pueblo* precedent."[96] The danger of this precedent had been clearly demonstrated to the Soviets in May, when the Brazilian navy captured an AGI operating two miles from shore. Within three weeks of the seizure, the Soviets apologized, and the ship was released.[97]

Since traditional forms of diplomatic pressure had accomplished little, the administration added a new tactic. For decades, fishing had been vital to North Korean life, providing employment, trade commodities, and almost 70 percent of the protein in the national diet. However, years of overworking their coastal waters began to take its toll in the 1960s, and DPRK fishing intake declined. Accordingly, North Korean fishing boats began to foray into more distant areas, requiring large factory ships to process and deep-freeze their catch while they remained at sea. Since North Korea's only factory ship had been built in 1955, Kim ordered two more from Rotterdam's Verlome United Shipyards in 1967, at a cost of $14 million. In late 1968, Verlome announced that the ships were close to completion and promised to launch them in early 1969 under a Dutch flag and with a joint DPRK-Dutch crew.

Kim's need for these ships was tremendous, especially since it appeared that the 1968 fish intake would be less than that of the previous year, despite the government's pledge of a dramatic increase.[98] Recognizing this, the Johnson team believed that the threat of capture might put some badly needed pressure on Kim. The idea, explained one official, was that "North Korea has already milked about as much propaganda from the seizure as it can expect. Rather than run the risk of a black eye and loss of an expensive vessel on the high seas, it may be willing to turn the *Pueblo* crewmen back and close the book on the incident."[99] In reality, the administration had no intention of hijacking the ships, which would not only antagonize the Netherlands but also be a violation of international law and likely spark considerable protest at home and abroad. Still, there seemed nothing to lose by making such threats, and in September,

Rusk ordered the American ambassador to the Hague to inquire of Dutch officials when the ship would sail and when the title would officially pass into DPRK hands. The "ultimate object, of course, would be that such an inquiry on our part get back to [the] North Korean government," wrote the secretary of state.[100] Throughout the winter, American officials made a conscious effort to be seen snooping around the ships and making inquiries of relevant authorities, acting, the *New York Times* reported, "ostentatiously . . . in part to raise some apprehension that one or both of the vessels might be seized on their trip to the Far East."[101] Rusk also ordered the American embassy in London to contact the ships' insurer, Lloyd's of London, to express interest in the transfer of their titles to North Korea, and he reminded the staff to request that Lloyd's mention these inquiries to the DPRK government.[102] At the same time, the administration pressured other nations not to provide North Korea with any assistance. James Leonard informed the British ambassador to the United States that the Johnson administration "very much hoped that their friends would not develop their trade with North Korea."[103] The State Department also asked the Japanese government to prohibit private dealers from selling Kim a small refrigerated fishing vessel, even suggesting that the United States might capture the ship while under way if the sale were made. Although pessimistic about its ability to block a private sale, the Japanese government pledged to do everything it could to help.[104]

One can only speculate about the effectiveness of these threats, but it seems likely that they had some influence. *Juche* did not exist merely in foreign policy; Kim needed to provide evidence of independent development in the economic realm *(charip)* as well. These ships, which could each process seventy-five tons of fish per day, offered a significant contribution to this effort, not only by providing additional food and helping local economies but also by allowing the nation to satisfy its international trade agreements, which had been a problem since the beginning of the fishing downturn. Additionally, the government could use the presence of such modern technology as a symbol of the nation's economic advancement. Since the *Pueblo* crew had provided steady doses of *juche* in different forms for almost a year, it seems likely that Kim would have recognized that the ships, not the men, now provided him with the greater opportunity to demonstrate his ability to advance the DPRK along that promised track. Finally, it seems, the Johnson administration had discovered—albeit inadvertently—that the key to pressuring Kim lay not in using the tools of traditional Cold War diplomacy but in attacking his ability to conform to the defining paradigm of North Korean life.

On December 17, the two sides sat down to discuss the *Pueblo* for the twenty-sixth time.[105] Pak began by reiterating the demands that American representatives had heard so many times: "If your side wants to have the question of the crew of the *Pueblo* practically settled, it should sign the document put forth by us as it is. . . . There can be no alternative." Woodward responded by offering two solutions from which Pak could choose. The first option was to reconsider the overwrite formula; however, Woodward continued:

> If your authorities prefer to avoid the use of this additional phrase, I am authorized to simply sign my name on the place provided, but under one specific condition. This condition relates to the fact that . . . (1) The United States government does not consider that the *Pueblo* was engaged in illegal activities, (2) the United States government has not seen convincing evidence that the ship intruded into the waters claimed by your authorities, and (3) the United States government cannot apologize for an action unless such action actually took place. If I were to sign your document without first adding the phrase mentioned earlier in proposal A, I would have to make a formal statement just before signing to clarify those three points.

He also reminded Pak that Christmas, which the administration considered a deadline for the crew's release, was only eight days away. "These offers," Woodward concluded, "will all be withdrawn on December 23, 1968."

After a fifty-minute recess, Pak returned to the conference room with a single question: "Where are you going to sign?" When Woodward agreed to sign to the right of his printed name and title, as traditionally done in Korean documents, Pak accepted the second offer. "An agreement has now been reached," he announced, "upon the question of principle. Therefore, from now on we can enter into the discussion on the question of procedure." Quickly, the details fell into place. Woodward agreed to allow three DPRK photographers into the room during the signing and twenty-five others to stand at the north end of the Sachon Bridge. The administration recognized that the presence of the journalists would help Kim's propaganda efforts but decided that the North Koreans would be less likely to disrupt the smooth transfer with the media present.[106] Both sides also agreed that Bucher would be the first man across the bridge, followed by the body of Duane Hodges and then the rest of the crew, which would be released starting with the lowest rank and proceeding upward. Bucher would stay at the south end of the bridge to acknowledge each man's return, while Woodward and Pak remained in the conference room until the exchange was completed.

The North Korean decision left many within the Johnson administration stupefied. "We regarded the North Koreans," Rostow recalled, "as nuts."[107] By American standards, choosing an apology that had already been publicly repudiated instead of one that merely contained a note acknowledging receipt seemed foolish. Why, a reporter asked Katzenbach, would North Korea "accept this proposal, as opposed to the overwrite, which would seem more favorable to their position?" "So it seemed to us," answered the attorney general.[108] "I don't think any of us," he added later, "would have thought this would be particularly attractive to them." Rusk agreed. "It is as though a kidnapper kidnaps your child and asks for fifty thousand dollars ransom. You give him a check for fifty thousand dollars and you tell him at the time that you've stopped payment on the check, and then he delivers your child to you."[109] This attitude derived from the administration's failure to understand the central role that domestic ideology played in North Korea, unlike the Cold War focus of the U.S. government. The Leonard proposal, in terms of its ability to generate *juche*-related propaganda, was superior to the overwrite formula, because Kim's iron fist ensured that the American denial would never reach North Korean society. The handwritten receipt statement called for in the overwrite plan, especially if written across the text of the letter itself, would have been much more difficult to conceal. Writing over a decade later, Clifford finally seemed to have grasped the reason for the decision. "The North Koreans," he concluded, "accepted our offer, presumably because they could control their own media completely and wanted to be rid of the problem."[110]

Had the U.S. government recognized the importance of domestic ideology in DPRK behavior, it seems likely that it would have offered this solution earlier. At a press conference shortly after the release, reporters asked Katzenbach if this proposal had been extended previously. "No," he replied. "We had tried other approaches before. We had not broached this one. I think, quite frankly, we had not broached it because we didn't see how they could accept that." Yet, even if they had advanced such a proposition earlier, Kim would likely have rejected it. For months he had milked the hostages for every possible drop of *juche;* it seems unlikely that he would have agreed to any solution until he believed that this resource had been depleted. Not until autumn did the DPRK's attitude toward the men suggest that this point had been reached. "They had exhausted their propaganda efforts," recalled Murphy. "And we were no longer an asset to them. In fact, it was evident we were becoming an increasing burden."[111] Further, there were no factory ships for the United States to threaten in early 1968. Thus, although the administration's failure to recognize the complexity of the situation may have delayed its presentation of the Leonard plan, it still had no means of persuading Kim to release the men before it was in his best interests to do so.

The two sides met again on December 19 to finalize the details.[112] Pak demanded the right to make a statement after Woodward signed the letter and, citing administrative reasons and a need to "comply with North Korean law," also insisted on a two-hour interval between the signing and the release of the men. Both sides pledged to keep the details secret until the deal was consummated, an agreement the United States quickly broke. "Go ahead," Woodward told Katzenbach after the meeting. "You can make the announcement. They'll turn 'em loose. They won't dare back up now."[113] Still, the press continued to relegate the matter to the back pages. On December 20, the *New York Times* reported on page seven that a solution appeared close, while the front page carried stories about the installation of new automatic meters for cab drivers and a decision by the city's Board of Estimates to allow local television stations to create their own programs.[114]

On December 22, Woodward and Pak met in the MAC conference room for final discussions regarding the release of the men of the USS *Pueblo*. They resolved last-minute details, including the number of microphones allowed on the table during the signing, the timing of each side's verbal statement, and the size of the conference table. When Woodward mentioned that he needed room for some papers, Pak, perhaps remembering the last time an agreement seemed imminent, grew suspicious. "I have no objection to your placing the papers to be used by you for speaking," he warned. "But as I have already stated, the stationery to be used for the signing of the document will be furnished by our side and the signing will be done with the stationery to be prepared by our side." Pak rambled on about the exchange of paper and then stopped abruptly: "Do you have anything which is not clear to you and have you anything which you cannot understand and do you agree to this?" Woodward offered no complaints, and the two men resolved to meet again at 9:00 the following morning for statements and signing, after which Pak would provide written assurance that the crew would be released within two hours.[115] It had taken eleven months and twenty-eight meetings, but the two sides seemed on the verge of ending the standoff. The *Pueblo* men stood on the brink of freedom.

CHAPTER TEN

Climbing Out of Hell

If some night you're pub-crawlin',
And into gutters you're fallin',
And in that gutter are 82 gaffers;
It's only the crew,
of AGER-2,
We answer to the name Bucher's Bastards.

While the Johnson administration desperately tried to get the *Pueblo* crew home by Christmas, the men had begun to wonder whether they would make it home at all. Their attempt to undercut DPRK propaganda through subtle hints and messages had helped them survive the ordeal emotionally, but it also led them closer and closer toward disaster. In October, Quartermaster First Class Charles Law sent a letter to his uncle, Earl Hopkins, which included a photograph of eight crewmen, three of whom had extended their middle fingers. This time, the "Hawaiian good-luck symbol" carried only bad luck. Hopkins brought the gesture to the attention of his local newspaper, the *Tacoma News-Tribune*, which ran the story on October 10. A week later, *Time* magazine reprinted the picture over the caption: "The North Koreans are having a hard time proving to the world that the captive crewmen of the USS *Pueblo* are a contrite and cooperative lot. Last week, Pyongyang's flacks tried again—and lost to the US Navy. In this class reunion picture, three of the crewmen have managed to use the medium for a message, furtively getting off the US hand signal of obscene derisiveness and contempt."[1] President Johnson and his advisers were furious. They had recognized the finger gesture and other signs much earlier but had not mentioned them publicly for fear of sparking DPRK retribution against the prisoners.[2] Now, the American press had revealed the secret. "If the Koreans ever see this," thought James Leonard, "it'll be curtains for the crew."[3]

His fear proved justified. In early December, while MAC negotiations hovered on the brink of success, Super C summoned the ship's officers to a meeting room. Glaring at them, he dumped a thick envelope of papers onto his desk and announced, "You have ruined your own chances for repatriation." The men stared at the papers blankly until they noticed a copy of the *Time* article.

"You play us for the fool?" their tormentor asked in a quiet but menacing voice. Super C then began reciting a long litany of supposed offenses the men had committed, which proved that they were not "sincere." "I knew we had accomplished our mission," Bucher later wrote, "but I thought this might result in the death of some of the crew." After they were dismissed, the commander pulled Charles Law aside and warned him that they had been discovered. Law was to spread the word to expect the worst. "If you are beaten," Bucher told him to inform the other crewmen, "you may tell the Koreans what you have done yourself, but not what others have done."[4]

Retribution began the next day, as North Korean guards launched a ten-day wave of brutal attacks that the prisoners labeled "Hell Week."[5] Soldiers assigned the men new rooms in groups of twelve, while the officers were separated in individual rooms. Most of their privileges were revoked. Lights again remained on constantly, sports and recreation periods were canceled, and no movement was allowed without explicit permission. For the rest of Hell Week, the men were required to sit in their chairs at all times, except for meals, bathroom visits, and beatings, with their feet on the floor and their legs together. Guards wandered the halls, dispensing violent retribution for even the slightest sound or movement. Super C also ordered the crew to compose new confessions, which, he demanded, must include "everything you have done to try to discredit the DPRK, all you had planned to do in the future to discredit us, and what every one of your comrades has done and was planning. . . . Interrogations to test your sincerity," he added ominously, "will be resumed."[6]

The torment of the first few weeks of captivity now paled in comparison to the wave of brutality that swept through the Country Club; in fact, the injuries suffered during Hell Week surpassed those accumulated during the previous ten months combined. "It was," Bucher recalled, "the most concentrated form of terror that I've ever seen or dreamed is possible."[7] Harry Iredale endured a thirty-six-hour interrogation during which DPRK soldiers pounded his head with a hammer handle and then forced him to lie on the ground with a board over his knees, which they jumped on repeatedly. Following the beatings, Iredale recalled, "My head looked like a pumpkin. My lower lip was curled downward, swollen three times its normal size, and severely lacerated, my left upper lip paper thin. My left eye was swollen shut and completely bloodshot and the right eye had a red halo around the pupil. There was a contusion on the right side of my head between the ear and temple and lumps around the entire circumference of my head. My shins were cut and bruised, and the flesh over my ribs, hips, and knees were also bruised and aching."[8] When guards finished with Iredale, they gave him a bucket of water and a brush and ordered him to wash his own blood off the walls and floor.[9] Earl Kisler was forced to sit in a chair with his feet on the floor, hands on his legs, and chin on his chest for seventeen hours while North Korean guards took turns thrashing him. Soldiers beat Donnie Tuck with a three-foot stake, pummeled Skip Schumacher for approximately fifteen minutes every six hours for five consecutive days, and choked Tim Harris so badly that he tried to commit suicide. Still, the men took some solace in the knowledge that their actions had so obviously upset their captors. "At least we've rattled these bastards by making them look stupid to the outside world," Bucher told his crew. "That's something we can all be proud of."[10]

Although almost every prisoner was severely beaten during Hell Week, a few were singled out as special targets. Monroe Goldman, James Layton, and Howard Bland, the three who had made the finger gesture in the photo, attracted special interest. Goldman, who had served on a minesweeper that mined Wonsan Harbor during the Korean War, emerged from one beating with his ear almost torn off the side of his head. Charles Law, another suspected troublemaker, composed a twenty-five-page confession that Super C rejected. Instead, guards began questioning him on the crew's opposition, demanding to know who was leading it and what their plans involved. Dissatisfied with his answers, guards beat him for thirty-nine hours, dispensing over 250 blows with a two-by-four block of wood. When it finally broke over his back, they punched and kicked him and then smashed him across the face with a four-by-four wooden post, leaving him lying on the floor, bleeding and only semiconscious. Finally, Law confessed to almost every offense the crew had committed and some they had not, including an escape plan he remembered from a James Bond movie. Others did the same, many of them naming other crewmen who had supposedly helped organize the resistance or inventing conspiracies that had never existed. Despite their best efforts to resist, the incredible brutality of the North Koreans overwhelmed the men. For ten days, survival was the only thing that mattered.

In room thirteen, Hell Week sparked another problem. In the midst of the beatings, guards insisted that the occupants admit that the middle-finger gesture had been part of an organized conspiracy and demanded to know who was behind it. The men denied the charge until one of the roommates stepped forward. The others feared the worst. This man had tried to ingratiate himself to the North Koreans almost from the start, and on numerous occasions he had provided them with information about the crew's plans and transgressions. Lately, he had been showing an increasing inability to handle the stress of the ordeal, and Hell Week had broken him. The finger gesture had been an organized plot, he announced, one that had gone forward despite his attempts to prevent it. Two guards grabbed Lee Roy Hayes, just back from a devastating beating, and began dragging him out for another. Hayes yanked free for a moment and turned to face his tormentors. "You can have me taken across the hall and beat me all you want," he declared. "Eventually I will tell you what ever you want to know. If you want me to say it was organized, I will. But it will all be bullshit. This one," he said, pointing toward his accuser, "is lying to you to save his own skin."[11] It made no difference. A guard quickly paralyzed Hayes with a blow to the throat and then broke his jaw with a single punch.

This action forced the occupants of room thirteen into a painful decision. This particular man had seemed ready to betray them before but had never fully crossed the line. Now he had. The others considered their options and came to a painful decision: they would have to kill their shipmate. They debated specific plans, including throwing him out the window or smothering him with a pillow. Problems emerged, however, since neither method would look like suicide, which they considered vital in order to avoid further North Korean punishment and possible criminal charges in the United States. After much debate, the men decided to give their roommate a final chance, with a clear warning of the dire consequences that awaited the next betrayal. The men drew straws to decide who would issue the admonition, and Stu Russell got the short one. He pulled Hayes's accuser aside and issued an ultimatum: if he ever betrayed them again, they would strangle him and throw his body out the window. The stunned man withdrew in silence and rarely spoke to anyone for the remainder of the imprisonment.

Hell Week subsided as swiftly as it had begun, almost certainly because of the impending release of the men. On December 19, the same day that Woodward and Pak finalized the details of the Panmunjom agreement, guards suddenly became concerned about the physical condition of the men they had been beating with leather belts one day earlier. "It was like a faucet being turned off," recalled Bucher. "The prison which had been echoing for ten days with the sounds of blows and cries of pain, fell silent within the hour, leaving only the mournful moan of the wind."[12] Doctors arrived to treat obvious injuries, usually by dispensing hard-boiled eggs to be rubbed over bruises, and Hospital Corpsman First Class Herman Baldridge, whom the Koreans had forbidden to help with medical problems, suddenly found himself solicited for emergency opinions. "This could be it," thought Murphy, "the beginning of our long trek to freedom. But we were almost afraid to hope that it was."[13]

On Sunday, December 22, Super C gathered the entire crew in the movie room. "As I knew and told you from the beginning of this shameful imperialist intrigue against our peace-loving Korean people," he announced proudly, "it has ended with the warmongering US on its knees apologizing to us and assuring that no such provocation and many intrusions into our sovereign territorial waters shall occur again."[14] Finally, they would be going home. The Americans looked at one another warily, almost unsure how to respond. For most of them, the joyous news was tempered by the thought that this could be another North Korean trick, an attempt to get them angry at the United States when the fictitious agreement collapsed. Still, Super C seemed sincere. Finally, a subdued round of applause swept through the hall, before soldiers hustled the men back to their rooms. Later that night, guards led the men onto waiting buses, which returned them to the Pyongyang train station where DPRK soldiers had so brutally welcomed them to North Korea eleven months earlier. After an overnight ride to Kaesong and then a three-hour bus ride to Panmunjom, the men finally arrived at their destination, the northern end of the Bridge of No Return, at 10:30 on the morning of December 23.

Ninety minutes before their arrival, Woodward and Pak met to consummate the agreement. The American opened by reading a prepared statement. "The position of the United States government with regard to the *Pueblo*," he began, "as consistently expressed in the negotiations at Panmunjom and in public, has been that the ship was not engaged in any illegal activity, that there is no convincing evidence that the ship at any time intruded into the territorial waters claimed by North Korea, and that we could not apologize for actions which we did not believe took place. The document which I am going to sign was prepared by the North Koreans and is at variance with the above position, but my signature will not and cannot alter the facts. I will sign the document to free the crew and only to free the crew."[15] Woodward then signed the letter proffered by Pak, which, except for a few minor changes, was essentially the same one he had provided on September 30. The U.S. government, it acknowledged, "Shoulders full responsibility and solemnly apologizes for the grave acts of espionage committed by the US ship against the Democratic People's Republic of Korea after intruding into the territorial waters of the Democratic People's Republic of Korea." Woodward handed the paper back across the table and waited expectantly as the air grew thick with tension. Suddenly, Pak announced that his government would not be releasing the crew as agreed, because the United States had leaked the information to the press, despite promising not to do so. This action, he explained, had "insulted the entire Korean people," and the return would now have to be renegotiated. Woodward glared at him but sensed that his counterpart was just trying to start an argument. He chose not to rise to the bait. "Is there anything I can do to assist you?" he asked. "If you are having administrative delays, if you cannot release the crew at eleven o'clock, then eleven-thirty would be acceptable. But I will need a receipt." Seeing that Woodward would not be provoked, Pak did not respond. Silently, he picked up the paper and filled in the time of release: 11:30.[16]

While the minutes ticked off until their repatriation, the *Pueblo* crewmen sat nervously in their buses. There was little conversation, and sheets hanging over the windows prevented them from even seeing any of their surroundings. As they waited, a guard distributed copies of the apology letter. "Here it is," he announced. "You can see for yourselves." One thing jumped out at them immediately: the last two lines of the letter, which acknowledged "receipt of eighty-two former crew members of the *Pueblo* and one corpse," had been crudely erased.[17] Other captors continued to harangue the men with lectures about the evils of capitalism. Finally, guards led Bucher from the bus and walked him to the north end of the bridge. They waited in silence for twenty minutes. A North Korean soldier approached at 11:30. "Now walk across that bridge, captain," he ordered. "Not stop. Not look back. Not make any bad move. Just walk across sincerely. Go now!"[18] Fighting the urge to run, Bucher slowly began his march home while North Korean loudspeakers blasted a tape of his confession in the background. Soon after, DPRK soldiers began broadcasting other confessions the crewmen had given, including the one in which the men proclaimed their desire to paean (pee on) the DPRK government.[19] A cascade of flashbulbs filled the air as the commander reached the American side. First to greet him was army colonel John Lucas, the American secretary of the Military Armistice Commission, who spoke the words Bucher had waited 335 days to hear: "Welcome back, Commander Bucher."[20]

Turning back to the bridge, Bucher identified his men as they crossed over at thirty-second intervals. They walked, remarked one South Korean observer, "the way only Americans walk."[21] The first of the *Pueblo* men to follow Bucher was Duane Hodges, carried across the bridge in a plain wooden coffin. As each subsequent man reached the end, Bucher loudly pronounced his name and greeted him with a strong handshake and a broad smile. "It's just like," Law announced upon reaching the American side, "climbing out of Hell into Heaven."[22] After the entire crew finished the 250-foot march, three navy buses rushed them to an advance camp four miles south of the bridge for a quick medical examination and lunch. When Bucher walked into the mess hall, his crew rose as one to give him a standing ovation. Helicopters then flew them to the 121st Army Evacuation Hospital in Amscom City, ten miles west of Seoul, for a more thorough examination. Arriving in Amscom, Bucher held an impromptu press conference. "I would like to say," he began, "that I had perhaps the finest bunch of men that I've ever had the pleasure to serve with together with me in captivity in North Korea.... They never once lost their spirit or faith in the United States of America." Reporters put down their pens and listened as Bucher told the story of the seizure and their captivity. How would he describe North Korea, asked one? "Completely devoid of humanity," the commander responded, "completely devoted to [the] enslavement of men's minds."[23] The next morning, Rear Admiral Edwin Rosenberg, who was overseeing the crew's transport home, held his own conference. Bucher, he announced, was "a hero among heroes," and the men had "at all times acted in an extremely honorable fashion."[24]

The agreement received a generally favorable response internationally. The independent *Times* of London described it as "a triumph of patience and diplomacy," and "an encouraging sign that American public opinion is mature enough to endure this kind of provocation . . . without automatically resorting to rash countermeasures." The liberal *Guardian* (England) called it "another welcome relaxation of tension between the U.S. and the communist world," and the *Berita Harian* (Kuala Lumpur) praised LBJ for his "restraint in facing pressure from Pyongyang. . . . It has been proven once again that diplomacy is still not bankrupt, and that restraint in the face of a crisis such as this can benefit mankind."[25] Most nations quickly dismissed the apology. "Only a malicious observer could maintain that the American confession had any truth," wrote the *Berliner Morgenpost.* "The whole odious matter can be reduced to a simple conclusion: the North Koreans scored a propaganda success for home consumption." South Korea was the only American ally to voice displeasure. Porter had briefed Park on the resolution in advance, and the unhappy ROK president had accepted it, provided that it would "not lead to the impairment of the security of the Republic of Korea."[26] Still, criticism flowed from below the 38th parallel. *Donga Ilbo* called the agreement "dishonorable," and *Chosun Ilbo* lamented the decision to make "a secret deal . . . with an insignificant communist group in North Korea instead of punishing them." "The US," added one ROK official, "seems to be engrossed more in the release of the *Pueblo* crewmen than in the security of the free world."[27]

The communist reaction varied. The Soviet Union gave the resolution little coverage, failing even to list it in its year-end summary of important events in 1968.[28] Most likely, Moscow hoped to see the whole issue disappear without Soviet involvement attracting attention. Other communist nations were more outspoken. *Nhan Dan,* Hanoi's official paper, called the agreement "an ignominious defeat for the United States" and described the repudiation as "a base act that exposes further the obstinate and treacherous features of the United States imperialists."[29] Hanoi also distributed copies of the signed statement to Americans held in North Vietnamese prison camps. The letter, recalled an American prisoner of war who spent six years in captivity, "was far worse than anything I ever confessed to in my many confrontations, and he [Woodward] was permitted to make that statement without being tortured, and here we're being tortured . . . to prevent ourselves from saying even less. We felt really bad at that. We wondered in our own minds was it worth all that we took, to keep from making statements."[30]

Consistent to the end, the DPRK stressed the signing in the domestic media, milking the incident for every possible ounce of *juche* by portraying the letter as a demonstration of North Korean strength and audacity forcing a great power to yield.[31] The United States had "solemnly apologized," reported Radio Pyongyang, and in doing so had "signed a document . . . [which] will remain forever in history as the evidence of the brigandish crimes committed by the US imperialists and their disgraceful defeat and a record of the great victory of the Korean people."[32] A Korean Central News Agency report boasted, "The US imperialists bent the knee again to the Korean people"; the signing, it concluded, was an "ignominious defeat of the United States imperialist aggressors and constitutes another great victory of the Korean people, who have crushed the myth of the mightiness of United States imperialism to smithereens."[33] *Nodong Sinmun* also covered the agreement, often in *juche* terms, writing on January 8 that "peace must not be begged for but should be won by the struggle of the masses of the people. . . . Proof of this was furnished by the incident of the US imperialist armed spy ship *Pueblo*. . . . Thus our people once again humbled the arrogant pride of the US imperialists . . . and thus our party and people are not only defending the honor and dignity of our nation but the interests of the world revolution."[34]

Most Americans applauded the solution. The *New York Times* called it "a wise decision . . . to accept some sacrifice of American pride as preferable to a resolution by military force."[35] The president of the Veterans of Foreign Wars wrote to Johnson to "express the delight of the 1,450,000 members. . . . The nation's restraint and patience have paid off, and the men have been returned."[36] Still, concerns existed. "It is both delusive and dishonest," wrote the *Times*, "to pretend that world respect for America's integrity will not be injured by the willingness of this government to put its signature to a document it insists is a fraud."[37] Others blasted the administration for taking so long to reach the solution. "If we intended," asked Senator Gordon Allott (R-Colo.), "to admit before the whole world that we were wrong, and then deny that we were wrong, and then to deny that our apology was valid, did we have to wait eleven months to do it?"[38] Nor did the resolution of this one crisis placate the many who were unhappy with LBJ. "*Pueblo* taken care of," wrote the League of Wives of American Prisoners in Vietnam. "When will you effect release of prisoners of war and take action on missing personnel in Vietnam and Laos?"[39]

The men remained overnight in Amscom City, desperately hoping that the medical staff would clear them for the long flight home the next morning so that they could spend Christmas with their families. Visitors flooded the hospital, including ROK Prime Minister Chung-Il Kwon, who told Law that anyone hated so much by the North Koreans must be "the greatest people in the world." The Filipino ambassador came to visit the Filipino crewmen, but doctors, citing their need for rest, not only refused to let him enter but would not let the men drink the six-pack of San Miguel beer he left.[40] Good news came the next morning. Despite finding that almost one-third of the crew suffered from malnutrition, and many others sported various bruises and lacerations, the doctors approved the whole crew for an immediate flight home.[41] That afternoon, the men piled onto two air force C-141 Starlifters destined for San Diego, while in the background, loudspeakers blared Al Jolson's "California, Here I Come." The navy had thoughtfully stocked the planes with reading materials, including newspapers, comic books, the Bible, and *Playboy* magazines. Each man also received a small book entitled *World News Roundup,* which summarized the major events of 1968, including the election of Richard Nixon and the marriage of Jacqueline Kennedy to Aristotle Onasis. "Miniskirts," the crew was happy to read, "are still very much in style."[42]

The plane landed at Miramar Naval Air Station, twelve miles north of San Diego, at 2:00 P.M. on December 24. As the men descended onto American soil for the first time in over a year, the San Diego Naval Training Center band launched into a boisterous rendition of the *Pueblo*'s theme song, "The Lonely Bull." "That feeling of security when I felt the wheels touch down was tremendous," recalled Fireman Michael O'Bannon. "It was home. It didn't make any difference what state it was—it was home."[43] Five hundred family members and almost as many reporters were there to greet them. "Today," wrote the *San Diego Union,* "San Diego is happy again with tears as eighty-two men whose names will be permanently inscribed in the history of the United States come home to San Diego." Residents, the paper also noted, "shed mental tears for that blotch in American military-civilian relations that permitted the piracy of a ship of the United States Navy."[44]

After leading the crew out of the plane, Bucher marched into the chaos, his eyes searching for his family while he repeatedly muttered "thank you so much" to the well-wishing crowds. Finally spotting his wife and sons, he grabbed them all in a desperate embrace. "I love you, Rose," he muttered, tears running down his cheeks; it was the same line he had repeated eleven months earlier with a North Korean gun in his ear. Other families flocked to him. "Thank you, skipper," gushed one mother, "for bringing my boy back."[45] Shouts of joy rang out as men found their families, including five children who had been born while their fathers were in captivity. A note of sobriety interrupted the celebration when a navy honor guard carried Duane Hodges's casket off the plane and loaded it into a gray hearse while the navy band played "Taps." Bucher approached Hodges's parents and gave his mother a hug. "Your son," he told them, "was a great American."[46] Five days later, the great American was buried at Creswell Junior High School in Creswell, Oregon. In a town of 917 people, approximately 800 attended the funeral.[47]

For many, the jubilation proved fleeting. Despite the boisterous reception they received in San Diego, the *Pueblo* crewmen quickly sensed that they were persona non grata to many in the military and intelligence communities. "Overall," recalled one CT, "they seemed disappointed that we hadn't gone down with the ship. The younger ones seemed to understand our situation, but the majority of the old navy had this 'win or die' attitude."[48] Within a few days of their return, the men were debriefed by personnel from Navy Intelligence, the Naval Security Group, the NSA, and the Marine Corps Counter Intelligence Command, in an attempt to determine the specific ramifications of their capture. The questions were extensive (eventually covering 270 miles of tapes), and the questioners antagonistic. One enlisted man assigned to the debriefing team was shocked by the attitude of some of his colleagues:

> At first, it seemed to be a fact finding operation seeking information. Later on, after overhearing two of the civilian debriefers talking, I got the impression that they viewed the crew members as something less than U.S. Navy men. They said they wanted to use more forceful methods of debriefing and to me it sounded like interrogation. . . . I got the impression that they wanted to treat the crew members as criminals rather than as released prisoners. They seemed to think that the crew was being handled with "kid gloves" and that it was wasting time. I heard one of them say that if they could run the debriefing the way they wanted to that they would get the answers.[49]

The treatment left the men angry and confused. "I wanted [to go] back to North Korea," recalled one CT. "At least those guys didn't know what to ask!"[50]

On December 24, Admiral John Hyland of CINCPACFLT ordered the formation of a formal court of inquiry to investigate the circumstances of the seizure. To ward off the expected public protest, the navy hierarchy insisted that it was merely a routine inquiry. "The navy," Admiral Moorer insisted, "is searching for facts, not scapegoats."[51] In reality, however, the navy was determined to make an example of Bucher for surrendering his ship. "The military," recalled one vice admiral, "had blood in its eye to try to get Commander Bucher and bring him to justice."[52] Hyland appointed a panel of five admirals to investigate the matter, directing them to "inquire into all the facts and circumstances relating to the subject incident . . . [and] recommend administrative or disciplinary action as appropriate."[53] Heading the investigation was Vice Admiral Harold Bowen, Jr.

The inquiry horrified the American public. "Judging from what happened to the *Liberty* and the *Pueblo*," wrote the *New Republic*, "the navy prefers to accept the loss of these ships one by one, and then to court-martial the skipper if he survives."[54] "The navy and the Pentagon," echoed the *Newark (Ohio) Advocate,* "are at this moment trying to make Commander Lloyd M. Bucher scapegoat of the whole affair with the dishonest hope that this will satisfy the American people."[55] Still, the military insisted that Bucher would not be treated unfairly. "We may well end up pinning a medal on the commander," explained a ranking Pentagon official.[56] Few found these assurances convincing. "Commander Bucher," wrote a Tulsa woman to her congressman, "is getting a raw deal and we know it."[57]

Hearings began on January 20, 1969, at the U.S. Naval Amphibious Base in Coronado, California, and lasted almost two months.[58] Commander Bucher testified first and made it clear that he believed the navy had failed the *Pueblo,* not the other way around.

> I had a difficult time preparing for the type of operation I was scheduled to conduct. . . . There were many improvements that we were not permitted due to money and time. . . . I did request a destruct system . . . [but] was turned down. . . . I had lost steering as many as sixty times in two weeks . . . we did have a stability problem . . . did not have a watertight door although I had requested one. . . . I had no collision alarm. I had requested it and was turned down . . . the .50 caliber machine guns were unfamiliar to my gunner's mate, who had never had any formal training in their use . . . we went to sea without any destruct device of an explosive nature.[59]

On the third day of testimony, he was questioned about his decision to relinquish the ship without a fight. "In making the decision to surrender," asked Captain William Newsome, the counsel to the court, "you also made the calculated decision that you would also surrender this additional classified element of your ship, the personnel?" "Yes sir," Bucher answered. "That is right." Ominously, the court called for an immediate recess. Soon it returned to session, and Captain Newsome addressed the *Pueblo*'s captain:

> It is my duty to inform you that the facts revealed . . . render you to be a suspect of a violation of the United States Naval Regulations, article 0730, which reads "the commanding officer shall not submit his command to be searched by any persons representing a foreign state; will not permit any of the personnel under his command to be removed . . . by such persons as long as he has the power to resist." You are further advised that having been so informed of that offense, you do not have to make any statements with respect to it. And any statement that you make . . . thereafter can be used as evidence against you in a subsequent trial.[60]

The next day, Bucher continued his testimony while admirals peppered him with questions and comments, sometimes accompanied with not-so-subtle hints that they held him personally responsible for the debacle. "The commanding officer," asked Bowen, "was ultimately responsible that all classified material on the ship was disposed of. Is that right, Commander Bucher?"[61] The weary captain did his best to answer the charges, but the year of confinement and the stress of the inquiry had clearly taken their toll, and he struggled to keep himself composed under the deluge of insinuation. He broke down only once, while relaying how the Koreans had first gotten him to confess by threatening to kill the crew, but his exhaustion was apparent throughout. During one recess, Tim Harris crept into the hearing room and passed him a note: "We've made it this far together," it read, "and we'll finish it together." The note was signed: "Bucher's Bastards."[62]

After Bucher, the admirals interviewed others who were either involved with the incident or had some relevant expertise in the field. The five admirals found much to criticize in the *Pueblo*'s premission preparation. When asked about his plans to protect the *Pueblo*, Admiral Johnson explained that "I had this on-call arrangement with the Fifth Air Force and Commander Seventh Fleet." Admiral Marshall White shook his head. "So when we add it up," he responded, "then we really had a contingency plan to use forces which do not exist?"[63] White also took issue with the risk evaluation procedure. "The ship received a hazardous duty allowance for classified publications," he noted, "yet the risk of this mission was estimated to be minimal. How does hazardous jibe with minimal?" he asked. "This is outside my field," responded Rear Admiral George Cassell, the former assistant chief of staff for operations at CINC-PACFLT. "I'm not able to explain that rationale."[64] Others found different aspects to criticize. "It seems to me," declared Bowen, "that in a highly technological navy, in the area of classified material and equipment we haven't moved very far since the Stone Age."[65]

The hearings lasted almost two months. The admirals called 104 witnesses, who produced over 4,300 pages of testimony.[66] A host of navy officers testified, including Admiral Johnson, Rear Admiral George Cassell of CINCPACFLT, and Captains Thomas Dwyer and William Everett of COMNAVFORJAPAN. For advice on specific issues, the board summoned a navy expert on emergency destruction, a former submarine commander, and the former commander of the *Banner*. To get a feel for the ship, they traveled to Little Creek, Virginia, to tour the *Palm Beach*. They also questioned the *Pueblo* crewmen. "What kept you going during detention?" one admiral asked Seaman Ramon Rosales. "My faith in God and my country," he answered, "and the decisions of my CO." Bucher's head fell into his hands, and he quietly wept.[67]

The investigation closed on March 13, and the court released its findings four weeks later. It was not good news for the men of the *Pueblo*. After listing the many failings of the ship's officers, the two-and-a-half-pound report recommended court-martial for Bucher and Stephen Harris. "He just didn't try," the court wrote of Bucher. "This was his greatest fault." The admirals also suggested formal letters of admonition for Murphy for "dereliction in the performance of his duties as executive officer," for Admiral Johnson for "derelict[ion] in the performance of duty in negligently failing to plan properly," and for Captain Everett Gladding of the Naval Security Group for failing to "provide intelligence support." Although the rest of the crew escaped formal punishment, the court noted that "with few exceptions, the performance of the men was unimpressive."[68] Eleven were singled out for exemplary conduct while in captivity, and five were criticized for revealing too much classified information. Ironically, the crewman who had cooperated with the North Koreans to such an extent that he was almost murdered by his shipmates avoided censure completely, since Bucher, after the release, requested that the men keep his actions secret.[69]

In early April, the court sent its formal conclusions to Admiral Hyland, who, citing the length of a court-martial and the likely public outcry, recommended instead letters of admonition for the three *Pueblo* officers and Admiral Johnson, and no punishment for Gladding. On April 18, he forwarded these reports to John Chafee, the secretary of the navy, for a final decision. Three weeks later, Chafee released his verdict. "As a result of my review," he announced at a press conference, "I have decided that no disciplinary actions will be taken against any of the personnel involved in the *Pueblo* Incident. . . . It is my opinion," he concluded, "that they have suffered enough, and further punishment would not be justified."[70] The decision infuriated many officers. "I was appalled," recalled the chief of the U.S. Naval Advisory Group in Korea, "[when] Chafee threw out the recommendation." "The decision by SECNAV to clear Commander Bucher," wrote another officer, "was good news to many folks including my dear wife, but to me he will remain always as a coward disgracing the navy and blackening our glorious naval tradition." Chafee, agreed Admiral Hyland, was a "politician . . . [lacking] any deep feelings for the navy." The secretary's explanation that the men had "suffered enough" did not satisfy Hyland, since, he later explained, "They really didn't look all that bad to me when they got back."[71]

With Hyland's decision, the *Pueblo* Incident drew to a close. Although the House of Representatives undertook its own investigation, the military offered little cooperation, refusing to release documents, failing to provide complete information, and frequently requesting closed sessions to provide even the slightest details. These constant demands for secrecy, concluded the head of the investigation, were designed "not to protect national security but to protect individuals or groups from embarrassment."[72] In June, after three months of hearings, the committee released a report that leveled a barrage of criticism at the military and emphasized the serious consequences of its errors. "The damage this incident has caused our nation," the committee concluded, "is, in truth, incalculable."[73] The *Pueblo* men either left or were quietly driven from the service. "The results of the Court of Inquiry . . . and subsequent actions of the navy in regard to my career," declared Murphy when he resigned in May, "seem to leave no alternative."[74]

For most of them, however, the year of confinement left scars that could not be so easily forgotten. Some of the men returned to personal problems with devastating consequences. One man found his wife four months pregnant, and another returned to a still incomplete family; his brother had been killed in Vietnam a week after the *Pueblo* capture. Navy psychiatrists diagnosed three men—Bucher, Goldman, and Mack—with reactive depression, and the whole crew, concluded one naval officer who debriefed them, went through "mental torture. . . . Something was set up between the captors and the crewman—a psychological fear that these men still have. . . . The North Koreans took the will out of a lot of people."[75] For some, physical reminders of the ordeal continued for years, including loss of feeling in or control of their extremities, vision problems, and various forms of nerve damage. Bucher himself had only 40 percent use of his hip as a result of the beatings and torture. A large number could never hold steady jobs because of their physical disabilities. Most found even greater problems adjusting emotionally, and divorce, alcoholism, drug abuse, and suicide took a major toll on the survivors. The American military did little to help them through the difficult adjustment period. "I was never even warned that there might be residual effects of the imprisonment," lamented one, "so I wasn't even aware that what I was experiencing wasn't normal."[76] "The second they opened fire on us," recalled another, "the whole world changed completely and forever."[77]

The *Pueblo* itself remained in North Korean hands. In 1999, the DPRK relocated it to a spot in the Taedong River, outside Pyongyang. The ship, the captors' claimed, now occupied the same position where Kim Il Sung's grandfather had led an attack against the USS *General Sherman* in 1866. The new spot, however, did not change the ship's role as a propaganda instrument, as approved guests could climb aboard for a tour that included a twenty-minute video shown in the mess hall celebrating the capture and release of the crew. In 1992, North Korea even offered the men a chance to return to see the ship and to be guests at Kim's eightieth birthday party. Consistent to the end, however, the trip was reported to the international press as a journey of repentant spies seeking forgiveness from a former enemy. Unsurprisingly, no one accepted the offer.

It would be over twenty years before the *Pueblo* crew again assembled for an official navy ceremony. In 1969, the navy awarded the Legion of Merit to Captain William Newsome, the Board of Inquiry's legal adviser, but gave only a few Purple Hearts to those *Pueblo* men who had been seriously wounded during the attack, including one that went posthumously to Duane Hodges.[78] Bucher was incensed. "Many people," he wrote in 1970, "including the counsel for the court of inquiry, the commanding officer of the naval hospital which initially cared for us, and all those who participated in the navy response to our capture on board ship in the Sea of Japan have been awarded some medal for performance or service. It seems to me that everyone connected even remotely to *Pueblo,* with the exception of its crew, has been somehow rewarded for their service."[79] For two decades, he lobbied for similar recognition for his men. In the early 1970s, the navy granted some additional awards, including a Navy Cross, two Silver Stars, five Bronze Stars, and numerous Navy Achievement Medals; yet most went for actions taken on the day of the seizure.[80] The navy also granted Civilian Service Medals to the two civilians, Harry Iredale and Donnie Tuck. In 1985, Congress created the Prisoner of War Medal, specifically to honor those who had suffered in enemy captivity, but the Pentagon ruled the *Pueblo* crew ineligible, explaining that they had merely been detained in North Korea rather than being POWs, since there was no formal conflict between the two nations at the time of the capture.[81]

Their exclusion left the men hurt and angry, especially since a formal state of war did exist between the United States and North Korea, because the Korean War had been resolved with only a military armistice rather than a formal peace treaty. Many others also found the decision objectionable. After the first medal presentations in 1988, the *San Diego Union-Tribune* noted that the *Pueblo* men were "disturbingly absent" and reminded readers that "the bottom line is that those eighty-two men would not have found themselves in that situation if they had not been serving their country."[82] Shortly thereafter, Stephen Woelk wrote to his congressman, Jim Slattery (D-Kans.), to protest the crew's exclusion. In 1988, Slattery introduced unsuccessful legislation specifically declaring the *Pueblo* men eligible for the POW Medal, and the following year, he pushed for a House of Representatives investigation of the decision. Congress agreed, and on June 23, 1989, the Investigations Subcommittee of the House Committee on Armed Services held hearings on the decision to exclude the men.[83] Four *Pueblo* crewmen testified, including Bucher, who protested the decision vehemently. "Those men," Bucher concluded, "were America's sons."[84] Congress agreed. "In our eyes and in the eyes of the American people, let me assure you—not that you want to hear this—but you are heroes each and every one of you," concluded Congressman Nicholas Mavroules (D-Mass.). "We appreciate what you have done for our country."[85] Under pressure from Congress and the public to reverse the decision, the navy yielded and agreed to award the men their medals.

On May 5, 1990, sixty-four members of the *Pueblo* crew gathered in Washington, D.C., to receive POW Medals in full-dress navy ceremonies at the County Administration Building. Assistant Secretary of the Navy Barbara Pope read a statement from President George Bush, which commended them for their "unfailing resolve" and acknowledged that "America owes a debt of gratitude to the crew of the *Pueblo.*"[86] Pope then yielded to Schumacher, who announced to the men that the medal demonstrated that which they had already known, "that this crew did serve honorably." As the men lined up to receive their medal from Assistant Secretary Pope, they and their families took turns congratulating one another and cheering each man as he walked onto the stage. The loudest cheers came for Commander Bucher.

Conclusion

In 1796, President John Adams signed a treaty with Tripoli pledging the United States to pay an annual tribute in return for a promise from the Barbary state to refrain from plundering American commerce in the Mediterranean Sea. When the pasha of Tripoli, Yusuf Karamanli, broke the agreement five years later, President Thomas Jefferson responded with force, dispatching the American navy to the region with the order to "protect our commerce and chastise their insolence—by sinking, burning or destroying their ships and vessels wherever you shall find them."[1] The two sides fought a number of battles over the next few years, and in 1803, Tripoli captured the frigate *Philadelphia* and her crew of over 300 men. The ship's physician described their treatment in blunt terms: "Our seamen were immediately put to hard labor, without mercy, and they have suffered much for the necessities of life. Five have paid their last debt to nature."[2] Quickly, the American consul in Tunis led an army of mercenaries and U.S. Marines that seized the Tripolitan town of Derne. In 1805, the pasha relented and signed a treaty allowing American shipping to continue unfettered.

One hundred sixty-five years later, American foreign policy had become much more complicated. The nation's rise to global superpower status brought increased responsibilities and interests, while advances in military technology brought increased dangers. An interdependent world economy, expanding cultural relations, improvements in communication and transportation, and a series of alliances and rivalries linked the United States with the rest of the world in ways the founding fathers could never have envisioned. Two world wars had shattered the era of imperial control, freeing many small countries to act in accordance with their own traditions and values rather than at the dictate of a foreign authority, and unleashing a Third World nationalism that resented the exercise of force by the great powers anywhere around the globe. In such a world, where every American action had global and complex ramifications, Jefferson's aggressive "gunboat diplomacy" would have been sorely out of place.

As international relations evolved, American policy makers responded by seeking a "one size fits all" paradigm that could provide simple answers to complex questions. They thus forced disparate international situations to fit within a single framework that was based on the immediate threat of the Cold War and the global rivalry between capitalism and communism. Instability and opposition, regardless of their specific form, became automatically associated with an international plot whose ultimate objective was the destruction of the United States. While this paradigm brought order and comprehensibility to the increasingly complicated international arena, it also hindered recognition of the importance of indigenous values and local circumstances in world affairs. Thus, American policy makers saw no need to distinguish Soviet communism from other more nationalistic variants, since, as Secretary of State Dean Acheson explained of Ho Chi Minh in 1949, "[The] question of whether Ho [is] as much nationalist as Commie is irrelevant. All Stalinists in colonial areas are nationalists." "The assault on free institutions is worldwide now," echoed the National Security Council the following year, "and in the context of the present polarization of power a defeat of free institutions anywhere is a defeat everywhere."[3]

Accordingly, American military, intelligence, and political leaders often ignored local factors in dealing with communist nations, whose defining characteristic was thought to be membership in the larger communist bloc. The ramifications of this belief were most clearly demonstrated in Vietnam, but the same failure lay at the heart of the *Pueblo* Incident. In planning and executing the *Pueblo* mission, American advisers neglected to do the one thing that was needed above all else: evaluate North Korea as North Korea rather than as a generic communist nation. Had they done so, they might have recognized the possibility that emerging problems in the nation's economic and political life could spark Kim to more aggressive actions in foreign relations, in accordance with the nation's defining ideological tenets. Their failure to do so reflected basic American perceptions of the world and the way it operated. It also sealed the fate of the eighty-three men of the USS *Pueblo*.

After the release of the crew, American policy makers returned to their comfortable Cold War worldview and settled for superficial reforms that failed to acknowledge the shortcomings inherent in this simplistic method of conducting foreign policy. The *Pueblo* Incident was quickly glossed over, viewed as an unfortunate aberration whose blame lay primarily with Commander Pete Bucher. "He [Bucher] didn't do anything," explained Admiral Hyland. "It was absolutely inexcusable."[4] "All made mistakes of judgement," wrote syndicated columnist James Reston, "but only Commander Bucher was held accountable and put through a medieval trial which exposed his agony and broke his spirit."[5] Thus armed with a convenient scapegoat, government officials saw no need for a structural reexamination of American intelligence-collection programs and continued to approve superfluous missions characterized by ill-equipped vehicles, inadequate risk assessment, and insufficient contingency planning.

Although Lyndon Johnson abandoned the Clickbeetle program soon after the *Pueblo* capture, reconnaissance planes and specifically configured submarines continued to run similar missions. The night before the release of the *Pueblo* crew, DPRK guards gave Seaman Stu Russell a warning to pass along to the United States. "The Sea of Japan is the Sea of Korea," they told him. Any American ships or planes entering would be destroyed. When Russell relayed the message to the intelligence officers who debriefed him, they laughingly dismissed the threat: "The United States can do what we want where we want."[6] On April 14, 1969, North Korea shot down an American EC-121 reconnaissance plane over the Sea of Japan, with thirty-one Americans on board. The aircraft had been conducting intelligence collection about seventy miles southeast of Chongjin. The similarities with the *Pueblo* were eerie. The plane was virtually unarmed, suffered from communications problems, reported to the Naval Security Group in Kamiseya, and was not supported by any covering forces. "It appears abundantly clear," noted a House of Representatives Armed Services Subcommittee, "that the same degree of confusion existed in the military command organization in respect to the EC-121 incident that occurred previously in the case of the USS *Pueblo*."[7] Once again, the system had failed to protect those who had sworn to protect the system. There was one major difference between the EC-121 and the *Pueblo*, however; this time, there were no survivors.[8]

This failure to heed the lessons of the *Pueblo* continued to hinder intelligence missions over the next decade. Operations bearing such code names as "Binnacle" and "Holystone" converted submarines for use in intelligence-collection missions by adding new sections filled with special eavesdropping equipment and communications specialists similar to the SOD-Huts.[9] The programs, which actually predated the AGERs but assumed a more important position in the late 1960s, were—like Clickbeetle—directed by the chief of naval operations, with missions subject to the approval of the 303 Committee (now called the 40 Committee). The similar process led to similar results, as shortcomings plagued the operations. Submarines (sometimes referred to as "underwater U-2s") were often sent on dangerous assignments, despite obvious physical deficiencies and despite the sometimes redundant nature and questionable worth of their missions. In many ways, American intelligence had just moved the AGER program underwater.

The undersea program's most notable tragedy involved the USS *Scorpion*, a 3,500-ton nuclear submarine that disappeared in the summer of 1968.[10] Like the *Pueblo*, the *Scorpion* had serious physical deficiencies; in fact, it was so

badly in need of repairs that the crew had nicknamed it the "USS *Scrap Iron.*"
Recognizing the problems, the navy limited the sub's operations to a depth of
300 feet, less than one-third of the operational depth of similar vessels, but
budget constraints and a desire for immediate information led it to delay badly
needed repair work. After completing an assignment in the Mediterranean Sea
in April 1968, the *Scorpion* was scheduled to return to Virginia, but instead, the
navy sent her on another eavesdropping mission, this time monitoring Soviet
ships just outside of the Mediterranean. In late May, the *Scorpion* finished her
work and finally headed home. It was a trip she would never complete. Investigators found the sub near the Sargasso Sea in the North Atlantic Ocean on October 29, half buried in sand and separated into two pieces, the result of an ex-
plosion caused by a faulty torpedo battery. Engineers had warned of problems
with the battery design for years, but no one in the chain of command had
taken action. This time, the death toll was ninety-nine.

Other events also reflected the problems endemic to the program. Ill-
equipped ships sent on dangerous missions (many of which could have been
accomplished by satellite technology) repeatedly avoided disaster by the slim-
mest of margins. In 1968, the USS *Scamp* narrowly avoided destruction when,
in a hurry to monitor a Soviet missile test, it rammed an underwater mountain
in the Pacific. One sub was damaged when it surfaced into the bottom of a Soviet ship that was in the middle of fleet naval exercises; another ran aground
within three miles of Soviet territory; and a third collided with a Soviet submarine in the North Sea in 1974 while carrying sixteen nuclear missiles. In late
1969, the USS *Gato,* operating as close as one mile off the Soviet coast, collided
with a Soviet missile submarine a mere two days before arms-control talks
were scheduled to begin in Helsinki, Finland. Soviet and Chinese officials, who
were aware of the program, occasionally launched operations to find the subs,
and on a number of occasions, such a loss seemed imminent. Yet these dangers
were overlooked by those in direct control of the missions, despite criticism
from a number of government and intelligence officials familiar with the program. "What bothers me," explained one, "is the fact that the Soviets know
we're there. This isn't like overhead intelligence. This is provocative."[11]

There is no doubt that some of these operations provided vital information
that could not have been collected in any other manner. In 1971, the USS *Hali-
but* tapped into Soviet underwater telephone cables in the Sea of Okhotsk,
gaining unprecedented access to strategic information. Yet other missions
seemed less vital and more easily accomplished by technical means. Even when
assignments were merited, they were plagued by the same types of physical and
support problems that had characterized the *Pueblo.* The American government
had asked the men operating these submarines to risk their lives in missions

that were deemed critical to the future of the United States. If the operations were that vital, surely those conducting them deserved to have the full resources of the American government behind them. Pinching pennies and carelessly evaluating risks violated the principles that these men were risking their lives to defend. The fact that a number of submariners came forward in the early 1970s to provide classified information to reporters and congressional investigators suggests that even those at the front lines had begun to question the way the program was being run.

Although many military and intelligence officials ignored the lessons of the *Pueblo*, its significance was not lost on those seeking to provide greater oversight of future intelligence operations. The criticisms leveled at the military and intelligence communities by the House subcommittee that investigated the *Pueblo* Incident were echoed throughout the halls of Congress, as many began demanding a greater degree of accountability from the nation's intelligence agencies. Other examples of shoddy, unnecessary, or unconstitutional operations by American intelligence services continued to emerge in the late 1960s and early 1970s, steadily turning public opinion against them.[12] In 1975, Congress decided to take action. In January, the Senate created a Select Committee to Study Governmental Operations with Respect to Intelligence Activities, under the chairmanship of Idaho Democrat Frank Church. The committee's charter demanded that it investigate "whether there is unnecessary duplication of expenditure and effort in the collection and processing of intelligence information by United States agencies," and consider "the need for improved, strengthened, or consolidated oversight of United States intelligence activities by the Congress."[13] The House appointed a similar committee in February, this one chaired by Otis Pike, who had led the House subcommittee investigation of the *Pueblo* Incident. Extensive hearings filled the air with dramatic information about murder plots, domestic spying, incompetence, and carelessness and left both committees convinced that the American intelligence community needed to start answering to congressional authorities. The Church Committee's 651-page final report, released in April 1976, concluded that intelligence operations had become "excessive, and at times self-defeating. . . . In addition, covert action has become a routine program with a bureaucratic momentum of its own."[14] It was a conclusion the *Pueblo* crewmen had learned the hard way eight years earlier.

In the end, the committee proposed eighty-seven specific reforms designed to create greater oversight of the intelligence apparatus. The suggestions included requiring the approval of the NSC, the executive branch, and all "appropriate congressional committees" before any covert operation could be launched. That summer, both houses of Congress established permanent committees on intelligence and required intelligence agencies keep them "fully and currently informed" of their operations. Although in the end these measures had only limited success, the decade of the 1970s brought the most serious attempt of the post–World War II era to enforce civilian control of America's intelligence operations. The "Era of Trust," as one leading intelligence historian has termed the years from 1947 until 1974, had collapsed, replaced in 1976 by an "Era of Uneasy Partnership."[15] The *Pueblo* had played a small but not unimportant part in the transition.

The *Pueblo* Incident also helps shed some light on the foreign policies of the Johnson administration. Although there is not yet a true consensus, Johnson's diplomacy generally receives poor marks from both historians and the general public. A major component of this criticism is the contention that LBJ overreacted to perceived communist threats and thus involved the country in foreign crises that did not represent legitimate dangers to American interests. "Lacking a sophisticated perception of international relations," concluded one historian, "Johnson . . . remained captive of Cold War illusions shaped by a Munich analogy where distinctions between communism and fascism blurred and a strong America that was always ready to counter aggression was essential."[16] Such obvious cases as the Vietnam War and the American intervention in the Dominican Republic present clear examples in support of the idea that Johnson, in accordance with basic Cold War precepts, neither recognized nor cared about the relationship between communism and nationalism in Third World countries. "He [LBJ] would not take the openings offered," wrote one leading historian of the Vietnam War, "he would not act, and thus he was finally unable to escape the Cold War definition of the world that he had helped to construct for so many years."[17]

The president's handling of the *Pueblo* Incident reinforces this perception. In a crisis that offered little evidence of a larger communist conspiracy, LBJ and most of his advisers nevertheless remained wedded to the belief that one existed. Yet such criticism does not tell the whole story and, in fact, can distract from another, more positive aspect of Johnson's diplomacy. In his handling of the *Pueblo* Incident, LBJ had failed to consider the event from a North Korean worldview, and for this, his administration certainly deserves censure. Yet, within his Cold War framework, the president handled the crisis remarkably well. In the face of loud (albeit brief) public demands for retribution, he wisely stuck to a diplomatic course that avoided another costly Asian war. In the face of growing unhappiness and pressure from South Korea, he kept his allies in line with a skillful combination of the carrot and the stick. In the face of lengthy and discouraging negotiations, he continued to try new approaches until finally stumbling across the right one. In the end, then, Johnson may not have always made the right decisions for the right reasons, but he made the right decisions nonetheless.

In fact, Johnson's patient handling of the *Pueblo* Incident in 1968, combined with his increased efforts that year to achieve peace in Vietnam and his moves toward arms control and other agreements with the Soviet Union, suggests that perhaps the president had grown as a foreign policy leader by the end of his term. The brash and confident LBJ who had sent troops to Vietnam in 1965 while loudly predicting victory was now nowhere to be seen. By 1968, his actions in Korea and elsewhere suggest that he had grasped the more complex nature of foreign policy in the modern world. Johnson, the *Pueblo* Incident indicates, had perhaps realized that power is relative; possession of a certain type or degree of power in one situation does not necessarily translate into the ability to apply it in another. North Korea was no match for the United States by any traditional measure of power, yet the world situation in 1968 and Kim's possession of eighty-two hostages made such traditional measures irrelevant. For a man of action and bluster like Lyndon Johnson, the idea that a great power like the United States might not hold all the cards during a crisis with a smaller nation like North Korea was no doubt a difficult one to accept. Yet he recognized this reality and sought a peaceful solution that in the end solved the crisis without damaging larger American interests. The "new" LBJ thus avoided another Asian war, maintained and even solidified America's alliances, dodged a potential rift with the Soviets and the Chinese, and won worldwide accolades for his patient diplomacy. These foreign policy lessons may have been learned too late to help over 500,000 American soldiers fighting in Vietnam, but they likely saved the lives of eighty-two sailors trapped in North Korea.

Much as American political and military leaders quickly forgot the lessons of the *Pueblo,* the American people quickly forgot the *Pueblo* itself. The incident became just another vague memory of unwarranted communist aggression against heroic Americans, a tragic but unavoidable part of the Cold War struggle. Had they paid more attention, Americans might have realized that there was more to the tale of the *Pueblo* than appeared at first glance. It was a story of heroes and villains, but also of many others who belonged somewhere in between. It was a story of spectacular triumphs and disasters, but also of less noticeable mistakes and misperceptions. It was a story of a Cold War crisis that at the same time had little to do with the Cold War. And it was the story of a group of men who did their jobs as they had been instructed and, as a reward, suffered the harsh ramifications of the failures of others. Perhaps Commander Bucher put it best, writing twenty years after his release, "Our country and our navy were served honorably and loyally by all the officers and men of the *Pueblo*—and if I may say so, one hell of a sight better than they were served in turn."[18]

Notes

INTRODUCTION

1 Quoted in Lloyd Bucher with Mark Rascovich, *Bucher* (Garden City, N.Y.: Doubleday, 1970), p. 141.

2 This exchange is quoted in Trevor Armbrister, *A Matter of Accountability* (New York: Coward-McCann, 1970), p. 17. The risk assessment is from the *Pueblo's* operational orders, December 1967, p. 2, reprinted in "Inquiry into the USS *Pueblo* and EC-121 Plane Incidents," *Report of the Special Subcommittee on the U.S.S.* Pueblo *of the Committee on Armed Services,* House of Representatives, Ninety-first Congress, First Session, July 28, 1969 (Washington, D.C.: U.S. Government Printing Office, 1969), p. 1644; hereafter referred to as House *Pueblo* Report. On the *Pueblo's* problems mentioned above, see Bucher, *Bucher,* pp. 139–141; Edward Murphy with Curt Gentry, *Second in Command* (New York: Holt, Rinehart and Winston, 1971), pp. 79–81; Armbrister, *Matter of Accountability,* p. 14.

3 The TV movie "*Pueblo*" aired on ABC on March 29, 1973.

4 Dan Hearn, "A Career Built on SIGINT," *American Intelligence Journal,* Spring/Summer 1994, p. 69.

CHAPTER 1. A CLASSIFIED OPERATION

1 Bucher, *Bucher,* p. 1.

2 This exchange is reprinted in ibid., pp. 2–4.

3 For the purposes of this book, the term *signals intelligence* includes both communications intelligence (COMINT), which is technical and intelligence information derived from intercepting communications such as telephone, satellite, or undersea cable contacts, and electronic intelligence (ELINT), which is technical and intelligence information obtained from noncommunications-related sources, such as radar and other air defense systems, missile signals, and infrared and light signals.

4 House *Pueblo* Report, p. 1631. The ship that first detected the missiles was either the USS *Oxford* or the USS *Muller,* but it is not known which, since they frequently covered for each other in this area.

5 On wartime SIGINT programs, see *History of the Special Branch, MIS, War Department,* National Archives II, College Park, Md., record group 457, stack 190, box 17, SRH-035 (hereafter this archive is referred to as NA2). See also James Bamford, *The Puzzle Palace* (New York: Penguin Books, 1983), chap. 2; Edward Drea, *MacArthur's*

Ultra (Lawrence: University Press of Kansas, 1993); John Winton, *Ultra in the Pacific* (London: Leo Copper, 1993). On intelligence matters prior to Pearl Harbor, see especially Gordon Prange, *At Dawn We Slept* (Middlesex, England: Penguin Books, 1981). Other good sources include Jonathan Utley, *Going to War with Japan* (Knoxville: University of Tennessee Press, 1985); Waldo Heinrich, *Threshold of War* (New York: Oxford University Press, 1988); Ladislas Farago, *The Broken Seal* (New York: Bantam Books, 1968); John Tolland, *Infamy* (New York: Berkley Books, 1982). For a more thorough examination of the evolution of SIGINT in general during and after World War II, see William Corson, *Armies of Ignorance* (New York: Dial Press, 1977), chaps. 4 and 5; David Kahn, *The Codebreakers* (New York: Macmillan, 1973), especially chaps. 1, 2, and 17; Bamford, *Puzzle Palace*. On the intelligence failures of the Korean War, see Joseph Goulden, *Korea* (New York: McGraw-Hill, 1982), chap. 1; Ed Evanhoe, *Dark Moon* (Annapolis, Md.: Naval Institute Press, 1995); William Breuer, *Shadow Warriors* (New York: John Wiley and Sons, 1996).

6 National Security Council Intelligence Directive #6 quoted in Jeffrey Richelson, *The U.S. Intelligence Community* (Cambridge: Ballinger Publishing, 1985), p. 301.

7 Tyrus Fain, ed., *The Intelligence Community* (New York: R. R. Bowker, 1977), p. 361; Bamford, *Puzzle Palace*, p. 122.

8 Loch Johnson, *America's Secret Power* (New York: Oxford University Press, 1989), p. 53.

9 Ibid., p. 52; Victor Marchetti and John Marks, *The CIA and the Cult of Intelligence* (New York: Dell Publishing, 1974), p. 196; Richelson, *U.S. Intelligence Community*, pp. 16–17; Bamford, *Puzzle Palace*, p. 273.

10 House *Pueblo* Report, pp. 1631–34. See also Bamford, *Puzzle Palace*, chap. 5; David Hannum, Jr., "The *Pueblo* Incident" (unpublished research project, National War College, Washington, D.C., 1974); Richard Deacon, *The Silent War* (New York: Hippocrene Books, 1978), p. 224.

11 McNamara to Senate Appropriations Committee, February 1, 1968, Lyndon B. Johnson Presidential Library, Austin, Tex., National Security File, NSC Histories, *Pueblo* Crisis, 1968, boxes 31–33, vol. 13, public statements, tabs D–F, "Compilation of Statements Concerning USS *Pueblo* Incident." Hereafter this library is referred to as JL.

12 *Congressional Record*, January 31, 1968, vol. 114, pt. 2, p. 1668; telegram to American Embassy Tokyo from State Department, #108362, February 1, 1968, NA2, 1967–69 central files, pol 33-6, box 2256, folder 2/1/68; oral history of Vice Admiral Edwin Hooper, Naval Historical Center, Washington, D.C., Operational Archives branch, pp. 430–32 (hereafter this archive is referred to as NHC); Bamford, *Puzzle Palace*, pp. 273–74.

13 Oral history of Captain Phil Bucklew, NHC, Operational Archives branch; notes of the president's meeting with Senator Dirksen and Congressman Ford, JL, Tom Johnson's notes of meetings, box 2, January 30, 1968, 6:04 P.M., p. 4.

14 Telegram from State Department to American Embassy Moscow, #106055, January 27, 1968, JL, National Security File, NSC Histories, *Pueblo* Crisis, 1968, box 29 and 30, vol. 6, day by day documents, pt. 10.

15 Transcript of news briefing, February 6, 1968, JL, National Security File, NSC Histories, *Pueblo* Crisis, 1968, boxes 29, 30, vol. 6, day by day documents, pt. 10; telegram to State Department from American Embassy Moscow, #106055, January 27, 1968, JL, National Security File, NSC Histories, *Pueblo* Crisis, 1968, boxes 29, 30, vol. 6, day by day documents, pt. 10.

16 Meeting notes, January 30, 1968, 8:30 A.M., JL, Tom Johnson's notes of meetings, box 2.

17 *Congressional Record,* January 31, 1968, vol. 14, pt. 2, p. 1668.

18 Oral history of Admiral Thomas Moorer, vol. 2, NHC, Operational Archives branch, p. 700.

19 Frank Raven quoted in Bamford, *Puzzle Palace,* p. 275.

20 Bamford, *Puzzle Palace,* pp. 274–76.

21 Ibid., p. 276.

22 Oral history of Vice Admiral Edwin Hooper, NHC, Operational Archives branch, pp. 430–32; House *Pueblo* Report, p. 1632; Bamford, *Puzzle Palace,* pp. 277–93; Richelson, *U.S. Intelligence Community,* pp. 127–29; *Jane's Fighting Ships, 1967/68* (New York: McGraw-Hill, 1970).

23 Armbrister, *Matter of Accountability,* pp. 81–83; Bamford, *Puzzle Palace,* pp. 294–95.

24 F. Carl Schumacher with George Wilson, *Bridge of No Return* (New York: Harcourt Brace Jovanovich, 1971), p. 60; Armbrister, *Matter of Accountability,* pp. 82–85; Bamford, *Puzzle Palace,* pp. 294–96.

25 Statement by Rear Admiral Frank Johnson, *Hearings before the Special Subcommittee on the U.S.S.* Pueblo *of the Committee on Armed Services,* House of Representatives (Washington, D.C.: U.S. Government Printing Office, 1969), p. 733; hereafter these proceedings are referred to as House *Pueblo* hearings.

26 Technically, the *Banner* maintained its designation as an AKL until 1967, when AGERs were officially sanctioned to exist.

27 House *Pueblo* Report, p. 1634.

28 "Legal Issues in the *Pueblo* Seizure," JL, National Security File, NSC Histories, *Pueblo* Crisis, 1968, boxes 31–33, vol. 12, summary press reaction, representative press folder.

29 Armbrister, *Matter of Accountability,* pp. 116–17.

30 McDonald quoted in ibid., p. 84.

31 Oseth quoted in ibid., p. 85.

32 House *Pueblo* Report, pp. 1632–35; Bamford, *Puzzle Palace,* pp. 295–96; Bucher, *Bucher,* pp. 4–6.

33 Bamford, *Puzzle Palace,* pp. 295–96. Oseth quoted in Armbrister, *Matter of Accountability,* pp. 86–87.

34 Chief engineer quoted in Don Tuthill, "Operational Planning, Pre-*Pueblo,*" *Naval Intelligence Professionals Quarterly,* Winter 1994.

35 Oral history of Vice Admiral Edwin Hooper, NHC, Operational Archives branch, p. 433.

36 The problems of the *Banner* can be found in more detail in Bucher, *Bucher,* pp. 4–6; Armbrister, *Matter of Accountability,* pp. 86–87; House *Pueblo* Report, pp. 1647–48; "Finding of Facts, Opinions, and Recommendations of a Court of Inquiry," NHC, command file, post 1 Jan. 1946, USS *Pueblo,* pp. 8–10 (hereafter referred to as "Finding of Facts").

37 House *Pueblo* Report, p. 1636.

38 Oral History of Vice Admiral Edwin B. Hooper, NHC, Operational Archives branch, p. 431.

39 Armbrister, *Matter of Accountability,* p. 117; Bamford, *Puzzle Palace,* p. 298.

40 House *Pueblo* hearings, pp. 735–37, 779; Bamford, *Puzzle Palace,* pp. 297–98.

41 Lloyd Bucher, "Commander Bucher Replies," *Naval History,* Winter 1989, pp. 44–45; letter to Senator Wayne Morse from Glen Hancock, February 29, 1968, Wayne Morse

Papers, University of Oregon Library, Eugene, Oreg., Special Collections branch, collection 1, robo file series L, box 22, foreign relations: *Pueblo* Incident; CINPAC Command History, 1968, vol. 4, NHC, Operational Archives branch, p. 231; Bucher, *Bucher,* pp. 129–30; Armbrister, *Matter of Accountability,* pp. 168–69.

42 "Q and A" book, JL, National Security File, NSC Histories, *Pueblo* Crisis, 1968, boxes 31–33, vol. 13, public statements, tabs G–I; "Report on the *Pueblo* Incident," NA2, record group 200, papers of Robert McNamara (hereafter referred to as NSC *Pueblo* Report).

43 Testimony of Admiral Frank Johnson, House *Pueblo* hearings, p. 734; Bucher, *Bucher,* pp. 23, 130; Armbrister, *Matter of Accountability,* pp. 116–22.

44 Letter to Senator Wayne Morse from Glen Hancock, February 29, 1968, Wayne Morse Papers, University of Oregon Library, Special Collections branch, collection 1, robo file series L, box 22, foreign relations: *Pueblo* Incident.

45 Enclosure 7, House *Pueblo* hearings, p. 766; House *Pueblo* Report, p. 1639.

46 Author's telephone interview with Jack Stuchell, November 2, 2000.

47 Johnson quoted in Armbrister, *Matter of Accountability,* p. 117.

48 Testimony of Admiral Frank Johnson, House *Pueblo* hearings, p. 735.

49 Testimony of Lieutenant General Seth McKee, House *Pueblo* hearings, p. 863; Armbrister, *Matter of Accountability,* pp. 117–18.

50 Rusk quoted in George Herring, *America's Longest War,* 2nd ed. (New York: Alfred A. Knopf, 1986), p. 120.

51 *Congressional Record,* August 5, 1964, vol. 111, pp. 18132–33.

52 The best history of the program and the Gulf of Tonkin Incident itself is Edwin Moise, *Tonkin Gulf and the Escalation of the Vietnam War* (Chapel Hill: University of North Carolina Press, 1996). See also Ezra Siff, *Why the Senate Slept* (Westport, Conn.: Praeger Publishing, 1999); Joseph Goulden, *Truth Is the First Casualty* (Chicago: Rand McNally, 1969); Eugene Windchy, *Tonkin Gulf* (Garden City, N.Y., Doubleday, 1971); Anthony Austin, *The President's War* (Philadelphia: Lippincott Press, 1971).

53 Lieutenant Gerrell Moore quoted in Moise, *Tonkin Gulf,* pp. 52–53.

54 *New York Times,* February 4, 1968, p. 3.

55 Goulden, *Truth Is the First Casualty,* chap. 5.

56 Moise, *Tonkin Gulf,* p. 55.

57 The story of the *Liberty* is best described in James Ennes, Jr., *Assault on the* Liberty (New York: Random House, 1979). See also John Borne, *The USS* Liberty (New York: Reconsideration Press, 1995); William Gerhard, *Attack on the USS* Liberty (New York: Aegean Park, 1996); Donald Neff, *Warriors for Jerusalem* (New York: Simon and Schuster, 1984).

58 Ennes, *Assault on the* Liberty, p. 43.

59 Ibid., p. 21.

60 This response came from Vice Admiral William Martin, commander of the Sixth Fleet, quoted in ibid., pp. 42–43.

61 Testimony of Admiral Frank Johnson, House *Pueblo* hearings, p. 786.

62 Testimony of Admiral Thomas Moorer, House *Pueblo* hearings, p. 686.

63 Oral history of Admiral Thomas Moorer, JL, interview #2, pp. 1–4; testimony of Admiral Thomas Moorer, House *Pueblo* hearings, pp. 635–36.

64 Ennes, *Assault on the* Liberty, p. ix.

65 Roosevelt quoted in J. Garry Clifford, "Institutions and the Policy Process," in *American Foreign Relations Reconsidered,* ed. Gordon Martel (New York: Routledge, 1994), p. 29.

CHAPTER 2. THE UGLY DUCKLING

1 Bucher, *Bucher,* pp. 19–20.
2 Bucher quoted in Armbrister, *Matter of Accountability,* p. 115.
3 Fitness report from *Fitness Report for LCDR Lloyd Bucher for February–June 1967,* reprinted in Bucher, *Bucher,* p. 13.
4 Testimony of Admiral Frank Johnson, House *Pueblo* hearings, p. 734.
5 Admiral Frank Johnson quoted in "Statements by Various Officers," NHC, Operational Archives branch, command file, post 1 Jan. 46, individual ships, USS *Pueblo.*
6 Bucher, *Bucher,* pp. 27–28. *FP-344* was smaller and lighter than *FS-389,* had a higher bow and a deeper well deck, and had a very different interior design.
7 The *Pueblo's* early history can be found in "Finding of Facts," p. 12. See also *Dictionary of American Naval Fighting Ships,* vol. 5 (Washington, D.C.: U.S. Government Printing Office, 1970), p. 400; "Joint Commissioning . . . USS *Pueblo* [and] USS *Palm Beach*" (pamphlet in author's possession).
8 Armbrister, *Matter of Accountability,* pp. 88–89.
9 The descriptions of the *Pueblo's* early condition come from Murphy, *Second in Command,* p. 46; Armbrister, *Matter of Accountability,* pp. 114–16; Bucher, *Bucher,* pp. 19–20; Robert Liston, *The* Pueblo *Surrender* (New York: M. Evans, 1988), p. 26; Stu Russell, unpublished manuscript in author's possession (hereafter referred to as Russell manuscript).
10 Bucher, *Bucher,* p. 22.
11 "Finding of Facts," p. 13; Murphy, *Second in Command,* p. 29; Armbrister, *Matter of Accountability,* pp. 88–90.
12 On the problems facing the early part of the ship's conversion, see Command Information Bureau (CIB) #48-69, February 5, 1969, NHC, Operational Archives branch, command file, post 1 Jan. 1946, individual ships, USS *Pueblo,* CIB news releases, #57-69 through #1-169; Murphy, *Second in Command,* p. 24; Armbrister, *Matter of Accountability,* pp. 122–23; Bucher, *Bucher,* pp. 20, 28–30; *New York Times,* January 21, 1969, p. 1.
13 Bucher, "Commander Bucher Replies," pp. 44–45; CIB #48-69, February 5, 1969; Bucher, *Bucher,* p. 29.
14 Bucher, *Bucher,* pp. 65–69.
15 Murphy, *Second in Command,* p. 51.
16 Bucher, *Bucher,* pp. 20–22.
17 Murphy, *Second in Command,* p. 103; Bucher, *Bucher,* pp. 152–53.
18 House *Pueblo* Report, p. 1647; Bucher, *Bucher,* p. 20; Armbrister, *Matter of Accountability,* p. 125.
19 Murphy, *Second in Command,* p. 25.
20 Letter to author from John Grant, May 14, 1999, in author's possession.
21 *Christian Science Monitor,* June 10, 1969, p. 1.

22 Schumacher, *Bridge of No Return,* pp. 48–49.

23 Bucher, *Bucher,* p. 21.

24 Stu Russell quoted in Russell manuscript, p. 8.

25 Murphy, *Second in Command,* pp. 27–28.

26 Bucher, *Bucher,* p. 128.

27 Bucher, "Commander Bucher Replies," pp. 44–45; "Finding of Facts," pp. 24–27; Ed Brandt, *The Last Voyage of the USS* Pueblo (New York: W. W. Norton, 1969), p. 39.

28 *New York Times,* January 21, 1969; Armbrister, *Matter of Accountability,* p. 129; Murphy, *Second in Command,* p. 139.

29 Amount of material from "Finding of Facts," pp. 24–27; estimated time from CIB #47-69, February 4, 1969.

30 "Finding of Facts," pp. 25–27; testimony of Captain John Williams in CIB #53-69.

31 "Finding of Facts," p. 9.

32 Oral history of Admiral U. S. Grant Sharp, NHC, vol. 2, p. 575; testimony of Admiral Frank Johnson, House *Pueblo* hearings, p. 756.

33 CIB #43-69, January 29, 1969; Ennes, *Assault on the* Liberty, pp. 71–72.

34 Testimony of Captain John Williams, CIB #53-69.

35 Testimony of Admiral Frank Johnson, House *Pueblo* hearings, pp. 753–54.

36 Murphy, *Second in Command,* p. 105. On the overload of classified documents, see also Armbrister, *Matter of Accountability,* pp. 12–13, 202–3; Murphy, *Second in Command,* pp. 77–78; "Finding of Facts," p. 7; Bucher, *Bucher,* pp. 110–11.

37 Hearn, "A Career Built on SIGINT," p. 69.

38 "Finding of Facts," pp. 14–18, 24–27; Murphy, *Second in Command,* p. 78.

39 Unnamed official quoted in *New York Times,* February 4, 1968, p. 8.

40 "Finding of Facts," pp. 24–27; Murphy, *Second in Command,* p. 3.

41 Time estimates from CIB #48-69; testimony of Gene Lacy in "Finding of Facts," p. 32; scuttling method from Bucher, *Bucher,* pp. 131, 182.

42 Letter quoted in House *Pueblo* hearings, p. 729.

43 House *Pueblo* hearings, pp. 729–30; oral history of Admiral Edwin Hooper, NHC, Operational Archives branch, pp. 221–23, 435–36.

44 House *Pueblo* Report, p. 1648; Bucher, *Bucher,* p. 132.

45 Bucher, *Bucher,* p. 133.

46 Testimony of Admiral Thomas Moorer, House *Pueblo* hearings, p. 655.

47 Ibid.; undated UPI report, headline: "Ships Now Equipped to Destroy Secrets," NHC, Operational Archives branch, records of CINCPACFLT, 1941–75, series 1, box 5, file "*Pueblo* Newspaper Clippings (25 Jan.– July 1969)"; "Bucher Returns to Sea," *Washington Post,* March 9, 1969.

48 "Finding of Facts," pp. 14–18, 26–27; House *Pueblo* Report, p. 1648; undated UPI report, headline: "Ships Now Equipped to Destroy Secrets"; *Honolulu Star Bulletin,* January 27, 1969; letter to author from Rick Darsay, July 26, 1999.

49 Oral history of Admiral Thomas Moorer, NHC, Operational Archives branch, vol. 2, p. 703.

50 *New York Times,* January 21, 1969, p. 4; Murphy, *Second in Command,* p. 29.

51 "Finding of Facts," p. 13; Bucher, *Bucher,* pp. 67–68; Murphy, *Second in Command,* p. 61.

52 "Finding of Facts," p. 33; "*Pueblo,*" *Electronic News,* February 24, 1969; various letters to author from *Pueblo* crewmen.

53 Letter to author from Don McClarren, April 19, 1999; Schumacher, *Bridge of No Return*, p. 79.

54 Armbrister, *Matter of Accountability*, p. 36; Schumacher, *Bridge of No Return*, pp. 79 –80.

55 "Finding of Facts," p. 33; "*Pueblo*," *Electronic News*, February 24, 1969; letter to author from Dan Spry, November 1, 2000.

56 Letter to author from Don McClarren, April 29, 1999; House *Pueblo* Report, p. 1662; Armbrister, *Matter of Accountability*, pp. 35 –36.

57 House *Pueblo* Report, p. 1662; Schumacher, *Bridge of No Return*, p. 80; Armbrister, *Matter of Accountability*, pp. 35 –36.

58 Letter to author from Don McClarren, May 6, 1999.

59 Bucher, *Bucher*, pp. 82–83, 129.

60 Ibid., pp. 26, 62–68; letter to author from John Grant, May 14, 1999; letter to author from Ralph McClintock, May 31, 1999. Installation dates and Bucher quote from Armbrister, *Matter of Accountability*, pp. 127 –28.

61 Armbrister, *Matter of Accountability*, p. 138.

62 Quoted in Bucher, *Bucher*, p. 57. The above problems are cited in Armbrister, *Matter of Accountability*, pp. 14, 18, 148 –49, 161–62, and Bucher, *Bucher*, p. 81. Five-mile loran estimate from CIB #45-69.

63 On naval operations and the Vietnam War, see R. L. Schreadley, *From the Rivers to the Sea* (Annapolis, Md.: Naval Institute Press, 1992), chap. 7; Thomas Cutler, *Brown Water, Black Berets* (Annapolis, Md.: Naval Institute Press, 1988); Edward Marolda and Oscar Fitzgerald, *The US Navy and the Vietnam Conflict* (Washington, D.C.: Naval Historical Center Press, 1986); Edwin Hooper, *Mobility, Support, Endurance* (Washington, D.C.: U.S. Government Printing Office, 1972).

64 Rear Admiral William Petrovic quoted in Armbrister, *Matter of Accountability*, p. 123.

65 Bucher, *Bucher*, pp. 74 –78; Murphy, *Second in Command*, pp. 45 –46. There is some dispute over the exact date of the first trial. Murphy (p. 45) and Armbrister (p. 72) claim June, but Bucher claims July (p. 73). Schumacher does not mention the trial at all, which may be revealing, since he did not report until July. Navy records are vague, but most indications are that the first official trial run was in late June.

66 INSURV report from Bucher, *Bucher*, p. 81, and Armbrister, *Matter of Accountability*, pp. 148 –49.

67 Letter to author from Don McClarren, June 3, 1999; Bucher, *Bucher*, p. 81.

68 Murphy, *Second in Command*, p. 50.

69 Ibid., p. 61.

70 Ibid., p. 51; Armbrister, *Matter of Accountability*, p. 149.

71 Bucher, *Bucher*, p. 99.

72 Letter to author from Stu Russell, June 4, 1999.

73 Bucher, *Bucher*, p. 106.

74 TRAPAC report from Bucher, *Bucher*, p. 107; propulsion problems in *Newsweek*, February 5, 1968; interview with Lieutenant Jack Alderson, June 21, 1999.

75 *Pueblo* deck log remarks sheet, November 12, 1967, NHC, Ships History branch.

76 Ibid., November 24, 1967.

77 Test runs in Brandt, *Last Voyage of the* Pueblo, p. 22; documents and crew quarters in Bucher, *Bucher*, pp. 110–11.

78 Murphy, *Second in Command*, p. 70.

79 *Pueblo* deck log remarks sheet, November 24, 1967, NHC, Ships History branch; Bucher, *Bucher,* p. 115; Brandt, *Last Voyage of the* Pueblo, p. 20.

80 Letter to author from James Layton, October 31, 2000.

81 Bucher, *Bucher,* p. 125.

82 Russell manuscript, pp. 25–26.

83 House *Pueblo* Report, pp. 1632–34; McNamara to Senate Appropriations Committee, February 1, 1968, JL, National Security File, NSC Histories, *Pueblo* Crisis, 1968, boxes 31–33, vol. 13, public statements, tabs D–F, "Compilation of Statements Concerning USS *Pueblo* Incident"; testimony of Admiral Thomas Moorer, House *Pueblo* hearings, p. 686.

84 House *Pueblo* hearings, p. 747.

85 Bucher, *Bucher,* pp. 86–87.

86 CIB #30-69; Bucher, *Bucher,* pp. 87–88; House *Pueblo* Report, pp. 737, 1648.

87 "Finding of Facts," pp. 28–29; Bucher, *Bucher,* p. 140; *New York Times,* January 21, 1969, p. 4.

88 Armor in oral history of Vice Admiral Edwin Hooper, NHC, Operational Archive branch, pp. 434–35; gun tubes in Armbrister, *Matter of Accountability,* p. 172.

89 Admiral Frank Johnson, March 14, 1969, NHC, Operational Archives branch, command file, post 1 Jan. 46, individual ships, USS *Pueblo,* "Statements by Various Officers"; testimony of Admiral Frank Johnson, House *Pueblo* Report, p. 737.

90 "Finding of Facts," pp. 28–29; House *Pueblo* Report, p. 1646.

91 Phares quoted in *Stars and Stripes,* March 5, 1969; lack of general quarters drills in *Christian Science Monitor,* June 10, 1969, p. 5.

92 House *Pueblo* Report, p. 1646; Armbrister, *Matter of Accountability,* pp. 14–15.

93 Oral history of Admiral John Hyland, U.S. Naval Institute, Annapolis, Md., vol. 2, p. 455.

94 "Finding of Facts," pp. 83–85.

95 Bucher, *Bucher,* p. 141.

96 Testimony of Frank Johnson, House *Pueblo* hearings, p. 740.

97 Murphy, *Second in Command,* p. 105; Brandt, *Last Voyage of the* Pueblo, p. 25; Armbrister, *Matter of Accountability,* pp. 7–10.

98 Testimony of Admiral Frank Johnson, House *Pueblo* hearings, p. 740.

99 "Finding of Facts," pp. 2, 78–81; oral history of Vice Admiral Edwin Hooper, NHC, Operational Archives branch, pp. 434–35.

100 Oral history of Admiral Thomas Moorer, NHC, Operational Archives branch, p. 709; oral history of Admiral John Hyland, NHC, Operational Archives branch, p. 468.

101 Bucher, "Commander Bucher Replies," p. 44.

102 CIB #81-69.

103 Testimony of Gene Lacy, CIB #48-69.

104 *Christian Science Monitor,* June 10, 1969, p. 5; Armbrister, *Matter of Accountability,* pp. 115–16.

105 "Finding of Facts," pp. 14–18, 26–27, 91.

106 Letter to author from Stu Russell, June 2, 1999.

107 Lawrence Mack quoted in Armbrister, *Matter of Accountability,* p. 25.

108 Murphy quoted in CIB #45-69, February 4, 1969; Mack quoted in Liston, *The* Pueblo *Surrender,* p. 41.

109 "Finding of Facts," pp. 28–32.

110 Statement by Robert Hammond, JL, Papers of Clark Clifford, box 17, "North Korea—*Pueblo* Incident"; Armbrister, *Matter of Accountability*, p. 21; Liston, *The Pueblo Surrender*, p. 48.

111 Harris quoted in James Bamford, *Body of Secrets* (New York: Doubleday, 2001), p. 252.

112 Letter to author from Ralph McClintock, May 31, 1999; Bucher, *Bucher*, p. 387.

113 Bucher, *Bucher*, p. 387; emphasis in original.

114 Letter to author from Ralph McClintock, April 28, 1999.

115 Ibid.

116 Executive Officer Dave Behr quoted in Armbrister, *Matter of Accountability*, p. 126; Radioman Lee Hayes quoted in Liston, *The Pueblo Surrender*, p. 15.

117 Oral history of Admiral John Hyland, U.S. Naval Institute, vol. 2, p. 453.

118 "Finding of Facts," pp. 78–81.

119 Bucher, *Bucher*, pp. 81–82.

120 Murphy, *Second in Command*, p. 40.

121 Ibid., p. 89; letter to author from Stu Russell, March 29, 1999.

122 *Christian Science Monitor*, June 10, 1969, p. 5; Russell manuscript, p. 20; letter to author from Stu Russell, June 2, 1999; Armbrister, *Matter of Accountability*, p. 18.

123 Bucher quoted in Murphy, *Second in Command*, pp. 410–11.

124 Murphy, *Second in Command*, p. 55.

125 Statement of Rear Admiral Frank Johnson, NHC, Operational Archives branch, command file, post 1 Jan. 46, individual ships, USS *Pueblo*, "Statements by Various Officers."

126 Oral history of Vice Admiral Kent Lee, U.S. Naval Institute, vol. 2, p. 409.

127 Daniel Gallery, *The Pueblo Incident* (Garden City, N.Y.: Doubleday, 1970), pp. 16–17.

128 "Finding of Facts," pp. 21–23. There has been much dispute over Bucher's claim that he was denied access to certain areas because of security restrictions, since he held the same security classification as Harris. While this is technically true, Bucher did not hold the same "need to know" classifications within that security clearance that would empower him to be involved in all aspects of the ship. Instead, it was up to Harris to determine whether Bucher, or anyone else, needed certain information.

129 Murphy, *Second in Command*, p. 34; Armbrister, *Matter of Accountability*, pp. 23, 153.

130 Bucher, *Bucher*, p. 113.

131 Armbrister, *Matter of Accountability*, pp. 110–11.

CHAPTER 3. A MINIMAL RISK

1 Oral history of Admiral John Hyland, U.S. Naval Institute, vol. 2, p. 457, reprinted in *Naval History*, Spring 1989; Bucher, "Commander Bucher Replies," p. 48.

2 "Finding of Facts," pp. 1–3; statement of Rear Admiral Frank Johnson, NHC, Operational Archives branch, command file, post 1 Jan. 1946, individual ships file, USS *Pueblo*, "Statements by Various Officers"; testimony of Admiral Frank Johnson, House *Pueblo* hearings, p. 733; testimony of Captain W. H. Everett, House *Pueblo* hearings, pp. 771–75.

3 Testimony of Admiral Frank Johnson, House *Pueblo* hearings, pp. 736–37; testimony of Captain W. H. Everett, House *Pueblo* hearings, p. 766; House *Pueblo* hearings, pp. 771–72.

4 "The Operational Assessment of Risk: A Case Study of the *Pueblo* Mission" (Santa Monica, Calif.: RAND Corporation, 1971), NHC, Operational Archives branch, pp. 10–12; hereafter referred to as RAND report.

5 Testimony of Captain W. H. Everett, House *Pueblo* hearings, p. 774; testimony of Admiral Frank Johnson, House *Pueblo* hearings, p. 734.

6 Chester Cooper Papers, Carl Macy report, "The Seizure of the USS *Pueblo*," January 6, 1969, for the Senate Foreign Relations Committee (hereafter referred to as Macy report; testimony of Captain William Everett, House *Pueblo* hearings, p. 774.

7 Testimony of Lieutenant General Seth McKee, House *Pueblo* hearings, pp. 874–75; Armbrister, *Matter of Accountability*, pp. 118–21; Commander Charles Clark in Murphy, *Second in Command*, pp. 85–86.

8 See chapter 4 for a more detailed discussion of the redundancy of this mission.

9 Testimony of Admiral Frank Johnson, House *Pueblo* hearings, pp. 734–36.

10 Rear Admiral George Cassell of CINCPACFLT in Murphy, *Second in Command*, p. 378.

11 Testimony of Admiral Frank Johnson, House *Pueblo* hearings, p. 777.

12 Oral history of Admiral U. S. Grant Sharp, NHC, Operational Archives branch, vol. 2, pp. 568–69; author's interview with Donald Showers, July 20, 1999.

13 Oral history of Vice Admiral John Chew, NHC, Operational Archives branch, pp. 381–85.

14 Testimony of Admiral Frank Johnson, House *Pueblo* hearings, p. 777; RAND report, pp. 17–19, 27–28.

15 Patrick McGarvey, *CIA* (New York: Saturday Review Press, 1972), pp. 106–7.

16 Testimony of Admiral Frank Johnson, House *Pueblo* hearings, p. 760.

17 Ibid., p. 778.

18 Testimony of Captain William Everett, House *Pueblo* hearings, pp. 772–74; RAND report, p. 34.

19 RAND report, p. 18; Assistant Chief of Staff for Intelligence Captain John Marocchi quoted in Armbrister, *Matter of Accountability*, p. 189.

20 "Finding of Facts," pp. 10–11.

21 RAND report, pp. 19–20.

22 McGarvey, *CIA*, pp. 104–7.

23 House *Pueblo* Report, p. 1645; testimony of General Earle Wheeler, House *Pueblo* hearings, pp. 885–89; testimony of Admiral Thomas Moorer, House *Pueblo* hearings, pp. 699–700; RAND report, pp. 10–12, 19–20; Bamford, *Puzzle Palace*, p. 299. The other absent officers were General Harold Johnson of the army and Marine Corps General Wallace Greene.

24 House *Pueblo* Report, p. 1645; testimony of General Earle Wheeler, House *Pueblo* hearings, p. 892; Wendt quoted in Armbrister, *Matter of Accountability*, p. 194.

25 Author's telephone interview with Walt Rostow, January 14, 1998; House *Pueblo* Report, p. 1645; testimony of Admiral Thomas Moorer, House *Pueblo* hearings, pp. 699–700; RAND report, pp. 10–12, 19–20; Bamford, *Puzzle Palace*, p. 299; testimony of General Earle Wheeler, House *Pueblo* hearings, p. 885.

26 Testimony of Admiral Thomas Moorer, House *Pueblo* hearings, pp. 693–94.

27 House *Pueblo* hearings, p. 728.

28 Testimony of Admiral Thomas Moorer, House *Pueblo* hearings, p. 644.

29 *Pueblo*'s operational orders, December 18, 1967, reprinted in House *Pueblo* Report, p. 1644. The other reports are quoted in House *Pueblo* Report, pp. 1650–51.

30 McGarvey, *CIA,* pp. 104–7.

31 Marchetti and Marks, *CIA and Cult of Intelligence,* p. 314.

32 Charles Bonesteel oral history, U.S. Army Military History Institute, Carlyle Barracks, Pa., Charles H. Bonesteel III papers, p. 347.

33 House *Pueblo* Report, p. 1654.

34 Gene Sheck quoted in Bamford, *Body of Secrets,* p. 250.

35 House *Pueblo* Report, pp. 1655–56.

36 Bamford, *Body of Secrets,* p. 250.

37 RAND report, pp. 12–13; testimony of Admiral Moorer, House *Pueblo* hearings, p. 710. The story of the NSA warning is different, depending on what source is consulted, and will probably never be satisfactorily resolved. I have pieced it together, as well as I could, from the following sources: testimony of Admiral Thomas Moorer, House *Pueblo* hearings, pp. 704–6; testimony of Admiral U.S. Grant Sharp, House *Pueblo* hearings, p. 825; House *Pueblo* Report, pp. 1654–56; Armbrister, *Matter of Accountability,* pp. 196–98.

38 House *Pueblo* Report, p. 1656.

39 Testimony of Admiral Thomas Moorer, House *Pueblo* hearings, pp. 704–6.

40 "Finding of Facts," p. 3; testimony of Admiral U.S. Grant Sharp, House *Pueblo* hearings, p. 825.

41 This more militant period of DPRK policies is examined more fully in chapter 5. See especially "North Korean Intentions and Capabilities with Respect to South Korea," NA2, NSC *Pueblo* Report; MAC to JCS, January 27, 1968, JL, NSF, Korea country file, boxes 263–64, military cables I; Nick Sarantakes, "The Quiet War," *Journal of Military History,* April 2000. The number of incidents in 1967 actually varies, depending on what source is consulted. Regardless of the specific number, however, it certainly represented a significant increase.

42 Schumacher, *Bridge of No Return,* p. 65; Armbrister, *Matter of Accountability,* pp. 87–88.

43 Memo to Rostow from Marshall Wright, October 20, 1967, JL, NSF, country file: Korea cables and memos, box 255, vol. 5.

44 Macy report.

45 Details of Blue House raid from "The Seoul Raid," JL, NSC Histories, *Pueblo* Crisis, 1968, boxes 31–33, vol. 12, draft white paper, summary press reaction, representative press, document #3; MAC to JCS, January 27, 1968, JL, NSF, Korea country file, boxes 263–64, military cables I file; telegram #3649 from American Embassy Seoul to State Dept., January 1968, JL, NSC Histories, *Pueblo* Crisis, 1968, boxes 34–35, vol. 15, telegrams to Seoul, tabs 9–17; Nicholas Sarantakes, "The Quiet War" (paper presented at Society for Historians of American Foreign Relations conference, Washington, D.C., June 18–20, 1998); CINCPAC Command History, 1968, vol. 4, pp. 223–25, NHC, Operational Archives branch; oral history of Vice Admiral J. V. Smith, NHC, pp. 427–31; *New York Times,* January 23, 1968.

46 Anonymous general quoted in *New York Times,* August 16, 1968.

47 Armbrister, *Matter of Accountability,* pp. 33–34.

48 Bucher, *Bucher,* p. 387.

49 Testimony of Admiral Thomas Moorer, House *Pueblo* hearings, p. 685.

50 Message to RVEP JS/JCS Washington from INCUNC/CGUUSQKOREA, January 24, 1968, NA2, records of the US JCS, records of Chairman (Gen.) Earle Wheeler, 1964–70, 091 Korea, box 160, chairman's messages, 1–31 January 1968.

51 McNamara in House *Pueblo* hearings, p. 703.

52 Testimony of Admiral Frank Johnson, House *Pueblo* hearings, p. 737; testimony of Captain William Everett, House *Pueblo* hearings, p. 774.

53 Macy report.

54 Armbrister, *Matter of Accountability*, p. 27.

55 *New York Times*, January 27, 1968, p. 7.

56 Macy report.

57 Ibid.

58 CIB # 38–69; Armbrister, *Matter of Accountability*, p. 27; Schumacher, *Bridge of No Return*, p. 70.

59 House *Pueblo* Report, p. 1619; Armbrister, *Matter of Accountability*, p. 27; Schumacher, *Bridge of No Return*, p. 70.

60 Fulbright letter, March 25, 1968, JL, NSC Histories, *Pueblo* Crisis, 1968, boxes 31–33, vol. 10; *New York Times*, February 5, 1969, p. 14.

61 "Finding of Facts," p. 11.

62 House *Pueblo* Report, p. 1656.

63 Ibid., pp. 1622–23.

64 Johnson quoted in Liston, *The* Pueblo *Surrender*, p. 251.

65 Oral history of Admiral John Hyland, U.S. Naval Institute, vol. 2, p. 451, and appendix, p. 3.

66 Oral history of Rear Admiral Kemp Tolley, NHC, Operational Archives branch, vol. 2, pp. 839–40.

67 Omar Bradley, *A General's Life* (New York: Simon and Schuster, 1983), p. 535; NSC-68 reprinted in *Foreign Relations of the United States*, 1950, vol. 1 (Washington, D.C.: U.S. Government Printing Office, 1977), pp. 237–40; *Infantry Journal*, May 1948, p. 42.

68 The depiction of the Vietnam War as a consequence of America's failure to recognize Vietnamese nationalism can be found in Herring, *America's Longest War;* Gabriel Kolko, *Anatomy of a War* (New York: W. W. Norton, 1985); Stanley Karnow, *Vietnam* (Middlesex, England: Penguin Books, 1984); Marilyn Young, *The Vietnam Wars* (New York: HarperCollins, 1991); Jeffrey Race, *War Comes to Long An* (Berkeley: University of California Press, 1972); Loren Baritz, *Backfire* (New York: Ballantine Books, 1985).

69 Memorandum for the secretary of defense, "The Strategic Importance of the Southeast Asian Mainland," January 13, 1962, in *The Pentagon Papers*, Gravel ed. (New York: Bantam Books, 1971), vol. 2, p. 664.

70 General Taylor's report to President Kennedy, November 3, 1961, reprinted in *Pentagon Papers, New York Times* ed. (New York: Bantam Books, 1971), p. 148; NSAM 288 in Robert McMahon, *Major Problems in the History of the Vietnam War* (Lexington, Mass.: D. C. Heath, 1990), p. 225.

71 On the American intervention in Iran, see especially Barry Rubin, *Paved with Good Intentions* (New York: Oxford University Press, 1981), and Mark Lytle, *The Origins of the Iranian-American Alliance* (New York: Holmes and Meier, 1987). See also Amin Saikal, *The Rise and Fall of the Shah* (Princeton, N.J.: Princeton University Press, 1980), James Bill, *The Eagle and the Lion* (New Haven, Conn.: Yale University Press, 1988); Stephen McFarland, "A Peripheral View of the Origins of the Cold War," *Diplomatic History*, Fall 1980.

72 Guzman quoted in Richard Immerman, *The CIA in Guatemala* (Austin: University

of Texas Press, 1982), p. 63; Peurifoy quoted in *Time,* January 11, 1954, p. 27. Other good sources on the U.S. intervention in Guatemala include Pierro Gleijeses, *Shattered Hope* (Princeton, N.J.: Princeton University Press, 1991); Stephen Schlesinger and Stephen Kinzer, *Bitter Fruit* (Garden City, N.Y.: Doubleday, 1982); Blanche Wiesen Cook, *The Declassified Eisenhower* (New York: Penguin Books, 1984).

73 *Pueblo*'s operational orders reprinted in House *Pueblo* hearings, p. 767, enclosure 8; *Pueblo*'s sailing orders reprinted in House *Pueblo* hearings, p. 639; author's interview with Jim Herbert, December 18, 1999.

74 Annex P—special instructions to operation order CTF 96, #301-58, NA2, RG 218, records of the US JCS, records of Chairman (Gen.) Earle Wheeler, 1964–70, box 160.

75 Oral history of Thomas Moorer, JL, interview #2, p. 1.

76 General Earle Wheeler quoted in Moise, *Tonkin Gulf,* p. 67.

77 Johnson quoted in *Washington Post* editorial, February 2, 1969.

CHAPTER 4. WE ARE BEING BOARDED

1 Travel problems from *Washington Post* and *New York Times,* January 12, 1968.

2 From navy pamphlet marking the *Pueblo*'s commissioning, in author's possession.

3 Murphy, *Second in Command,* p. 109.

4 *Pueblo*'s operational orders reprinted in House *Pueblo* hearings, p. 767, enclosure 8; *Pueblo*'s sailing orders reprinted in House *Pueblo* hearings, pp. 639–40.

5 *Pueblo*'s sailing orders, House *Pueblo* hearings, pp. 639–40. This order to stay beyond thirteen miles from shore overrode an earlier and more general order, sailing order 003120.24A, which authorized "patrols to the 3-mile limit." Although such an order is grist for the mill of conspiracy theorists, this two-year-old order was intended only to establish general rules for the program and was clearly superseded by the more specific sailing orders for each mission.

6 *Pueblo*'s operational orders, House *Pueblo* hearings, p. 767, enclosure 8.

7 Oral history of Captain Phil Bucklew, NHC, Operational Archives branch; testimony of Admiral U. S. Grant Sharp, House *Pueblo* hearings, p. 795; Schumacher, *Bridge of No Return,* pp. 60–61; Murphy, *Second in Command,* p. 53.

8 On the ship's specific goals, see "Finding of Facts," p. 19; testimony of Admiral U. S. Grant Sharp, House *Pueblo* hearings, p. 797; oral history of Admiral U. S. Grant Sharp, vol. 2, NHC, Operational Archives branch, p. 568; McNamara and Wheeler testimony before the Senate Foreign Relations Committee, February 1, 1968, JL, NSC Histories, *Pueblo* Crisis, 1968, boxes 31–33, vol. 13, public statements, tabs D–F, "Compilation of Statements Concerning the USS *Pueblo* Incident"; Bucher, *Bucher,* p. 165; Murphy, *Second in Command,* p. 115; Schumacher, *Bridge of No Return,* pp. 61–62; Armbrister, *Matter of Accountability,* p. 20.

9 NSA intercept stations in McGarvey, *CIA,* pp. 98–99; National Reconnaissance Office in Fain, *The Intelligence Community,* chap. 7; Corona in Jeffrey Richelson, National Security Archive Electronic Briefing Book Number 13, "U.S. Satellite Imagery, 1960–1999," 1999, reprinted at http://www.gwu.edu/~nsarchiv/NSAEBB/NSAEBB13/index.html; air force in Marchetti and Marks, *CIA and Cult of Intelligence,* pp. 202–3, and Fain, *The Intelligence Community,* chap. 7; CIA in Christopher Andrew, *For the*

President's Eyes Only (New York: HarperCollins, 1995), p. 332; Oxcart in Jeffrey Richelson, "The Wizards of Langley," in *Eternal Vigilance,* ed. Rhodri Jeffreys-Jones and Christopher Andrew (London: Frank Cass, 1997), p. 95.

10 Bucher quoted in Armbrister, *Matter of Accountability,* p. 200.

11 Oral history of General Charles Bonesteel, Military History Institute, pp. 345–46.

12 Letter to author from Ralph McClintock, April 28, 1999. The other was the submarine facilities in Petropovlosk.

13 Letter to author from John Grant, April 29, 1999.

14 *Pueblo*'s operational orders, House *Pueblo* hearings, p. 767, enclosure 8.

15 It should be noted that all the evidence suggesting that the Soviet Union was the true target is circumstantial. It remains quite possible that the *Pueblo* was merely sent on an unnecessary and redundant mission due to failures within the American intelligence community.

16 Unless otherwise indicated, details of the *Pueblo*'s mission prior to January 23 are from Bucher, *Bucher,* chaps. 8–9; Armbrister, *Matter of Accountability,* chaps. 1–5, Murphy, *Second in Command,* pp. 100–23; Schumacher, *Bridge of No Return,* pp. 67–84; "Finding of Facts," pp. 2–4.

17 House *Pueblo* Report, p. 1657.

18 Letter to author from Ralph McClintock, June 29, 1999; Bucher, *Bucher,* pp. 160–64.

19 Bucher, *Bucher,* p. 165.

20 "Finding of Facts," p. 19; Bucher, *Bucher,* p. 165; Murphy, *Second in Command,* p. 115.

21 Bucher, *Bucher,* p. 167; Murphy, *Second in Command,* pp. 116–17. Only Gene Lacy rejected the contention that they had been overlooked, and the rest of the officers easily overrode his warnings.

22 Schumacher quoted in Armbrister, *Matter of Accountability,* p. 30.

23 Schumacher, *Bridge of No Return,* p. 71.

24 Bucher, *Bucher,* p. 168.

25 Armbrister, *Matter of Accountability,* p. 36.

26 SITREP-1, reprinted in House *Pueblo* hearings, pp. 841–42; Russell manuscript, p. 30.

27 This incident is described in Bucher, *Bucher,* pp. 168–70. See also CIB #57-69 to #1-69; Murphy, *Second in Command,* pp. 118–19; SITREP-1 reproduced in House *Pueblo* hearings, pp. 841–42.

28 SITREP-1, House *Pueblo* hearings, pp. 841–42; Armbrister, *Matter of Accountability,* pp. 38–39.

29 Letter to author from Don McClarren, April 29, 1999; Brandt, *Last Voyage of the* Pueblo, pp. 33–35.

30 CIB #51-69; Bucher, *Bucher,* p. 174.

31 Their position, as recorded by Murphy (*Second in Command,* p. 122), was 39 degrees 25.2 minutes north, 127 degrees 55.0 minutes east, roughly 15.8 miles from the offshore island of Ung-do. Bucher's test of the depth sounder confirmed this approximate position ("The Seizure of the USS PUEBLO," staff memo to all members of the Senate Foreign Relations Committee, William Fulbright Papers, University of Arkansas at Fayetteville, series 72, box 30, January 6, 1969, p. 5); Schumacher, *Bridge of No Return,* pp. 84–85.

32 The accounts of the seizure itself are extensive but vary in specific detail. I have compiled the most accurate picture I could by utilizing all of them, but many

details remain sketchy, as should be expected, considering the circumstances. Still, a general picture can be discerned, despite the occasional contradiction. Among the best sources are House *Pueblo* hearings, pp. 699–72; "Finding of Facts," pp. 37–46; CIB releases #57-69 through #1-69, especially CIB #32-69, 33-69, and 34-69; "On Watch" (National Cryptologic School report in author's possession), pp. 67–71; NA2, "NSC Pueblo Report"; Armbrister, *Matter of Accountability,* chaps. 5–9; Bucher, *Bucher,* chaps. 9–11; Murphy, *Second in Command,* chaps. 11–14; Schumacher, *Bridge of No Return,* chap. 5; Russell manuscript, pp. 30–36. I also relied on a collection of interviews I conducted with the *Pueblo* crewmen, copies of which remain in my possession.

33 Law quoted in Bucher, *Bucher,* p. 177. The conversation is from Bucher, *Bucher,* pp. 176–78, and Murphy, *Second in Command,* pp. 122–24; "Finding of Facts," p. 37. Murphy (p. 123) and Armbrister (p. 40) claim that Bucher ordered Law to contact him if the ship approached three miles. However, all sources agree that Law called back to warn Bucher that the point had been reached within five minutes, meaning that the ship would have had to travel five miles in less than five minutes. Hence Bucher's account seems more likely.

34 Bamford, *Body of Secrets,* p. 258.

35 "Chronology of Events Concerning the Seizure of the USS *Pueblo,*" JL, National Security files, NSC Histories, *Pueblo* Crisis 1968, boxes 27–28, vol. 1, basic study and presidential decisions file.

36 Quoted in Bucher, *Bucher,* p. 181.

37 This exchange is reprinted in Bucher, *Bucher,* p. 182. See also CIB #32-69.

38 "Analysis of Communications/Command/Control Functions Involved in USS PUEBLO Capture," NA2, pol 33-6, KoreaN-US, 1/1/68 file. PINNACLE 1 also reprinted in House *Pueblo* hearings, p. 842.

39 House *Pueblo* hearings, p. 670; notes of president's meeting, January 31, 1968, 8:40 A.M., JL, Tom Johnson's notes of meetings, box 2; Schumacher, *Bridge of No Return,* p. 86.

40 Quoted in Armbrister, *Matter of Accountability,* pp. 43–44.

41 Notes of president's meeting with Senator Ev Dirksen and Congressman Gerald Ford, January 30, 1968, 6:04 P.M., JL, Tom Johnson's notes of meetings, box 2. This transmission and others by the North Korean ships were intercepted, although there is some question about who was doing the intercepting. Some were intercepted by South Korean intelligence, while others were obtained by American intelligence, presumably NSA satellites in the area, or by the occasional C-130 intelligence aircraft flown by the air force. See undated "chronology of events," JL, NSF, country file, Asia and the Pacific, Korea box 259, "Korea—*Pueblo* Incident," vol. 5, 12/68, Cactus misc. papers; *New York Times,* February 2, 1968; House *Pueblo* hearings, p. 692; draft copy of Arthur Goldberg speech to UN, January 26, 1968, JL, White House Aides file, George Christian, box 12, *Pueblo* misc; Schumacher, *Bridge of No Return,* p. 86. The *Pueblo* gave her position as approximately seventeen miles off the coast at the same time. Most accounts of this message claim that it actually read, "It is American guys," rather than "It is Americans," but that is most likely an error stemming from a mistranslation of "*MiGuk saram,*" which means simply "American" or "Americans."

42 Lacy quoted in Armbrister, *Matter of Accountability,* p. 44.

43 Notes of president's meeting with Senator Ev Dirksen and Congressman Gerald Ford, January 30, 1968, 6:04 P.M., JL, Tom Johnson's notes of meetings, box 2; Schumacher, *Bridge of No Return*, p. 89.

44 Army unit from Dae-Sook Suh, *Kim Il-Sung* (New York: Columbia University Press, 1988), p. 234.

45 Bucher, *Bucher*, p. 185.

46 Schumacher, *Bridge of No Return*, p. 89; Murphy, *Second in Command*, p. 131.

47 Brandt, *Last Voyage of the* Pueblo, p. 40.

48 Ibid., p. 48; Armbrister, *Matter of Accountability*, p. 47. Liston makes much of this message, suggesting that the ship was actually boarded at this time by the Chinese, and then the Soviets seized it from them. However, all evidence suggests that Bailey just made a mistake.

49 Murphy, *Second in Command*, p. 134.

50 Analysis of Communications/Command/Control Functions Involved in USS PUEBLO Capture," NA2, pol 33-6, KoreaN-US, 1/1/68 file; House *Pueblo* hearings, p. 843; time sent from "Finding of Facts," p. 40.

51 Testimony of McNamara and Wheeler before the Senate Foreign Relations Committee, February 1, 1968, JL, NSC Histories, *Pueblo Crisis*, 1968, boxes 31–33, vol. 13, public statements, tabs D–F, "Compilation of Statements Concerning the USS PUEBLO Incident."

52 Armbrister, *Matter of Accountability*, p. 49.

53 Don Crawford, Pueblo *Intrigue* (New York: Pyramid Books, 1969), p. 22.

54 Bucher, "Commander Bucher Replies," p. 44.

55 Berens quoted in Schumacher, *Bridge of No Return*, p. 91.

56 Bucher claims that he ordered the emergency destruct earlier, immediately after the boarding attempt. Other accounts, including Murphy (*Second in Command*, p. 134), however, suggest that the order was not given until after the firing, a difference of less than thirty minutes. It is possible that because of the poor communications facilities, Bucher did give the order, but in the chaos of the moment, it went unheard.

57 Quoted in *New Republic*, February 15, 1969, p. 8.

58 Harris in CIB #47-69.

59 See, for example, "Finding of Facts," pp. 87–88.

60 Ennes, *Assault on the* Liberty, pp. 84–85.

61 "Finding of Facts," pp. 53, 59.

62 Bucher, *Bucher*, pp. 191–92; Murphy, *Second in Command*, pp. 138–39; "On Watch," p. 70.

63 Chicca in Bucher, *Bucher*, p. 196.

64 Bucher claims that it was Gene Lacy who actually stopped the ship without orders to do so (Bucher, *Bucher*, pp. 191–92). Most accounts, however, suggest that Bucher did it himself (Murphy, *Second in Command*, pp. 138–39, Brandt, *Last Voyage of the* Pueblo, pp. 47–48). It seems unlikely that, regardless of the circumstances, a chief warrant officer would take it upon himself to stop a ship without the captain's consent.

65 Flash telegram, Ager-2/JOPREP/OPREP-3/001, NA2, record group 218, 091 Korea.

66 Murphy, *Second in Command*, p. 100.

67 House *Pueblo* hearings, p. 671; Murphy, *Second in Command*, p. 139.

68 Bucher, *Bucher*, p. 194.

69 Ibid., p. 198; Murphy, *Second in Command*, p. 142.

70 CIB #52-69; Bucher, *Bucher,* pp. 203–4; last words from the *New York Times,* December 25, 1969, p. 2. Hodges appears to have died just before 3:00 P.M.

71 "Finding of Facts," p. 44; House *Pueblo* hearings, p. 672.

72 Ibid.; Murphy, *Second in Command,* p. 151.

73 CIA Intelligence Information Cable, "Implications of Reported Relocation of USS *Pueblo,*" 12 February 1968, document #0651, fiche 56, DDRS, 1999; telegram dated February 22, 1968, no citations, NA2, 1967–69 central files, pol 33-6, box 2255, 2/21/68 folder; Bucher, *Bucher,* pp. 207–16; Murphy, *Second in Command,* p. 153; Schumacher, *Bridge of No Return,* pp. 100–5.

74 Dean Rusk oral history, Russell Library, tape CCC CCC, February 1986.

75 Testimony of McNamara and Wheeler before the Senate Foreign Relations Committee, February 1, 1968, JL, NSC Histories, *Pueblo* Crisis, 1968, boxes 31–33, vol. 13, public statements, tabs D–F.

76 WTOP radio interview, 1-27-68, in NHC, Operational Archives branch, oo files, box 122–1969.

77 CBS News interview with Oleg Kalugin, unpublished tape #3, p. 9.

78 Aircraft and fax in meeting notes of LBJ's luncheon meeting January 25, 1968, JL, Tom Johnson's notes of meetings, box 2; author's telephone interview with Jack Stuchell, November 2, 2000; Seymour Hersh, *The Target Is Destroyed* (New York: Random House, 1986), p. 59; crewmen in "Finding of Facts," p. 57, and *"Pueblo," Electronic News,* February 24, 1969; Crandell in CIB #53-69; Murphy in Murphy, *Second in Command,* pp. 154–56; hundreds of pounds in *Christian Science Monitor,* July 15, 1969; pilothouse in "Finding of Facts," p. 57; file cabinet in "Finding of Facts," p. 57, and Schumacher, *Bridge of No Return,* p. 94; ACP and JANAPS in letter to author from Don McClarren, May 6, 1999; Schumacher in Schumacher, *Bridge of No Return,* p. 124.

79 CIB #53-69 and #47-69; Schumacher, *Bridge of No Return,* p. 124; Murphy, *Second in Command,* p. 248; Hersh, *The Target Is Destroyed,* p. 59; Andrew, *For the President's Eyes Only,* p. 340; Peter Early, *Family of Spies* (New York: Bantam Books, 1988); letter to author from Stu Russell, March 28, 1999; letters to author from Don McClarren, May 6, 1999, and May 16, 1999; CBS News interview with Oleg Kalugin, unpublished tape #3, 4/WO #00533; meeting notes of NSC meeting, February 7, 1968, 12:29 P.M., JL, Tom Johnson's notes of meetings, box 2, set II.

80 Ralph McClintock quoted at http://users.erols.com/engineer/new390A.html.

81 CIA cable 316-309-2, "Comments of North Korean . . . Concerning the *Pueblo* Incident," JL, NSF, NSC Histories, vol. 12, CIA documents [II], box 32.

82 Bucher, *Bucher,* p. 215.

83 *New York Times,* February 16, 1969, p. 16; *New York Times Magazine,* May 11, 1969; "On Watch," p. 71.

84 Armbrister, *Matter of Accountability,* pp. 73, 226; Bucher, *Bucher,* p. 195.

85 NSA cable to DIA and JCS, January 24, 1968, JL, NSF, country file, Korea—Pueblo Incident, codeword material, vol. I, pt. B (through January).

86 Bamford, *Body of Secrets,* p. 268.

87 "Finding of Facts," p. 69; meeting notes of NSC meeting, February 7, 1968, 12:29 P.M., JL, Tom Johnson's notes of meetings, box 2, set II.

88 Quoted in Hersh, *The Target Is Destroyed,* p. 59.

89 June 1968 telegram to Wheeler from Admiral Sharp, CINCPAC (reference numbers missing), NA2, Records of the US JCS, Records of Chairman (Gen.) Earle Wheeler, 1964–70, 091 Korea, box 30, "Korea visits" file. It is likely that the ten-week delay came about because the DPRK had to construct new land lines to carry the messages.

90 Telegram from CSAF to SAC, #68838, JL, NSF, country file, Asia and the Pacific, Korea, box 263, "Korea—*Pueblo* Incident," military cables vol. I, January 30, 1968; undated response to Fulbright letter, question 12b, JL, NSF, NSC Histories, *Pueblo* Crisis, vol. 10, box 31.

91 "In the know" and intelligence official in Corson, *Armies of Ignorance,* pp. 410–11; Ford in notes of president's meeting with Senator Everett Dirksen and Congressman Gerald Ford, January 30, 1968, 6:04 P.M., JL, Tom Johnson's notes of meetings, box 2; Johnson in JL, Drew Pearson Papers, box 6294, "*Pueblo* Crisis."

92 CBS News interview with Oleg Kalugin, unpublished tape #3, 4/WO #00533; letter to author from Stu Russell, March 28, 1999; letters to author from Don McClarren, May 6, 1999, and May 16, 1999; Hersh, *The Target Is Destroyed,* p. 59; Andrew, *For the President's Eyes Only,* p. 340; Early, *Family of Spies; Soundoff,* September 10, 1998, p. 3.

93 *Seattle Post-Intelligencer,* May 21, 1998.

94 On the Walker case, see Early, *Family of Spies;* Howard Blum, *I Pledge Allegiance* (New York: Simon and Schuster, 1987); Oleg Kalugin with Fen Motaigne, *The First Directorate* (New York: St. Martin's Press, 1994), especially chap. 4; Jack Kneece, *Family Treason* (New York: Stein and Day, 1986). There remains much debate about the exact role Walker's espionage played in the *Pueblo* seizure and the importance of the ship's lost KW-7. Oleg Kalugin, former head of the KGB, claims that the Soviets did not need the KW-7 from the *Pueblo,* since Walker's case officer, Andrei Krasavin, was able to build a working replica of the machine (for which he received the Lenin Medal, the highest honor granted by the Soviet government). Yet questions remain about the timing of the three events (the *Pueblo* seizure, the Walker espionage, and the Krasavin model) that make it impossible to determine the relationship with any certainty. However, it can be assumed that regardless of the specifics of Krasavin's model, having an actual KW-7, along with the repair manuals, would have benefited the Soviets enormously.

95 Bamford, *Body of Secrets.*

96 Admiral William Studeman quoted in Blum, *I Pledge Allegiance,* p. 140.

97 Moorer in testimony of Admiral Thomas Moorer, House *Pueblo* hearings, p. 673; House Subcommittee in House *Pueblo* Report, p. 1661; Murphy in Murphy, *Second in Command,* p. 127, Bucher in *Bucher,* p. 157.

98 Fulbright in telegram #3704, from American Embassy Seoul to State Department, January 1968, JL, NSC Histories, *Pueblo* Crisis, 1968, boxes 34–35, vol. 15, telegrams to Seoul, tabs 9–17; Ribicoff in *New Haven Register,* October 20, 1968, and *New York Times,* October 28, 1968, JL, NSC Histories, *Pueblo* Crisis, 1968, boxes 31–33, vol. 12, draft White House paper, "Summary Press Reaction, Representative Press"; *Newsweek,* February 5, 1968, p. 15; *Kansas City Star* and *Minneapolis Tribune* in *Sunday News Survey,* JL, White House Central Files, subject file, defense, ND 19/CO 151, box 211, January 28, 1968; nurse in telegram from Donna Hudson, JL, White House Central Files, subject file, defense, ND 19/CO 151, box 208, February 5, 1968; junior high school telegram in JL, White House Central Files, subject file, defense, ND 19/CO 151,

box 213, March 23, 1968; McNamara in notes of LBJ's meeting, January 24 1968, 1:00 P.M., JL, Tom Johnson's notes of meetings, box 2, set II; Clifford in notes of LBJ's meeting on January 25, 1968, 6:30 P.M., JL, Tom Johnson's notes of meetings, box 2.

99 Analysis of PUEBLO navigational photographs (c), JL, Papers of Clark Clifford, boxes 23–24, "*Pueblo*—March 1, 1968–Jan. 20, 1969" folder; telegram #4653 from American Embassy Seoul to State Department, March 4, 1968, NA2, 1967–69 central files, pol 33-6, box 2254, 3/1/68 folder; "Navy analysis of *Pueblo* Documents," telegram #120759 from State Department to Seoul Embassy, February 26, 1968, NA2, 1967–69 central files, pol 33-6, box 2254, 2/25/68 folder.

100 "Navy analysis of *Pueblo* Documents," telegram #120759 from State Department to Seoul Embassy, February 26, 1968, NA2, 1967–69 central files, pol 33-6, box 2254, 2/25/68 folder.

101 SO-1 in notes of president's meeting with Senator Ev Dirksen and Congressman Gerald Ford, January 30, 1968, 6:04 P.M., JL, Tom Johnson's notes of meetings, box 2; undated chronology of events, JL, NSF, country file, Asia and the Pacific, Korea box 259, Korea—*Pueblo* Incident, vol. V, 12/68, Cactus misc. papers; House *Pueblo* hearings, p. 692; draft copy of Arthur Goldberg speech to UN, January 26, 1968, JL, White House Aides file, George Christian, box 12, *Pueblo* Misc.; radar in NA2, NSC *Pueblo* Report; ambassador in report from J. B. Denson, February 28, 1968, Public Records Office, Kew Gardens, England, FCO 21/347, reference FK 10/19.

102 AP release, January 25, 1968, NHC, Operational Archives branch, 00 files series, box 122. The close friend referred to was Lieutenant Commander Alan Hemphill.

103 Analysis of PUEBLO navigational photographs (c), JL, Papers of Clark Clifford, boxes 23–24, "*Pueblo*—March 1, 1968–Jan. 20, 1969" folder; "Navy analysis of *Pueblo* Documents," telegram #120759 from State Department to Seoul Embassy, February 26, 1968, NA2, 1967–69 central files, pol 33-6, box 2254, 2/25/68 folder.

104 Analysis of PUEBLO navigational photographs (c), JL, Papers of Clark Clifford, boxes 23–24, "*Pueblo*—March 1, 1968–Jan. 20, 1969" folder; Murphy, *Second in Command*, pp. 194–97.

105 Analysis of PUEBLO navigational photographs (c), JL, Papers of Clark Clifford, boxes 23–24, "*Pueblo*—March 1, 1968–Jan. 20, 1969" folder.

106 "Navy analysis of *Pueblo* Documents," telegram #120759 from State Department to Seoul Embassy, February 26, 1968, NA2, 1967–69 central files, pol 33-6, box 2254, 2/25/68 folder.

107 Ibid.

108 Bucher, *Bucher*, p. 148.

109 CIB #45-69.

110 On the loran problems, see "Finding of Facts," pp. 28–32; CIB #31-69; Murphy, *Second in Command*, pp. 81, 100; Armbrister, *Matter of Accountability*, p. 25; Bucher, *Bucher*, p. 165; Liston, *The* Pueblo *Surrender*, p. 82.

111 CIB #45-69 and #51-69; "Finding of Facts," pp. 28–32.

112 On straying closer, see, for example, James Bamford, "USS *Pueblo* Fraught with Lessons," *Dallas Times Herald*, January 17, 1988; navy's legal specialists from William Crowe and David Chanoff, *The Line of Fire* (New York: Simon and Schuster, 1993), pp. 65–66; COMINT stations in McGarvey, *CIA*, p. 97; Ball report in George Ball, *The Past Has Another Pattern* (New York: W. W. Norton, 1982), p. 436. So damaging

was this report that Ball destroyed all written copies of it to prevent it from leaking to the newspapers and reported to the president orally only. On the committee with Ball were General Mark Clark, Admiral George Anderson, and General Lawrence Kuter.

113 Oral history of Admiral U. S. Grant Sharp, vol. 2, NHC, Operational Archive branch, pp. 574–75.

114 Gallery, *The* Pueblo *Incident,* p. ix; Tuthill, "Operational Planning, Pre-*Pueblo,*" p. 10.

115 "Finding of Facts," pp. 83–88.

116 Schumacher, *Bridge of No Return,* p. 85.

117 Special Instructions, Operation Order CTF 96 No. 301-58, in House *Pueblo* hearings, pp. 760–61.

118 Testimony of Admiral Horace Epes, House *Pueblo* hearings, p. 898.

119 Time breakdown from "Analysis of Communications/Command/Control Functions Involved in USS *PUEBLO* Capture," NA2, pol 33-6, KoreaN-US, 1/22/68 file. See also "Review of Department of Defense Worldwide Communications—Phase I," report to the House Committee on Armed Services, March 24, 1971, in author's possession. I am grateful to Loyd Paton for bringing this report to my attention.

120 House *Pueblo* Report, p. 1624; "Analysis of Communications/Command/Control Functions Involved in USS *PUEBLO* Capture"; "Review of Department of Defense Worldwide Communications—Phase I."

121 Statement by Admiral Frank Johnson to House of Representatives, March 14, 1969, NHC, Operational Archives branch, command file, post 1 Jan. 1946, USS *Pueblo,* "Statements by Various Officers"; testimony of Admiral U. S. Grant Sharp, House *Pueblo* hearings, p. 796.

122 Testimony of General Earle Wheeler, House *Pueblo* hearings, p. 900.

123 House *Pueblo* Report, pp. 1668–72; testimony of General Earl Wheeler, House *Pueblo* hearings, p. 886.

124 Oral history of Vice Admiral Kent Lee, vol. 2, U.S. Naval Institute, pp. 406–9.

125 Ibid.

126 Testimony of Admiral Frank Johnson, House *Pueblo* hearings, pp. 741–42.

127 Testimony of Admiral Frank Johnson, House *Pueblo* hearings, p. 785.

128 Sailing orders reprinted in Bucher, *Bucher,* p. 422.

129 Testimony of Admiral Thomas Moorer in House *Pueblo* hearings, p. 637; Bucher in "Finding of Facts," p. 5; State Department in February 23, 1968, memo from State Department, Bourke Hickenlooper Papers, Foreign Relations Subseries—*Pueblo,* p. 2; Wheeler in notes of LBJ meeting January 30, 1968, 8:30 A.M., JL, Tom Johnson's notes of meetings, box 2.

130 Bucher, *Bucher,* p. 194.

131 CIB #89-69.

132 CIB #30-69; Bucher, *Bucher,* pp. 112–13. Similar exchanges are in Brandt, *Last Voyage of the* Pueblo, p. 19, and Armbrister, *Matter of Accountability,* p. 160.

133 Statement by Johnson to House of Representatives, March 14, 1969, NHC, Operational Archives branch, command file, post 1 Jan. 1946, USS *Pueblo,* "Statements by Various Officers"; Armbrister, *Matter of Accountability,* p. 204.

134 Bucher, *Bucher,* p. 113.

135 House *Pueblo* Report, p. 1644.

136 House *Pueblo* hearings, pp. 837–38.
137 "Finding of Facts," p. 81.

CHAPTER 5. THE KEY QUESTION

1 *New York Times,* January 28, 1968, sec. 4, p. 1.
2 A fuller account of how Americans explained the seizure can be found in chapter 7. Che Guevara quoted in "Vietnam and the World Struggle for Freedom," in George Lavan, ed., *Che Guevara Speaks* (New York: Grove Press, 1968), p. 159.
3 Notes of president's meeting, 1 P.M., January 24, 1968, JL, Tom Johnson's notes of meetings, box 2, set II.
4 Summary notes of president's January 31, 1968, meeting with congressional leaders, JL, Papers of Lyndon Johnson, President, 1963–69, meeting notes files, box 2.
5 Notes of January 31, 1968, cabinet meeting, JL, cabinet papers, box 12.
6 Compilation of statements concerning USS *Pueblo* Incident, JL, NSF, NSC Histories, *Pueblo* Crisis, 1968, boxes 31–33, vol. 13, public statements, tabs A–C. See also State Department Korean Task Force, February 24 situation report, JL, NSF, NSC Histories, *Pueblo* Crisis, 1968, boxes 29 and 30, vol. 7, day by day documents, pt. 13; telegram from LBJ to Kosygin, Tom Johnson's notes of meetings, January 25, 1968, 8:30 A.M., box 2, set II.
7 Author's telephone interview with Oleg Kalugin, January 27, 2000; CBS interview with Oleg Kalugin, tape #4,4/WO #00533, in which he explained, "The KGB did not plan the capture of the *Pueblo*. The KGB was not aware of the *Pueblo*'s capture until the North Koreans informed the Soviets"; Boris Solomatin, deputy director of the KGB's First Department and adviser to KGB chief Yuri Andropov, in an interview in the *Washington Post,* April 23, 1995, unpublished tapes 365 and 366. A different explanation is provided by William Corson and Robert Crowley in *The New KGB* (New York: William Morrow, 1985), pp. 344–47. Corson and Crowley attribute the incident to Soviet fears that they had fallen too far behind the United States in the field of intelligence-collection technology and cite the incident as the event that brought Yuri Andropov to prominence. Yet Corson does not cite his sources on this matter and lists no evidence to support this supposition in the footnotes of his excellent book. Nonetheless, the two explanations are not wholly incompatible, as it is possible that the Soviets were interested in the ship for their reasons and the North Koreans interested in it for theirs. Nevertheless, without specific evidence, I remain unconvinced that the Soviets would have taken such a rash step.
8 Vadim Tkachenko quoted in Donald Oberdorfer, *The Two Koreas* (Reading, Mass.: Addison-Wesley, 1997), p. 154.
9 Author's telephone interview with Oleg Kalugin, January 28, 2000.
10 Ibid.
11 Oral history of Maxwell Taylor, JL, transcript #2, p. 15; author's interview with Walt Rostow, January 14, 1998.
12 Giap quoted in James Wirtz, *The Tet Offensive* (Ithaca, N.Y.: Cornell University Press, 1991), pp. 58–59.
13 Paulson quoted in William Westmoreland, *A Soldier Reports* (Garden City, N.Y.: Doubleday, 1976), p. 321.

14 "Authority Required from Congress in Relation to the *Pueblo* Incident," JL, NSF, NSC Histories, *Pueblo* Crisis, 1968, boxes 31–33, vol. 11, background documents; Wirtz, *Tet Offensive*, pp. 212–13.

15 Vo Nguyen Giap, *Big Victory, Great Task* (New York: Praeger Publishers, 1968), p. 97; Ronnie Ford, *Tet, 1968* (Portland, Oreg.: Frank Cass, 1995), chap. 9.

16 George Gallup, *The Gallup Poll, Public Opinion 1935–71* (New York: Random House, 1972).

17 The concept of *juche* is covered in a number of excellent works on North Korea. In spite of some specific interpretive differences, the most helpful include Robert Scalapino and Chong-Sik Lee, *Communism in Korea,* 2 vols. (Berkeley: University of California Press, 1972); Tai Sung An, *North Korea in Transition* (Westport, Conn.: Greenwood Press, 1983); Dae-Ho Byun, *North Korea's Foreign Policy* (Seoul: Research Center for Peace and Unification of Korea, 1991); Byung Chul Koh, *The Foreign Policy Systems of North and South Korea* (Berkeley: University of California Press, 1984); and Ilpyong Kim, *Communist Politics in North Korea* (New York: Praeger Publishers, 1975).

18 Kim Il Sung, *Revolution and Socialist Construction* (New York: International Publishers, 1971), p. 87.

19 From "Answers to the Questions Raised by Abdel Hamid Ahmed Hamrouche, General Manager of Dar-El-Tahrir for Printing and Publishing of the United Arab Republic," July 1, 1969, in Kim Il Sung, *On Juche in Our Revolution,* vol. 2 (New York: Weekly Guardian Associations, 1975), p. 196.

20 From "On Eliminating Dogmatism and Formalism and Establishing Juche in Ideological Work," December 28, 1955, in Kim, *On Juche in Our Revolution,* vol. 1, pp. 149–50.

21 Nikita Khrushchev, *Khrushchev Remembers* (Boston: Little, Brown, 1970), appendix 4; Moscow declaration in "Statement on Relations between the LCY and the CPSU," June 20, 1956, reprinted in Stephen Clissold, ed., *Yugoslavia and the Soviet Union: A Documentary Survey* (London: Oxford University Press, 1975), p. 261.

22 From "On Improving the Work Methods of the Country Party Organization in Accordance with the New Circumstances," February 18, 1969, in Kim, *On Juche in Our Revolution,* vol. 1, p. 221.

23 An, *North Korea in Transition,* pp. 20–31.

24 From "On the Orientation of the Compilation of an Encyclopedia and Maps," April 22, 1964, in Kim, *On Juche in Our Revolution,* vol. 1, p. 404.

25 Byun, *North Korea's Foreign Policy,* p. 70.

26 From "Let Us Embody the Revolutionary Spirit of Independence, Self-Sustenance, and Self-Defence More Thoroughly in All Fields of State Activity," December 16, 1967, in Kim, *On Juche in Our Revolution,* vol. 2, pp. 37–38.

27 An, *North Korea in Transition,* pp. 24, 131–37; Ralph Clough, *Embattled Korea* (Boulder, Colo.: Westview Press, 1987), pp. 52–53; Oberdorfer, *The Two Koreas,* pp. 20–21.

28 An, *North Korea in Transition,* pp. 23, 133–37; Kim, *Communist Politics in North Korea;* p. 17; Koh, *Foreign Policy Systems of North and South Korea,* p. 113; *New Republic,* June 7, 1969, pp. 9–10; Clough, *Embattled Korea,* pp. 57–58.

29 Clifford Geertz, "After the Revolution" in Geertz, *The Interpretation of Cultures* (New York: Basic Books, 1973), p. 237.

30 From "On Some Problems of Our Party's Juche Idea and the Government of the

Republic's Internal and External Policies," September 17, 1972, in Kim, *On Juche in Our Revolution,* vol. 2, p. 430.

31 From "On Creating Revolutionary Literature and Art," November 7, 1964, in Kim, *On Juche in Our Revolution,* vol. 1, pp. 431–32.

32 Gregory Winn, "Korean Foreign Policy," in *The Two Koreas in World Politics,* ed. Tae-Hwan Kwak, Wayne Patterson, and Edward Olsen (Seoul: Kyungnam University Press, 1983), pp. 27–28.

33 Geertz, *The Interpretation of Cultures,* p. 215.

34 From "On Some Problems of Our Party's Juche Idea and the Government of the Republic's Internal and External Policies," September 17, 1972, in Kim, *On Juche in Our Revolution,* vol. 2, p. 429.

35 From "On Present Political and Economic Policies of the DPRK and Some International Problems," January 10, 1972, in Kim, *On Juche in Our Revolution,* vol. 2, p. 395.

36 Kim Il Sung, *Juche!* (New York: Grossman Publishers, 1972), p. viii.

37 From "Let Us Further Strengthen the Socialist System of Our Country," December 25, 1972, in Kim, *On Juche in Our Revolution,* vol. 2, p. 472.

38 From "On Present Political and Economic Policies of the DPRK and Some International Problems," January 10, 1972, in Kim, *On Juche in Our Revolution,* vol. 2, p. 397.

39 Quoted in Wayne Kiyosaki, *North Korea's Foreign Relations* (New York: Praeger Publishers, 1976), p. 25.

40 See, for example, Kim's speech at the First Session of the Fifth Supreme People's Assembly of the Democratic People's Republic of Korea, December 25, 1972, in Kim, *On Juche in Our Revolution,* vol. 2, p. 452.

41 Byun, *North Korea's Foreign Policy,* chap. 3.

42 Quoted in Ibid., p. 72.

43 Koh, *Foreign Policy Systems of North and South Korea,* pp. 41–43, 60; Kim, *Communist Politics in North Korea,* pp. 16–17.

44 Kim, *Communist Politics in North Korea,* pp. 57–58.

45 From "Report on the Work of the Central Committee to the Fourth Congress of the Workers Party of Korea," September 11, 1961, in Kim, *On Juche in Our Revolution,* vol. 1, p. 226.

46 Ibid., pp. 305–11.

47 Ibid., pp. 306–11.

48 Ibid.

49 Koh, *Foreign Policy Systems of North and South Korea,* p. 41.

50 Clough, *Embattled Korea,* p. 85; Koh, *Foreign Policy Systems of North and South Korea,* pp. 35–48; Scalapino and Lee, *Communism in Korea,* p. 616. It should be obvious that specific statistics regarding the DPRK economy must be greeted with some skepticism, as little documentary evidence has emerged to confirm the numbers released by North Korea or estimated by outsiders. Nevertheless, these numbers are useful as a general source, if only to indicate the direction in which the economy, or other aspects of DPRK life, was moving.

51 Rinn-Sup Shinn, John Folan, John Henderson, Marilyn Hopkins, Edward Knobloch, and Robert Younglof, eds., *Area Handbook of North Korea,* 2nd ed. (Washington, D.C.: U.S. Government Printing Office, 1969), pp. 93, 110–11; Scalapino and Lee, *Communism in Korea,* pp. 1404–13.

52 Koh, *Foreign Policy Systems of North and South Korea,* p. 43.

53 Clough, *Embattled Korea,* p. 89.

54 Murphy, *Second in Command,* p. 243; Schumacher, *Bridge of No Return,* pp. 10, 163 – 67.

55 Suh, *Kim Il-Sung,* p. 218.

56 From "The Present Situation and the Tasks of Our Party," October 5, 1996, in Kim, *On Juche in Our Revolution,* vol. 1, p. 575.

57 *Area Handbook of North Korea,* pp. 110 – 11; Kim in "Report to the Fifth Congress of the Workers Party of Korea on the Work of the Central Committee," November 2, 1970, in Kim, *On Juche in Our Revolution,* vol. 2, p. 250.

58 Koh, *Foreign Policy Systems of North and South Korea,* pp. 34 – 48; An, *North Korea in Transition,* pp. 78 – 82; Clough, *Embattled Korea,* pp. 85 – 6; Donald Zagoria and Young Kum Kim, "North Korea and the Major Powers," in *The Two Koreas in East Asian Affairs,* ed. William Barnds (New York: New York University Press, 1976), p. 33.

59 Kim, *Communist Politics in North Korea,* pp. 95 – 98.

60 Koh, *Foreign Policy Systems of North and South Korea,* pp. 206 – 7; Byun, *North Korea's Foreign Policy,* pp. 75 – 76.

61 Kim, *Communist Politics in North Korea,* pp. 97 – 98, 104 – 5; Koh, *Foreign Policy Systems of North and South Korea,* pp. 206 – 7; Helen Louise Hunter, "The Myth of Equidistance," in Kwak, Patterson, and Olsen, *The Two Koreas in World Politics,* p. 196; Bruce Cumings, *Korea's Place in the Sun* (New York: W. W. Norton, 1997), p. 424; Seung-Hwan Kim, *The Soviet Union and North Korea* (Seoul: Research Center for Peace and Unification of Korea, 1988), chap. 2.

62 Cancellations in research memorandum from State Department Director of Intelligence and Research, "North Korea's Balancing Act between Russia and China," February 15, 1968, NA2, 1967 – 69 central files, pol 33-6, box 2258, 1/1/67 folder, p. 3; Soviet cutoff in *Area Handbook of North Korea,* p. 37, and Scalapino and Lee, *Communism in Korea,* pp. 647 – 50; MiGs in Kim, *Soviet Union and North Korea,* p. 20; next two years in Barnds, *Two Koreas in East Asian Affairs,* p. 46; Kim, *Soviet Union and North Korea,* chap. 2; Byun, *North Korea's Foreign Policy,* pp. 73 – 74; Kim, *Communist Politics in North Korea,* pp. 106 – 7.

63 Memo to Secretary of State from Director of Intelligence and Research Thomas Hughes, "Pyongyang Views the Vietnam War," JL, NSF, country file, Korea, box 255, Korea memos vol. 3, 11/65 – 12/66.

64 "Let Us Defend Our Independence," *Nodong Sinmun,* August 12, 1968, quoted in Kim, *Communist Politics in North Korea,* p. 109.

65 From "The Present Situation and the Tasks of Our Party," October 5, 1966, in Kim, *On Juche in Our Revolution,* vol. 1, p. 551. Note that the word "Their" in this sentence does not explicitly refer to the Chinese, but it is clear by implication where the comment was directed.

66 Research Memorandum from State Department Director of Intelligence and Research, February 15, 1968, "North Korea's Balancing Act between Russia and China," NA2, 1967 – 69 central files, pol 33-6, box 2258, 1/1/67 folder, p. 5; China in *Washington Post, Parade* magazine, July 14, 1968.

67 Chin-Wee Chung, "North Korea's Relations with China," in *The Foreign Relations of North Korea,* ed. Jae Kyu Park, Byung Chul Koh, and Tae-Hwan Kwak (Boulder,

Colo.: Westview Press, 1987), pp. 176–87; loudspeakers in Kim, *Soviet Union and North Korea,* p. 110.

68 Kim, *Communist Politics in North Korea,* pp. 110–112; Donald Zagoria and Young Kum Kim, "North Korea and the Major Powers," in Barnds, *Two Koreas in East Asian Affairs,* p. 47.

69 Kim, *Communist Politics in North Korea,* pp. 54–55, 73–76; Suh, *Kim Il-Sung,* p. 228.

70 Kim purged other notables as well, including Director of Propaganda and Agitation Kim To-man, Vice Premier of Arts and Sciences Ko Hyok, Director of North Korea's Central News Agency Pae Chun-ki, and Director of Culture and Arts Ho Sok-Son. *New York Times,* February 1, 1968, p. 15; Scalapino and Lee, *Communism in Korea,* pp. 609–10; Kim, *Communist Politics in North Korea,* pp. 36, 54–55, 74–75; An, *North Korea in Transition,* pp. 13–18, 36; Koon Woo Nam, *The North Korean Communist Leadership* (University: University of Alabama Press, 1974), p. 146.

71 From "On Some Theoretical Problems of the Socialist Economy," March 1, 1969, in Kim, *On Juche in Our Revolution,* vol. 2, pp. 209–18.

72 Scalapino and Lee, *Communism in Korea,* pp. 602–14; Byun, *North Korea's Foreign Policy,* p. 34; Nam, *North Korean Communist Leadership,* p. 146; Kim, *Communist Politics in North Korea,* pp. 36–7; An, *North Korea in Transition,* pp. 13–18.

73 Byun, *North Korea's Foreign Policy,* p. 34.

74 Jong-Chun Baek, "North Korea's Military Capabilities," in Park, Koh, and Kwak, *Foreign Relations of North Korea,* p. 91.

75 1964 in *Area Handbook of North Korea,* p. 37; Scalapino and Lee, *Communism in Korea,* pp. 647–50; 1966 in cable from Ambassador Brown to State Department, November 2, 1966, JL, NSF, country file: Korea, box 255, Korea cables, vol. III; oral history of Dean Rusk, transcript #3, JL, pp. 26–28; Byun, *North Korea's Foreign Policy,* p. 75; 1967 in House *Pueblo* Report, pp. 684–85; Zagoria and Kim, "North Korea and the Major Powers," pp. 24–25; 1968 in Donald Zagoria and Janet Zagoria, "Crises on the Korean Peninsula," in *Diplomacy of Power,* ed. Stephen Kaplan (Washington, D.C.: Brookings Institution, 1981), p. 386.

76 Koh, *Foreign Policy Systems of North and South Korea,* pp. 11, 59; Kiyosaki, *North Korea's Foreign Relations,* p. 80; Kook-Chin Kim, "An Overview of North Korean–Southeast Asian Relations," in Park, Koh, and Kwak, *Foreign Relations of North Korea,* p. 365. Byun, *North Korea's Foreign Policy,* pp. 4, 44, 95.

77 Statement by Edward Murphy, JL, Papers of Clark Clifford, box 17, North Korea—*Pueblo* Incident.

78 Murphy, *Second in Command,* p. 248.

79 Schumacher, *Bridge of No Return,* p. 158.

80 Layton quoted in Brandt, *Last Voyage of the* Pueblo, p. 176.

81 Report on *Pueblo* Crew in North Korea, JL, Papers of Clark Clifford, box 17, North Korea—*Pueblo* Incident; Brandt, *Last Voyage of the* Pueblo, p. 83; Murphy, *Second in Command,* pp. 216–17.

82 Schumacher, *Bridge of No Return,* p. 123.

83 Murphy, *Second in Command,* pp. 175, 215–17.

84 CIB #60-69; "Finding of Facts," p. 69; letter to author from Ralph McClintock, July 8, 1999; Bucher, *Bucher,* p. 324.

85 *Time,* January 3, 1969.

86 Bucher, *Bucher,* p. 333; Brandt, *Last Voyage of the* Pueblo, p. 139.

87 See, for example, the confessions of Bucher, Stephen Harris, Schumacher, Murphy, Tuck, and Hammond, held at JL, NSF, NSC Histories, *Pueblo* Crisis, vol. 13, public statements, tabs G–I.

88 "Alleged 'Joint Letter of Apology' by Crew of USS *Pueblo* to North Korean Government," JL, NSF, NSC Histories, *Pueblo* Crisis, vol. 13, public statements, tabs G–I.

89 "First Confession of Commander Lloyd M. Bucher," JL, NSF, NSC Histories, *Pueblo* Crisis, vol. 13, public statements, tabs G–I.

90 "Text of *Pueblo* Crew Press Conference," JL, NSF, NSC Histories, *Pueblo* Crisis, 1968, vol. 13, public statements, tabs G–I, document #285.

91 *Pyongyang Times* in Bucher, *Bucher,* p. 293.

92 Korean Task Force Situation Report, February 4, 1968, JL, NSC Histories, *Pueblo* Crisis, 1968, boxes 29 and 30, vol. 6, day by day documents, pt. 10; "The *Pueblo* Incident and the South Korean Revolution," *Asian Forum* 2, no. 3 (1970), p. 207.

93 "The *Pueblo* Incident and the South Korean Revolution," p. 207.

94 Ibid., pp. 201, 203–5.

95 Ibid., p. 212.

96 Publicly stressed in State Department Korean Task Force Situation Report, March 6, 1968, JL, NSF, NSC Histories, *Pueblo* Crisis, 1968, vol. 7, boxes 29 and 30, day by day documents, pt. 14, and "The *Pueblo* Incident in Perspective," *Asian Survey,* April 1969, p. 276; February and March attacks in JL, NSF, NSC Histories, *Pueblo* Crisis, 1968, vol. 7, boxes 29 and 30, day by day documents, pt. 13; other spy ships in State Department Korean Task Force Situation Report, February 16, 1968, JL, NSF, NSC Histories, *Pueblo* Crisis, 1968, vol. 7, boxes 29 and 30, day by day documents, pt. 12; propaganda in Zagoria and Zagoria, "Crises on the Korean Peninsula," p. 369.

97 CBS News interview with Oleg Kalugin, 1995, tape #3, 4/WO #00533, copy in author's possession.

CHAPTER 6. JAW TO JAW

1 Oral history of Vice Admiral J. V. Smith, NHC, pp. 422–23.

2 CIB #87-69, March 10, 1968.

3 Oral history of Vice Admiral J. V. Smith, NHC, p. 426; CIA intelligence memorandum, January 24, 1968, 1300 EST, JL, NSF, NSC Histories, *Pueblo* Crisis 1968, boxes 27–28, vol. 3, day by day documents, pt. II. Smith quoted in Armbrister, *Matter of Accountability,* p. 246.

4 Oral history of Vice Admiral J. V. Smith, NHC, p. 464; CIA intelligence memorandum, January 24, 1968, 1300 EST, JL, NSF, NSC Histories, *Pueblo* Crisis 1968, boxes 27–28, vol. 3, day by day documents, pt. II.

5 Telegram #3624 from American Embassy Seoul to State Department, January 24, 1968, JL, NSF, NSC Histories, *Pueblo* Crisis, boxes 34–35, vol. 15, telegrams to Seoul, tabs 9–17.

6 Telegram #103961 from American Embassy Seoul to State Department, January 25, 1968, JL, NSF, country file: Korea, box 255, Korea cables and memos, vol. 5, tab 9/67–3/68.

7   CIB #87-69, March 10, 1968.

8   Author's interview with Walt Rostow, March 18, 1998; Brandt, *Last Voyage of the Pueblo*, pp. 9–11; Armbrister, *Matter of Accountability*, pp. 66–68, 222–23.

9   Radio message from *Pueblo* to Naval Communications Station, Kamiseya, Japan, January 23, 1968, 1430 hours, reprinted in House *Pueblo* hearings, p. 672.

10 Telegram #8517 from American Embassy Seoul to State Department, January 24, 1968, JL, NSF, country file: Asia and the Pacific, box 257, Korea—*Pueblo* Incident pt. A, vol. I (through January).

11 Lyndon Johnson, *The Vantage Point* (New York: Holt, Rinehart and Winston, 1971), pp. 532–34; author's interview with Walt Rostow, January 19, 1998; Armbrister, *Matter of Accountability*, p. 237.

12 Johnson, *Vantage Point*, p. 532; Clark Clifford with Richard Holbrooke, *Counsel to the President* (New York: Random House, 1991), pp. 465–66. The B-52 referred to here had crashed seven miles short of the runway at Thule, Greenland.

13 Report on meeting of the advisory group, January 29, 1968, JL, NSF, Files of Walt Rostow, box 10, the president's file for Korea and Vietnam.

14 Oral history of Admiral Thomas Moorer, NHC, Operational Archives branch, vol. 3, p. 1414.

15 CINCPACFLT in oral history of Admiral U. S. Grant Sharp, NHC, vol. II, pp. 582–85; Bonesteel in Daniel Bolger, *Scenes from an Unfinished War* (Fort Leavenworth, Kans.: Combat Studies Institute, 1991). See Armbrister, *Matter of Accountability*, pp. 237–41, for a more detailed discussion.

16 Letters to author from John Perry, February 15, 2000, and February 19, 2000; CINCPACFLT cable 2400008Z, JL, NSF, country file: Korea—*Pueblo* Incident, military cables, vol. I, boxes 263–64; CINCPAC telegram 230909Z, JL, NSF, country file: Asia and the Pacific, box 257; CINCPAC telegram 231021Z, JL, NSF, country file: Asia and the Pacific, box 257. I am indebted to Richard Mobley for bringing the details of this operation to my attention.

17 Miller in "Compilation of Statements Concerning USS *Pueblo* Incident," JL, NSC Histories, *Pueblo* Crisis, 1968, boxes 31–33, vol. 13, public statements, tabs D–F; Thurmond in *Congressional Record*, January 23, 1968, vol. 14, pt. 1, p. 679.

18 Watson in *Congressional Record*, February 1, 1968, vol. 14, pt. 2, p. 1901.

19 Quoted in Armbrister, *Matter of Accountability*, p. 303.

20 Los Angeles telegram from Irving Pell, Philadelphia telegram from Herbert Trulick, in JL, White House Central Files, subject file, defense, ND 19/CO 151, box 210.

21 *New York Times*, February 11, 1968. Specifically, 40 percent of those responding said that force should be used to get the ship back, and another 6 percent favored using force later if diplomacy failed. Only 21 percent favored continuing negotiations as at present.

22 LBJ in meeting notes of president's February 2 breakfast with Democratic congressional leaders, JL, Tom Johnson's notes of meetings, box 2, set II, "February 6, 1968, 8:30 A.M. folder"; Rusk ("If you just") in oral history of Dean Rusk, tape CCC CCC, Richard Russell Library, University of Georgia, Athens, Ga.; Dulles in *Washington Star*, February 22, 1968, and *Baltimore Sun*, February 24, 1968; Rusk ("we ourselves") in Dean Rusk with Richard Rusk, *As I Saw It* (New York: W. W. Norton, 1991), p. 392.

23 CIA intelligence memorandum, "Disposition of North Korean Merchant and Fishing Ships," January 26, 1968, JL, NSF, country file: Asia and the Pacific, Korea, box 259,

Korea—*Pueblo* Incident; minutes of the Korean Working Group meeting, January 27, noon, NA2, 1967–69 central files, pol 33-6, box 2257, 1/27/68 folder; Dean Rusk oral history, tape CCC CCC, Richard Russell Library; memo to Rostow from Alfred Jenkins, January 31, 1968, JL, NSF, country file: Asia and the Pacific, box 257, Korea—*Pueblo* Incident, pt. B, vol. I (through January); "Chronology of Diplomatic Activity in the *Pueblo* Crisis," NA2, p. 316; Rostow in meeting notes of January 25, 1968, 6:30 P.M. meeting, JL, Tom Johnson's notes of meetings, box 2. The DPRK fleet contained only three standard merchant ships, the *Wisung Ho,* the *P'yong Hwa,* and the *Paektu San,* and two refrigerated ships, the *MAG* I, and the *MAG* II. In addition, they had about thirty medium-size trawlers, the seizure of which not only would have raised international protest but likely would have had virtually no impact on North Korea.

24 Telegram #68838 from CSAF to SAC, January 30, 1968, JL, NSF, country file: Asia and the Pacific, Korea, box 263, Korea—*Pueblo* Incident, military cables, vol. I, 1/68 folder.

25 *Pueblo* Incident question and answer briefing book, JL, George Christian Papers, box 4; sitrep—1700 hours EST, January 26, 1968, JL, NSF, NSC Histories, *Pueblo* Crisis 1968, vol. 3, day by day documents, pt. 3, box 28; "Compilation of Statements Concerning USS *Pueblo* Incident," JL, NSC Histories, *Pueblo* Crisis, 1968, boxes 31–33, vol. 13, public statements, tabs A–C; *Time,* April 26, 1968, pp. 28–29; *New York Times,* February 1, 1968, p. 15; memorandum for the Korean working group, January 27, 1968, 12:00 noon, NA2, 1967–69 central files, pol 33-6, box 2257, folder 1/27/68.

26 Minutes of the Korean working group meeting, January 27, 1968, noon, NA2, 1967–69 central files, pol 33-6, box 2257, 1/27/68 folder.

27 Telegram #8527 from American Embassy Tokyo to State Department, February 1, 1968, JL, NSC History, *Pueblo* Crisis, 1968, boxes 36–37, vol. 19, telegrams from Asia, tabs 8–9; *Time,* May 3, 1968, pp. 27–28; *New Republic,* November 16, 1968, pp. 11–12; Zagoria and Kim, "North Korea and the Major Powers," p. 46.

28 Notes of president's January 25, 1968 luncheon meeting, JL, Tom Johnson's notes of meetings, box 2.

29 Oral history of Dean Rusk, JL, interview #3, p. 27; oral history of Nicholas Katzenbach, JL, interview #3, p. 4.

30 *St. Louis Globe-Democrat,* January 26, 1968.

31 Telegrams in JL, White House Central Files, subject file, defense, ND 19/CO 151, box 205.

32 Johnson, *Vantage Point,* p. 536.

33 CINCPAC command history, 1968, NHC, vol. 4, pp. 246–50; "Historical Reports Relating to Diplomacy during the Lyndon Johnson Administration," NA2, p. 67; notes of White House meeting, January 26, 1968, 11:00 A.M., JL, NSC Histories, *Pueblo* Crisis, 1968, boxes 27 and 28, vol. 3, day by day documents, pt. 3; "Q and A" book, JL, NSC Histories, *Pueblo* Crisis, 1968, boxes 31–33, vol. 13, public statements, tabs G–I; Zagoria and Zagoria, "Crises on the Korean Peninsula," pp. 356–60; telegram #60176 from COMSEVENTHFLT to RUHHBRA/CINCPACFLT, January 25, 1968, and telegram #65553 from COMSEVENTHFLT to CNO, January 28, 1968, JL, NSC Histories, country file: Asia and the Pacific, box 257, Korea—*Pueblo* Incident, pt. A, vol. 1 (through January); Bolger, *Scenes from an Unfinished War,* p. 72; Armbrister, *Matter of Accountability,* p. 262.

34 See Richard Mobley, "The *Pueblo* Crisis" (unpublished paper in author's possession).

35 Notes of president's meeting, January 24, 1968, 7:50 P.M., JL, Tom Johnson's notes of

meetings, box 2; "Report on Meeting of Advisory Group, January 29, 1968," JL, NSF, country file: Asia and the Pacific, Korea—*Pueblo* Incident, vol. I, pt. B, box 257; "Summary Minutes of *Pueblo* Group," January 24, 1968, document #3410, fiche 282, Declassified Documents Reference System (Woodbridge, Conn.: Research Publications, 1998); "Meeting on Korean Crisis without President," January 24, 1968, document 3411, fiche 282, Declassified Documents Reference System (Woodbridge, Conn.: Research Publications, 1998).

36 Memorandum for the Korean working group, January 26 1968, JL, NSF, country file: Korea—*Pueblo* Incident miscellaneous, vol. I.

37 Notes of president's breakfast meeting, January 25, 1968, JL, Tom Johnson's notes of meetings, box 2.

38 Information memo from National Military Command Center, February 6, 1968, "Current Summary of Korean Situation," NA2, 1967–69 central files, pol 33-6, box 2254, 3/1/68 folder; undated report, document #56, JL, NSF, NSC Histories, boxes 27–28, vol. 6, pt. 11.

39 CINCPACFLT telegram #240008Z, JL, country file: Korea—*Pueblo* Incident, military cables, vol. I, boxes 263–64; numerous letters in author's possession from American servicemen involved in the operation.

40 Telegram to Wheeler from Sharp, January 31, 1968, NA2, RG 218, Records of the US JCS, records of Chairman (Gen.) Earle Wheeler, 1964–70, 091 Korea, box 29, Chairman Wheeler's files.

41 Letter to author from George Howe, October 27, 2000.

42 *New York Times,* February 1, 1968, p. 15.

43 Shots in *New York Times,* February 8, 1969, and notes of State Department press briefing, JL, NSC Histories, *Pueblo* Crisis, 1968, boxes 29 and 30, vol. 6, day by day documents, pt. 11; students in "Chronology of Diplomatic Activity in the *Pueblo* Crisis," NA2, p. 322.

44 Telegram #4015 from American Embassy Seoul to State Department, February 6, 1968, JL, NSC Histories, *Pueblo* Crisis, 1968, boxes 34–35, vol. 16, telegrams from Seoul, tabs 1–5; telegram from American Embassy Seoul to State Department, January 24, 1968, JL, NSC Histories, *Pueblo* Crisis, 1968, boxes 34–35, vol. 15, telegrams to Seoul, tabs 9–17; *New York Times,* February 8, 1968, p. 15.

45 Telegram #9193 from American Embassy Seoul to State Department, February 20, 1968, JL, NSF, country file, Asia and the Pacific, Korea, box 262, Korea—*Pueblo* Incident, Seoul cables, vol. II, 2/11/68–3/68 folder.

46 Telegram #8515 from American Embassy Seoul to State Department, January 24, 1968, NA2, 1967–69 central files, pol 33-6, box 2258, 1/1/68 file; *New York Times,* January 27, 1968, p. 9; cable from Ambassador Porter to White House, January 24, 1968, JL, Korea cables and memos, vol. 5, NSF, country file: Asia and the Pacific, Korea, box 255, document #14a.

47 Telegram #8582 from American Embassy Seoul to State Department, January 26, 1968, NA2, 1967–69 central files, pol 33-6, box 2258, 1/30/68 folder.

48 Telegram #3976 from American Embassy Seoul to State Department, February 5, 1968, NA2, 1967–69 central files, pol 33-6, box 2256, 2/4/68 folder; speech in telegram #3894 from American Embassy Seoul to State Department, February 1968, JL, NSC Histories, *Pueblo* Crisis, 1968, boxes 34–35, vol. 16, telegrams from Seoul, tabs 1–5.

49 February 6, 1968, FBIS report, JL, NSC Histories, *Pueblo* Crisis, 1968, boxes 29 and 30, vol. 6, day by day documents, pt. 10; *Washington Post,* February 7, 1968.

50 "Chronology of Diplomatic Activity in the *Pueblo* Crisis," NA2, p. 204; telegram #3895 from American Embassy Seoul to State Department, February 1, 1968, JL, NSC Histories, *Pueblo* Crisis, 1968, boxes 34–35, vol. 16, telegrams from Seoul, tabs 1–5.

51 Memo from Komer to Bundy, December 9, 1963, JL, NSF, country file: Korea, box 256, filed by LBJ Library; Sung-Joo Han, "Policy towards the United States," in *The Foreign Policy of the Republic of Korea,* ed. Young-nok Koo and Sung-Joo Han (New York: Columbia University Press, 1985), pp. 150–51.

52 Infantry divisions in McNamara to Johnson, November 25, 1963, JL, NSF, country file: Korea, box 256, filed by LBJ Library, and memo to LBJ from Robert McNamara, "Study of Possible Redeployment of US Division Now in Korea," JL, NSF, NSA memorandums, box 4; funding in Park briefing book, briefing paper: "Korean Force Levels and the MAP," May 11, 1965, JL, NSF, country file: Korea, box 256.

53 Clifford, *Counsel to the President,* p. 450.

54 Memo to LBJ from William Guad, "Authorization to Make a New Commodity Assistance Commitment to Korea," February 15, 1967, JL, NSF, country file, Korea, box 255, Korea cables and memos, vol. 4, 1/67–8/67. The Johnson Library is full of evidence documenting the nature of this relationship. See, for example, memo to Johnson from M. Bundy, "Sweetener for Another ROK Division in Vietnam," JL, NSF, country file, Korea, box 255, Korea memos, vol. 3, 11/65–12/66; memo to M. Bundy from David Bell, January 26, 1966, JL, NSF, country file, Korea, box 255, Korea memos, vol. 13, 11/65–12/66; memo to W. Bundy from Francis Bator, December 29, 1965, JL, NSF, country file, Korea, box 255, Korea memos, vol. 3, 11/65–12/66; telegram #1120 from Seoul to State Department, September 6, 1967, JL, NSF, country file, Korea, box 255, Korea memos, vol. 5, 9/67–3/68; Bundy to Johnson, April 16, 1968, and Porter to Rusk, January 15, 1968, JL, NSF, country file, Vietnam, box 91, Vietnam allies 5D (3).

55 Memo to LBJ from M. Bundy, "Sweetener for Another ROK Division in Vietnam," February 3, 1966, JL, NSF, country file: Korea, box 255, Korea memos, vol. 3, 11/65–12/66 folder.

56 Notes of president's meeting, April 30, 1968, 1:25 P.M., JL, Tom Johnson's notes of meetings, box 3, set III.

57 Park in airgram #A-350 from American Embassy Seoul to State Department, January 26, 1968, "ROKG Note on North Korean Acts," NA2, 1967–69 central files, pol 33-6, box 2258, 1/26/68 folder. See also message #86876 to RUEKDA/JCS from CINCPAC, May 6, 1968, NA2, Record Group 218, Records of the US JCS, records of Chairman (Gen.) Earle Wheeler, 1964–70, box 160, chairman's messages, 1 May 1968–31 May 1968; telegram #4088 to State Department from American Embassy Seoul, NA2, 1967–69 central files, pol 33-6, box 2255, file 2-8-68; CINCPAC Command History, 1968, NHC, vol. 2, p. 220; telegram #2769 from American Embassy Seoul to State Department, December 7, 1967, JL, NSF, memos to the president, box 26, Walt Rostow, vol. 53, December 1–10, 1967.

58 ROK JCS request in Air Force Chief of Staff memo to subordinate commands, January 29, 1968, JL, NSF, country file, Korea—*Pueblo* Incident, boxes 263–64, military cables vol. I; assembly in telegram #4015 from American Embassy Seoul to State Department, February 6, 1968, JL, NSF, NSC Histories, *Pueblo* Crisis, boxes 34–35, vol.

16, telegrams from Seoul, tabs 1–5. Although Korean documents are hard to obtain, the newspaper *Chosun Ilbo* recently examined a collection of ROK government documents related to the crisis, most of which indicated that the government had consciously demanded additional assistance from the United States in exchange for its acceptance of the passive American position on DPRK aggression (*Chosun Ilbo,* January 19, 1999). I am indebted to Dr. Gordon Bennett of the University of Texas for bringing these articles to my attention.

59 On the mission, see Clifford, *Counsel to the President,* p. 448; on LBJ's desire to maintain ROK troops, see notes of president's meeting, February 13, 1968, 1:12 P.M., JL, Tom Johnson's notes of meetings, box 2, set II, and notes of meeting of senior foreign policy advisers, February 12, 1968, 1:45 P.M., JL, Tom Johnson's notes of meetings, box 2, set II.

60 Quoted in Marvin Kalb and Elie Abel, *Roots of Involvement* (New York: W. W. Norton, 1971), p. 213.

61 See, for example, telegram #3901 from American Embassy Seoul to State Department, February 3, 1968, NA2, 1967–69 central files, pol 33-6, box 2256, 2/2/68 folder; telegram #4008 from American Embassy Seoul to State Department, NA2, 1967–69 central files, pol 33-6, box 2256, 2/6/68 folder. Rusk in Dean Rusk oral history, Richard Russell Library, tape CCC CCC.

62 Transcript of press conference #118, February 3, 1968, JL, NSC Histories, *Pueblo* Crisis, 1968, boxes 31-33, vol. 13, public statements, tabs A–C.

63 Telegram #109821 from Johnson to Park, February 4, 1968, NA2, 1967–69 central files, pol 33-6, box 2256, 2/4/68 folder.

64 Telegram #3935 to State Department from American Embassy Seoul, February 4, 1968, NA2, 1967–69 central files, pol 33-6, box 2256, 2/4/68 folder.

65 Telegram #3935 to State Department from American Embassy Seoul, February 4, 1968, NA2, 1967–69 central files, pol 33-6, box 2256, 2/4/68 folder.

66 Telegram #106085 from State Department to American Embassy Seoul, January 28, 1968, NA2, 1967–69 central files, pol 33-6, box 2261.

67 Vance report, "Memorandum for the President," February 20, 1968, JL, NSF, files of Walt Rostow, box 10; February 8, 1968, message to Congress, JL, NSF, NSC History, *Pueblo* Crisis, 1968, boxes 29 and 30, vol. 6, day by day documents, pt. 11; *Chicago Sun-Times,* February 9, 1968.

68 Memo, "Authority Required from Congress in Relation to the *Pueblo* Incident," January 1968, JL, NSF, NSC History, *Pueblo* Crisis, 1968, boxes 31–33, vol. 11, background documents.

69 Notes of LBJ's meeting with the Democratic congressional leadership, February 5, 1968, JL, president's appointment file, diary backup, box 89, and backup daily log, February 6, 1968.

70 Notes of meeting of senior foreign policy advisers, February 12, 1968, 1:45 P.M., JL, Tom Johnson's notes of meetings, box 2, set II; letter from Rusk to LBJ, "Themes for the Mission of Cyrus Vance," NA2, 1967–69 central files, pol 33-6, box 2255, 2-8-68 folder; Cy Vance report, "Memorandum for the President," February 20, 1968, JL, NSF, files of Walt Rostow, box 10; oral history of Cyrus Vance, JL, vol. 2, p. 15.

71 Chronology of Diplomatic Activity in the *Pueblo* Crisis, NA2, pp. 338, 341; notes of president's meeting with Cy Vance, February 15, 1968, 6:06 P.M., JL, Tom Johnson's notes of meetings, box 2.

72 Vance Report, "Memorandum for the President," February 20, 1968, JL, NSF, files of Walt Rostow, box 10.

73 Notes of president's meeting with Cy Vance, February 15, 1968, 6:06 P.M., JL, Tom Johnson's notes of meetings, box 2.

74 On Vance meetings with ROK officials, see telegram #4315 from American Embassy Seoul to State Department, February 17, 1968, NA2, 1967–69 central files, pol 33-6, box 2255, 2/15/68 file; telegram #4207 from American Embassy Seoul to State Department, February 13, 1968, NA2, 1967–69 central files, pol 33-6, box 2255, 2nd file in box (no label); report from State Department, "Vance—Korean Cabinet Meeting," February 13, 1968, NA2, 1967–69 central files, pol 33-6, box 2255, 2/15/68 folder. John Walsh in Armbrister, *Matter of Accountability,* p. 277.

75 Telegram #4229 from American Embassy Seoul to State Department, February 14, 1968, NA2, 1967–69 central files, pol 33-6, box 2255, 2nd file in box (unlabeled).

76 Telegram #4315 from American Embassy Seoul to State Department, February 17, 1968, NA2, 1967–69 central files, pol 33-6, box 2255, 2/15/68 file.

77 Vance Report, "Memorandum for the President," February 20, 1968, JL, NSF, files of Walt Rostow, box 10.

78 Ibid.; telegram #4315 from American Embassy Seoul to State Department, February 17, 1968, NA2, 1967–69 central files, pol 33-6, box 2255, 2/15/68 file.

79 Memo from JCS, "Korean Forces," document #5, JL, Tom Johnson's notes of meetings, box 2, set II, March 11, 1968, 6:57 P.M. folder.

80 Memo to Johnson from Rostow, June 19, 1968, JL, NSF, country file, Vietnam, box 91, Vietnam 5D (3), 1967–69, allies: troop commitments.

81 Meeting notes, April 16, 1968, 10:25 A.M. meeting, JL, Tom Johnson's notes of meetings, box 3, set III; telegram from White House Situation Room to Rostow, April 17, 1968, JL, NSF, country file, Vietnam, box 91, Vietnam, 5D (3), 1967–69, allies: troop commitments.

82 Briefing material, tab 14, "ROK Prime Minister's Idea of 2 Additional ROK Divisions for Vietnam," JL, NSF, international meetings and travel file, box 21, meeting with President Park folder.

83 Cable #7104 from State Department to American Embassy Seoul, January 15, 1969, JL, NSF, country file, Asia and the Pacific, box 256, Korea, filed by the LBJ Library folder.

84 CINCPAC Command History, 1968, NHC, vol. 2, pp. 192–97; telegram #111263 from State Department to American Embassy Seoul, February 7, 1968, NA2, 1967–69 central files, pol 33-6, box 2256, 2/6/68 folder.

85 CINCPAC Command History, 1968, NHC, vol. 2, pp. 192–97; memo—attachment A, "Korea—Additional US Commitments," March 11, 1968, 6:57 P.M., JL, Tom Johnson's notes of meetings, box 2. Counterinsurgency in telegram #111264 from State Department to American Embassy Seoul, February 7, 1968, NA2, 1967–69 central files, pol 33-6, box 2255, 2/8/68 folder.

86 Memo—attachment A, "Korea—Additional US Commitments," March 11, 1968, 6:57 P.M., JL, Tom Johnson's notes of meetings, box 2; memo from Bundy to Johnson, "Additional Korean Forces in Vietnam," April 16, 1968, JL, NSF, country file, Vietnam, box 91, Vietnam, 5D (3), 1967–69, allies: troop commitments; CINCPAC Command History, 1968, NHC, vol. 2, pp. 209–16, and vol. 4, p. 222; briefing book, tab 18, "Foreign Ministers Choi's Request to Vance . . . for Further US Commitments," JL, NSF, international meetings and travel file, box 21, meeting with President Park folder.

87 Telegram #815 from Defense Department to JCS, February 3, 1968, JL, NSF, country file, Asia and the Pacific, Korea, box 263, Korea—*Pueblo* Incident, military cables, vol. II, 2/68–3/68 folder.

88 Telegram #4714 from American Embassy Seoul to State Department, March 6, 1968, JL, NSC Histories, *Pueblo* Crisis, 1968, boxes 34–35, vol. 17, telegrams from Seoul folder, tab 1; telegrams #9216 and #9282 from American Embassy Seoul to State Department, February 22 and 26, 1968, JL, NSF, NSC Histories, *Pueblo* Crisis, 1968, box 35, vol. 7.

89 Oral history of Rutherford Poats, JL, pp. 17–19.

90 Nancy Bernkopf Tucker, "Threats, Opportunities, and Frustrations in East Asia," in Warren Cohen and Nancy Bernkopf Tucker, *Lyndon Johnson Confronts the World* (Cambridge: Cambridge University Press, 1994), p. 131.

91 Telegrams #4453 and #4463 from Porter to State Department, February 23, 1968, NA2, 1967–69 central files, pol 33-6, box 2255, 2/21/68 folder; telegram #4501 from American Embassy Seoul to State Department, February 26, 1968, NA2, 1967–69 central files, pol 33-6, box 2254, 2/25/68 folder; telegram #110353 to American Embassy Seoul from State Department, February 6, 1968, NA2 1967–69 central files, pol 33-6, box 2256, folder 2/6/68.

92 Clifford, *Counsel to the President,* p. 466.

93 Notes from meeting of the *Pueblo* Group, 1/24/68, 10:30 A.M., JL, NSF, files of Bromley K. Smith, box 1.

94 Ibid.; meeting notes, January 24, 1968—1:00 P.M., JL, Tom Johnson's notes of meetings, box 2, set II.

95 January 24, 1968, memo from Hughes to Rusk, "Soviet Policy towards North Korea and the *Pueblo* Incident," JL, NSF, country file, Asia and the Pacific, box 257, Korea—*Pueblo* Incident, pt. B, vol. I (through January).

96 Defense Department news release #73-68, JL, NSF, NSC History, *Pueblo* Crisis, 1968, boxes 27 and 28, "*Pueblo* Crisis, 1968, vol. 3, day by day documents, pt. I; "Chronology of Diplomatic Activity in *Pueblo* Crisis," NA2, p. 10.

97 Chronology of Diplomatic Activity in *Pueblo* Crisis, NA2, p. 15; telegram #1272 from State Department to American Embassy Seoul, January 23, 1968, NA2, 1967–69 central files, pol 33-6, box 2258, 1/1/68 folder.

98 Johnson, *Vantage Point,* p. 535.

99 Meeting notes of State Department meeting on *Pueblo,* January 24, 1968, JL, Papers of Lyndon Johnson, President, meeting notes files, box 2. See also "Backup Daily Log for January 24, 1968," JL, President's Appointment File, diary backup, box 87, appointment file, January 23, 1968, folder.

100 Johnson, *Vantage Point,* p. 180.

101 LBJ speech at Johns Hopkins University, April 7, 1965, reprinted in William Williams et al., *America in Vietnam* (New York: Anchor Books, 1985).

102 Doris Kearns, *Lyndon Johnson and the American Dream* (New York: Harper and Row, 1976), p. 330.

103 Jack Valenti in report for the president, April 30, 1965, JL, White House Central Files, executive file, CO 1-8; LBJ in Johnson, *Vantage Point,* pp. 193, 200.

104 Telegram #2566 from State Department to American Embassy Seoul, January 25, 1968, NA2, 1967–69 central files, pol 33-6, box 2258, 1/1/68 folder; telegram #1272 from

State Department to American Embassy Seoul, January 23, 1968, NA2, 1967–69 central files, pol 33-6, box 2258, 1/1/68 folder; summary of 1:00 P.M. cabinet room meeting, JL, NSF, NSC Histories, *Pueblo* Crisis, 1968, vol. 3, day by day documents, pt. 2.

105 Information in CIA intelligence information cable, February 5, 1968, JL, NSF, NSC Histories, *Pueblo* Crisis, vol. 12, CIA documents [I], box 32, document #102. See also telegram #2913 from American Embassy Moscow to State Department, February 25, 1968, NA2, 1967–69 central files, pol 33-6, box 2254, 2/25/68 folder, for signs that the North Koreans were not sharing information about the crisis with the Soviet Union. Return in telegram #113552 to American Embassy Moscow from State Department, February 10, 1968, NA2, 1967–69 central files, pol 33-6, box 2255, 2nd file in box (unlabeled); memo regarding February 15 meeting between Soviet Ambassador Anatoly Dobrynin and Deputy Undersecretary of State Charles Bohlen, NA2, 1967–69 central files, pol 33-6, box 2255, 2/15/68 folder; memorandum from Rostow to LBJ, February 9, 1968, JL, NSC Histories, *Pueblo* Crisis, 1968, boxes 29 and 30, vol. 6, day by day documents, pt. 11.

106 CIA intelligence information cable, February 2, 1968, JL, NSF, NSC Histories, *Pueblo* Crisis, vol. 12, CIA documents [I], box 32, document #93. On the restrained Soviet response, see memo to LBJ from Bromley Smith, February 3, 1968, JL, NSC Histories, *Pueblo* Crisis, 1968, boxes 29 and 30, vol. 5, day by day documents, pt. 9; telegram #4212, from American Embassy Vientiane to State Department, February 2, 1968, NA2, 1967–69 central files, pol 33-6, box 2256, 2/1/68 folder; telegram #7307 from American Embassy Moscow to State Department, January 26, 1968, NA2, 1967–69 central files, pol 33-6, box 2258, 1/30/68 folder.

107 Zagoria and Zagoria, "Crises on the Korean Peninsula," p. 378.

108 EC-121 in House *Pueblo* hearings, p. 890; Budapest in Zagoria and Zagoria, "Crises on the Korean Peninsula," p. 387.

109 See, for example, statement by Defense Department, news release #73-68, JL, NSF, NSC History, *Pueblo* Crisis, 1968, boxes 27 and 28, vol. 3, day by day documents, pt. I.

110 Mondale in Chronology of Diplomatic Activity in the *Pueblo* Crisis, NA2, p. 65; memo from Thompson to George Christian, January 26, 1968, JL, White House Aides Files, George Christian, box 12, *Pueblo* misc. file; embassy officer in telegram #2839 from American Embassy New Delhi to State Department, January 27, 1968, JL, NSF, country file, Asia and the Pacific, box 257, Korea—*Pueblo* Incident, pt. B, vol. I (through January); telegram #2839 to State Department from American Embassy New Delhi, January 27, 1968, NA2, 1967–69 central files, pol 33-6, box 2257, 1/27/68 folder (the writers were Adam Clymer of the *Sun* and Bernard Nossiter of the *Post*); Clymer in information memo to the president, January 26, 1968, JL, NSC Histories, *Pueblo* Crisis, 1968, boxes 27 and 28, vol. 3, day by day documents, pt. 3; telegram #745 from US Mission UN to State Department, NA2, 1967–69 central files, pol 33-6, box 2257, 1/27/68 folder; telegram #3593 from US Mission UN to State Department, February 1, 1968, NA2, 1967–69 central files, pol 33-6, box 2256, 2/1/68 folder; Chronology of Diplomatic Activity in the *Pueblo* Crisis, NA2, pp. 96, 171; telegram #1236 from American Embassy Ouagadougou to State Department, February 7, 1968, NA2, 1967–69 central files, pol 33-6, box 2256, folder 2/6/68.

111 Department of State memorandum, intelligence note #75, "The Emerging Soviet Line on the *Pueblo* Incident," JL, NSC Histories, *Pueblo* Crisis, 1968, boxes 27 and 28,

vol. 4, day by day documents, pt. 6; memo to Rusk from George Denney, "North Korea's Balancing Act between Russia and China," February 15, 1968, NA2, 1967–69 central files, pol 33-6, box 2255, 2/15/68 folder.

112 Thompson in telegram from American Embassy Moscow to State Department, January 27, 1968, JL, NSF, country file, Asia and the Pacific, box 257, Korea—*Pueblo* Incident, pt. A, vol. 1a (through January); advisers in *New York Times,* January 28, 1968, p. 30.

113 Transcript of press and news radio briefing, January 30, 1968, 12:40 P.M., JL, NSC Histories, *Pueblo* Crisis, 1968, boxes 27 and 28, vol. 4, day by day documents, pt. 6; State Department press conference, January 24, 1968, 12:44 P.M., JL, NSF, NSC History, *Pueblo* Crisis, 1968, boxes 27 and 28, vol. 3, day by day documents, pt. 2.

114 Telegram #2579 from American Embassy Moscow, January 26, 1968, NA2, RG 59, 1967–69 central files, pol 33-6, KOR N–US.

115 Note from Rostow to Helms, January 26, 1968, JL, NSC Histories, *Pueblo* Crisis, 1968, boxes 27 and 28, vol. 3, day by day documents, pt. 3; telegram #112161 from American Embassy Tehran to State Department, February 15, 1968, NA2, 1967–69 central files, pol 33-6, box 2255, 2nd file (unlabeled); blunder in CIA cable #17863-171-4, "Comments . . . Concerning the *Pueblo* Incident," and CIA cable #17052 81-3, "Views of a West European on the USS *Pueblo* Incident," JL, NSF, NSC Histories, *Pueblo* Crisis, vol. 12, CIA documents [II], box 32.

116 Although Soviet efforts to assist the situation were never spelled out directly, they are suggested in a number of places, including telegram #120035 to American Embassy Moscow from State Department, February 24, 1968, NA2, 1967–69, central files, pol 33-6, box 2255, 2/21/68 folder, which describes a meeting between Soviet Ambassador Anatoly Dobrynin and Deputy Undersecretary for Political Affairs Charles Bohlen. See also telegram from State Department to American Embassy Brussels, January 28, 1968, NA2, 1967–69 central files, pol 33-6, box 2257, 1/28/68 folder; telegram from American Embassy Rabat #2695 to State, February 2, 1968, NA2, 1967–69 central files, pol 33-6, box 2256, 2/2/68 folder; "Memo of Conversation between Secretary Rusk and Ambassador Charles Lucet," February 2, 1968, NA2, 1967–69 central files, pol 33-6, box 2256, 2/2/68 folder; *New York Times,* January 29, 1968, and November 26, 1968; telegram #3645 from US Mission UN to State Department, February 3, 1968, NA2, 1967–69 central files, pol 33-6, box 2256, 2/2/68 folder.

117 Quoted in *New York Times,* February 3, 1968.

118 Summary meeting notes, January 31, 1968, meeting with congressional leaders, JL, Papers of Lyndon Johnson, President, 1963–69, meeting notes files, box 2.

119 Johnson, *Vantage Point,* pp. 534–35. For similar comments, see oral history of Charles Roberts, interview #3, JL, pp. 86–89.

120 Clifford in notes of meeting with National Alliance of Businessmen, January 27, 1968, 1:25 P.M., JL, Tom Johnson's notes of meetings, box 2, set II; Rusk in meeting notes, January 24, 1968, 1:00 P.M., Tom Johnson's notes of meetings, box 2, set II.

121 Porter in telegram #8517 from American Embassy Seoul to State Department, January 24, 1968, JL, NSF, country file, Asia and the Pacific, box 257, Korea—*Pueblo* Incident, pt. A, vol. I (through January); Westmoreland in Wirtz, *Tet Offensive,* p. 213.

122 Summary meeting notes, January 24, 1968, 10:30 A.M. meeting, JL, NSF, files of Bromley Smith, meeting of *Pueblo* Group.

123 Author's interview with Walt Rostow, January 14, 1998.

124 Transcript of minutes of Security Council meeting, January 26, 1968, JL, NSF, NSC Histories, *Pueblo* Crisis, 1968, boxes 31–33, vol. 13, public statements folder; "Chronology of Diplomatic Activity in the *Pueblo* Crisis," NA2, p. 95; memo to Christian from Dick Moose, January 26, 1968, JL, Christian Papers, box 4, *Pueblo* folder.

125 State Department telegram #1862 to US Mission UN, January 25, 1968, JL, NSF, country file, Asia and the Pacific, box 257, Korea—*Pueblo* Incident, pt. A, vol. 1 (through January); UN telegram #074 to State Department, January 28, 1968, NA2, 1967–69 central files, pol 33-6, box 2257, 1/28/68 folder; State Department telegram #104660 to US Mission UN, January 25, 1968, NA2, 1967–69 central files, pol 33-6, box 2258, 1/1/68 folder; "Chronology of Diplomatic Activity in the *Pueblo* Case," NA2, pp. 51–53, 56, 125, 140, 159; memo to LBJ from Rostow, January 29, 1968, 6:30 P.M., JL, NSF, country file, Asia and the Pacific, box 257, Korea—*Pueblo* Incident, pt. B, vol. 1 (through January); sitrep—January 31, 1968, 0600 hours, JL, NSF, NSC, History, *Pueblo* Crisis, 1968, vol. 5, day by day documents, pt. 7, box 9; State Department telegram #108199 to UN, February 1, 1968, NA2, 1967–69 central files, pol 33-6, box 2256, 2/1/68 folder; KTF sitrep, January 28, 1968—0600 hours, NA2, 1967–69 central files, pol 33-6, box 2257, folder 1/28/68; *New York Times,* January 28, 1968, p. 1.

126 Telegram #104827 to US Mission Geneva from State Department, January 26, 1968, NA2, 1967–69 central files, pol 33-6, box 2258, 1/30/68 folder.

127 Press briefing, January 31, 1968, 12:50 P.M., JL, NSC Histories, *Pueblo* Crisis, 1968, boxes 29 and 30, vol. 5, day by day documents, pt. 7; editorial in telegram #2650 from US Mission Geneva to State Department, February 23, 1968, NA2, 1967–69 central files, pol 33-6, box 2255, 2/21/68 folder.

128 Undated memo from Meeker to Rusk, "North Korean Seizure of the USS *Pueblo,*" JL, WH Aides Files, office files of Harry Macpherson, box 10, Korea folder; memo to Walt Rostow from Benjamin Reed, "Replies to Our Demarche," NA2, 1967–69 central files, pol 33-6, box 2256, 2/2/68 folder.

129 Telegram #8610 from American Embassy Seoul to State Department, January 27, 1968, JL, NSF, country file, Asia and the Pacific, box 257, Korea—*Pueblo* Incident, pt. A, vol. 1a (through January); unsigned report, "The *Pueblo* Case," February 2, 1968, NA2, 1967–69 central files, pol 33-6, box 2256, 2/4/68 folder; *Los Angeles Times,* May 17, 1964, p. 16.

130 Oral history of Arthur Goldberg, JL, p. 20.

131 "Chronology of Diplomatic Activity in the *Pueblo* Case," NA2, p. 170.

132 Information memorandum to Rostow from LBJ, January 27, 1968, JL, NSF, country file, Asia and the Pacific, box 257, Korea—*Pueblo* Incident, pt. A, vol. 1a (through January).

133 Telegram #106085 from State Department to American Embassy Seoul, January 28, 1968, NA2, 1967–69 central files, pol 33-6, box 2257, 1/28/68 folder; Rusk in meeting with congressional leaders, January 31, 1968, JL, Papers of Lyndon Johnson, President, 1963–69, meeting notes files, box 2; 50–50 in memo of conversation of Secretary Rusk and Ambassador Charles Lucet, February 2, 1968, NA2, 1967–69 central files, pol 33-6, box 2256, 2/2/68 folder.

134 Unsigned report, "The *Pueblo* Case," February 5, 1968, NA2, 1967–69 central files, pol 33-6, box 2256, 2/4/68 folder.

135 Telegram #108338 to American Embassy Seoul from State Department, February 1,

1968, NA2, 1967–69 central files, pol 33-6, box 2256, 2/1/68 folder; telegram #3597 from US Mission UN to State Department, February 1, 1968, NA2, 1967–69 central files, pol 33-6, box 2256, 2/1/68 folder; telegram #074 from US Mission UN to State Department, January 28, 1968, NA2, 1967–69 central files, pol 33-6, box 2257, 1/28/68 folder; memo to Rusk from Joseph Sisco, February 2, 1968, "Diplomatic Track: UN," NA2, 1967–69 central files, pol 33-6, box 2256, 2/1/68 folder; January 31, 1968, report, "*Pueblo* Situation as of 5:30 PM, Wednesday, January 31," JL, NSF, country file, Asia and the Pacific, box 257, Korea—*Pueblo* Incident, pt. B, vol. 1 (through January); memorandum #18a (no citations), JL, NSC Histories, *Pueblo* Crisis, 1968, boxes 29 and 30, vol. 5, day by day documents, pt. 7; telegram #3578 from US Mission UN to State Department, January 31, 1968, NA2, 1967–69 central files, pol 33-6, box 2261; undated telegram #3532 from US Mission UN to State Department, JL, NSC Histories, *Pueblo* Crisis, 1968, boxes 36–37, vol. 21.

136 February 2, 1968, memo, "Developments beyond the Next Meeting in Panmunjom," JL, NSF, NSC History, *Pueblo* Crisis, 1968, vol. 5, day by day documents, pt. 9, box 29; telegram #3890/1 from American Embassy Seoul to State Department, February 2, 1968, NA2, 1967–69 central files, pol 33-6, box 2256, 2/2/68 folder.

137 February 2, 1968, memo to Rusk from Berger, "UNC–NK meeting on the *Pueblo* Incident," NA2, 1967–69 central files, pol 33-6, box 2256, 2/2/68 folder.

138 Telegram #3925 from American Embassy Seoul to State Department, February 4, 1968, NA2, 1967–69 central files, pol 33-6, box 2256, 2/4/68 folder; telegram #3927 from American Embassy Seoul to State Department, February 4, 1968, NA2, 1967–69 central files, pol 33-6, box 2256, 2/4/68 folder; telegram #3970 from American Embassy Seoul to State Department, February 5, 1968, NA2, 1967–69 central files, pol 33-6, box 2256, 2/5/68 folder; telegram #3974 from American Embassy Seoul to State Department, February 5, 1968, NA2, 1967–69 central files, pol 33-6, box 2256, 2/5/68 folder; telegram #4051 from American Embassy Seoul to State Department, February 7, 1968, NA2, 1967–69 central files, pol 33-6, box 2261; telegram #4136 from American Embassy Seoul to State Department, February 10, 1968, NA2, 1967–69 central files, pol 33-6, box 2255, 2–10–68 folder. Specifically, the two sides met on February 4, 5, 7, and 10.

139 Polite in telegram #4136 from American Embassy Seoul to State Department, February 10, 1968, NA2, 1967–69 central files, pol 33-6, box 2255, 2-10-68 folder; names in telegram #4051 from American Embassy Seoul to State Department, NA2, 1967–69 central files, pol 33-6, box 2261.

140 Telegram #3927 from American Embassy Seoul to State Department, February 4, 1968, NA2, 1967–69 central files, pol 33-6, box 2256, 2/4/68 folder.

141 Telegram #4062 from American Embassy Seoul to State Department, February 6, 1968, NA2, 1967–69 central files, pol 33-6, box 2256, 2/6/68 folder.

142 Telegram from American Embassy Seoul to State Department, February 4, 1968, NA2, 1967–69 central files, pol 33-6, box 2261.

143 Telegram #3794 from American Embassy Seoul to State Department, January 31, 1968, NA2, 1967–69 central files, pol 33-6, box 2256, 2/1/68 folder.

144 Telegram #3794 from American Embassy Seoul to State Department, January 31, 1968, NA2, 1967–69 central files, pol 33-6, box 2256, 2/1/68 folder.

145 Telegram #4261 from American Embassy Seoul to State Department, February 15, 1968, NA2, 1967–69 central files, pol 33-6, box 2255, 2/15/68 folder. On LBJ's response,

see, for example, George Aldrich, quoted in Armbrister, *Matter of Accountability,* p. 299; telegram #119560 to various embassies from State Department, February 22, 1968, NA2, 1967–69 central files, pol 33-6, box 2255, 2/21/68 folder.

146   Telegram #106096 from State Department to American Embassy Seoul, January 29, 1968, NA2, 1967–69 central files, pol 33-6, box 2261; telegram #3712 from American Embassy Seoul to State Dept., January 28, 1968, NA2, 1967–69 central files, pol 33-6, box 2257, 1/28/68 folder; telegram #109856 from State Department to American Embassy Seoul, February 4, 1968, NA2, 1967–69 central files, pol 33-6, box 2256, 2/4/68 folder.

147   Telegram #111812 from State Department to American Embassy Seoul, February 8, 1968, NA2, 1967–69 central files, pol 33-6, box 2255, 2/8/68 folder; telegram #4136 from American Embassy Seoul to State Department, February 10, 1968, NA2, 1967–69 central files, pol 33-6, box 2255, 2/10/68 folder.

148   Telegram #9121 from American Embassy Seoul to State Department, February 16, 1968, NA2, 1967–69 central files, pol 33-6, box 2255, 2/15/68 folder; telegram #117393 from State Department to American Embassy Seoul, February 19, 1968, NA2, 1967–69 central files, pol 33-6, box 2254, 1st folder (unlabeled).

149   CIA Intelligence Information Cable, "Implications of Reported Relocation of USS *Pueblo,*" February 12, 1968, document #0651, fiche 56, DDRS, 1999.

150   U.S. State Department, "Chronology of Diplomatic Activity in Pueblo Crisis," April 29, 1968, document #2713, fiche 226, DDRS, 1999.

151   Telegram #120291 to American Embassy Moscow from State Department, February 24, 1968, NA2, 1967–69 central files, pol 33-6, box 2255, 2/21/68 folder.

152   Verbatim text of March 4, 1968, Panmunjom meeting, NA2, 1967–69 central files, pol 33-6, box 2254, 3/1/68 folder; verbatim text of February 26, 1968, Panmunjom meeting, NA2, 1967–69 central files, pol 33-6, box 2254, 2/25/68 folder.

153   Draft white paper, summary press reaction, representative press, JL, NSC Histories, *Pueblo* Crisis, 1968, boxes 31–33, vol. 12; quote from *Washington Post,* March 13, 1968.

154   Telegram from American Embassy, Soviet Union to State Department, February 6, 1968, reprinted in *Foreign Relations of the United States, 1964–1968,* vol. 29, Korea, document #269 (Washington, D.C.: U.S. Government Printing Office, 2001).

155   Information memorandum from the President's Special Assistant (Rostow) to Johnson, February 8, 1968, reprinted in *Foreign Relations of the United States,* vol. 29, document #273.

156   "Remarks at the Presidential Prayer Breakfast," *Public Papers of the President,* Lyndon Johnson, 1968 (Washington, D.C.: U.S. Government Printing Office, 1970), vol. 1, p. 121.

157   Press conference #118, February 3, 1968, JL, NSC Histories, *Pueblo* Crisis, 1968, boxes 31–33, vol. 13, public statements, tabs A–C.

158   February 22, 1968, telegram from UN to State Department, response to State Department telegram #119560, NA2, 1967–69 central files, pol 33-6, box 2255, 2/21/68 folder.

CHAPTER 7. FORGOTTEN MEN

1   *Buffalo Daily News,* January 24, 1968, p. 12.

2   Telegrams from JL, White House Central Files, subject file, defense, ND 19/CO 151,

box 205. The Georgia telegram is from Vincent Guy; the Florida telegram is from Hugh Moreland.

3 Bourke Hickenlooper in *Des Moines Register-Tribune,* January 24, 1968; Long in *Philadelphia Enquirer,* January 29, 1968; Bennett in *Newsweek,* February 5, 1968, p. 19; Rivers in *Washington Post,* January 27, 1968.

4 *Lynchburg News,* January 30, 1968; *Milwaukee Sentinel,* January 25, 1968, p. 14; Reagan in *Los Angeles Times,* January 25, 1968, p. 8; Dirksen in *Congressional Record,* January 24, 1968, vol. 114, pt. 1, p. 818; telegram from Arthur Hannam in JL, White House Central Files, subject file, defense, ND 19/CO 151, box 205.

5 The "Long Telegram," February 22, 1946, reprinted in George Kennan, *Memoirs: 1925–1950* (Boston: Little, Brown, 1967), pp. 547–60.

6 "The Sources of Soviet Conduct," *Foreign Affairs,* July 1947.

7 From Truman's speech before Congress, March 12, 1947, reprinted in *Public Papers of the President,* Harry Truman, 1947 (Washington, D.C.: U.S. Government Printing Office, 1954), pp. 176–80.

8 Acheson in Daniel Yergin, *Shattered Peace* (New York: Penguin Books, 1990), p. 308.

9 NSC-68 reprinted in *Foreign Relations of the United States, 1950,* vol. 1 (Washington, D.C.: U.S. Government Printing Office, 1977), pp. 237–40.

10 *Public Papers of the President,* Harry Truman, 1948, pp. 336–40.

11 "Aggressive" in Yergin, *Shattered Peace,* p. 285; *Newsweek,* March 22, 1948; McMahon in Stephen Whitfield, *The Culture of the Cold War* (Baltimore: Johns Hopkins University Press, 1991), p. 5; atomic bomb in August 8, 1949, Gallup poll, reprinted in Gallup, *Gallup Poll,* vol. 2; military training in March 4, 1949, Gallup poll, reprinted in Gallup, *Gallup Poll,* vol. 2; president of the AHA Conyers Read in Whitfield, *Culture of the Cold War,* p. 58.

12 Commager quoted in Michael Sherry, *In the Shadow of War* (New Haven, Conn.: Yale University Press, 1995), p. 176; loyalty oaths in Whitfield, *Culture of the Cold War,* p. 45; Communist Control Act in *Congressional Record,* August 16, 1954, vol. 100, pt. II, p. 14640; Eisenhower in "Annual Message to Congress on the State of the Union," January 7, 1954, in *Public Papers of the President,* 1954 (Washington, D.C.: U.S. Government Printing Office, 1960), pp. 12–13.

13 Robert Divine, ed., *Foreign Policy and U.S. Presidential Elections, 1940–48* (New York: New Viewpoints, 1974), pp. 270–76.

14 Kennedy in "Address before the American Society of Newspaper Editors," *Public Papers of the President,* 1961 (Washington, D.C.: U.S. Government Printing Office, 1962), pp. 305–6; approval ratings in Richard Reeves, *President Kennedy* (New York: Simon and Schuster, 1993), p. 106; 72 percent and "debate on Vietnam" in Leslie Gelb with Richard Betts, *The Irony of Vietnam* (Washington, D.C.: Brookings Institution, 1979), p. 212. For perhaps the best discussion of this Cold War consensus and Vietnam, see David Levy, *The Debate over Vietnam* (Baltimore: Johns Hopkins University Press, 1995).

15 On the Iran crisis and American public opinion, see especially Mark Rozel, *The Press and the Carter Presidency* (Boulder, Colo.: Westview Press, 1989), chap. 6. See also Kenneth Morns, *Jimmy Carter* (Athens: University of Georgia Press, 1996); Theodore White, *America in Search of Itself* (New York: Warner Books, 1982), chaps. 13, 14; Richard Thornton, *The Carter Years* (New York: Paragon House, 1991), chaps. 9, 10; Austin

Ranney, ed., *The American Election of 1980* (Washington, D.C.: American Enterprise Institute, 1981). Hamilton Jordan, *Crisis* (New York: Putnam, 1982), pp. 42, 55; White, *America in Search of Itself,* p. 17.

16 Letter from G. McMurtrie Godley, deputy assistant secretary of state, to the parents of Richard Arnold, from Armbrister, *Matter of Accountability,* p. 297.

17 All telegrams from JL, White House Central Files, subject file, defense, ND 19/CO 151, box 205.

18 See, for example, telegram from Felice Rubine, JL, White House Central Files, subject file, defense, ND 19/CO 151, box 213. *Pueblo*-related songs included "Song from the USS *Pueblo,*" by Dave McEnerny; "Ballad of the USS *Pueblo,*" by Robert Dobbs; and "USS *Pueblo,*" by Bob Terry. The stanza quoted is from McEnerny and can be found at http://www.usspueblo.org/v2f/memorabilia/memobiframe.html.

19 *New York Times,* February 2, 1968.

20 *Congressional Record,* March 11, 1968, vol. 114, pt. 5, pp. 6050–52.

21 "The Bill Gordon Report," WPTV, Palm Beach, Fla., March 13, 1968, in *Congressional Record,* 1968, vol. 114, pt. 6, p. 6908.

22 Letter to Johnson from Bradley Crowe, JL, White House Central Files, subject file, defense, ND 19/CO 151, box 213, March 15, 1968; letter from Mrs. Kenneth Olson, Frank Church Papers, Boise State University, Boise, Idaho, series 2.2, box 25.

23 *New York Times,* April 17, 1968.

24 *New York Times,* May 26, 1968, p. 14, and May 27, 1968, p. 6.

25 Murphy, *Second in Command,* p. 293. Of course, not everyone forgot about the *Pueblo.* One fourteen-year-old California girl used donations and her own baby-sitting money to rent ten billboards asking local residents to "Please remember the men of the USS *Pueblo.*" "Remember the *Pueblo*" Committees sold bumper stickers, held bake sales, and organized rallies, all designed to remind the nation of its overlooked soldiers. Their efforts were not entirely ineffective; without them, wrote the *Virginian Pilot* on June 22, 1968, "The nation might accomplish what it seems inclined to— forget the whole business." Still, the mere fact that such committees were necessary suggests the nation's overall lack of attention.

26 Reid in *Congressional Record,* vol. 114, pt. 14, p. 18098; *Time* magazine, October 18, 1968, December 6, 1968, and December 27, 1968.

27 See, for example, Corson, *Armies of Ignorance,* p. 410, which concludes that "public attention was diverted away from the *Pueblo* by the month long Tet offensive." See also Russell Library, Rusk oral history, tape CCC CCC, February 1986, in which Rusk concluded that the lack of attention stemmed from "the news media being swamped with Vietnam material."

28 Stokely Carmichael and Charles Hamilton, *Black Power* (New York: Random House, 1967), p. 65; Pucinski in Allen Matusow, *The Unraveling of America* (New York: Harper and Row, 1984), p. 214.

29 U.S. Bureau of the Census, *Statistical Abstract of the United States* (Washington, D.C.: U.S. Government Printing Office, 1990), p. 265.

30 *Chicago Tribune,* February 7, 1968.

31 Letter from Gary Miranda in *Los Angeles Times,* January 26, 1968, pt. 2, p. 4.

32 News conference #1106-A, 12:35 P.M., January 24, 1968, JL, NSF, NSC History, *Pueblo Crisis,* 1968, boxes 27 and 28, vol. 3, day by day documents, pt. 2.

33 On the Dominican intervention, see especially Peter Felton, "The 1963–65 United
States Intervention in the Dominican Republic" (dissertation, University of Texas,
1995). See also Abraham Lowenthal, *The Dominican Intervention* (Cambridge: Harvard University Press, 1972); Pierro Gleijeses, *The Dominican Crisis* (Baltimore: Johns
Hopkins University Press, 1978). For statements suggesting that the intervention was
designed to protect American lives, see, for example, "The President's News Conference of April 27, 1965," *Public Papers of the President,* Lyndon Johnson, 1965, vol. 1,
p. 451, and "Statement by the President upon Ordering Troops into the Dominican
Republic," April 28, 1965, p. 461. For reference to anti-communism as the driving
force behind the action, see, for example, "Radio and Television Report to the American People on the Situation in the Dominican Republic," *Public Papers of the President,* Lyndon Johnson, 1965, vol. 1, p. 471.

34 For a more detailed breakdown of the list, see *Christian Science Monitor,* May 18,
1965, p. 1.

35 "Remarks to Committee Members on the Need for Additional Appropriations for
Military Purposes in Viet-Nam and the Dominican Republic," *Public Papers of the
President,* Lyndon Johnson, 1965, vol. 1, pp. 484–92.

36 *Christian Science Monitor,* May 22, 1965, p. 3.

37 Quoted in Robert Dallek, *Flawed Giant* (New York: Oxford University Press, 1998),
pp. 266–67.

38 *New Republic,* March 23, 1968, p. 6; Alamo in "Remarks to American and Korean Servicemen at Camp Stanley, Korea," November 1, 1966, *Public Papers of the President,*
Lyndon Johnson, 1966, vol. 2, p. 1287, and Kathleen Turner, *Lyndon Johnson's Dual
War* (Chicago: University of Chicago Press, 1985), p. 167; letter from Wyoming
woman (Elizabeth Jensen, La Grange, Wyo.) in JL, White House Central Files, subject
file, defense, ND 19/CO 151, box 209, February 5, 1968.

39 Press conference in "President's News Conference of July 28, 1965," *Public Papers of
the President,* Lyndon Johnson, 1965, vol. 2, pp. 794–803; Merle Miller, *Lyndon* (New
York: G. P. Putnam's Sons, 1980), p. 501; Westmoreland in Patrick Hearden, *The Tragedy of Vietnam* (New York: Longman, 1991), p. 129; LBJ in "Address on Vietnam before
the National Legislative Conference, San Antonio Texas," September 29, 1967, *Public
Papers of the President,* Lyndon Johnson, 1967, vol. 2, p. 878; Harold Johnson quoted
in Robert Pisor, *The End of the Line* (New York: Ballantine Books, 1982), p. 52.

40 Goodwin in *New Yorker,* April 16, 1966; Gallup poll in Gallup, *Gallup Poll,* vol. 3,
p. 2058; Harris poll from *Los Angeles Times,* December 4, 1967.

41 Joseph Califano, Jr., *The Triumph and Tragedy of Lyndon Johnson* (New York: Simon
and Schuster, 1991), p. 257.

42 Letter from George Wilden to Bourke Hickenlooper, January 25, 1968, Herbert
Hoover Presidential Library, West Branch, Iowa, Bourke Hickenlooper Papers, foreign relations—*Pueblo* file.

43 Letter to the editor, *New Republic,* August 10, 1968, p. 20.

44 Letter from H. Jeremy Wintersteen, JL, White House Central Files, subject file, defense, ND 19/CO 151, box 211.

45 Quoted in Matusow, *Unraveling of America,* p. 390.

46 Transcript of *Meet the Press* interview with Rusk and McNamara, February 4, 1968,
JL, NSC Histories, *Pueblo* Crisis, 1968, boxes 29 and 30, vol. 6, day by day documents,

pt. 10. Ironically, LBJ had arranged this appearance in order to present the administration's version of events to the American people.

47 State Department in news briefing at the White House, February 5, 1968, 12:52 P.M., JL, NSC Histories, *Pueblo* Crisis, 1968, boxes 29 and 30, vol. 6, day by day documents, pt. 10; Bundy in "transcript of W. Bundy interview on 'Today' show," February 5, 1968, JL, NSC Histories, *Pueblo* Crisis, 1968, boxes 29 and 30, vol. 6, day by day documents, pt. 10; telegram from David Kershaw in JL, White House Central Files, subject file, defense, ND 19/CO 151, box 210; *Washington Post,* February 5, 1968. On the public response to the Gulf of Tonkin Incident, see especially Moise, *Tonkin Gulf,* chap. 9. See also Goulden, *Truth Is the First Casualty;* Randall Woods, *Fulbright* (New York: Cambridge University Press, 1995; Austin, *The President's War;* and John Galloway, *The Gulf of Tonkin Resolution* (Rutherford, N.J.: Fairleigh Dickinson University Press, 1970).

48 Telegram from Betty Gildoff in JL, White House Central Files, subject file, defense, ND 19/CO 151, box 208, February 5, 1968; letter from Oliver Schroeder, Jr., to Assistant Secretary of State Eugene Rostow in NA2, 1967–69 central files, pol 33-6, box 2254, folder 3/1/68; Indiana letter from R. Soms, JL, White House Central Files, subject file, defense, ND 19/CO 151, box 212, January 24, 1968; Oregon letter from Luther Dearborn in Wayne Morse Papers, collection #1, robo file series L, box 22, foreign relations: *Pueblo* Incident, January 26, 1968; *Birmingham News,* February 7, 1968.

49 Kempton quoted in *Newsweek,* February 5, 1968, p. 16, and *Washington Evening Star,* January 31, 1968; letter from Ralston Brown in JL, White House Central Files, subject file, defense, ND 19/CO 151, box 205, January 26, 1968.

50 Ronald Steel, *Pax Americana* (New York: Viking Press, 1967), p. 7; David Potter quoted in Thomas Powers, *Vietnam: The War at Home* (Boston: G. K. Hall, 1973), p. 76; letter from John Kyper, *New Republic,* August 10, 1968.

51 Levy, *Debate over Vietnam,* pp. 47–51.

52 Fulbright in ibid., p. 58.

53 Quoted in Taylor Branch, *Parting the Waters* (New York: Simon and Schuster, 1988), pp. 138–39.

54 Quoted in John Blum, *Years of Discord* (New York: W. W. Norton, 1991), p. 254.

55 Huey Newton quoted in Matusow, *Unraveling of America,* p. 368.

56 George Katsiaficas, *The Imagination of the New Left* (Boston: South End Press, 1987), pp. 74–76.

57 Quoted in Clayborne Carson, *In Struggle* (Cambridge: Harvard University Press, 1981), p. 136.

58 Carmichael in *New York Review of Books,* September 22, 1966, p. 6.

59 Carmichael quoted in Matusow, *Unraveling of America,* p. 370.

60 "We believe" in Alvin Josephy, *Red Power* (New York: American Heritage Press, 1971); Bellecourt in Peter Matthiessen, *In the Spirit of Crazy Horse* (New York: Viking Press, 1980).

61 From "Meet the Women of the Revolution," *New York Times,* February 9, 1969.

62 Richard Scammon in *Washington Post,* September 22, 1968; Dan Carter, *Politics of Rage* (New York: Simon and Schuster, 1995), pp. 28–29, 345.

63 *Time,* May 10, 1968, p. 72. While *Hair* garnered the bulk of the attention, other shows quickly followed its example, and by the end of the year, nudity could be seen in

Scuba Duba, The Prime of Miss Jean Brodie, Tom Paine, The Christmas Turkey, and *Tennis Anyone.*

64 Quoted in *Time,* October 8, 1968, p. 72.

65 These films first emerged in mainstream society in 1961, when Shirley Clarke's *The Connection* became the first to achieve traditional commercial success. Others followed, most of which broke taboos regarding sex and nudity, including *The Orgy at Lil's Place* (1962), *The Chelsea Girls* (1966), and *The Nude Restaurant* (1967), which, despite their sexuality, were shown at some of the larger movie houses in the nation. Sadistic themes also emerged, incorporating sexuality with violence, as in *Sinderella and the Golden Bra* (1966) and Russ Meyer's *Faster Pussycat, Kill! Kill!* (1967). On this underground movie trend, see especially Paul Michael, ed., *The American Movies Reference Book* (New York: Garland Books, 1969). See also John Mason, *The Identity Crisis Theme in American Feature Films, 1960–1969* (New York: Arno Press, 1977).

66 Quoted in Seth Cagin and Philip Dray, *Hollywood Films of the Seventies* (New York: Harper and Row, 1984), p. 67.

67 Other popular films that celebrated the new values included *Guess Who's Coming to Dinner* (1967), which portrayed the African American not as an equal but as a superior to his white counterpart; *Alice's Restaurant* (1968), which celebrated the community and solidarity of those who rejected traditional American values; and *M*A*S*H* (1970), which won the Best Picture Oscar for suggesting that the real enemy in the Korean War was the American military itself. On the films of this period, see especially Cagin and Dray, *Hollywood Films of the Seventies;* Mason, *The Identity Crisis Theme;* and Robert Bray, *A Certain Tendency* (Princeton, N.J.: Princeton University Press, 1985).

68 David Gerrold, *The World of Star Trek,* 2nd ed. (New York: Bluejay Books, 1984), p. 155.

69 Memo from Gene Roddenberry to Justin Freiberger, April 3, 1968, and memo from Justman to Freiberger, April 2, 1968, Roddenberry Papers, University of California at Los Angeles, box 21, folder 7. I am indebted to Nicholas Sarantakes of Texas A&M University—Commerce for bringing these materials to my attention.

70 Memo from Justman to Freiberger, April 2, 1968, Roddenberry Papers, box 21, folder 7; Gerrold, *World of Star Trek,* pp. 159–60.

71 Gerrold, *World of Star Trek,* pp. 159–60.

72 Harris poll in *Nation,* December 30, 1968, p. 708; Gallup in *New York Times,* February 10, 1968, p. 12; Rovere in *Atlantic Monthly,* May 1968, p. 39.

73 Bray in *Congressional Record,* February 8, 1968, vol. 114, pt. 3, p. 2792; Edwards in *Congressional Record,* February 1, 1968, vol. 114, pt. 2, p. 1887; Gurney in *Congressional Record,* January 25, 1968, vol. 114, pt. 1, p. 1062; Symington in *Des Moines Register Tribune,* January 24, 1968; Long in *Philadelphia Inquirer,* January 29, 1968.

74 Kuykendall in *Congressional Record,* January 29, 1968, vol. 114, pt. 1, p. 1211; Taft in JL, oral history of Robert Taft, vol. 1, pp. 11–12; Pucinski in *Congressional Record,* January 25, 1968, vol. 114, pt. 1, p. 1042.

75 *New York Times,* January 29, 1968; *Richmond News Leader,* January 24, 1968; *Newsweek,* February 5, 1968, p. 15; KONO radio in JL, White House Central Files, subject file, defense, ND 19/CO 151, box 205; Thurmond in *Congressional Record,* January 30, 1968, vol. 14, pt. 2, pp. 1397–98.

1 Telegram #4653 from American Embassy Seoul to State Department, March 4, 1968, NA2, 1967–69 central files, pol 33-6, box 2254, folder 3/1/68; *New York Times*, March 5, 1968.

2 *Washington Star*, December 31, 1968.

3 From "Code of Conduct for Members of the Armed Forces of the United States," Article V, reprinted in House *Pueblo* hearings, pp. 955–66.

4 Except where otherwise noted, the description of the *Pueblo*'s arrival is from Bucher, *Bucher*, pp. 218–21; Armbrister, *Matter of Accountability*, pp. 232–34; Murphy, *Second in Command*, pp. 156–58; Crawford, Pueblo *Intrigue*, pp. 34–37; Stephen Harris and James Hefley, *My Anchor Held* (Old Tappan, N.J.: Fleming H. Revell, 1970), pp. 14–17; Brandt, *Last Voyage of the* Pueblo, pp. 60–65; and Schumacher, *Bridge of No Return*, pp. 105–7.

5 Brandt, *Last Voyage of the* Pueblo, p. 61.

6 Statements of Earl Kisler and Lloyd Bucher, JL, Clifford Papers, box 17, North Korea—*Pueblo* Incident.

7 Statement of Stephen Woelk, JL, Clifford Papers, box 17, North Korea—*Pueblo* Incident.

8 Statements of Earl Kisler and Robert Hammond, JL, Clifford Papers, box 17, North Korea—*Pueblo* Incident.

9 Bucher, *Bucher*, p. 220.

10 Armbrister, *Matter of Accountability*, p. 234.

11 Pyongyang described in CIB #36-69, January 23, 1969; statement by Bucher to Naval Investigators, December 24, 1968, JL, Clifford Papers, box 17, North Korea—*Pueblo* Incident; Bucher, *Bucher*, pp. 223–25; Murphy, *Second in Command*, p. 163.

12 Schumacher, *Bridge of No Return*, p. 11.

13 Statement by Bucher to Naval Investigators, December 24, 1968, JL, Clifford Papers, box 17, North Korea—*Pueblo* Incident.

14 Unless otherwise indicated, description of the Barn come from the crew's memoirs, especially Murphy, *Second in Command*, chaps. 14–19; and Bucher, *Bucher*, chaps. 11–14. See also Armbrister, *Matter of Accountability*, chaps. 26–30; Brandt, *Last Voyage of the* Pueblo, chaps. 13–24; Schumacher, *Bridge of No Return*, p. 12.

15 Rooms described in CIB #36-69, January 23, 1969; Schumacher, *Bridge of No Return*, p. 13; and Murphy, *Second in Command*, p. 165.

16 Murphy, *Second in Command*, p. 165.

17 *Navy Times*, March 7, 1969.

18 Statement of Lloyd Bucher, JL, Clifford Papers, box 17, North Korea—*Pueblo* Incident; Bucher, *Bucher*, pp. 221, 230–31.

19 Although the specific details vary, this meeting is described in Schumacher, *Bridge of No Return*, pp. 15–17; Bucher, *Bucher*, pp. 232–35; and Murphy, *Second in Command*, pp. 168–70.

20 Statement of Lloyd Bucher, JL, Clifford Papers, box 17, North Korea—*Pueblo* Incident; Bucher, *Bucher*, pp. 240–42; CIB #36-69, January 23, 1969.

21 CIB #36-69, January 23, 1969; Bucher, *Bucher*, pp. 242–45; Crawford, Pueblo *Intrigue*, p. 122. In fact, the youngest crewman was Larry Marshall, who was only nineteen.

22 Quoted in *New York Times Magazine*, May 11, 1969.

23 Statement of Lloyd Bucher, JL, Clifford Papers, box 17, North Korea—*Pueblo* Incident; CIB #36-69, January 23, 1969; Bucher, *Bucher,* pp. 244-45.

24 "First Confession of Commander Lloyd M. Bucher," JL, NSF, NSC Histories, *Pueblo* Crisis, 1968, boxes 31–33, vol. 13, public statements, tabs G–I, document #264; Notes of January 24, 1968, 1 P.M. meeting, JL, Tom Johnson's notes of meetings, box 2; NSC memo, "Confession of Commander Bucher, January 24, 1968," JL, NSF, NSC Histories Folder, *Pueblo* Crisis, 1968, vol. 3, day by day documents, pt. 2.

25 NSC memo, "Confession of Commander Bucher, January 24, 1968," notes of January 24, 1968, 1 P.M. meeting, JL, Tom Johnson's notes of meetings, box 2, *Pueblo* II; Murphy, *Second in Command,* pp. 209-10, 333; "First Confession of Commander Lloyd M. Bucher," JL, NSF, NSC Histories, *Pueblo* Crisis, 1968, boxes 31–33, vol. 13, public statements, tabs G–I, document #264.

26 Bucher listed his serial number as 58215401, but it was really 582154, and he claimed to be thirty-eight years old, despite the fact that he was forty. NSC memo, "Confession of Commander Bucher, January 24, 1968," notes of January 24, 1968, 1 P.M. meeting, JL, Tom Johnson's notes of meetings, box 2, *Pueblo* II; "Q and A" book, JL, NSC Histories, *Pueblo* Crisis, 1968, boxes 31–33, vol. 13, public statements, tabs G–I; "Analysis of Bucher's Confession," NA2, 1967-69 central files, pol 33-6, box 2255, 2/15/68 file.

27 Bucher press interview transcript, JL, NSC Histories, *Pueblo* Crisis, 1968, boxes 31–33, vol. 13, public statements, tabs G–I; Walt Rostow memo to Lyndon Johnson, January 26, 1968, JL, NSC Histories, *Pueblo* Crisis, 1968, boxes 27 and 28, vol. 3, day by day documents, pt. 3; CIB #37-69, January 23, 1969; Bucher, *Bucher,* pp. 248-52; "Finding of Facts," p. 65.

28 "Finding of Facts," pp. 63-65; Murphy, *Second in Command,* pp. 180-84; *Christian Science Monitor,* June 19, 1968, p. 1; statement of Edward Murphy, JL, Clifford Papers, box 17, North Korea—*Pueblo* Incident.

29 "Finding of Facts," pp. 63-65; Brandt, *Last Voyage of the* Pueblo, pp. 83-88; CIB #60-69, February 19, 1969.

30 "Finding of Facts," pp. 63-65; radio broadcast in February 3 situation report, 0600 hours, JL, NSC Histories, *Pueblo* Crisis, 1968, boxes 29-30, vol. 5, day by day documents, pt. 9.

31 CIB #60-69, February 18, 1969; February 3, 1968, memo from Korean Task Force, JL, NSC Histories, *Pueblo* Crisis, 1968, boxes 29-30, vol. 5, day by day documents, pt. 9; Murphy, *Second in Command,* pp. 210-11; Schumacher, *Bridge of No Return,* pp. 110-37.

32 Murphy, *Second in Command,* p. 189.

33 Rigby in CIB #78-69, March 4, 1969; Law in *Baltimore Sun,* January 31, 1968; Ayling in Brandt, *Last Voyage of the* Pueblo, pp. 93-94.

34 *Congressional Record,* February 25, 1969, vol. 115, pt. 4, p. 4496; CIB #24-69, February 20, 1969.

35 Statements of Earl Kisler, Angelo Strano, and Robert Hammond, Clifford Papers, box 17, North Korea—*Pueblo* Incident; Armbrister, *Matter of Accountability,* p. 272.

36 *Congressional Record,* February 25, 1969, vol. 115, pt. 4, p. 4496.

37 I refer to three studies headed by Dr. Charles Ford and Captain Raymond Spaulding of the Naval Health Research Center in San Diego, where the crew was examined following their release. The studies relied on an initial interview of each man, usually lasting about one hour; a sentence completion test; and a Minnesota Multiphasic

Personality Inventory Test. Then there was another examination twelve weeks later. The results are summarized in Raymond Spaulding and Charles Ford, "The *Pueblo* Incident: Psychological Reactions to the Stresses of Imprisonment and Repatriation," *American Journal of Psychiatry,* July 1972; Raymond Spaulding and Charles Ford, "The *Pueblo* Incident: A Comparison of Factors Related to Coping with Extreme Stress," *Archives of General Psychiatry,* September 1973, pp. 340–44; and Raymond Spaulding, "Some Experiences Reported by the Crew of the USS *Pueblo* and American Prisoners of War from Vietnam," report #75-28 (San Diego, Calif.: Naval Health Research Center, January 1975). Each of these studies cites specific examples of how the men dealt with their powerlessness without considering the possibility that they were not completely powerless, at least not on a symbolic level. Furthermore, the conclusions drawn are, in my opinion, wholly inappropriate, considering the limited time spent with the men, the condition of the subjects at the time of the interviews, and the doctors' failure to consider the emotional makeups of the men before the ordeal.

38 Murphy, *Second in Command,* pp. 176–77.
39 "North Korean Press Conference with USS *Pueblo* Officers," JL, NSF, NSC Histories, *Pueblo* Crisis, boxes 31–33, vol. 13, public statements, tabs G–I; "Officers of Armed Spy Ship of US Imperialist Aggression Army Were Interviewed by Newspaper, News Agency, and Radio Reporters," NA2, 1967–69 central files, pol 33-6, box 2254, 3/6/68 folder; Brandt, *Last Voyage of the* Pueblo, p. 108.
40 "North Korean Press Conference with USS *Pueblo* Officers," JL, NSF, NSC Histories, *Pueblo* Crisis, boxes 31–33, vol. 13, public statements, tabs G–I; Murphy, *Second in Command,* p. 208.
41 "Alleged Joint Letter of Apology by Crew of U.S.S. *Pueblo* to North Korean Government," JL, NSF, NSC Histories, *Pueblo* Crisis, boxes 31–33, vol. 13, public statements, tabs G–I; Schumacher, *Bridge of No Return,* p. 149.
42 Information memorandum to LBJ from Rostow, February 16, 1968, JL, NSC Histories, *Pueblo* Crisis, 1968, boxes 29 and 30, vol. 6, day by day documents; "Alleged Joint Letter of Apology by Crew of U.S.S. *Pueblo* to North Korean Government," JL, NSF, NSC Histories, *Pueblo* Crisis, boxes 31–33, vol. 13, public statements, tabs G–I; CIB #77-69, March 3, 1969; Schumacher, *Bridge of No Return,* pp. 149–53; Bucher, *Bucher,* p. 305.
43 CIB #77-69, March 3, 1969; Bucher, *Bucher,* p. 309.
44 Bucher, *Bucher,* p. 310; Harris, *My Anchor Held,* p. 73.
45 CIB #64-69, February 24, 1969; Armbrister, *Matter of Accountability,* pp. 282–83.
46 Letter to LBJ from crew, February 29, 1968, JL, White House Central Files, subject file, defense, ND 19/CO 151, box 213; letter from Bucher to Lyndon Johnson, JL, White House Central Files, subject file, defense, ND 19/CO 151, box 205.
47 Statement of Earl Kisler, JL, Clifford Papers, box 17, North Korea—*Pueblo* Incident.
48 Unless otherwise indicated, descriptions of life in the Country Club are from Murphy, *Second in Command,* especially pp. 225–41; Bucher, *Bucher,* chaps. 15, 16; and Armbrister, *Matter of Accountability,* pp. 286–338, as well as the previously cited works by Brandt, Crawford, Harris, and Schumacher.
49 Schumacher, *Bridge of No Return,* pp. 194–95.
50 CIB #64-69, February 24, 1969.
51 Bucher, *Bucher,* p. 330; Armbrister, *Matter of Accountability,* p. 289.
52 Armbrister, *Matter of Accountability,* p. 289.

53 *Time,* April 12, 1968; twenty-four letters in *New York Times,* March 24, 1968, p. 44.

54 Ellis in *New York Times,* March 23, 1968, p. 6; Bouden in letter from Mrs. Grant Bouden to Senator Len Jordan, May 17, 1968, Papers of Len Jordan, Boise State University, Boise, Idaho, MSS 6, box 173, folder 3.

55 *New York Times,* March 23, 1968, p. 6.

56 "Finding of Facts"; statement of Earl Kisler, JL, Clifford Papers, box 17, North Korea—*Pueblo* Incident.

57 CIB #64-69, February 24, 1969.

58 *McCall's,* May 1969, p. 157.

59 Murphy, *Second in Command,* p. 236.

60 Hayes in *Baltimore Sun,* March 21, 1968; Rogala in *New York Times,* March 25, 1968, p. 11.

61 Bucher's statement to naval investigators, December 24, 1968, JL, Clifford Papers, box 17, North Korea—*Pueblo* Incident.

62 Spaulding and Ford, "The *Pueblo* Incident: Psychological Reactions."

63 CIB #78-69, March 4, 1969; Brandt, *Last Voyage of the* Pueblo, pp. 71, 98; Murphy, *Second in Command,* p. 238; "Finding of Facts," pp. 65-66.

64 Brandt, *Last Voyage of the* Pueblo, pp. 160, 177; CIB #61-69, February 20, 1969; Armbrister, *Matter of Accountability,* p. 317.

65 Letter from Robert Klepac to John Connally, March 22, 1968, JL, White House Central Files, subject file, defense, ND 19/CO 151, box 205.

66 Telegram #7682 from American Embassy Seoul to State Department, June 5, 1968, and telegram #177553 from State Department to American Embassy Seoul, June 6, 1968, NA2, 1967-69 central files, pol 33-6, box 2259.

67 *Chicago Daily News,* August 26, 1968; *New York Times,* July 27, 1968, p. 8; *Philadelphia Bulletin,* May 26, 1968; telegram #319 to State Department from American Embassy Seoul, April 23, 1968, NA2, 1967-69 central files, pol 33-6, box 2259.

68 Brandt, *Last Voyage of the* Pueblo, p. 154.

69 Schumacher, *Bridge of No Return,* p. 198.

70 Armbrister, *Matter of Accountability,* p. 309.

71 Draft white paper, "Summary Press Reaction: Representative Press," September 28, 1968, JL, NSC Histories, *Pueblo* Crisis, 1968, boxes 31-33, vol. 12; Schumacher, *Bridge of No Return,* pp. 185-87; Bucher, *Bucher,* pp. 341-45; Brandt, *Last Voyage of the* Pueblo, p. 181; Murphy, *Second in Command,* pp. 272-73; Armbrister, *Matter of Accountability,* pp. 318-20.

72 Armbrister, *Matter of Accountability,* p. 349; Bucher, *Bucher,* p. 345; Murphy, *Second in Command,* p. 273.

73 Intelligence information cable, "Reactions of *Pueblo* Crew Members at Press Conference on 12 September, 1968," JL, NSF, Country File: Korea, vol. 6, box 256.

74 Bucher, *Bucher,* p. 354; emphasis added.

75 Schumacher, *Bridge of No Return,* p. 188.

76 "Code of Conduct for Members of the Armed Forces of the United States," House *Pueblo* hearings, p. 964.

77 Schumacher, *Bridge of No Return,* p. 151.

78 James Scott, *Weapons of the Weak* (New Haven, Conn.: Yale University Press, 1985), p. 33.

79 Statement by Bucher, December 24, 1968, JL, Clifford Papers, box 17, North Korea—*Pueblo* Incident; Bucher, *Bucher,* pp. 284, 288-89; Murphy, *Second in Command,*

p. 199; Schumacher, *Bridge of No Return,* p. 143; Brandt, *Last Voyage of the* Pueblo, pp. 104–5.

80 Quoted in Armbrister, *Matter of Accountability,* p. 377.

81 CIB #50-68.

82 Russell in "The Whole World Was Watching," ABC TV, December 1998.

83 Schumacher, *Bridge of No Return,* p. 192.

84 CIB #60-69, February 18, 1969.

85 Schumacher, *Bridge of No Return,* p. 185.

CHAPTER 9. AT THE BRINK

1 Fulbright in *Newsweek,* August 21, 1967. Federal Reserve Chairman William McChesney Martin quoted in the *New York Times,* April 20, 1968, p. 1; approval rating in Gallup, *Gallup Poll,* vol. 2, September 4, 1968; Johnson in *Public Papers of the President,* 1968, vol. 2, p. 1129.

2 Johnson quoted in Kearns, *Lyndon Johnson and the American Dream,* p. 266.

3 Johnson, *Vantage Point,* pp. 532–33.

4 Ibid., p. 532.

5 Johnson to Art McCafferty, quoted in Armbrister, *Matter of Accountability,* p. 285.

6 Johnson, *Vantage Point,* pp. 536–37.

7 Humphrey in *New York Times,* May 19, 1968, p. 45; Nguyen Van Sao in *New York Times,* May 20, 1968, p. 16.

8 Telegram #4684 from American Embassy Seoul to State Department, March 5, 1968, NA2, 1967–69 central files, pol 33-6, box 2254, 3/1/68 folder.

9 Anatoly Dobrynin in State Department memorandum of conversation between Katzenbach, Dobrynin, Charles Bohlen, and Robert Homme, August 13, 1968, JL, Clifford Papers, boxes 23 and 24. Other representative appeals to the Soviets can be seen in telegram #173266 from State Department to American Embassy Moscow, May 29, 1968, NA2, 1967–69 central files, pol 33-6, box 2259; telegram #2913 from American Embassy Moscow to State Department, February 25, 1968, NA2, 1967–69 central files, pol 33-6, box 2254, 2/25/68 folder; telegram #3270 from American Embassy Moscow to State Department, March 26, 1968, NA2, 1967–69 central files, pol 33-6, box 2259; telegram #120035 to American Embassy Moscow from State Department, February 24, 1968, NA2, 1967–69 central files, pol 33-6, box 2255, 2/21/68 folder.

10 Telegram #9090 to State Department from American Embassy Seoul, February 15, 1968, NA2, 1967–69 central files, pol 33-6, box 2255, 2/15/68 folder. See also telegram #119560 from State Department to various embassies, February 22, 1968, NA2, 1967–69 central files, pol 33-6, box 2255, 2/21/68 folder.

11 Verbatim text from Panmunjom, tenth meeting, March 4, 1968, NA2, 1967–69 central files, pol 33-6, box 2254, 3/1/68 folder.

12 Telegram #9500 from American Embassy Seoul to State Department, March 7, 1968, JL, NSF, NSC Histories, *Pueblo* Crisis, 1968, vol. 17, telegrams from Seoul, tab 1.

13 Telegram #4624 from American Embassy Seoul to State Department, March 1, 1968, NA2, 1967–69 central files, pol 33-6, box 2254, 3/1/68 folder.

14 Telegram #9537 from American Embassy Seoul to State Department, March 9, 1968, NA2, 1967–69 central files, pol 33-6, box 2254, 3/6/68 folder.

15 State Department telegram #127759 to various embassies, March 9, 1968, JL, NSC Histories, *Pueblo* Crisis, 1968, vol. 15, boxes 34 and 35, telegrams to Seoul, tabs 1–3; memo to LBJ from Rostow, February 17, 1968, JL, NSC Histories, *Pueblo* Crisis, 1968, boxes 29 and 30, vol. 7, day by day documents, pt. 13.

16 Telegram #119560 to embassies in London, Moscow, Seoul, and Tokyo from State Department, February 22, 1968, NA2, 1967–69 central files, pol 33-6, box 2255, 2/21/68 folder.

17 Telegram #127760 from State Department to American Embassy Moscow, March 21, 1968, NA2, 1967–69 central files, pol 33-6, box 2259.

18 Telegram #9903 from American Embassy Seoul to State Department, March 28, 1968, NA2, 1967–69 central files, pol 33-6, box 2259.

19 Notes of Johnson's April 2, 1968, meeting with congressional leaders, JL, Tom Johnson's notes of meetings, box 3, set III.

20 Memo to Johnson from Dean Rusk, "USS *Pueblo*," March 14, 1968, NA2, 1967–69 central files, pol 33-6, box 2254, 3/6/68 folder.

21 Letter to State Department from Winthrop Brown of the Korean Task Force, "Next steps on *Pueblo*," March 4, 1968, NA2, 1967–69 central files, pol 33-6, box 2254, 3/1/68 folder.

22 Message #91955 from COMUSK to RUHKA/CINCPAC, March 24, 1968, NA2, Record Group 218, Records of the US JCS, Records of Chairman (Gen.) Earle Wheeler, 1964–70, box 160, "Chairman's messages," 1 March 1968–30 April 1968.

23 Letter to unnamed undersecretary of state from Winthrop Brown, Korean Task Force, March 7, 1968, NA2, 1967–69 central files, pol 33-6, box 2254, 3/6/68 folder.

24 Protest march in *Congressional Record*, July 22, 1968, vol. 114, pt. 17, p. 22645; prayer vigil in draft white paper, "Summary Press Reaction, Representative Press," *Washington Post*, June 20, 1968, and *New York Times*, May 3, 1968, p. 3, in JL, NSC Histories, *Pueblo* Crisis, 1968, boxes 31–33, vol. 12.

25 *McCall's*, May 1969, p. 74.

26 Ibid., p. 73. See also Crawford, Pueblo *Intrigue*, p. 82; Murphy, *Second in Command*, pp. 331–33; Brandt, *Last Voyage of the* Pueblo, pp. 115–16, 165; Armbrister, *Matter of Accountability*, p. 241.

27 Brandt, *Last Voyage of the* Pueblo, p. 116.

28 *McCall's*, May 1969, p. 75; Armbrister, *Matter of Accountability*, p. 300.

29 Letter to Mrs. Lloyd Bucher from the president, February 23, 1968, JL, Papers of LBJ, 1963–69, confidential file, name file, Bu, box 144.

30 *McCall's*, May 1969, p. 152.

31 Memo to LBJ from Walt Rostow, March 6, 1968, JL, White House Central Files, subject file, defense, ND 19/CO 151, box 205; memo to Rostow from Manatos, February 27, 1968, JL, White House Central Files, subject file, defense, ND 19/CO 151, box 205; memo to Manatos from Rick Raphael, February 24, 1968, JL, White House Central Files, subject file, defense, ND 19/CO 151, box 205; *McCall's*, May 1969, p. 75.

32 *McCall's*, May 1969, p. 152.

33 Letter to LBJ from parents of Lee Roy Hayes, April 15, 1968, JL, White House Central Files, subject file, defense, ND 19/CO 151, box 213.

34 *McCall's,* May 1969, pp. 150–52.

35 Crawford, Pueblo *Intrigue,* pp. 96–97.

36 Letter to Johnson from Karl Smedegard, March 14, 1968, JL, White House Central Files, subject file, defense, ND 19/CO 151, box 213; letter to Johnson from Ben Ellis, February 17, 1968, JL, White House Central Files, subject file, defense, ND 19/CO 151, box 213.

37 Quoted in Crawford, Pueblo *Intrigue,* p. 69.

38 Series of letters (April 8, April 9, April 12) between Devine and the White House, JL, White House Central Files, subject file, defense, ND 19/CO 151, box 213.

39 Memo to Johnson from Barefoot Sanders, July 23, 1968, JL, White House Central Files, subject file, defense, ND 19/CO 151, box 205.

40 *New York Times,* September 18, 1968, p. 50; author's telephone interview with the Reverend Paul Lindstrom, June 21, 2001.

41 Memo of conversation between Rusk, Lindstrom, and others, July 15, 1968, NA2, 1967–69 central files, pol 33-6, box 2258, 1/1/67 folder; *Congressional Record,* March 20, 1969, vol. 115, pt. 6, p. 7004; author's telephone interview with the Reverend Paul Lindstrom, June 21, 2001.

42 Draft white paper, "Summary Press Reaction, Representative Press," *Baltimore Sun,* July 23, 1968, JL, NSC Histories, *Pueblo* Crisis, 1968, boxes 31–33, vol. 12.

43 UPI release, July 25, 1968, JL, Clifford Papers, boxes 23 and 24, *Pueblo* folder.

44 *Congressional Record,* July 3, 1968, vol. 114, pt. 15, p. 19986.

45 July 26, 1968, press conference, JL, Clifford Papers, boxes 23 and 24, *Pueblo* folder.

46 Memo to LBJ from Rostow, "Public Opinion Poll on *Pueblo* Tactics," September 16, 1968, JL, NSC Histories, *Pueblo* Crisis, 1968, boxes 29 and 30, day by day documents, pt. 15.

47 State in NA2, State Department *Pueblo* chronology, p. 430; Rusk in telegram #120315 from Rusk to Porter, February 24, 1968, NA2, 1967–69 central files, pol 33-6, box 2255, 2/21/68 folder.

48 *New York Times,* February 16, 1968, p. 4.

49 Telegram #114429 to American Embassy Seoul from State Department, February 13, 1968, NA2, 1967–69 central files, pol 33-6, box 2255, 2nd file (unlabeled).

50 State Department telegram #144339 to American Embassy Seoul, April 10, 1968, JL, NSC Histories, *Pueblo* Crisis, 1968, vol. 15, boxes 34 and 35, telegrams to Seoul, tabs 1–3; telegram #120315 from Rusk to Porter, February 24, 1968, NA2, 1967–69 central files, pol 33-6, box 2255, 2/21/68 folder; Honolulu briefing book, pp. 35, 44–46, NA2, Record Group 59, Conference Files, 1966–72, CF 282–287, box 47, lot 69D182, LBJ—Pres. of Korea, Honolulu file.

51 Report from K. M. Wilford, March 18, 1968, Public Records Office, Kew Gardens, England, FCO 21/345, reference FK 10/16.

52 Telegram #9794 to State Department from American Embassy Seoul, March 22, 1968, NA2, 1967–69 central files, pol 33-6, box 2259.

53 Letter from Park, "North Korean Intention for the Communization of the Republic of Korea," NA2, 1967–69 central files, pol 33-6, box 2254, 3/6/68 folder; February 28, 1968, letter to Speaker of House John McCormack, JL, Clifford Papers, box 23–24, *Pueblo* folder.

54 Text of joint communiqué, April 18, 1968, JL, NSC Histories, *Pueblo* Crisis, 1968,

boxes 29 and 30, vol. 8, day by day documents, pt. 15; telegram #5813 from American Embassy Seoul to State Department, April 19, 1968, JL, NSC Histories, *Pueblo* Crisis, 1968, boxes 34 and 35, vol. 18, telegrams from Seoul, tab 1.

55 Memo to Lt. Col. Haywood Smith from J. R. Thurman, July 26, 1968, JL, White House Central Files, EX CO 150, box 49, CO151, 7/1/68 folder; State Department telegram #144339 to American Embassy Seoul, April 10, 1968, JL, NSC Histories, *Pueblo* Crisis, 1968, volume 15, boxes 34 and 35, telegrams to Seoul, tabs 1–3.

56 Pisor, *End of the Line,* p. 37.

57 Unnamed senator quoted in *Newsweek,* February 5, 1968, p. 17.

58 Telegram #125332 from State Department to American Embassy Seoul, March 6, 1968, NA2, 1967–69 central files, pol 33-6, box 2254, 3/1/68 folder.

59 *New York Times,* August 14, 1968, p. 25.

60 "Eyes only" telegram #109845 from Rusk to Porter, and telegrams #3938 and #3945, from Porter to Rusk, February 4, 1968, NA2, 1967–69 central files, pol 33-6, box 2256, 2/4/68 folder; NA2, State Department *Pueblo* chronology, p. 254.

61 Telegram #160103 from State Department to American Embassy Moscow, May 8 1968, NA2, 1967–69 central files, pol 33-6, box 2259.

62 Telegram #1465 from American Embassy Seoul to State Department, June 27, 1968, NA2, 1967–69 central files, pol 33-6, box 2259.

63 Telegram #160103 from State Department to American Embassy Moscow, May 8, 1968, NA2, 1967–69 central files, pol 33-6, box 2259; telegram #7078 from American Embassy Seoul to State Department, May 8, 1968, NA2, 1967–69 central files, pol 33-6, box 2259. The apology letter as reproduced in these telegrams appears to be missing a few words at the end of the first paragraph, apparently because of a copying error prior to transmission. I reproduced it as I believe it was written, based on the final draft of the letter and other transcripts of the negotiations. Regardless, the few words that I included that did not appear in the State Department telegrams are minor and in no way change the meaning of the document.

64 Notes of president's meeting, May 21, 1968, 1:15 P.M., JL, Tom Johnson's notes of meetings, box 3, set III.

65 Telegram #7491 from American Embassy Seoul to State Department, May 28, 1968, NA2, 1967–69 central files, pol 33-6, box 2259.

66 *Congressional Record,* April 8, 1968, vol. 114, pt. 7, p. 9181; telegram from State Department to American Embassy Seoul, April 1968, JL, NSC Histories, *Pueblo* Crisis, 1968, boxes 34 and 35, vol. 15, telegrams to Seoul, tabs 1–3.

67 Young in *New York Times,* July 13, 1968, p. 7; McCloskey in *Chicago Tribune,* July 13, 1968.

68 Notes from president's meeting, September 9, 1968, JL, Tom Johnson's notes of meetings, box 4, set II, September 17, 1968, folder.

69 Telegram from Ambassador Brown to Porter, May 17, 1968, NA2, Records of the US JCS, Records of Chairman (Gen.) Earle Wheeler, 1964–70, 091 Korea, box 29, tab 335.

70 Notes from president's meeting, September 9, 1968, JL, Tom Johnson's notes of meetings, box 4, set II, September 17, 1968, folder.

71 Memo to LBJ from Katzenbach, "*Pueblo* Action Memorandum," October 1968, JL, NSF, country file, Asia and the Pacific, box 256, Korea, filed by the LBJ Library folder.

72 Telegram #234620 to American Embassy Seoul from State Department, September 7, 1968, NA2, 1967–69 central files, pol 33-6, box 2259.

73　Telegram #2235 from American Embassy Seoul to State Department, NA2, 1967–69 central files, pol 33-6, box 2259; telegram #2230 from American Embassy Seoul to State Department, August 16, 1968, NA2, 1967–69 central files, pol 33-6, box 2259.

74　Telegrams to State Department from American Embassy Seoul, August 27, 1968, and August 29, 1968, JL, Clifford Papers, boxes 23 and 24, *Pueblo* folder; telegrams #9416 and #2230, August 27, 1968, from American Embassy Seoul to State Department, NA2, 1967–69 central files, pol 33-6, box 2259.

75　Telegram #2429 to State Department from American Embassy Seoul, August 29, 1968, NA2, 1967–69 central files, pol 33-6, box 2259; *New York Times,* September 12, 1968, p. 2.

76　Telegram to State Department from American Embassy Seoul, September 17, 1968, JL, Clifford Papers, boxes 23 and 24; telegram #2737 from American Embassy Seoul to State Department, September 17, 1968, NA2, 1967–69 central files, pol 33-6, box 2259; telegram #242959 to American Embassy Moscow from State Department, September 21, 1968, NA2, 1967–69 central files, pol 33-6, box 2259; Porter in telegram #242963 to American Embassy Seoul from State Department, September 12, 1968, NA2, 1967–69 central files, pol 33-6, box 2259. There is, of course, no documentation released yet by the North Koreans confirming that they left this meeting convinced that the agreement had been reached, but their actions suggest that they did, especially since at the next meeting, they provided the document they expected the United States to sign and seemed genuinely shocked by the explanation of American intentions.

77　Telegram #247443 to American Embassy Seoul from State Department, September 30, 1968, NA2, 1967–69 central files, pol 33-6, box 2259.

78　Telegram #251495 from State Department to American Embassy Moscow, October 8, 1968, NA2, 1967–69 central files, pol 33-6, box 2259.

79　Telegram #253715 from State Department to American Embassy Moscow, October 10, 1968, NA2, 1967–69 central files, pol 33-6, box 2259.

80　Telegram #3241 from American Embassy Seoul to State Department, October 10, 1968, NA2, 1967–69 central files, pol 33-6, box 2260.

81　Telegram #254615 to American Embassy Seoul from State Department, October 12, 1968, NA2, 1967–69 central files, pol 33-6, box 2259.

82　State Department telegram #255324 to American Embassy Seoul, October 15, 1968, JL, NSC Histories, *Pueblo* Crisis, 1968, vol. 15, boxes 34 and 35, telegrams to Seoul, tabs 1–3.

83　Telegram #261409 from State Department to American Embassy Moscow, October 23, 1968, NA2, 1967–69 central files, pol 33-6, box 2259; cable #10633 from American Embassy Seoul to State Department, October 24, 1968, JL, NSC Histories, *Pueblo* Crisis, 1968, boxes 34 and 35, vol. 18, telegrams from Seoul, tab 1.

84　Memo to LBJ from Katzenbach, "*Pueblo* Action Memorandum," October 1968, JL, NSF, country file, Asia and the Pacific, box 256, Korea, filed by the LBJ Library folder.

85　Oral history of Nicholas Katzenbach, JL, interview #3, p. 5.

86　*Newsweek,* December 2, 1968, p. 23.

87　November 20, 1968, telegram to Johnson, JL, White House Central Files, subject file, defense, ND 19/CO 151, box 213.

88　Oral history of Nicholas Katzenbach, JL, interview #3, pp. 4–5.

89　Telegram #265604 to American Embassy Seoul from State Department, November 1, 1968, NA2, 1967–69 central files, pol 33-6, box 2259.

90 Oral history of James Leonard, Georgetown University, Washington, D.C., pp. 2–4; Armbrister, *Matter of Accountability,* pp. 334–35.

91 Memo to Warnke from Steadman, December 10, 1968, JL, Clifford Papers, boxes 23 and 24, *Pueblo* folder.

92 Telegram #285230 to American Embassy Seoul from State Department, December 11, 1968, NA2, 1967–69 central files, pol 33-6, box 2260.

93 Telegram #285426 to American Embassy Seoul from State Department, December 11, 1968, NA2, 1967–69 central files, pol 33-6, box 2260.

94 Woodward quoted in Armbrister, *Matter of Accountability,* p. 335.

95 Telegram #5290 from US Mission UN to State Department, December 9, 1968, NA2, 1967–69 central files, pol 33-6, box 2260.

96 Memo to Nitze from Charles Havens, December 11, 1968, JL, Clifford Papers, boxes 23 and 24, *Pueblo* folder; *New York Times,* September 12, 1968, and November 26, 1968.

97 *New York Times,* June 12, 1968, p. 6.

98 CIA cable "North Korean fears of fishing in international waters," August 10, 1968, JL, NSC Histories, *Pueblo* Crisis, 1968, box 32, vol. 12, CIA Documents [II]; *New York Times,* November 26, 1968, p. 1.

99 Official in *New York Times,* November 26, 1968, p. 1; telegram #236092 from Rusk to Ambassador Tyler, September 11, 1968, NA2, 1967–69 central files, pol 33-6, box 2259.

100 Telegrams #10395 and #10393 from American Embassy Seoul to State Department, October 14, 1968, NA2, 1967–69 central files, pol 33-6, box 2259; telegram #236092 to American Embassy Hague from State Department, September 11, 1968, NA2, 1967–69 central files, pol 33-6, box 2259; telegram #7103 to State Department from Ambassador Tyler, the Hague, September 11, 1968, NA2, 1967–69 central files, pol 33-6, box 2259.

101 *New York Times,* November 25, 1968.

102 Telegram #274630 from State Department to American Embassy London, November 20, 1968, NA2, 1967–69 central files, pol 33-6, box 2259.

103 September 26, 1968, report from J. B. Denson, Public Records Office, Kew Gardens, England, FCO 21/346, reference FK 10/16.

104 Telegram #262347 from State Department to American Embassy Tokyo, October 26, 1968, NA2, 1967–69 central files, pol 33-6, box 2259; telegram #14359 from American Embassy Tokyo to State Department, December 2, 1968, NA2, 1967–69 central files, pol 33-6, box 2259.

105 Telegram #288931 to American Embassies in London, Paris, and Saigon from State Department, December 18, 1968, NA2, 1967–69 central files, pol 33-6, box 2260.

106 Telegram #3156 from American Embassy Seoul to State Department, October 15, 1968, NA2, 1967–69 central files, pol 33-6, box 2260.

107 Author's interview with Walt Rostow, January 14, 1998.

108 State Department telegram #291121 to American Embassy Seoul, December 23, 1968, JL, NSC Histories, *Pueblo* Crisis, 1968, boxes 34 and 35, vol. 15, telegrams to Seoul, tabs 4–8.

109 Oral history of Dean Rusk, JL, transcript #3, pp. 28–29.

110 Clifford, *Counsel to the President,* pp. 466–67.

111 *Christian Science Monitor,* July 10, 1969, p. 1.

112 Telegram #289783 to American Embassy Moscow from State Department, December 19, 1968, NA2, 1967–69 central files, pol 33-6, box 2260.

113 Armbrister, *Matter of Accountability*, p. 335.

114 *New York Times*, December 20, 1968.

115 Telegram #291107 to American Embassies in London, Moscow, Paris, Saigon, and Tokyo, from State Department, December 22, 1968, NA2, 1967–69 central files, pol 33-6, box 2260.

CHAPTER 10. CLIMBING OUT OF HELL

1 *Time*, October 18, 1968, p. 38.

2 See, for example, telegram #120759 from State Department to American Embassy Seoul, February 26, 1968, JL, NSF, NSC Histories, *Pueblo* Crisis, 1968, box 35, vol. 15, telegrams to Seoul, tabs 1–3.

3 Leonard in Armbrister, *Matter of Accountability*, p. 327.

4 Bucher quoted in Armbrister, *Matter of Accountability*, pp. 329–30. On this meeting, see Schumacher, *Bridge of No Return*, p. 200; Bucher, *Bucher*, pp. 356–57; Armbrister, *Matter of Accountability*, pp. 329–30; Murphy, *Second in Command*, pp. 296–97.

5 Hell Week description, except where otherwise noted, from Armbrister, *Matter of Accountability*, pp. 329–32; Schumacher, *Bridge of No Return*, pp. 200–9; Murphy, *Second in Command*, pp. 295–310; Bucher, *Bucher*, pp. 355–61; Brandt, *Last Voyage of the Pueblo*, pp. 216–18; statements of Lloyd Bucher, Earl Kisler, Donnie Tuck, Angelo Strano, and Edward Murphy, JL, Clifford Papers, box 17, North Korea—*Pueblo* Incident.

6 Schumacher, *Bridge of No Return*, p. 202.

7 Memorandum to Clark Clifford from Moorer, "Physical Abuse of the *Pueblo* Crew," December 24, 1968, NA2, 1967–69 central files, pol 33-6, box 29, tab 307; Bucher in *Washington Star*, December 23, 1968.

8 Quoted from the *Pueblo* Web site, at http://www.usspueblo.org/v2f/captivity/incapacity.html.

9 *Portsmouth Herald*, December 26, 1968.

10 "Finding of Facts," p. 71; statements of Earl Kisler and Donnie Tusk, JL, Clifford Papers, box 17, North Korea—*Pueblo* Incident folder; CIB #60-69, February 19, 1969.

11 Quoted from http://www.usspueblo.org/v2f/captivity/incaptivity.html.

12 Bucher, *Bucher*, p. 360.

13 *Christian Science Monitor*, July 10, 1969, p. 3.

14 Bucher, *Bucher*, pp. 361–62; Murphy, *Second in Command*, p. 309.

15 *New York Times*, December 23, 1968, p. 3.

16 Telegram #291107 to American Embassies London, Moscow, Paris, Saigon, and Tokyo, from State Department, NA 2, 1967–69 central files, pol 33-6, box 2260; CINCPAC Command History, 1968, NHC, vol. 4, p. 231; *New York Times*, December 23, 1968, p. 3; Armbrister, *Matter of Accountability*, pp. 340–41.

17 Bucher, *Bucher*, p. 363; *Christian Science Monitor*, July 10, 1969, p.3; Schumacher, *Bridge of No Return*, p. 215.

18 Bucher, *Bucher*, p. 364.

19 *USS* Pueblo *Hearings before the Investigations Subcommittee of the Committee on Armed Services House of Representatives*, June 23, 1989 (Washington, D.C.: U.S. Government Printing Office, 1989).

20 Bucher, *Bucher*, p. 364; Armbrister, *Matter of Accountability*, p. 341.

21 *New York Times*, December 24, 1968, p. 3.

22 Law in *Newsweek*, January 6, 1969, p. 9.

23 *New York Times*, December 24, 1968, p. 3, and December 25, 1968, p. 1; CIB #09-68.

24 On Amscom, see CINCPAC Command History, 1968, NHC, vol. 4, p. 231; Bucher, *Bucher*, pp. 365–73; *Time*, January 3, 1969, p. 18; *New York Times*, December 23, 1968, p. 3, and December 24, 1968, p. 1; *Newsweek*, January 6, 1969, p. 9; *Washington Star*, December 23, 1968; CIB #09-68.

25 "Worldwide Treatment of Current Issues," reports on December 23 and December 27, 1968, JL, White House Aides Files, Fred Panzer, box 224.

26 Telegram #11824 from American Embassy Seoul to State Department, December 17, 1968, NA2, 1967–69 central files, pol 33-6, box 2260; Park in *New York Times*, December 22, 1968, p. 3.

27 "Worldwide Treatment of Current Issues," reports on December 23 and December 27, 1968, JL, White House Aides Files, Fred Panzer, box 224.

28 Sheldon Simon, "The *Pueblo* Incident and the South Korean Revolution," *Asian Forum* 2, no. 3 (1970), p. 207.

29 *New York Times*, December 26, 1969, p. 6.

30 Oral history of Captain Richard Stratton, U.S. Naval Institute, Annapolis, Md., p. 70.

31 *Washington Post*, February 11, 1969; Scalapino and Lee, *Communism in Korea*, p. 644.

32 "Worldwide Treatment of Current Issues," December 23, 1968, report, JL, White House Aides Files, Fred Panzer, box 224.

33 *Washington Star*, December 23, 1968, p. 3; *New York Times*, December 23, 1968, p. 1.

34 Simon, "The *Pueblo* Incident and the South Korean Revolution," p. 206.

35 *New York Times*, December 24, 1968, p. 22.

36 Letter to Lyndon Johnson from Richard Homan, December 23, 1968, JL, NSF, Defense, ND 19/CO 151, box 205.

37 *New York Times*, December 23, 1968, p. 38.

38 *Congressional Record*, January 10, 1969, vol. 115, pt. 1, p. 432.

39 Telegram to LBJ from the League of Wives of American Prisoners of War, December 22, 1968, JL, White House Central Files, subject file, defense, ND 19/CO 151, box 205.

40 CIB #09-68.

41 Telegram #11953 to State Department from American Embassy Seoul, December 24, 1968, NA2, RG 218, Records of the US JCS, Records of Chairman, (Gen.) Earle Wheeler, 1964–70, 091 Korea.

42 Records of CINCPACFLT, 1941–75, NHC, series I, box 7, "*Pueblo*—Duplicate material"; CIB #09-68.

43 CIB #50-68.

44 San Diego in *New York Times*, December 25, 1968, p. 2; CINCPAC Command History, 1968, NHC, vol. 4, p. 231; CIB #49-68; Bucher, *Bucher*, pp. 370–72; *Time*, January 3, 1968, p. 18; *San Diego Union*, December 24, 1968.

45 *Newsweek*, January 6, 1969, p. 9.

46 Armbrister, *Matter of Accountability*, p. 345.

47 *New York Times*, December 29, 1968, p. 3; Armbrister, *Matter of Accountability*, p. 348.

48 Letter to author from John Grant, April 29, 1999.

49 Letter to author from Rick Darsey, June 26, 1999.

50 Letter to author from Ralph McClintock, April 4, 1999.

51 Armbrister, *Matter of Accountability,* p. 368.

52 Vice Admiral George Steel, quoted in *Naval History,* Fall 1988, pp. 58–59.

53 House *Pueblo* hearings, pp. 661–62.

54 *New Republic,* February 8, 1969, p. 12.

55 *Newark (Ohio) Advocate,* January 23, 1969.

56 Quoted in *New York Times,* December 25, 1969, p. 3.

57 Letter to Fred Harris from Hazel Boudreau, Carl Albert Papers, Fred Harris Collection, box 166, folder 18.

58 Pueblo hearings from "Finding of Facts"; CIB news releases #57-69 through #1–69; Armbrister, *Matter of Accountability,* chaps. 41–43; Bucher, *Bucher,* pp. 385–400.

59 Armbrister, *Matter of Accountability,* pp. 358–59; *New York Times Magazine,* May 11, 1969.

60 *New York Times,* January 23, 1969.

61 Quoted in Armbrister, *Matter of Accountability,* p. 366.

62 A photograph of this note can be found at htpp://www.usspueblo.org/y2f/coi/court ofinquiry.html.

63 This exchange is reproduced at htpp://www.usspueblo.org/y2f/coi/courtofinquiry.html.

64 Armbrister, *Matter of Accountability,* p. 370.

65 Ibid., p. 371.

66 CIB #104-69.

67 CIB #74-69.

68 "Finding of Facts," pp. 88–94.

69 The eleven men praised for their behavior in captivity were Lloyd Bucher, Charles Law, Carl Schumacher, Robert Hammond, Dale Rigby, Don Bailey, Earl Kisler, Robert Chicca, Charles Sterling, Gerald Hagenson, and Monroe Goldman. The five criticized were Don McClarren, Charles Ayling, Angelo Strano, James Shepard, and Ralph Bouden.

70 "Statement of John Chafee," May 6, 1969, Carl Albert Papers, Departmental Series, box 74, folder 71.

71 "Appalled" from Vice Admiral George Steel, in *Naval History,* Fall 1988, p. 59; "coward" in letter from Lieutenant Hector Constantine to Admiral Duncan, Chief of Naval Personnel, May 12, 1969, NHC, Ships History Branch, subject files, box 493, CDR Bucher—Transfer/retirement folder; Hyland in oral history of Admiral John Hyland, U.S. Naval Institute, vol. 2, p. 461.

72 Otis Pike, quoted in House *Pueblo* hearings, p. 630. The navy's unwillingness to cooperate was a recurrent theme in these hearings. See also *New York Times,* January 25, 1969, p. 3.

73 House *Pueblo* Report, p. 1674.

74 "*Pueblo* Crew Reassignment Data," NHC, Ships History Branch, subject files, box 483, *Pueblo* Incident.

75 Memo to Clark Clifford from Colonel Robert Pursley, military assistant, USAF, January 6, 1969, "Summary of Navy Compendium on Treatment of *Pueblo* Crew," JL, Clifford Papers, box 17, North Korea—*Pueblo* Incident; *New York Times,* January 9, 1969, p. 5.

76 Letter to author from John Grant, April 29, 1999.

77 Russell in "The Whole World Was Watching," December 10, 1998, ABC news special.

78 CIB #49-68; *New York Times,* January 3, 1969, p. 30. Soon, the navy gave Purple Hearts to the rest of the crewmen for their suffering while in captivity, although it did so begrudgingly.

79 Bucher, *Bucher,* p. 405.

80 September 1973 news release #430-73, Office of the Assistant Secretary of Defense, NHC, Ships History Branch, subject files, box 493, CDR Bucher—Transfer/retirement folder; *Washington Star,* September 8, 1973.

81 *New York Times,* May 7, 1990, p. B-15; *St. Louis Post Dispatch,* June 25, 1989.

82 *San Diego Union-Tribune,* September 17, 1988.

83 See especially *USS* Pueblo *Hearings before the Investigations Subcommittee of the Committee on Armed Services House of Representatives,* June 23, 1989 (Washington, D.C.: U.S. Government Printing Office, 1989). See also House Resolution 819, *Congressional Record,* February 2, 1989, vol. 135, p. 167; *New York Times,* May 7, 1990, p. 13; *San Diego Union-Tribune,* May 4, 1990, p. B1.

84 *St. Louis Post Dispatch,* June 25, 1989.

85 *USS* Pueblo *Hearings before the Investigations Subcommittee.*

86 *New York Times,* May 7, 1990, p. B-15.

CONCLUSION

1 Acting Secretary of the Navy Samuel Smith to Captain Richard Dale, May 20, 1801, in *Naval Documents Related to the United States War with the Barbary Powers* (Washington, D.C.: U.S. Government Printing Office, 1939), p. 467. On the war with the Barbary pirates, see Ray Irwin, *The Diplomatic Relations of the United States with the Barbary Powers* (Chapel Hill: University of North Carolina Press, 1931); Michael Kitzen, *Tripoli and the United States at War* (Jefferson, N.C.: McFarland, 1993); and Louis Wright and Julia Macleod, *The First Americans in North Africa* (Princeton, N.J.: Princeton University Press, 1945).

2 Irwin, *Diplomatic Relations with the Barbary Powers,* p. 134.

3 NSC-68 reprinted in *Foreign Relations of the United States,* 1950, vol. 1 (Washington, D.C.: U.S. Government Printing Office, 1977), pp. 237–40; Acheson quoted in Lloyd Gardner, *Architects of Illusion* (Chicago: Quadrangle Books, 1970), p. 210.

4 Oral history of Admiral John Hyland, U.S. Naval Institute, Annapolis, Md., vol. II, p. 454.

5 *New York Times,* May 7, 1969.

6 Letter to author from Stu Russell, June 26, 1999.

7 House *Pueblo* Report, p. 1681.

8 For the EC-121 crisis, see especially House *Pueblo* hearings, pp. 889–954.

9 Much of the information on these programs comes from Sherry Sontag and Christopher Drew, *Blind Man's Bluff* (New York: Public Affairs, 1998). See also *New York Times,* May 25, 1975, and July 6, 1975.

10 Although the disappearance of the *Scorpion* remains the subject of much debate, the presentation by Sontag and Drew provides what appears to be a definitive, if disputed by the navy, account.

11 *New York Times,* May 25, 1975; Deacon, *The Silent War,* chap. 14.

12 Some examples of rumored intelligence activities that aroused public indignation include the overthrow of a democratically elected government in Chile, infiltration of American universities and the National Students Association, the hiring of American journalists, and the supposed assassination of numerous foreign leaders. In the early 1970s, press reports linked the CIA with the Voice of America and Radio Free Europe and suggested that the agency had contracted with organized crime in an attempt to assassinate Fidel Castro. The most damaging blow came in December 1974, when reporter Seymour Hersh disclosed details of an extensive operation that involved various agencies spying on American citizens within the United States.

13 Quoted in Corson, *Armies of Ignorance,* p. 437.

14 From "Summary: Findings and Recommendations of the Church Committee," reprinted in Fain, *Intelligence Community,* p. 99.

15 Johnson, *America's Secret Power,* p. 208.

16 Nancy Bernkopf Tucker, "Lyndon Johnson: A Final Reckoning," in Cohen and Tucker, *Lyndon Johnson Confronts the World,* p. 313.

17 Lloyd Gardner, "Lyndon Johnson and Vietnam," in *The Johnson Years,* vol. 3, ed. Robert Divine (Lawrence: University Press of Kansas, 1994), p. 231.

18 Bucher, "Commander Bucher Replies," p. 50.

Bibliography

ARCHIVAL HOLDINGS

Bourke Hickenlooper Papers, Herbert Hoover Presidential Library, West Branch, Iowa
  Foreign Relations Subseries—*Pueblo*
Carl Albert Congressional Resource and Studies Center, Congressional Archive, University of Oklahoma, Norman, Okla.
    Carl Albert Collection, Department of Defense Series, boxes 72, 74
    John Camp Collection, box 3
    Fred Harris Papers, boxes 109, 133, 166
Frank Church Papers, Boise State University, Boise, Idaho
    Series 2.2, box 25
Gene Roddenberry Papers, University of California at Los Angeles
    Box 21
Georgetown University Foreign Affairs Oral History Collection, Washington, D.C.
    Oral Histories of Walter Cutler, James Leonard, Francis Underhill
Karl Mundt Papers, Karl Mundt Historical and Educational Foundation, Dakota State University, Madison, S.D.
    Record Group I, State Subgroup, Microfilm #44
    Record Group III, Armed Services Committee Subgroup, Microfilm #75/76
    Record Group III, Foreign Relations Committee Subgroup, Microfilm #91
Lyndon Johnson Presidential Library, Austin, Tex.
    Cabinet Papers, box 12
    Handwriting File, boxes 27, 28
    NSF, Country File, Korea, boxes 255–64
    NSF, Country File, Vietnam, box 91
    NSF, Files of Bromley Smith, box 1
    NSF, Files of Walt Rostow, boxes 1, 7, 10
    NSF, International Meetings and Travel File, box 21
    NSF, Memos to the President; Walt Rostow, boxes 26, 27, 28, 30, 34, 36, 40
    NSF, National Security Action Memos, box 4
    NSF, NSC History, Pueblo Crisis, 1968, boxes 27–37
    Oral Histories of E. Ross Adair, Interview #1; Samuel Adams #1; George Ball #2; George Christian #2; Clark Clifford #3; Arthur Goldberg #1; Nicholas Katzenbach #3; Thomas Moorer; Rutherford Poats; Charles Roberts #1; Dean Rusk #3; Robert Taft, Jr.; Maxwell Taylor #2; Cyrus Vance #2; Paul Warnke #2
    Papers of Clark Clifford, boxes 17, 23

Papers of Drew Pearson, box 6294

President's Appointment File, Daily Diary, boxes 14, 17, 18

President's Appointment File, Diary Backup, boxes 87–91

Special Files, 1927–73, Meeting Notes File, boxes 2, 3

Tom Johnson's Notes of Meetings, boxes 2, 3, 4

White House Aides Files, Fred Panzer, boxes 224, 359, 406

White House Aides Files, George Christian, boxes 4, 12

White House Aides Files, Harry MacPherson, box 10

White House Central Files, Confidential Files, ND 19/CO 151, box 10

White House Central Files, Country Files, EX CO 150, box 49

White House Central Files, Defense, Gen ND 19-3/CO 56, box 421

White House Central Files, Defense Files, ND 19/CO 151, boxes 205–13

White House Central Files, Judicial, JL3/CO, box 37

Military History Institute, Carlisle Barracks, Pa.

Charles Bonesteel III oral history

National Archives II, College Park, Md.

"History of the Special Branch, MIS, War Dept., 1942–44," Record Group 457, Stack 190, Row 36, box 17, SRH-035

National Security Council Report on the Pueblo Incident, Papers of Robert McNamara, Record Group 200

1967–69 Central Files, Korea, boxes 2254–61

Record Group 59, Conference Files, 1966–72, CF 282 through CF 287, box 47, lot 69D182

Record Group 59, Historical Reports Relating to Diplomacy during the Lyndon Johnson Administration, 1963–69, Entry 3034 (lot 69D217)

Record Group 59, NSC Meeting Files, Memoranda to and from the NSC Special Committee, June 1967 to NSC Meetings, April 1969, box 2

Record Group 218, Records of the US JCS, Records of Chairman (Gen.) Earle Wheeler, 1964–70, boxes 160, 161

Record Group 218, Records of the US JCS, Records of Chairman (Gen.) Earle Wheeler, 1964–70, 091 Korea, boxes 29, 30

Navy Historical Center, Washington, D.C.

CINCPAC Command History 1968, vols. 1–4

Command File Post 1 Jan. 46, Ind. Ships, USS Pueblo (Command Information Bureau [CIB] News Releases, #57-69 through #1-69)

Command File Post 1 Jan. 46, Ind. Ships, USS Pueblo (Command Information Bureau [CIB] News Releases, #104-69 through #58-69)

Command File Post 1 Jan. 46, Ind. Ships, USS Pueblo, Confidential Memorandums

Command File Post 1 Jan. 46, Ind. Ships, USS Pueblo, Finding of Facts

Command File Post 1 Jan. 46, Ind. Ships, USS Pueblo, Newspaper Articles

Command File Post 1 Jan. 46, Ind. Ships, USS Pueblo, Statements by Various Officers

Deck Log Book of the USS Pueblo, May 1 through November 30, 1967

Oral Histories of Vice Admiral Philip Beshany, vol. 2 (1983); Captain Phil Bucklew (1982); Vice Admiral John L. Chew (1979); Vice Admiral Edwin B. Hooper (1979); Vice Admiral Andrew McBurney Jackson, Jr. (1979); Rear Admiral George Miller (1975); Admiral Thomas Moorer (1976); Admiral U. S. Grant

Sharp (1976); Vice Admiral J. Victor Smith (1977); Rear Admiral Kent Tolley (1984)

Records of CINCPACFLT, 1941–75, Series I, boxes 1, 3, 4, 5, 7, and Series II, box 12

"USS Pueblo," Subject Files, boxes 492, 493, 494

00 Files, box 122-1969

Public Records Office, Kew Gardens, England

Foreign Office and FCO Registered Files, FCO File, folders 344, 345, 346, 349

Records of Prime Minister's Office, Correspondence and Papers 1964–70, File 13, folder 3019

Richard Russell Library for Political Research and Studies, University of Georgia, Athens, Ga.

Dean Rusk Oral History, #CCC CCC

U.S. Naval Institute, Annapolis, Md.

Oral Histories of Admiral John Hyland (1989); Vice Admiral Kent Lee (1990); Vice Admiral Gerald Miller (1984); Captain John Noel (1987)

Wayne Morse Papers, University of Oregon, Eugene, Ore.

Robo File, Series L, box 22, Foreign Relations: Pueblo Incident

William Fulbright Papers, University of Arkansas, Fayetteville, Ark.

Series 48: 6, box 28

Series 72, box 30

GOVERNMENT DOCUMENTS AND PUBLICATIONS

Congressional Record. Washington, D.C.: U.S. Government Printing Office.

Dictionary of American Naval Fighting Ships. Vol. 5. Washington, D.C.: U.S. Government Printing Office, Naval History Division, Office of the Chief of Naval Operations, 1979.

Finding of Facts, Opinions, and Recommendations of a Court of Inquiry Convened by Order of Commander in Chief, United States Pacific Fleet to Inquire into the Circumstances Relating to the Seizure of USS *Pueblo* (AGER 2) by North Korean Naval Forces which Occurred in the Sea of Japan on 23 January 1968 and the Subsequent Detention of the Vessel and the Officers and Crew. Washington, D.C.: Department of the Navy, Office of the Judge Advocate General, 1969.

Foreign Relations of the United States. Washington, D.C.: U.S. Government Printing Office.

Inquiry into the USS *Pueblo* and EC-121 Plane Incidents. *Hearings before the Special Subcommittee on the U.S.S.* Pueblo *of the Committee on Armed Services,* House of Representatives, Ninety-first Congress, First Session, 1969. Washington, D.C.: U.S. Government Printing Office, 1969.

Inquiry into the USS *Pueblo* and EC-121 Plane Incidents. *Report of the Special Subcommittee on the U.S.S.* Pueblo *of the Committee on Armed Services,* House of Representatives, Ninety-first Congress, First Session, July 28, 1969. Washington, D.C.: U.S. Government Printing Office, 1969.

Navy Documents Related to the United States War with the Barbary Powers. Washington, D.C.: U.S. Government Printing Office, 1939.

On Watch. Report by the National Cryptologic School, Fort Meade, Md.

"The Operational Assessment of Risk: A Case Study of the *Pueblo* Mission." Santa Monica, Calif.: RAND Corporation, 1971.

The Pentagon Papers. New York Times ed. New York: Bantam Books, 1971.

Public Papers of the President of the United States. Dwight Eisenhower. Washington, D.C.: U.S. Government Printing Office, 1960.

Public Papers of the President of the United States. Lyndon B. Johnson. Washington, D.C.: U.S. Government Printing Office, 1970.

Public Papers of the President of the United States. Harry Truman. Washington, D.C.: U.S. Government Printing Office, 1954.

Review of Department of Defense Worldwide Communications—Phase I. Report to the House Committee on Armed Services, March 24, 1971, in author's possession.

Spaulding, R. C. "Some Experiences Reported by the Crew of the USS Pueblo and American Prisoners of War from Vietnam." Report # 75-28. San Diego, Calif.: Naval Health Research Center, January 1975.

U.S. Bureau of the Census. *Statistical Abstract of the United States.* Washington, D.C.: U.S. Government Printing Office, 1990.

Vreeland, Nena, with Rinn-Sup Shinn, Peter Just, and Phillip Moeller. *Area Handbook of North Korea.* 2nd ed. Washington, D.C.: U.S. Government Printing Office, 1976.

SECONDARY SOURCES

Aitken, Jonathan. *Nixon.* London: Weidenfeld and Nicolson, 1993.

Alperovitz, Gar. *Atomic Diplomacy.* New York: Simon and Schuster, 1965.

Ambrose, Stephen. *Nixon.* New York: Simon and Schuster, 1989.

An, Tai Sung. *North Korea in Transition.* Westport, Conn.: Greenwood Press, 1983.

Anderson, David, ed. *Shadow on the White House.* Lawrence: University Press of Kansas, 1993.

Andrew, Christopher. *For the President's Eyes Only.* New York: HarperCollins, 1995.

Armbrister, Trevor. *A Matter of Accountability.* New York: Coward-McCann, 1970.

Austin, Anthony. *The President's War.* Philadelphia: Lippincott Press, 1971.

Ball, George. *The Past Has Another Pattern.* New York: W. W. Norton, 1982.

Bamford, James. *Body of Secrets.* New York: Doubleday, 2001.

———. *The Puzzle Palace.* New York: Penguin Books, 1983.

Banner, Lois. American Beauty. New York: Alfred A. Knopf, 1983.

———. *Women in Modern America.* New York: Harcourt Brace Jovanovich, 1974.

Baritz, Loren. *Backfire.* New York: Ballantine Books, 1985.

Barnds, William, ed. *The Two Koreas in East Asian Affairs.* New York: New York University Press, 1976.

Berdahl, Robert. *The Politics of Prussian Nobility.* Princeton, N.J.: Princeton University Press, 1988.

Berg, Dorothy, ed. *Pearl Harbor as History.* New York: Columbia University Press, 1973.

Berman, Larry. *Lyndon Johnson's War.* New York: W. W. Norton, 1990.

———. *Planning a Tragedy.* New York: W. W. Norton, 1982.

Bernstein, Irving. *Guns or Butter.* New York: Oxford University Press, 1996.

Beschloss, Michael. *Mayday.* New York: Harper and Row, 1986.

Bill, James. *The Eagle and the Lion.* New Haven, Conn.: Yale University Press, 1988.

Blackbourne, David, and Geoff Eley. *The Peculiarities of German History.* Oxford: Oxford University Press, 1985.

Blum, Howard. *I Pledge Allegiance.* New York: Simon and Schuster, 1987.

Blum, John. *Years of Discord.* New York: W. W. Norton, 1991.

Bolger, Daniel. *Scenes from an Unfinished War.* Fort Leavenworth, Kans.: Combat Studies Institute, 1991.

Borne, John. *The USS Liberty.* New York: Reconsideration Press, 1995.

Bornet, Vaughn. *The Presidency of Lyndon Johnson.* Lawrence: University Press of Kansas, 1983.

Bowman, S. D. *Masters and Lords.* New York: Oxford University Press, 1993.

Bradley, Omar. *A General's Life.* New York: Simon and Schuster, 1983.

Branch, Taylor. *Parting the Waters.* New York: Simon and Schuster, 1988.

Brands, H. W. *The Wages of Globalism.* New York: Oxford University Press, 1995.

Brandt, Ed. *The Last Voyage of the USS* Pueblo. New York: W. W. Norton, 1969.

Bray, Robert. *A Certain Tendency.* Princeton, N.J.: Princeton University Press, 1985.

Breuer, William. *Shadow Warriors.* New York: John Wiley and Sons, 1996.

Bridges, Brian. *Korea and the West.* London: Routledge and Kegan Paul, 1986.

Brodie, Fawn. *Richard Nixon.* New York: W. W. Norton, 1981.

Bucher, Lloyd. "Commander Bucher Replies." *Naval History,* Winter 1989.

Bucher, Lloyd, with Mark Rascovich. *Bucher.* Garden City, N.Y.: Doubleday, 1970.

Byun, Dae-Ho. *North Korea's Foreign Policy.* Seoul: Research Center for Peace and Unification of Korea, 1991.

Cable, James. *Gunboat Diplomacy.* 3rd ed. New York: St. Martin's Press, 1994.

Cagin, Seth, and Philip Dray. *Hollywood Films of the Seventies.* New York: Harper and Row, 1984.

Califano, Joseph Jr. *The Triumph and Tragedy of Lyndon Johnson.* New York: Simon and Schuster, 1991.

Carmichael, Stokely, and Charles Hamilton. *Black Power.* New York: Random House, 1967.

Carson, Clayborne. *In Struggle.* Cambridge: Harvard University Press, 1981.

Carter, Dan. *Politics of Rage.* New York: Simon and Schuster, 1995.

Chafe, William. *The American Woman.* New York: Oxford University Press, 1972.

Chang, Gordon. *Friends and Enemies.* Stanford, Calif.: Stanford University Press, 1990.

Chung, Chin. *Pyongyang between Peking and Moscow.* University: University of Alabama Press, 1978.

Chung, Joseph Sang-hoon. *The North Korean Economy.* Stanford, Calif.: Hoover Institute Press, 1974.

Clifford, Clark, with Richard Holbrooke. *Counsel to the President.* New York: Random House, 1991.

Clissold, Stephen, ed. *Yugoslavia and the Soviet Union: A Documentary Survey.* London: Oxford University Press, 1975.

Clodfelter, Mark. *The Limits of Air Power.* New York: Free Press, 1989.

Clough, Ralph. *Embattled Korea.* Boulder, Colo.: Westview Press, 1987.

Cohen, Warren, and Nancy Bernkopf-Tucker. *Lyndon Johnson Confronts the World.* Cambridge: Cambridge University Press, 1994.

Colby, William, and Peter Forbath. *Honorable Men.* New York: Simon and Schuster, 1978.

Cook, Blanche Wiesen. *The Declassified Eisenhower.* New York: Penguin Books, 1984.

Corson, William. *Armies of Ignorance.* New York: Dial Press, 1977.

Corson, William, and Robert Crowley. *The New KGB.* New York: William Morrow, 1985.

Crawford, Don. Pueblo *Intrigue.* New York: Pyramid Books, 1969.

Crowe, William, with David Chanoff. *The Line of Fire*. New York: Simon and Schuster, 1993.

Cumings, Bruce. *Korea's Place in the Sun*. New York: W. W. Norton, 1997.

Cutler, Thomas. *Brown Water, Black Berets*. Annapolis, Md.: Naval Institute Press, 1988.

Dallek, Robert. *Flawed Giant*. New York: Oxford University Press, 1998.

Deacon, Richard. *The Silent War*. New York: Hippocrene Books, 1978.

DeBenedetti, Charles. *An American Ordeal*. Syracuse, N.Y.: Syracuse University Press, 1990.

Divine, Robert. *The Johnson Years*. Vol. 3. Lawrence: University Press of Kansas, 1994.

——, ed. *Foreign Policy and U.S. Presidential Elections, 1940–48*. New York: New Viewpoints, 1974.

Draper, Theodore. *The Dominican Revolt*. New York: Commentary, 1968.

Drea, Edward. *MacArthur's Ultra*. Lawrence: University Press of Kansas, 1993.

Duffett, John, ed. *Against the Crime of Silence*. New York: Simon and Schuster, 1970.

Early, Peter. *Family of Spies*. New York: Bantam Books, 1988.

Echols, Alice. *Daring to Be Bad*. Minneapolis: University of Minnesota Press, 1989.

Ennes, James Jr. *Assault on the* Liberty. New York: Random House, 1979.

Evanhoe, Ed. *Dark Moon*. Annapolis, Md.: Naval Institute Press, 1995.

Evans, Sara. *Born for Liberty*. New York: Free Press, 1989.

Fain, Tyrus, ed. *The Intelligence Community*. New York: R. R. Bowker, 1977.

Farago, Ladislas. *The Broken Seal*. New York: Bantam Books, 1968.

Felton, Peter. "The 1963–65 United States Intervention in the Dominican Republic." Dissertation, University of Texas, 1995.

Filene, Peter. *Him/Her/Self*. Baltimore: Johns Hopkins University Press, 1986.

Ford, Ronnie. *Tet, 1968*. Portland, Oreg.: Frank Cass, 1995.

Forman, James. *The Making of Black Revolutionaries*. Washington, D.C.: Open Hand Publishers, 1985.

Frady, Marshall. *Wallace*. New York: New American Library, 1968.

Frentzos, Chris. "The *Pueblo* Incident." Master's thesis, University of New Orleans, 1996.

Gaddis, John. "Intelligence, Espionage and the Cold War." *Diplomatic History*, Spring 1989.

——. *The United States and the Origins of the Cold War*. New York: Columbia University Press, 1972.

Gallery, Daniel. *The* Pueblo *Incident*. Garden City, N.Y.: Doubleday, 1970.

Galloway, John. *The Gulf of Tonkin Resolution*. Rutherford, N.J.: Fairleigh Dickinson University Press, 1970.

Gallup, George. *The Gallup Poll, Public Opinion 1935–71*. New York: Random House, 1972.

Gardner, Lloyd. *Architects of Illusion*. Chicago: Quadrangle Books, 1970.

——. *Pay Any Price*. Chicago: Ivan Dee Publishers, 1995.

Garrow, David. *Bearing the Cross*. New York: Morrow Publishers, 1986.

Geertz, Clifford. *The Interpretation of Cultures*. New York: Basic Books, 1973.

Gelb, Leslie, with Richard Betts. *The Irony of Vietnam*. Washington, D.C.: Brookings Institution, 1979.

Genovese, Eugene. *Roll Jordan, Roll*. New York: Pantheon Books, 1974.

Gerhard, William. *Attack of the USS* Liberty. New York: Aegean Park, 1996.

Gerrold, David. *The World of Star Trek*. 2nd ed. New York: Bluejay Books, 1984.

Giap, Vo Nguyen, and David Schoenbrun, eds. *Big Victory, Great Task*. New York: Praeger Publishers, 1968.

Giap, Vo Nguyen, with Russell Stetler, eds. *The Military Art of People's War.* New York: Monthly Review Press, 1970.

Gilbert, Marc, and William Head, eds. *The Tet Offensive.* Westport, Conn.: Praeger Publishers, 1996.

Gitlin, Todd. *The Sixties.* New York: Bantam Books, 1987.

Gleijeses, Pierro. *The Dominican Crisis.* Baltimore: Johns Hopkins University Press, 1978.

———. *Shattered Hope.* Princeton, N.J.: Princeton University Press, 1991.

Gordievsky, Oleg, and Christopher Andrew. *KGB.* New York: HarperCollins, 1990.

Goulden, Joseph. *Korea.* New York: McGraw-Hill, 1982.

———. *Truth Is the First Casualty.* Chicago: Rand McNally, 1969.

Guttmann, Allen, ed. *Korea.* Lexington, Mass.: D. C. Heath, 1972.

Hannum, David Jr. "The *Pueblo* Incident." Unpublished research project, National War College, Washington, D.C., 1974.

Harris, R. Scott. "The *Pueblo* Incident." Unpublished paper in author's possession.

Harris, Stephen, and James Hefley. *My Anchor Held.* Old Tappan, N.J.: Fleming H. Revell, 1970.

Heardon, Patrick. *The Tragedy of Vietnam.* New York: Longman, 1991.

Hearn, Dan. "A Career Built on SIGINT." *American Intelligence Journal,* Spring/Summer 1994.

Heinrich, Waldo. *Threshold of War.* New York: Oxford University Press, 1988.

Herring, George. *America's Longest War.* 2nd ed. New York: Alfred A. Knopf, 1986.

Hersh, Seymour. *The Target Is Destroyed.* New York: Random House, 1986.

Hooper, Edwin. *Mobility, Support, Endurance.* Washington, D.C.: U.S. Government Printing Office, 1972.

Horsman, Reginald. *The Diplomacy of the New Republic.* Arlington Heights, Ill.: Harlan Davidson, 1985.

Hunt, Michael. *Ideology and U.S. Foreign Policy.* New Haven, Conn.: Yale University Press, 1987.

Immerman, Richard. *The CIA in Guatemala.* Austin: University of Texas Press, 1982.

Irwin, Ray. *The Diplomatic Relations of the United States with the Barbary Powers.* Chapel Hill: University of North Carolina Press, 1931.

Jane's Fighting Ships. New York: McGraw-Hill, 1970.

Jeffreys-Jones, Rhodri, and Christopher Andrew, eds. *Eternal Vigilance.* London: Frank Cass, 1997.

Johnson, Loch. *America's Secret Power.* New York: Oxford University Press, 1989.

Johnson, Lyndon. *The Vantage Point.* New York: Holt, Rinehart and Winston, 1971.

Jordan, Hamilton. *Crisis.* New York: Putnam, 1982.

Josephy, Alvin. *Red Power.* New York: American Heritage Press, 1971.

Joyner, Charles. *Down by the Riverside.* Urbana: University of Illinois Press, 1984.

Kahn, David. *The Codebreakers.* New York: Macmillan, 1973.

———. *Kahn on Codes.* New York: Macmillan, 1983.

Kalb, Marvin, with Elie Abel. *Roots of Involvement.* New York: W. W. Norton, 1971.

Kalugin, Oleg, with Fen Motaigne. *The First Directorate.* New York: St. Martin's Press, 1994.

Kaplan, Stephen, ed. *Diplomacy of Power.* Washington, D.C.: Brookings Institution, 1981.

Kaplan, Stephen, and Barry Blechman, eds. *Force without War.* Washington, D.C.: Brookings Institution, 1978.

Karnow, Stanley. *Vietnam*. Middlesex, England: Penguin Books, 1984.

Katsiaficas, George. *The Imagination of the New Left*. Boston: South End Press, 1987.

Kearns, Doris. *Lyndon Johnson and the American Dream*. New York: Harper and Row, 1976.

Kennan, George. *Memoirs: 1925–1950*. Boston: Little, Brown, 1967.

Khrushchev, Nikita. *Khrushchev Remembers*. Boston: Little, Brown, 1970.

Kihl, Young Whan. *Politics and Policies in Divided Korea*. Boulder, Colo.: Westview Press, 1984.

Kim, Ilpyong. *Communist Politics in North Korea*. New York: Praeger Publishers, 1975.

Kim, Seung-Hwan. *The Soviet Union and North Korea*. Seoul: Research Center for Peace and Unification of Korea, 1988.

Kim Il Sung. *Juche!* New York: Grossman Publishers, 1972.

——. *On Juche in Our Revolution*. New York: Weekly Guardian Associations, 1977.

——. *Revolution and Socialist Construction*. New York: International Publishers, 1971.

Kinnard, Douglas. *The War Managers*. Hanover, N.H.: Da Capo Press, 1977.

Kitzen, Michael. *Tripoli and the United States at War*. Jefferson, N.C.: McFarland, 1993.

Kiyosaki, Wayne. *North Korea's Foreign Relations*. New York: Praeger Publishers, 1976.

Kneece, Jack. *Family Treason*. New York: Stein and Day, 1986.

Knoll, Erwin, and Judith McFadden, eds. *War Crimes and the American Conscience*. New York: Holt, Rinehart and Winston, 1970.

Koh, Byung Chul. *The Foreign Policy Systems of North and South Korea*. Berkeley: University of California Press, 1984.

——. "The *Pueblo* Incident in Perspective." *Asian Survey,* April 1969.

Kolko, Gabriel. *Anatomy of a War*. New York: W. W. Norton, 1985.

——. *The Roots of American Foreign Policy*. Boston: Beacon Press, 1969.

Koning, Hans. *1968*. New York: W. W. Norton, 1987.

Koo, Young-nok, and Sung-Joo Han, eds. *The Foreign Policy of the Republic of Korea*. New York: Columbia University Press, 1985.

Kwak, Tae-Hwan, Wayne Patterson, and Edward Olsen. *The Two Koreas in World Politics*. Seoul: Kyungnam University Press, 1983.

LaFeber, Walter. *The Clash*. New York: W. W. Norton, 1997.

Lavan, George, ed. *Che Guevara Speaks*. New York: Grove Press, 1968.

Leffler, Melvin. *A Preponderance of Power*. Stanford, Calif.: Stanford University Press, 1991.

Levy, David. *The Debate over Vietnam*. Baltimore: Johns Hopkins University Press, 1995.

Linden, Carl. *Khrushchev and the Soviet Leadership*. Baltimore: Johns Hopkins University Press, 1990.

Liston, Robert. *The Pueblo Surrender*. New York: M. Evans, 1988.

Littauer, Raphael, and Norman Uphoff, eds. *The Air War in Indochina*. Boston: Beacon Press, 1972.

London, Kurt, ed. *The Soviet Union and World Politics*. Boulder, Colo.: Westview Press, 1980.

Lowenthal, Abraham. *The Dominican Intervention*. Cambridge: Harvard University Press, 1972.

Lytle, Mark. *The Origins of the Iranian-American Alliance*. New York: Holmes and Meier, 1987.

MacDonald, Donald. *The Koreans*. Boulder, Colo.: Westview Press, 1988.

MacDonald, Peter. *Giap*. New York: W. W. Norton, 1993.

Marable, Manning. *Race, Reform and Rebellion*. Jackson: University Press of Mississippi, 1991.

Marchetti, Victor, and John Marks. *The CIA and the Cult of Intelligence.* New York: Dell, 1974.

Marolda, Edward, and Oscar Fitzgerald. *The U.S. Navy and the Vietnam Conflict.* Washington, D.C.: Naval Historical Center Press, 1986.

Martel, Gordon, ed. *American Foreign Relations Reconsidered.* New York: Routledge, 1994.

Mason, John. *The Identity Crisis Theme in American Feature Films, 1960–1969.* New York, Arno Press, 1977.

Matthiessen, Peter. *In the Spirit of Crazy Horse.* New York: Viking Press, 1980.

Matusow, Allen. *The Unraveling of America.* New York: Harper and Row, 1984.

May, Elaine Tyler. *Homeward Bound.* New York: Basic Books, 1988.

May, Ernest. *"Lessons" of the Past.* Oxford: Oxford University Press, 1973.

McCauley, Martin, ed. *Khrushchev and Khrushchevism.* London: Macmillan, 1987.

McFarland, Stephen. "A Peripheral View of the Origins of the Cold War." *Diplomatic History,* Fall 1980.

McGarvey, Patrick. *CIA.* New York: Saturday Review Press, 1972.

McMahon, Robert. *Major Problems in the History of the Vietnam War.* Lexington, Mass.: D. C. Heath, 1990.

Mersky, Peter, and Normal Polmar. *The Naval Air War in Vietnam.* Annapolis, Md.: Nautical and Aviation Publishing Company of America, 1981.

Michael, Paul, ed. *The American Movies Reference Book.* New York: Garland Books, 1969.

Miller, James. *Democracy Is in the Streets.* New York: Simon and Schuster, 1987.

Miller, Merle. *Lyndon.* New York: G. P. Putnam's Sons, 1980.

Miller, R. F., and F. Feher, eds. *Khrushchev and the Communist World.* Totowa, N.J.: Barnes and Noble, 1984.

Millet, Kate. *Sexual Politics.* Garden City, N.Y.: Doubleday, 1970.

Mills, Kay. *This Little Light of Mine.* New York: Dutton Publishers, 1993.

Mobley, Richard. "The *Pueblo* Crisis: A (De)classified Retrospective of the Initial U.S. Response." Unpublished article in author's possession.

Moise, Edwin. *Tonkin Gulf and the Escalation of the Vietnam War.* Chapel Hill: University of North Carolina Press, 1996.

Morns, Kenneth. *Jimmy Carter.* Athens: University of Georgia Press, 1996.

Moynihan, Daniel. *Secrecy.* New Haven, Conn.: Yale University Press, 1998.

Murphy, Edward, with Curt Gentry. *Second in Command.* New York: Holt, Rinehart and Winston, 1971.

Nam, Koon Woo. *The North Korean Communist Leadership.* University: University of Alabama Press, 1974.

Neff, Donald. *Warriors for Jerusalem.* New York: Simon and Schuster, 1984.

Nietzsche, Friedrich. *Beyond Good and Evil.* Edited by Walter Kaufmann. New York: Vintage Books, 1966.

———. *The Gay Science.* Edited by Walter Kaufmann. New York: Vintage Books, 1974.

Nitze, Paul, with Ann Smith and Steven Rearden. *From Hiroshima to Glasnost.* New York: Grove Weidenfeld, 1989.

Norris, Robert, et al. "Where They Were." *Bulletin of Atomic Scientists,* November/December 1999.

Oberdorfer, Donald. *Tet!* New York: Doubleday, 1971.

———. *The Two Koreas.* Reading, Mass.: Addison-Wesley, 1997.

Olmstead, Kathryn. *Challenging the Secret Government.* Chapel Hill: University of North Carolina Press, 1996.

Oshinsky, David. *A Conspiracy So Immense.* New York: Free Press, 1983.

Packard, Wyman. *A Century of U.S. Naval Intelligence.* Washington, D.C.: Naval Historical Center Press, 1996.

Park, Jae Kyu, Byung Chul Koh, and Tae-Hwan Kwak, eds. *The Foreign Relations of North Korea.* Boulder, Colo.: Westview Press, 1987.

Patterson, Thomas. *On Every Front.* New York: W. W. Norton, 1979.

Patton, William. "Command Control and Communications." Unpublished article in author's possession.

Pisor, Ronald. *The End of the Line.* New York: Ballantine Books, 1982.

Powers, Francis Gary, and Curt Gentry. *Operation Overflight.* New York: Holt, Rinehart and Winston, 1970.

Powers, Thomas. *Vietnam: The War at Home.* Boston: G. K. Hall, 1973.

Prange, Gordon. *At Dawn We Slept.* Middlesex, England: Penguin Books, 1981.

Race, Jeffrey. *War Comes to Long An.* Berkeley: University of California Press, 1972.

Ranney, Austin, ed. *The American Election of 1980.* Washington, D.C.: American Enterprise Institute, 1981.

Reeves, Richard. *President Kennedy.* New York: Simon and Schuster, 1993.

Richelson, Jeffrey. *The U.S. Intelligence Community.* Cambridge, England: Ballinger Publishing, 1985.

Robertson, Jack. "*Pueblo.*" *Electronic News,* February 24, 1969.

Rostow, Walt. *Diffusion of Power.* New York: Macmillan, 1972.

Rozel, Mark. *The Press and the Carter Presidency.* Boulder, Colo.: Westview Press, 1989.

Rubin, Barry. *Paved with Good Intentions.* New York: Oxford University Press, 1981.

Rusk, Dean, with Richard Rusk. *As I Saw It.* New York: W. W. Norton, 1991.

Said, Edward. *Culture and Imperialism.* New York: Alfred A. Knopf, 1994.

Saikal, Amin. *The Rise and Fall of the Shah.* Princeton, N.J.: Princeton University Press, 1980.

Sale, Kirkpatrick. *SDS.* New York: Vintage Books, 1973.

Sarantakes, Nicholas. "In the Service of Pharaoh." Unpublished paper in author's possession.

———. "The Quiet War." *Journal of Military History,* April 2000.

Scalapino, Robert, and Chong-Sik Lee. *Communism in Korea.* 2 vols. Berkeley: University of California Press, 1972.

Schlesinger, Arthur Jr. "Origins of the Cold War." *Foreign Affairs,* October 1967.

Schlesinger, Stephen, and Stephen Kinzer. *Bitter Fruit.* Garden City, N.Y.: Doubleday, 1982.

Schreadley, R. L. *From the Rivers to the Sea.* Annapolis, Md.: Naval Institute Press, 1992.

Schumacher, F. Carl, with George Wilson. *Bridge of No Return.* New York: Harcourt Brace Jovanovich, 1971.

Scott, James. *Weapons of the Weak.* New Haven, Conn.: Yale University Press, 1985.

Sellers, Cleveland. *The River of No Return.* New York: Morrow Publishers, 1971.

Sherry, Michael. *In the Shadow of War.* New Haven, Conn.: Yale University Press, 1995.

Siff, Ezra. *Why the Senate Slept.* Westport, Conn.: Praeger Publishing, 1999.

Simon, Sheldon. "The *Pueblo* Incident and the South Korean Revolution." *Asian Forum* 2, no. 3 (1970).

Sitkoff, Harvard. *The Struggle for Black Equality.* New York: Hill and Wang, 1981.

Small, Melvin. *Johnson, Nixon, and the Doves.* New Brunswick, N.J.: Rutgers University Press, 1988.

Smist, Frank. *Congress Oversees the United States Intelligence Community.* Knoxville: University of Tennessee Press, 1994.

Song, Byung-Nak. *The Rise of the Korean Economy.* Oxford: Oxford University Press, 1990.

Sontag, Sherry, and Christopher Drew. *Blind Man's Bluff.* New York: Public Affairs, 1998.

Spanier, John. *The Truman-MacArthur Controversy and the Korean War.* New York: W. W. Norton, 1965.

Spaulding, Raymond, and Charles Ford. "The *Pueblo* Incident." *American Journal of Psychiatry,* July 1972.

———. "The *Pueblo* Incident." *Archives of General Psychiatry,* September 1973.

Staar, Richard. *Communist Regimes in Eastern Europe.* 3rd ed. Stanford, Calif.: Hoover Institution Press, 1977.

Steel, Ronald. *Pax Americana.* New York: Viking Press, 1967.

Suh, Dae-Sook. *Kim Il-Sung.* New York: Columbia University Press, 1988.

Taylor, Maxwell. *Swords and Plowshares.* New York: Da Capo Press, 1972.

Thornton, Richard. *The Carter Years.* New York: Paragon House, 1991.

Tolland, John. *Infamy.* New York: Berkley Books, 1982.

Trimble, Bo. *The Star Trek Concordance.* New York: Ballantine Books, 1976.

Tucker, Robert, and David Hendrickson. *Empire of Liberty.* New York: Oxford University Press, 1990.

Turner, Kathleen. *Lyndon Johnson's Dual War.* Chicago: University of Chicago Press, 1985.

Tuthill, Don. "Operational Planning, Pre-*Pueblo*." *Naval Intelligence Professionals Quarterly,* Winter 1994.

Unger, Irving, and Debbi Unger. *Turning Point, 1968.* New York: Charles Scribner and Sons, 1988.

Unger, Irwin. *The Movement.* New York: Dodd Press, 1974.

Utley, Jonathan. *Going to War with Japan.* Knoxville: University of Tennessee Press, 1985.

VandeMark, Brian. *Into the Quagmire.* New York: Oxford University Press, 1991.

Viorst, Milton. *Fire in the Streets.* New York: Simon and Schuster, 1979.

Wainstock, Dennis. "The 1968 Presidential Campaign and Election." Dissertation, University of West Virginia, 1984.

Westmoreland, William. *A Soldier Reports.* Garden City, N.Y.: Doubleday, 1976.

White, Theodore. *America in Search of Itself.* New York: Warner Books, 1982.

———. *The Making of the President, 1968.* New York: Pocket Books, 1968.

Whitfield, Stephen. *The Culture of the Cold War.* Baltimore: Johns Hopkins University Press, 1991.

Williams, William, et al. *America in Vietnam.* New York: Anchor Books, 1985.

Windchy, Eugene. *Tonkin Gulf.* Garden City, N.Y.: Doubleday, 1971.

Winton, John. *Ultra in the Pacific.* London: Leo Copper, 1993.

Wirtz, James. *The Tet Offensive.* Ithaca, N.Y.: Cornell University Press, 1991.

Wise, David, and Thomas Ross. *The U-2 Affair.* New York: Random House, 1962.

Woods, Randall. *Fulbright.* New York: Cambridge University Press, 1995.

Wright, Edward. *Korean Politics in Transition.* Seattle: University of Washington Press, 1975.

Wright, Louis, and Julia Macleod. *The First Americans in North Africa*. Princeton, N.J.:
Princeton University Press, 1945.

Yergin, Daniel. *Shattered Peace*. New York: Penguin Books, 1990.

Young, Marilyn. *The Vietnam Wars*. New York: HarperCollins, 1991.

Zaroulis, Nancy, and Gerald Sullivan. *Who Spoke Up*. New York: Holt, Rinehart and Winston, 1984.

Index

North Korea (Democratic People's Republic of Korea, DPRK), 16, 166
belligerence before *Pueblo* Incident, 52, 58–62
cult of personality around President Kim, 105–106
downing of U.S. reconnaissance plane in 1969, 233
economic performance, 109–112
fabrication of evidence regarding alleged intrusion of *Pueblo* into territorial waters, 87–90, 151
internal dissent, 115–116
Juche ("self-reliance") ideology, 103–122, 153
nationalism, 106–107
and negotiations for release of *Pueblo* crew, 123–146, 170, 194–214; demands, 194, 196
policy independence from Soviet line, 63, 64, 65, 97–98, 99–100, 109, 111, 112–114, 116, 137, 140, 213
possible motives for seizing *Pueblo*: domestic ideology *(juche)*, 117–122; promotion of Soviet communist line, 99–100, 120; intelligence value of ship and crew, 118, 272; tactical diversion of U.S. forces before Tet Offensive by North Vietnam, 100–102, 16
Pueblo seizure, 71–92
raid on Blue House in South Korea, 60, 124, 131, 133
relations with China, 109, 113, 114–115, 116
relations with South Korea, 116–117, 131
surveillance of, by United States, 68–71
treatment of *Pueblo* crew, 45, 153
and Vietnam War, 100–102, 117
North Vietnam
reaction to agreement ending *Pueblo* Incident, 221
response to surveillance by USS *Maddox*, 16–19, 22, 99
See also Vietnam War
NSA. *See* National Security Agency

O'Bannon, Michael, 78, 180, 186, 191, 223
Operation Clickbeetle, 5–6, 10–12, 16, 21, 26, 42, 58, 61, 92, 233
planning and risk assessment, 50–51
Operation Combat Fox, 130
Operation Market Time, 37
Operation Pierce Arrow, 17
OPLAN-34A, 16–17, 18
Osbourn, USS, 127
Oseth, John, 12
Oxcart spy plane, 69–70
Oxford, USS (AGTR-1), 9, 20

Pae Chun-ki, 263
Pak Chae-Sok, 131
Pak Chung Kuk, 123–124, 142–145, 169, 182, 195–197, 202–208, 211–214, 218, 219
Pak Keun, 201
Pak Kum-ch'ol, 115
Palm Beach (AGER-3, formerly FS-389), 10–11, 26, 36, 226
Panama, 138
Park Chung Hee, 60, 126, 131–137, 200–202, 221
Paulson, Philip, 101
Pearson, Drew, 83
Penthouse, The (Collinson), 163
Peppard, Don, 183
Peurifoy, John, 64
Phares, Earl, 42
Philadelphia (U.S. frigate), 231
Pickard, Lynn, 33
Pierce, Jim, 80
Pike, Otis, 22, 56–57, 235
PINNACLE reports, 76, 77, 78, 93
Poats, Rutherford, 136
Poland, 128
Ponomarev, Boris, 140
Pope, Barbara, 230
Porter, William, 125, 131, 133–134, 135, 142, 144, 195, 202–203, 208, 209, 221
Pucinski, Roman, 152, 167
Pueblo, USS (AGER-2, formerly FS-344), 16, 24–25
arming of, 41–43

United States (*continued*)
  public distrust of government and re-
    jection of liberal internationalism,
    154–168
  public support for Cold War, 149
  *See also specific government depart-
    ments and agencies*
United States Embassy, Seoul, Korea, 60, 61
USSR. *See* Soviet Union
U Thant, 210

Valdez, USNS *Jose F.,* 8–9
Vance, Cyrus, 10, 134–135
Vega (Soviet trawler), 8
Vega, USS, 47
Venezuela, 117
Verlome United Shipyards, Rotterdam, 210
Veterans of Foreign Wars, 222
Vietnam War, 8, 16–18, 37, 63–64, 70, 86,
    99, 114, 117, 129, 132, 137, 146, 150, 152,
    193, 194, 201, 202, 232, 236, 237
  Gulf of Tonkin Incident, 16–18, 129,
    155, 157
  Johnson's view of, 138–139
  and loss of public trust in U.S. govern-
    ment, 159–161
  and public apathy toward *Pueblo* crisis,
    152, 153, 155–157
  purported link between Tet Offensive
    and *Pueblo* Incident, 100–102, 141–
    142, 167
  reaction of prisoners of war to U.S.
    "apology" ending *Pueblo* Incident, 221
  South Korean involvement in, 126, 131–
    135, 194, 202

Virginian Pilot, 278
Volador, USS, 130

Wadley, Kenneth, 42
Walker, John, Jr., 86, 256
Wallace, George, 162
Wallace, Henry, 149
Ward, Norvell, 28, 48
Warner, Jack, 183, 188, 191
Warnke, Paul, 202, 209
Warren, Earl, 153
Washington Post, 140, 157, 162
Watson, Albert, 127
Wayne, John, 164
Wegner, Nicholas, 37
Wendt, Waldemar, 56
Westmoreland, William, 101, 133, 141–142,
    156
Wheeler, Earle, 56, 96, 135, 202
White, Marshall, 226
Whitworth, Jerry, 86
Wiedman, Don, 94
Woelk, Stephen, 81, 170–171, 187, 229
Women's movement, 161–162
Wonsan, 1, 60, 71, 72–74, 77, 81, 82, 83, 91,
    94, 126, 127, 128, 130, 145, 147, 166, 217
Wood, Elliot, 181
Woodward, Gilbert, 202–210, 212–210,
    212–214, 218, 219, 221
World Court, 124, 195
Wright, John, 128
Wyman, Louis, 200

Yi Hyo-sun, 115
Young, Stephen, 204